Obeying
the
Truth

OBEYING
THE
TRUTH

Paul's Ethics in Galatians

JOHN M. G. BARCLAY

FORTRESS PRESS
Minneapolis

OBEYING THE TRUTH
Paul's Ethics in Galatians

Library of Congress Cataloging-in-Publication Data

Barclay, John M. G.
   Obeying the truth : Paul's ethics in Galatians / John M. G. Barclay.
      p.   cm.
   Originally published: Edinburgh : T. & T. Clark, c1988, in series: Studies of the New Testament and its world.
   Includes bibliographical references and indexes.
   ISBN 0-8006-2523-4 (alk. paper)
   1. Bible. N.T. Galatians—Criticism, interpretation, etc.
2. Ethics in the Bible.   I. Title.
   (BS2685.2.B29   1991)
227'.406—dc20   91-32867
                                                                      CIP

The paper used in this publication meets the minimum requirements of American National Standard for Information Sciences—Permanence of Paper for Printed Library Materials, ANSI Z329.48-1984.   (∞)™

Manufactured in the U.S.A.   AF 1-2523

95   94   93   92   91   1   2   3   4   5   6   7   8   9   10

Contents

Preface

Since the church is nowadays almost exlusively Gentile, it is hard for us to appreciate that one of the most disputed issues in early Christianity was the status of Gentile Christians. My aim in this book is to shed new light on some of the central features of this dispute, as they are reflected in Paul's letter to the Galatians. By investigating the place of ethics in the Galatian dispute I hope to provide a satisfactory explanation for what has always been a puzzling aspect of this letter, while also clarifying some of the moral and social problems faced by the first generation of Christians. My discussion of the practical aspects of the Galatian crisis involves a sociological analysis of the Galatian Christians which is crucial for comprehending the sort of problems with which Paul is faced. An exegetical study of key texts in his letter can then lay bare his technique in responding to these problems and illuminate the central theological considerations which he applies to the debate. At various points, and especially in the final chapter, I have attempted to show the relevance of my findings in Galatians for our general understanding of Paul and his role in the development of Christianity.

This book has its origins in a doctoral thesis accepted by the University of Cambridge in January 1986. Thanks are due to a number of people who have aided its development in various ways. Professor Morna Hooker supervised my doctoral research with a fine balance of advice, encouragement and criticism which always caused me to clarify my thinking and writing. Many friends at Tyndale House in Cambridge added greatly to the stimulation and enjoyment of my years of research; among these Tim Savage and Walter Hansen deserve special mention. Moving to Glasgow University provided another stimulating environment; the opportunity of lecturing on Paul and on Galatians, and the questions and comments of numerous students, undoubtedly helped to broaden and clarify my perspective on the issues discussed here. Revising the thesis for publication turned out to be a much more extensive task than I had originally expected, so that much of the original has been rewritten and remolded. During this process of revision I was particularly grateful for the encouragement and advice of C. K. Barrett and my colleague John Riches. As the editor of this series, Studies of the New Testament and Its World, in which this volume first appeared, John Riches has also made many valuable suggestions and provided practical assistance in a variety of ways. Mrs. M. Balden has battled heroically with my illegible script and has typed the finished product with remarkable speed and skill. Throughout the time from the very beginning of my research, my wife, Diana, has been amazingly patient and supportive, and together with young Robert has helped to keep me (relatively) sane. Finally, I would like to dedicate this book to my father, Oliver Barclay, who first taught me where to look for truth and challenged me to work out how to obey it.

Abbreviations

AB	Analecta Biblica
ANRW	*Aufstieg und Niedergang der römischen Welt*, ed. H. Temporini and W. Haase, Berlin 1972-.
Apoc Abr	Apocalypse of Abraham
Aristotle, *Pol*	Aristotle, *Politics*
ATD	Acta Theologica Danica
AV	Authorised (King James) Version
b	Babylonian Talmud
BAG	*A Greek-English Lexicon of the New Testament and Other Early Christian Literature*, E.T. and adaptation of W. Bauer's 4th edition by W.F. Arndt and F.W. Gingrich, 2nd edition revised by F.W. Gingrich and F.W. Danker, Chicago 1979.
BBB	Bonner biblische Beiträge
BDF	F. Blass and A. Debrunner, *A Greek Grammar of the New Testament and Other Early Christian Literature*, E.T. and ed. by R.W. Funk from 19th German edition, Chicago 1961.
BETh	Beiträge zur evangelischen Theologie
BJRL	*Bulletin of the John Rylands Library*
BU	Biblische Untersuchungen
BZNW	Beihefte zur *Zeitschrift für die neutestamentliche Wissenschaft*
CBQ	*Catholic Biblical Quarterly*
Cicero, *Orat*	Cicero, *Orationes*
Demosthenes, *Cor*	Demosthenes, *De Corona*
Ep Arist	Epistle of Aristeas
Epictetus, *Diss*	Epictetus, *Dissertations*
EQ	Evangelical Quarterly

E.T.	English Translation
Eusebius, *P.E.*	Eusebius, *Praeparatio evangelica*
EvTh	*Evangelische Theologie*
ExT	*Expository Times*
FRLANT	Forschungen zur Religion und Literatur des Alten und Neuen Testaments
GNB	Good News Bible
GNT	Grundrisse zum Neuen Testament
Hippolytus, *Ref*	Hippolytus, *Refutatio Omnium Haeresium*
Horace, *Sat*	Horace, *Satires*
HTR	*Harvard Theological Review*
HTS	Harvard Theological Studies
IEJ	*Israel Exploration Journal*
Ignatius, *Eph*	Ignatius, *Letter to the Ephesians*
Mag	*Letter to the Magnesians*
Philad	*Letter to the Philadelphians*
Int	*Interpretation*
Irenaeus, *Haer*	Irenaeus, *Adversus Haereses*
j	Jerusalem Talmud
JB	Jerusalem Bible
JBL	*Journal of Biblical Literature*
JBLMS	*Journal of Biblical Literature* Monograph Series
JES	*Journal of Ecumenical Studies*
Josephus, *Ant*	Josephus, *Antiquitates*
Apion	*Contra Apionem*
Bell	*Bellum Iudaicum*
JQR	*Jewish Quarterly Review*
JSJ	*Journal for the Study of Judaism*
JSNT	*Journal for the Study of the New Testament*
JSNTS	*Journal for the Study of the New Testament* Supplement Series
JTS	*Journal of Theological Studies*
Juvenal, *Sat*	Juvenal, *Satires*
KuD	*Kerygma und Dogma*
LD	Lectio Divina

LSJ	*A Greek-English Lexicon*, compiled by H.G. Liddell and R. Scott, revised and augmented by H.S. Jones, 9th edition, Oxford 1940.
LXX	The Septuagint
M	Mishnah
Mek	Mekilta
MM	J.H. Moulton and G. Milligan, *The Vocabulary of the Greek Testament, Illustrated from the Papyri and Other Non-Literary Sources*, London 1930.
MT	Massoretic Text
NA	Neutestamentliche Abhandlungen
NEB	New English Bible
Nestle-Aland[26]	*Novum Testamentum Graece*, 26th edition, Stuttgart 1979.
NIDNTT	*New International Dictionary of New Testament Theology*, ed. C. Brown, 3 volumes, Exeter 1975-8.
NIV	New International Version
n.s.	new series
NT	*Novum Testamentum*
NTS	*New Testament Studies*
Philo, *Abr*	Philo, *De Abrahamo*
Agr	*De Agricultura*
Conf	*De Confusione Linguarum*
Det	*Quod Deterius Potiori insidiari solet*
Ebr	*De Ebrietate*
Gig	*De Gigantibus*
Leg All	*Legum Allegoriae*
Mig Abr	*De Migratione Abrahami*
Mos	*De Vita Mosis*
Op Mund	*De Opificio Mundi*
Praem	*De Praemiis et Poenis*
Quaest Gen	*Quaestiones in Genesin*
Quis Her	*Quis rerum divinarum Heres*

Quod Deus	*Quod Deus immutabilis sit*
Sacr	*De Sacrificiis Abelis et Caini*
Som	*De Somniis*
Spec Leg	*De Specialibus Legibus*
Virt	*De Virtutibus*
· Plato, *Phdr*	Plato, *Phaedrus*
Plautus, *Mer*	Plautus, *Mercator*
Pliny, *Ep*	Pliny, *Epistulae*
Plutarch, *Alex*	Plutarch, *Alexander*
Cic	*Cicero*
Them	*Themistocles*
Polycarp, *Phil*	Polycarp, *Epistle to th Philippians*
PW	*Paulys Real-Encyclopädie der classischen Altertumswissenschaft*, ed. G. Wisowa et al., Stuttgart/München 1894–1972.
Rabba	Midrash Rabba
RGG	*Die Religion in Geschichte und Gegenwart*, ed. K. Galling, 7 volumes, 3rd edition, 1957–65.
RQ	*Revue de Qumran*
RSV	Revised Standard Version
SB	Stuttgarter Bibelstudien
SBLDS	Society of Biblical Literature Dissertation Series
SBM	Stuttgarter biblische Monographien
SBT	Studies in Biblical Theology
SEÅ	*Svensk Exegetisk Årsbok*
Sib Or	Sibylline Oracles
SJT	*Scottish Journal of Theology*
SNT	Supplements to *Novum Testamentum*
SNTSMS	Society for New Testament Studies Monograph Series
SNTW	Studies in the New Testament and Its World
STh	*Studia Theologica*

Strack-Billerbeck	H.L. Strack and P. Billerbeck, *Kommentar zum Neuen Testament aus Talmud und Midrasch*, 4 volumes, München 1922-8.
SUNT	Studien zur Umwelt des Neuen Testaments
TDNT	*Theological Dictionary of the New Testament*, ed. G. Kittel and G. Friedrich, E.T. ed. G. Bromiley, 10 volumes, Grand Rapids 1964-76.
Tertullian, *Ad Nat*	Tertullian, *Ad Nationes*
TF	Theologische Forschung
ThZ	*Theologische Zeitschrift*
TLZ	*Theologische Literaturzeitung*
TQ	*Theologische Quartalschrift*
TU	Texte und Untersuchungen
UBS³	*The Greek New Testament*, United Bible Societies, 3rd edition, Stuttgart 1975.
WMANT	Wissenschaftliche Monographien zum Alten und Neuen Testament
WUNT	Wissenschaftliche Untersuchungen zum Neuen Testament
ZNW	*Zeitschrift für die neutestamentliche Wissenschaft*
ZTK	*Zeitschrift für Theologie und Kirche*

Chapter One

The Context of the Discussion

Galatian Debates

Paul's letter to the Galatians affords a fascinating insight into the development of the early Christian movement. Its six short chapters provide a mass of invaluable information about Paul himself, the Gentile churches he founded and some of the most important controversies among the first Christians. With regard to Paul, this letter contains almost all the first-hand information we have about his 'call', his activities in the years after that event and his troubled relationship with the Jerusalem apostles. As concerns his churches, the nature of the crisis in the Galatian congregations reveals some of the most fundamental problems faced by Gentile converts to Christianity. And in relation to the controversies reflected in the letter, we have here crucial information on the bitter disputes between Paul and Peter in Antioch, and Paul and 'the agitators' in Galatia, both of which concerned the relationship between Jewish and Gentile believers in Christ. Since these disputes involved the interpretation of Scripture, the significance of the law, the relationship of the churches to Judaism, and many related moral and theological issues, they drew forth from Paul in this letter one of his most impressive statements on 'the gospel' and its practical implications.

Although other New Testament documents afford some information on each of these issues (e.g. Acts, Romans, Colossians), their unique concentration in Galatians and the passionate character of this letter have always given it particular importance. Luther found himself drawn to Galatians both theologically and temperamentally and the special attention he gave to this letter has helped to boost its status in Protestant

1

theology ever since.[1] When in the 1830s F.C. Baur launched the modern era of historical study of Paul, the witness of Galatians was of fundamental importance to his investigations; the questions he raised about Paul's opponents in Galatia and the character of early Jewish Christianity have remained crucial for New Testament scholarship ever since.[2] But in the last ten years these and other Galatian issues have become the subject of particularly intense scholarly debate. In some circles, attention has focused on the historical references in the first two chapters in Galatians, and fresh interpretation of this evidence has resulted in new reconstructions of Pauline chronology.[3] Elsewhere the quest for the identity of Paul's opponents has gathered momentum.[4] Meanwhile, in his commentary on Galatians, H.D. Betz has pioneered an important new approach to the letter via its rhetorical structure;[5] his work has been widely acclaimed and used as a basis for other attempts at 'rhetorical criticism'.[6]

[1] Luther once described Galatians as 'my epistle; I have betrothed myself to it; it is my wife'. His commentary on Galatians (most accessible in the revised E.T., based on the 'Middleton' edition of 1575, Cambridge 1953) is one of the foundation documents of the Reformation.

[2] See especially Baur's seminal essay, 'Die Christuspartei in der korinthischen Gemeinde, der Gegensatz des petrinischen und paulinischen Christenthums in der ältesten Kirche, der Apostel Petrus in Rom', *Tübinger Zeitschrift für Theologie* 4 (1831) 61-206, reprinted in *Ausgewählte Werke in Einzelausgaben* I, Stuttgart 1963; also his *Paul, the Apostle of Jesus Christ*, I, E.T. London/Edinburgh 1876, 105-145, 250-7. The subsequent discussion has been well surveyed by F.F. Bruce in his series of articles on 'Galatian Problems' in *BJRL* 51-55 (1969-73).

[3] R. Jewett, *Dating Paul's Life*, London 1979; G. Lüdemann, *Paul, Apostle to the Gentiles. Studies in Chronology*, E.T. London 1984; N. Hyldahl, *Die paulinische Chronologie*, Leiden 1986. U. Borse has also made a new attempt to determine the chronological sequence of Paul's letters, *Der Standort des Galaterbriefes*, Köln 1972; cf. his commentary, *Der Brief an die Galater*, Regensburg 1984, 9-17.

[4] B.H. Brinsmead, *Galatians – Dialogical Response to Opponents*, Chico 1982. Note also J.L. Martyn's foretaste of his forthcoming commentary, 'A Law-Observant Mission to Gentiles: The Background of Galatians', *Michigan Quarterly Review* 22 (1983) 221-236, reprinted in *SJT* 38 (1985) 307-324.

[5] H.D. Betz, *Galatians*, Philadelphia 1979. Another major but less revolutionary commentary has appeared more recently: F.F. Bruce, *The Epistle of Paul to the Galatians*, Exeter 1982.

[6] The rhetorical approach has been pursued by Brinsmead, *Galatians* and is of importance to Lüdemann, *Paul*. R.B. Hays has attempted a more structuralist analysis, *The Faith of Jesus Christ. An Investigation of the Narrative Substructure of Galatians 3:1-4:11*, Chico 1983.

However, the most important debate in recent years has focused on the theological content of the letter, that is, Paul's attitude to the law and Judaism and the issues at stake between him and 'the agitators' in Galatia. According to a long tradition of interpretation, given particularly sharp focus in the Reformation, Paul was contending in this letter for the principle of salvation by grace and faith alone and against human dependence on works to earn salvation. This theological analysis was enthusiastically adopted in the dialectical theology of the 1920s and was developed with a particular existentialist emphasis by Bultmann and his many pupils and followers. To take but one example: Ebeling, in his study of Galatians, describes Paul's antithesis of faith and works of the law in the following terms: 'what matters is what I live by, what I rely upon, what I take as the ground of my existence, what I understand to be my purpose with respect to God: is it faith and therefore God himself in his grace, or is it my own demonstrable reality and therefore I myself in what I achieve and represent?'[7] One can easily observe here the tendency to interpret Paul's discussion of law and Judaism on a generalized and individualistic level. Paul's argument against justification by works of the law is taken as an attack on self-righteous and self-sufficient attitudes.[8]

While there have been a number of voices raised in protest against this line of interpretation,[9] the most influential in recent

---

[7] G. Ebeling, *The Truth of the Gospel. An Exposition of Galatians*, E.T. Philadelphia 1985, 176-7. Ebeling expressly aligns himself with the Lutheran tradition of interpretation, ix.

[8] H. Hübner provides a variant of the same approach: those who believe in Christ 'base their self-understanding on faith' and 'do not see their existence as believers ultimately as conditioned by immanent factors'. By contrast, those who live from the works of the law 'understand their existence in the fulfilment of the requisite total of works of the law . . . Their existence is "on the basis of" (ἐκ) quantity', *Law in Paul's Thought*, E.T. Edinburgh 1984, 18.

[9] See e.g. W.D. Davies, *Paul and Rabbinic Judaism. Some Elements in Pauline Theology*, Philadelphia 1980; *idem*, 'Paul and the Law: Reflections on Pitfalls in Interpretation', in *Paul and Paulinism*, ed. M.D. Hooker and S.G. Wilson, London 1982, 4-16; M. Barth, 'The Kerygma of Galatians', *Int* 21 (1967) 131-146; K. Stendahl, *Paul among Jews and Gentiles*, London 1977; G. Howard, *Paul: Crisis in Galatia. A Study in Early Christian Theology*, Cambridge 1979.

years has been that of E.P. Sanders. Sanders insists that first-century Judaism was not the 'legalistic' religion it is often represented as in New Testament scholarship and that Paul's theology was not centred on a rebuttal of self-righteousness. Paul's polemic against works of the law in Galatians and Romans is in fact rooted in, and remains solely concerned with, specific historical questions about the position of Gentiles within the Christian churches.[10] Thus Sanders sums up the essential issue in Galatians quite differently from Ebeling: 'The subject of Galatians is not whether or not humans, abstractly conceived, can by good deeds earn enough merit to be declared righteous at the judgment; it is the condition on which Gentiles enter the people of God.'[11] This analysis highlights the historical context of Galatians and Sanders lays particular emphasis on the *Jewish* character of the law: the dispute is about whether Gentile believers need to observe the Jewish law, the law of Moses. To some extent this harks back to the work of F.C. Baur, who also stressed the liberation of early Christianity from Jewish particularism. But whereas Baur discussed this within a general thesis on the evolution of religion,[12] Sanders eschews all attempts to overlay the specific historical issue in Galatians with generalized theological notions.

[10] See especially Sanders' two important books on Paul: *Paul and Palestinian Judaism*, London 1977; and *Paul, The Law and the Jewish People*, Philadelphia 1983.

[11] *Paul, The Law and the Jewish People*, 18; later he writes (159), 'The supposed conflict between "doing" as such and "faith" as such is simply not present in Galatians. What was at stake was not a way of life summarized by the word "trust" versus a mode of life summarized by "requirements", but whether or not the requirement for membership in to the Israel of God would result in there being "neither Jew nor Greek".'

[12] In *Paul, The Apostle of Jesus Christ*, Baur maintains that the debate in Galatians is 'the debate of the momentous question whether there was to be a Christianity free from Judaism and essentially different from it, or whether Christianity was to exist merely as a form of Judaism' (253). But on the same page it becomes clear what part this thesis holds in his theology of the evolution of religions, when he writes of Paul's opponents: 'the chief reason why their Judaistic position was so narrow was just their natural incapacity to raise themselves from a lower state of religious consciousness to a higher and freer one.'

Sanders' work is, in fact, representative of an increasing disenchantment with 'theological exegesis' of Paul's letters and a renewed concern to uncover the historical and social realities of his ministry (and his churches).[13] This is sometimes expressed in an explicit attack on the Lutheran theology which has dominated Pauline studies. H. Räisänen, for instance, submits Paul's various statements on the law to a detailed examination and argues that, far from representing a consistent 'Lutheran' theology, Paul's views on this crucial subject are full of self-contradictions.[14] F. Watson offers an even more devastating critique of Lutheran interpretations, accusing them of isolating theology from history.[15] He proposes instead a strictly historical and sociological approach to Galatians and Romans in which particular attention is given to the distinction between Paul's Gentile congregations and the Jewish life-style of those who observed the law. This has also been a major emphasis in the work of G. Howard, J.D.G. Dunn and others, who have highlighted the effect of the law in distinguishing Jews from Gentiles; they approach Paul's discussion of 'works of the law' in Galatians as an argument about whether Gentile Christians need to adopt the tokens of Jewish identity.[16] Watson clarifies this matter by stressing the social context of Paul's remarks: Paul's arguments in Galatians and Romans are his attempts to justify the existence of his Gentile churches outside the Jewish synagogues, and he is opposing those who wanted the Christian movement to remain within the legal and social bounds of Judaism. By employing some well-known sociological categories, Watson argues that

[13] See e.g. B. Holmberg, *Paul and Power. The Structure of Authority in the Primitive Church as Reflected in the Pauline Epistles*, Philadelphia 1980; W. Meeks, *The First Urban Christians. The Social World of the Apostle Paul*, New Haven/London 1983; G. Theissen, *The Social Setting of Pauline Christianity*, E.T. Edinburgh 1982.

[14] H. Räisänen, *Paul and the Law*, Tübingen 1983.

[15] *Paul, Judaism and the Gentiles. A Sociological Approach*, Cambridge 1986.

[16] G. Howard, *Paul: Crisis in Galatia*. There are several pertinent articles by Dunn: 'The Incident at Antioch' (Gal.2:11-18)', *JSNT* 18 (1983) 3-57; 'The New Perspective on Paul', *BJRL* 65 (1983) 95-122; 'Works of the Law and the Curse of the Law (Galatians 3.10-14)', *NTS* 31 (1985) 523-542. See also T.D. Gordon, 'The Problem at Galatia', *Int* 41 (1987) 32-43.

'the essential issue in Galatians is . . . whether the church should be a reform-movement within Judaism or a sect outside it'.[17] What is more, he uses the sociological notion of 'ideology' to argue that Paul's various statements on Israel and the law are 'secondary theological reflection on a primary historical and social reality', that is, 'an ideology legitimating its [the sect's] state of separation'.[18]

It should be clear that there are a range of fundamental issues at stake in this debate about Galatians. On one level it concerns the rationale behind Paul's attack on 'works of the law' and the reasons for his dissatisfaction with law-observant Judaism. On another it concerns the relationship between historical context and theological statement in Paul's letters and the extent to which Paul's historically-conditioned remarks can now be given a theological interpretation. Sanders' work has not gone unchallenged, and H. Hübner, in particular, has proved to be a staunch defender of the Lutheran and existentialist tradition.[19] Moreover, Watson's thesis could be seen as dangerously close to a sociological reductionism in which 'theory' is dismissed as secondary legitimation of established social fact.[20] In these and other respects, Galatians is engendering debates almost as impassioned as the debate it itself reflects!

In the present work I intend to discuss these and other issues primarily on an exegetical level and through a consideration of the *ethical* dimensions of the letter. In the debates about the historical context and theological content of the letter, ethics have been widely neglected, and this chiefly for two reasons. *In the first place*, there is continuing uncertainty among scholars about how to interpret the explicitly paraenetic section of the letter in chapters 5-6. Since Paul offers warnings against the misuse of freedom

---

[17] *Paul, Judaism and the Gentiles*, 49.
[18] *Paul, Judaism and the Gentiles*, 19-20, 31.
[19] See for instance his articles, 'Pauli Theologiae Proprium', *NTS* 26 (1979-80) 445-473 (against Sanders) and 'Was heisst bei Paulus "Werke des Gesetzes"?', in *Glaube und Eschatologie*, ed. E. Grässer and O. Merk, Tübingen 1985, 123-133 (against Dunn).
[20] See my review of Watson's book in *Themelios* 13 (1987) 28-9.

(5.13) and gives a famous list of 'the works of the flesh', it is often thought that the problem here addressed is libertinism, and this seems difficult to square with the attack on 'nomism' in the rest of the letter. A number of different solutions to this problem have been proposed, some of which involve a radical reappraisal of the whole Galatian crisis. We will explore the different approaches to this section of the letter shortly. But we may note here the importance of a correct interpretation of these verses for establishing both the nature of the Galatian crisis and the role of Paul's ethical instructions in his response to it. *Secondly*, the comparative neglect of the ethical dimensions of the letter is a by-product of the 'Lutheran' theological consensus. If one considers that the main thrust of Paul's attack on 'works of the law' is against human works and achievement, one is apt to conclude that his specific ethical instructions are a mere appendix or, perhaps, an attempt to prevent himself being misunderstood as antinomian. To give these instructions any more integral place would be to admit that Paul also is concerned to promote 'works'.[21]

Thus, in approaching Galatians with a particular interest in ethics, we will fasten on an aspect of the letter which still requires a full investigation. However, a proper treatment of this matter will also take us into many of the controversial debates about this letter. We will need to investigate afresh the historical context of the letter – both the message of 'the agitators' in Galatia and the social context of the Galatians themselves. I do not propose to reopen the old debates about the date of the letter and its 'North' or 'South' Galatian destination: in my opinion the evidence for dating the letter is too uncertain to enable us to reach a secure conclusion,[22] while, with the majority of scholars, I incline

---

[21] W. Marxsen, *Einleitung in das Neue Testament*, 4th edition, Gütersloh 1978, 64 notes the problem that, if Paul is attacking 'nomism' in the first part of the letter, 'dann treiben die ethischen Ermahnungen am Schluss des Briefes die Galater doch gerade wieder in einen Nomismus hinein'.

[22] I am thus inclined to share Betz's agnosticism, *Galatians*, 9-12. I am as unpersuaded by the various attempts to fix the date on stylistic grounds as I am by the efforts of Hyldahl and others to determine its relation to 1 Cor 16 through its reference to the collection (2.10); see Hyldahl, *Chronologie*, 64-75.

towards the 'North' Galatian thesis.[23] Unfortunately this latter judgment means consigning Paul's churches to an area of Anatolia concerning which our historical information is particularly sparse.[24] Nonetheless, judicious use of Paul's letter and analogy with contemporary situations may still enable us to comment on the social context of the letter.

Our study will therefore focus initially on the social and practical dimensions of Paul's dispute with his opponents about the law. Naturally, this will require taking the whole letter into account, not just its last two chapters. However, some of the new ways of approaching Galatians suggest how these final moral instructions can be better understood. If the letter is not about 'works' in general but about how Gentiles become members of the people of God and what life-style they should adopt, ethical exhortation no longer appears to be so misplaced. Our aim is to explore precisely what purpose such exhortation may serve.

Our first task, however, is to describe the variety of approaches to the paraenetic material in Gal 5-6 and the issues involved in the disputes about these verses. This can then be supplemented by some observations on the way Galatians contributes to our understanding of Pauline ethics in general. For our ultimate aim is not only to gain a better comprehension of this letter but also to clarify a number of wider issues concerning Paul's theology and ethics.

---

[23] Bruce, *Galatians*, 3-18, recently restated Ramsay's case for a destination in the southern cities of the Galatian province. I do not think this hypothesis can be confidently ruled out, especially as we do not know if Paul would have shared Acts' understanding of 'the region of Galatia' (Acts 16.6; 18.23). However, with W.G. Kümmel, *Introduction to the New Testament*, E.T. of 17th revised edition, London 1975, 296-298 and most modern interpreters, I think the arguments weigh just in favour of the northern Galatian territory.

[24] S. Mitchell, 'Population and Land in Roman Galatia', *ANRW* II.7.2, 1053-1081 analyses some of the epigraphic evidence from this area which suggests, among other things, that the majority of the rural population did not speak Greek. We should probably assume, then, that the recipients of Paul's letter lived in towns such as Ankyra, Tavium and Pessinus.

Antinomians ??

A Survey of Views on the Paraenetic Material in 5.13-6.10

Even when they agree about the main themes of the letter, interpreters of Galatians hold a wide spectrum of views on the function of the moral instructions contained in 5.13-6.10. The differences of opinion are partly related to judgments on the structure of the letter (see below pp.23-6), but chiefly concern the more fundamental question of the relevance of this material to the foregoing arguments in Galatians 1-4. One may divide the various interpretations roughly into two groups: i) those which treat this material as wholly or largely unrelated to the main argument of the letter; and ii) those which attempt to integrate this material into the interpretation of the letter as a whole. This twofold classification will serve to order our survey.

1. Galatians 5.13-6.10 as a wholly or largely unrelated section

a) *An interpolated section.* Perhaps the most radical attempt to distinguish 5.13-6.10 from its surrounding context has been made by J.C. O'Neill; he regards the whole section as an interpolation by a later editor of a wholly unrelated collection of moral instructions.[25] He takes this section to be a warning against antinomianism, and hence incongruous in a letter directed against nomism: 'This section is directed to all Christians, to meet the common human temptations. It has nothing in particular to do with the urgent problem Paul was trying to meet in his original letter' (67). Moreover, it is not bound together by any consistent or sustained argument; there are only formal and superficial links which do not constitute real connections. In designating this whole section as an interpolation O'Neill concludes: 'I can find nothing specifically Pauline in the collection, and nothing that would have had specific bearing on the situation facing the Galatians' (71). Such a drastic hypothesis has, understandably,

---

[25] J.C. O'Neill, *The Recovery of Paul's Letter to the Galatians*, London 1972, 65-71. O'Neill gives an historical survey of those who have considered all or parts of the letter to be inauthentic (1-15) and cites the work of Völter, Weisse and Cramer as precedents for excising some or all of 5.13-6.10 (71).

won little support from other scholars.[26] Its one merit is in raising, in the sharpest possible form, the question of the relevance of this exhortation to the main themes of the letter.

b) *'Paraenesis' unrelated to the rest of the letter.* Although O'Neill considers 5.13–6.10 too general and fragmentary to be Pauline, a different explanation of these same features has been offered by M. Dibelius and those who adopt his definition of early Christian 'paraenesis'. Building on the work of Wendland and Vetschera, and through analysis of a broad range of Jewish and Christian literature, Dibelius attempted to define the characteristic features of a literary genre called 'paraenesis': 'By paraenesis we mean a text which strings together admonitions of general ethical content'; it contains 'sayings and groups of sayings very diverse in content, lacking any particular order, and containing no emphasis upon a special thought of pressing importance for a particular situation'.[27] Although Dibelius discussed this genre in most detail in his analysis of the epistle of James, he also considered it to be an appropriate description of many Pauline passages. The hortatory sections of Paul's letters (e.g. Rom 12–13; Gal 5.13–6.10; Col 3.1–4.6; 1 Thess 4.1–12; 5.1ff) are authentically Pauline but 'have nothing to do with the theoretic foundation of the ethics of the Apostle, and very little with other ideas peculiar to him'.[28] In style and content they belong to a tradition of Christian exhortation also witnessed in other early Christian documents: 'In particular they lack an immediate relation with the circumstances of the letter. The rules and directions are not formulated for special churches and concrete cases, but for the general requirements of earliest Christendom. Their significance

[26] Most would share G.B.Caird's conviction that 'the application of surgery to a biblical text is more often than not an admission on the part of the surgeon that he has failed to comprehend it as it stands', *The Language and Imagery of the Bible*, London 1980, 114 n.3. J. Drane complains that, in O'Neill's hands, Galatians 'becomes little more than an implausible collection of theological titbits drawn from incredibly diverse sources', *Paul: Libertine or Legalist? A Study in the Theology of the Major Pauline Epistles*, London 1975, 93.

[27] *A Commentary on the Epistle of James* (revised by H. Greeven), E.T. Philadelphia 1976, 3; the whole section, 1–11, is important.

[28] *From Tradition to Gospel*, E.T. London 1934, 239.

10

is not factual but actual – not the momentary need but the universal principle'. (German: 'Sie haben nicht aktuelle, sondern usuelle Bedeutung.')[29] Dibelius explicitly included Gal 5.13–6.10 within this genre, 'paraenesis': he considered that in this section 'there is scarcely a trace remaining of the high emotion and the critical situation. It is just here that we see clearly to what degree these schematic parts of the Pauline letters are unconditioned by the particular situation'.[30] Moreover, the traditional lists (5.19–23) and the use of catchwords to hold together general maxims (6.1–10) seemed to confirm his arguments. Thus Dibelius could conclude that, as an example of 'paraenesis', 5.13–6.10 has no real connection with the Galatian crisis or Paul's earlier theological arguments.

Dibelius' innovative form-critical work in this connection has been influential on many other scholars.[31] Whether he was right in his definition of 'paraenesis' is, however, widely disputed; many would consider that there is no such readily definable genre to which we can allocate so many New Testament passages.[32]

[29] From Tradition, 238; original in Die Formgeschichte des Evangeliums, 3rd edition, Tübingen 1959, 239. Dibelius makes similar statements in A Fresh Approach to the New Testament and Early Christian Literature, E.T. London 1936, 143–4 and Paul (ed. and completed by W.G. Kümmel), E.T. London 1953, 93.

[30] Fresh Approach, 159.

[31] His statements on 'paraenesis' are echoed by A. Hunter, Paul and his Predecessors, revised edition, London 1961, 52–7; A. Schulz, 'Grundformen urchristlicher Paränese', in Gestalt und Anspruch des Neuen Testaments, ed. J. Schreiner and G. Dautzenberg, Würzburg 1969, 249–261; and P. Vielhauer in his influential book, Geschichte der urchristlichen Literatur, Berlin 1975, 49–57. E. Käsemann has applied Dibelius' thesis to Rom 12–13 in his two essays, 'Worship and Everyday Life. A Note on Romans 12' and 'Principles of the Interpretation of Romans 13', in New Testament Questions of Today, E.T. London 1969, 188–195 and 196–216 respectively. Among the commentators on Galatians, F. Mussner, Der Galaterbrief, Freiburg 1974, 396, 408 and J. Becker, Der Brief an die Galater, Göttingen 1981, 4, 67 are inclined to accept Dibelius' judgment on some or all of 5.13–6.10. Note also J. Eckert, Die urchristliche Verkündigung im Streit zwischen Paulus und seinen Gegnern nach dem Galaterbrief, Regensburg 1971, 149–152.

[32] See especially R. Schnackenburg, art. 'Paränese', in Lexikon für Theologie und Kirche, VIII, 2nd edition, Freiburg 1963, 80–82; L.G. Perdue, 'Paraenesis and the Epistle of James', ZNW 72 (1981) 241–256 and W. Schrage, Die konkreten Einzelgebote in der paulinischen Paränese. Ein Beitrag zur neutestamentlichen Ethik, Gütersloh 1961, 37–48. H.D. Betz criticizes Dibelius' treatment of the subject as consisting in 'little more than a random collection of diverse material from a wide range of authors', Galatians, 254 n.7.

Certainly in what follows I will use the terms 'paraenesis' and 'paraenetic' in a broader sense, to designate moral exhortation of any kind. More importantly, one should question whether a passage which makes repeated reference to the law (5.14,18,23; 6.2) and is built on the same dualism of Spirit and flesh as was encountered earlier in the letter (3.3; 4.29) is really as unrelated to the Galatian situation as Dibelius maintained. His case is probably strongest in relation to 5.25–6.10 and will receive careful scrutiny in our discussion of those verses in chapter five.

c) *A defence against possible objections or misunderstandings.* While few scholars would go as far as O'Neill and Dibelius in denying the relevance of 5.13–6.10 to the rest of the letter, a large number treat this section as an apologetic appendix designed to dispel possible misapprehension of the earlier part of the letter. E. de W. Burton, for instance, insists that 5.13–26 'deals with a new phase of the subject, connected, indeed, with the main theme of the letter, but not previously touched upon. Aware that on the one side it will probably be urged against his doctrine of freedom from law that it removes the restraints that keep men from immorality, and certainly on the other that those who accept it are in danger of misinterpreting it as if this were the case, he fervently exhorts the Galatians not to fall into this error, but, instead, through love to serve one another.'[33] Burton's view is echoed by a number of other scholars who maintain that 5.13 'introduces a digression to avoid a misunderstanding of or objection to the course of action demanded in the main argument',[34] or that 'Paul

---

[33] E. de W. Burton, *A Critical and Exegetical Commentary on the Epistle to the Galatians*, Edinburgh 1921, 290. He comments on μόνον in 5.13: 'On this word, as on a hinge, the thought of the epistle turns from freedom to a sharply contrasted aspect of the matter, the danger of abusing freedom' (291).

[34] W.A. Meeks in his review of H.D. Betz, *Galatians*, in *JBL* 100 (1981) 305–6.

was merely anticipating possible objections to his attitude towards the Jewish Law.'[35]

This common approach clearly has important supporting evidence: the careful definition of freedom in 5.13 looks like Paul's attempt to guard himself against misunderstanding, while the charge of 2.17 ('is Christ an agent of sin?') could also have induced Paul to explain his ethical stance.[36] Certainly in other letters Paul is aware of possible or actual misapprehension of his teaching about freedom from the law (Rom 3.8; 6.1,15; 1 Cor 6.12).

If there is an apologetic note in this section, we need to examine more closely how Paul defends himself and why he feels it necessary to do so. We should also inquire, however, whether this section can be understood solely on this basis. The fact that Paul gave such a range of moral instructions in 5.13–6.10, not all obviously related to an apologetic purpose, should cause us to investigate whether there were other factors in the Galatian situation which called forth such exhortation. To treat this section merely as a digression or appendix may therefore be unsatisfactory.[37]

---

[35] Drane, *Paul*, 81; Drane suggests that this section is 'almost an afterthought' (54) since its 'vague content' indicates that there were no actual libertine dangers in mind (81-2). Among the commentators this view that 5.13–6.10 is a distinct apologetic passage is advanced by F. Sieffert, *Der Brief an die Galater*, Göttingen 1899, 314-5, G. Duncan, *The Epistle of Paul to the Galatians*, London 1934, 172, D. Guthrie, *Galatians*, London 1969, 142, J. Bligh, *Galatians. A Discussion of St. Paul's Epistle*, London 1969, 416, H. Schlier, *Der Brief an die Galater*, Göttingen 1971, 242, U. Borse, *Galater*, 189-90, and Mussner, *Galaterbrief*, 367-8. Cf. Luther's comment: 'To the end . . . that it might appear that Christian doctrine doth not destroy good works, or fight against civil ordinances, the Apostle also exhorteth us to exercise ourselves in good works', *A Commentary on St. Paul's Epistle to the Galatians*, Cambridge 1953, 481.

[36] U. Wilckens, 'Zur Entwicklung des paulinischen Gesetzesverständnisses', *NTS* 28 (1982) 154-190 suggests that 5.13–6.10 is Paul's resistance to the charge in 2.17 of his 'blasphemische Legitimation heidnischer Sünde im Namen Christi' (176).

[37] D.K. Fletcher has given a fuller survey of those who consider this section largely defensive, in his unpublished dissertation, *The Singular Argument of Paul's Letter to the Galatians*, Princeton 1982, 5-44. He himself argues against this view (84-98) since he regards it as odd that Paul should 'begin to write so unreservedly for freedom only to qualify it at the end' (96).

d) *Exhortation directed against a second front.* One of the attractions of the suggestions we have investigated thus far is that they help to alleviate what many feel to be the essential problem with this section of Galatians: whereas the rest of the letter is manifestly directed against the dangers of law-observance, this part appears to warn against an opposite danger, the use of freedom as a licence for the flesh (5.13, 19-21) – i.e. libertinism. Jewett has summed up the problem well: 'The core of the dilemma is that the apparent presence of libertinistic tendencies in the Galatian congregation is difficult to reconcile with the main argument of the letter directed against an orthodox nomism.'[38] As we have just seen, O'Neill and Dibelius circumvent this problem by taking 5.13–6.10 as an interpolation or piece of general paraenesis unrelated to the rest of the letter, while many others regard it as Paul's defence against being misunderstood as a libertine.

Another attempt to come to terms with this apparent dichotomy was the 'two-front theory' propounded by W. Lütgert[39] and later taken up by J.H. Ropes.[40] Lütgert considered that Paul's position was threatened not only by nomists but also by a party of 'spirituals' ('Pneumatiker' or 'freie Geister'), who were exploiting their new-found spiritual freedom. The two parties were at loggerheads (9-21, 59-67; see Gal 5.15) and were united only in their hatred of Paul (106). The 'Pneumatiker' attacked him for being dependent on men and subservient to the Jerusalem apostles and complained that he now practised circumcision and re-established the law (22-58; Gal 5.11; 2.18). Paul responded to

---

[38] R. Jewett, 'The Agitators and the Galatian Congregation', *NTS* 17 (1970-71) 198-212, at 198.

[39] W. Lütgert, *Gesetz und Geist. Eine Untersuchung zur Vorgeschichte des Galaterbriefes*, Gütersloh 1919.

[40] J.H. Ropes, *The Singular Problem of the Epistle to the Galatians*, Cambridge, Mass. 1929. In fact the idea of a second party, consisting of libertines, had already been mooted by M.L. de Wette, *Kurze Erklärung des Briefes an die Galater*, Leipzig 1841, 76 and A. Bisping, *Erklärung des zweiten Briefes an die Korinther und des Briefes an die Galater*, Münster 1863, 292-3. J.B. Lightfoot, *Saint Paul's Epistle to the Galatians*, 2nd edition, London 1866, also comments on 5.13: 'It may be that here, as in the Corinthian Church, a party opposed to the Judaizers had shown a tendency to Antinomian excess' (205); but he does not insist on this point nor develop it (see *ibid.* 212 on 6.1).

them fiercely and charged them in 5.7–6.10 with pride and irresponsibility: they were reintroducing heathen vices and an ecstatic frenzy like that of the Phrygian Cybele-cult (31–4, 79–82; Gal 4.8–11; 5.12). Lütgert argues, further, that the success of the nomists in these Gentile congregations can only be explained on the hypothesis that, in an attempt to offset persecution for such heathen excesses, they urged the Galatians to be circumcised and so receive protection as a Jewish sect – a 'religio licita' (94–106). Since the two dangers were connected in this way, Paul had to counter them both with equal vigour in the same letter.

Lütgert's thesis was presented with forceful and original arguments and his analysis was ably supported by Ropes, though with some modifications. Ropes regards the whole argument from 3.1–5.10 as carefully balanced in order to counter both nomists and anti-Jewish radicals and insists that 5.13ff. 'sounds like a straightforward warning against lax tendencies, addressed to persons who really needed it; it does not sound like an exhibition, for the purposes of argument, of the way in which Paul *would be* capable of treating the matter if he were actually writing to readers who did need the warning.'[41] Thus, like Lütgert, Ropes divides up the letter into sections which alternately counter one set of opponents or the other (28–42).

These two scholars performed an important service in opening up the discussion of many questions which had been prematurely closed in nineteenth-century scholarship. Their discussion of the opponents provokes many worthwhile questions and their contention that 5.13–6.10 contains polemical as well as apologetic material deserves serious consideration. One should also recognize their major achievement in relating the whole letter to their reconstruction of circumstances in the Galatian churches. But their analysis of the letter depends on taking 5.13–6.10 as directed against a problem wholly distinct from the main target of the letter and in this 'second front' thesis they have won little

---

[41] *Singular Problem*, 23. Lütgert likewise maintained that in 5.13–6.10 'nicht nur eine Apologie, sondern eine Polemik zu erkennen ist', *Gesetz und Geist*, 15.

support.[42] The letter itself does not indicate any such sharp divisions,[43] and 1 Corinthians indicates that Paul's attacks on consciously libertine behaviour are considerably more forthright than such exhortation as Gal 5.13-6.10.

2. *Galatians 5.13-6.10 integrated within the whole letter*

The views which we have outlined so far have been united in separating this section from the rest of the letter to a greater or lesser degree. In conscious reaction against such a division of Galatians, and especially against any explicit or implicit two-front theory, a number of suggestions have been put forward to hold together the different parts of the letter.

a) *An attack on Gnostic opponents who combined circumcision with libertine morals.* In an article on 'The Heretics in Galatia', W. Schmithals set about exploring the question 'Against what one movement could the apparently differing motifs of the polemic [of Galatians] be directed?' His answer was novel: Jewish-Christian Gnostics who practised circumcision but had libertine morals.[44] In breaking away from the standard hypothesis which

[42] See, among the many critiques of their work, the review of Ropes, *Singular Problem* by J.M. Creed in *JTS* 31 (1930) 421-4 and the comments by Drane, *Paul*, 84-88 and W. Schmithals, *Paul and the Gnostics*, E.T. Nashville 1972, 15-17. They have found support, however, from M. Enslin, *Christian Beginnings. Part III, The Literature of the Christian Movement*, New York 1956, 218-224 and in the commentary by R.T. Stamm, *The Epistle to the Galatians* in *The Interpreter's Bible*, volume 10, New York 1953, 430. W. Foerster, 'Abfassungszeit und Ziel des Galaterbriefes', in *Apophoreta*, ed. W. Eltester and F.H. Kettler, Berlin 1964, 135-141 considers that Paul has libertinism directly in view in 5.13-6.10, but denies that this must imply 'eine widerstreitende *bewusste* Haltung' (140).

[43] The fact that Lütgert and Ropes designate different points as the beginning of Paul's attack on the libertines (Lütgert at 5.7; Ropes at 5.11) underlines the uncertainty of their case for a clear division in the letter.

[44] 'Die Häretiker in Galatien', *ZNW* 47 (1956) 25-67, revised and translated in *Paul and the Gnostics*, 13-64; the question is posed in n.15. Schmithals was apparently unaware that his solution had been anticipated to some extent by F.R. Crownfield, 'The Singular Problem of the Dual Galatians', *JBL* 64 (1945) 491-500. Crownfield detected libertine syncretists in Galatia but he could only explain 5.13-6.10 as Paul's attempt to show the Galatians that Christians will not 'flout the canons of ordinary morality' (496).

16

took the opponents to be 'Judaizers', Schmithals pointed out weaknesses in the current theories, particularly their failure to account adequately for the material in the letter 'directed more or less pointedly against the sarkic conduct of the Galatians' (54). Arguing from Paul's statements in 5.3 and 6.13, he insisted that the opponents were not serious or thorough-going Torah-observers, but advocated circumcision along with veneration of the στοιχεῖα as release from the shackles of the flesh (32–43). This identifies them as (Jewish-Christian) Gnostics whose pride in possession of the Spirit was matched by 'ecstatic licentiousness' (46) and an arrogant manner of behaviour (parallel to the 'Gnostic' problems in Corinth). Paul's attack, then, finds its sharpest point in the ethical warnings of Galatians 5–6, where he urges them to walk humbly in accordance with the Spirit and warns them of the dangers of mocking God.[45] Schmithals concludes that 'it is sufficiently clear that people in Galatia were preaching circumcision but for the rest were thinking and living in libertine rather than legalistic fashion' (52). In a subsequent article he has continued to argue his distinctive case. Among other points he still maintains that the ethical instruction of Gal 5–6 'enthält keinerlei Züge, die sich antijudaistisch deuten lassen'; but it is acutely relevant as a concrete attack against the same self-styled pneumatics (6.1) who are in view throughout the letter.[46]

It is impossible for us to enter here into Schmithals' evidence for Gnostic opponents (see the comments in chapter two below). We should, however, note his attempt to give a unified explanation for the polemic of the whole letter. Unfortunately his case is questionable on two grounds: i) he cannot satisfactorily account for Paul's arguments about the law in Gal 3–4 and, to this

---

[45] Schmithals insists that an explanation out of the concrete situation in Galatia 'is just as much demanded for Gal 5.13–6.10 as for the other parts of the epistle' (49) and he maintains that 'every one of these vices and virtues [5.19–23] fits precisely into the situation which we have shown to exist in Galatia' (53).

[46] 'Judaisten in Galatien?', ZNW 74 (1983) 27–58, at 33; he also puts forward a vigorous response to Vielhauer's treatment of these verses as general and unrelated 'paraenesis', 33–4.

extent, fails to explain *all* the differing motifs in Galatians;[47] ii) he assumes that Paul's moral instruction in 5.13-6.10 is directed against 'typically Gnostic manners of conduct' (52), although an unbiased reading of the text hardly supports such an interpretation.[48] Schmithals' thesis has been taken up by a number of scholars, with several variations and modifications; but few of these have entered into a fresh investigation of Gal 5-6.[49] One contribution we may note here, however, is that once advocated by Marxsen.[50] Marxsen followed Schmithals in assuming that Paul attacked Gnostic libertine excesses in Gal 5-6 but insisted that in . the earlier chapters he attacked his opponents on the understanding that they were Pharisaic Judaists. The inconsistency sprang from Paul's own inadequate knowledge of the Galatian crisis and his consequent confusion. The real problem in Galatia was the Gnostically-inspired veneration of world-elements and ethical laxity: Paul rightly attacked this, but mistakenly associated its circumcision rite with the desire to observe the law. In this way Marxsen held the letter together, but only at considerable expense. In effect he was all but reverting to a two-front

---

[47] See especially *Gnostics*, 33-4, 41 where he asserts that most of the material in Gal 3-4 merely represents current 'topoi' from Paul's discussion with Jews and 'contains hardly any direct references to the situation in Galatia'. He attempts to explain his position in 'Judaisten', 36-7, 43-51, without substantially modifying it. Understandably, his treatment of Gal 3-4 has been heavily criticized: see e.g. D. Georgi, *Die Geschichte der Kollekte des Paulus für Jerusalem*, Hamburg 1965, 35 and E. Güttgemanns, *Der leidende Apostel und sein Herr. Studien zur paulinischen Christologie*, Göttingen 1966, 184-5.

[48] See the general criticisms of Schmithals by Jewett, 'Agitators' and R.McL. Wilson, 'Gnostics – in Galatia?', in *Studia Evangelica IV*, ed. F.L. Cross, Berlin 1965, 358-367.

[49] Note especially Georgi, *Kollekte*, 35-7, K. Wegenast, *Das Verständnis der Tradition bei Paulus und in den Deuteropaulinen*, Neukirchen-Vluyn 1962, 36-40 and D. Lührmann, *Das Offenbarungsverständnis bei Paulus und in paulinischen Gemeinden*, Neukirchen-Vluyn 1965, 67-73; see the fuller survey in Mussner, *Galaterbrief*, 17-24. These all modify Schmithals' thesis by holding that these 'Gnostics' were also, at least to some degree, Torah-observers; but by so doing they undercut the basis of Schmithals' interpretation of Gal 5-6.

[50] W. Marxsen, *Introduction to the New Testament*, E.T. Oxford 1968, 50-58. He has since retracted this thesis in favour of one derived from Betz (see pp.20-2 below), *Einleitung*, 56-71.

hypothesis,[51] while building on the dangerous assumption that he could understand the Galatian situation much better than Paul.[52]

b) *An attempt to dispel the Galatians' moral confusion.* Why should people who are morally serious enough to want to observe the law need the sort of instructions we find in Gal 5.13–6.10? This is the question which our passage invites and of the various answers which we have reviewed thus far none has been free of serious problems. It seems that a satisfactory answer to our question will only be found by establishing more exactly what was going on in Galatia in relation to the law and what Paul's moral instructions are really about. This line of approach is pursued by R. Jewett and H.D. Betz, who both suggest, in different ways, that the Galatians were confused in their moral standards and that Paul was therefore obliged to issue a set of specific instructions.

In an intriguing article Jewett has argued that the Galatians' moral confusion is a continuation of their Gentile past since the law–observance required of them was very superficial.[53] Paul's opponents came to Galatia from Judaea on a rapid circumcising mission to avoid persecution from Zealot fanatics; and because of their desire for 'quick and observable results' (208) they were content to persuade the Galatians to follow the first visible steps of law–observance (circumcision and the cultic calendar) rather than the whole law. This enabled them to portray circumcision as a

---

[51] 'As far as exegesis is concerned . . . there are two opponents, although historically there was only one' (58); in other words, Paul's criticism of the conduct of the Galatians in 5.13–6.10 'does not really fit in with the legalism that he has been attacking' (57).

[52] In fact this was also one of Schmithals' presuppositions in *Gnostics*, 18, 47 n.98, 52 n.110, 54 n.125, but was partly retracted in his subsequent article, 'Judaisten'. R.McL. Wilson, 'Gnosis, Gnosticism and the New Testament', in *Le Origini dello Gnosticismo*, ed. U. Bianchi, Leiden 1967, 511–527 warns of the dangers 'when we endeavour to hold up a mirror to St. Paul in order to identify the opinions of this [sic] opponents and, failing to find what we seek, conclude that he was mistaken, or ill-informed, and that he was entertaining Gnostics unawares' (516).

[53] Jewett, 'Agitators'; cf. his *Paul's Anthropological Terms. A Study of Their Use in Conflict Settings*, Leiden 1971, 17–20. One of the quirks of Jewett's discussion is his constant reference to 'the Galatian congregation' (singular!).

mysterious rite of 'perfection' (ἐπιτελεῖσθε 3.3), thus neatly assimilating their message to the 'Hellenistic aspirations' of the Galatians. Jewett maintains that the whole letter is directed to all the Galatians, even though 3.6–4.31 argues against the nomistic threat and 5.13–6.10 against the libertine threat (209). His solution of this paradox is that 'the entire congregation was as much in danger from the one as from the other. The Hellenistic assumptions of this congregation were as susceptible to the propaganda of the agitators as to the lures of libertinism' (209). The first danger was imported from outside, while the second was a symptom of the Galatians' own Hellenistic misunderstanding of the Spirit; this latter led to 'static self-sufficiency', disregard of ethical distinctions, disdain of future judgment and a proud spiritual self-consciousness (210-2; Gal 6.1-10). When Paul attacks this 'pneumatic libertinism' in 5.13–6.10 he is also attacking the Hellenistic assumptions which made 'perfection' and 'entrance into the mythical seed of Abraham' so attractive (212).

Jewett's reconstruction of the Galatian crisis certainly deserves careful attention. But it is not without its weaknesses. In reality it is a compromise between a two-front thesis and Schmithals' hypothesis. Although Paul is not fighting on two fronts, the letter is taken to represent an attack on two quite different dangers, linked only by a rather loosely-defined entity, the Galatians' 'Hellenistic assumptions'. Like Schmithals, Jewett sees Gal 5-6 as directed against 'pneumatic libertinism' (although this is not specifically Gnostic) and he thinks the Galatians were never really serious about observing the law. Clearly we will need to examine more closely the Galatians' commitment to the law, especially in the light of 4.21 ('you who desire to be under the law') and Paul's repeated references to works of the law. We will also have to enquire whether libertinism is really the main issue in 5.13–6.10.

Betz has provided a different and perhaps more fruitful way of describing the Galatians' moral confusion. In his commentary on Galatians he suggests that one of the causes of the Galatian crisis was that the churches had encountered specific moral problems and were attracted to the law as a means of dealing with them.[54] After a period of 'initial enthusiasm', the Galatians had run into problems with the flesh which they were unable to explain or correct on the basis of Paul's teaching on the Spirit and freedom. Faced by a major problem of 'flagrant misconduct', they were attracted by the opponents' theology since 'entering into the Sinai covenant and obedience to the Torah would provide them with the means to deal with human failure and misconduct' (273). In warning them against this policy, 'Paul realizes that mere polemic against accepting circumcision and law . . . does not do justice to the Galatian trouble. There has to be a positive and viable proposal as to how to deal effectively with misconduct and failure, that is, with the "flesh" ' (273). Hence, although Paul is fighting to defend freedom from two different threats (one from the forces of the flesh and the other from the enslaving power of the law), these are intimately connected as the initial problem and the desired solution in the Galatian churches. In preserving freedom, then, Paul argues both against the law and for the sufficiency of the Spirit in dealing with the flesh.

There are many attractive features in this hypothesis which deserve careful consideration.[55] It helpfully highlights the moral

[54] See especially Betz, *Galatians*, 8-9, 273-4, 295-6; he set out a similar argument in 'Spirit, Freedom and Law. Paul's Message to the Galatian Churches', *SEÅ* 39 (1974) 145-160 and 'In Defense of the Spirit: Paul's Letter to the Galatians as a Document of Early Christian Apologetics', in *Aspects of Religious Propaganda in Judism and Early Christianity*, ed. E. Schüssler-Fiorenza, Notre Dame, Indiana 1976, 99-114. D.E.H. Whiteley, 'Galatians: Then and Now', in *Studia Evangelica VI*, ed. E.A. Livingstone, Berlin 1973, 619-627 makes a similar suggestion (626).

[55] M.-J. Lagrange, *Saint Paul, Epître aux Galates*, Paris 1918, seems to be thinking on similar lines when he comments on the Galatians' desire for rules of good behaviour and suggests that Paul intends his instruction in Gal 5-6 to show 'comment ces instincts généreux trouvent leur satisfaction dans la vie chrétienne, par la charité qui est toute la loi, par la vie de l'esprit' (144). Marxsen has largely adopted Betz's hypothesis (see above n.50).

value of Torah-observance and its possible attraction to the Galatians. We must examine, however, whether Paul had in view specific and flagrant misconduct among the Galatians, or whether their problem was more wide-ranging.[56] We must also investigate more fully the causes of their attraction to the law and circumcision (the latter is not readily explainable on Betz's view) and define more exactly wherein lay their moral confusion.[57]

c) *A continuation of Paul's ironical polemic against the law.* Finally, we may note that a number of scholars have recently emphasized the fact that Paul characterizes the law and circumcision as fleshly pursuits (see 3.3; 6.12-13). This being so, Paul's polemic against pursuing the law (5.1-12) and the flesh (5.13-6.10) could be directed against exactly the *same* object – especially as the latter passage constantly refers to the law (5.14,18,23; 6.2). G. Howard suggested the main outlines of this interpretation,[58] stressing that to be under the law is, for Paul, closely allied with the flesh and being sold under sin; in this case, Paul's ethical section is not an attack on libertinism, nor a defence against charges of antinomianism, but 'his words are directed specifically to a judaizing situation which would force the Galatians to complete their salvation by moving from the Spirit to the flesh' (14). A similar argument has been put forward by Lull and Brinsmead,[59] who both stress the irony of Paul's attack here: it is precisely the Galatians' attempt to avoid the flesh by observing the law which enmeshes them fully in the flesh. Brinsmead, in particular, insists that Galatians cannot be split apart into contrasting sections: the

---

[56] Betz cites Gal 6.1 as evidence for 'flagrant misconduct' but then himself admits that Paul does not seem overly concerned with any specific offence here, *Galatians*, 295-6. D.J. Lull, *The Spirit in Galatia. Paul's Interpretation of 'Pneuma' as Divine Power*, Chico 1980, 7-9, 38-39 criticizes Betz's scheme of 'initial enthusiasm' and subsequent disappointment as imposed on the text from a Weberian model.

[57] Gal 5.21 suggests some previous moral instruction. Meeks considers that 5.13-6.10 'are not novelties, but reminders of the life the Christians already enjoyed after their initiation by Paul', *First Urban Christians*, 116.

[58] *Paul: Crisis in Galatia*, 11-14.

[59] Lull, *Spirit in Galatia*, 113-130; Brinsmead, *Galatians*, 164-192.

whole letter is a 'dialogical response' to the opponents, including Gal 5.13–6.10. In fact here Paul takes up the ethical traditions of his opponents, turns such traditions against them and accuses them of 'fleshly' behaviour, especially in causing disputes among the Galatians.[60]

We will have occasion below to criticize much of Brinsmead's methodology. Given the positive aspects of much in Paul's description of life in the Spirit in 5.13–6.10, it seems somewhat forced to take this whole passage as a subtle and sustained piece of polemic against the opponents. Nevertheless, the terminological links between 'law' and 'flesh' could well be significant and Brinsmead is right to point out that this passage contains repeated warnings about disunity (5.15,19–21,26; 6.1–2). Our task will be to investigate if all this varied material can be explained in relation to the crisis in the Galatian churches.

3. The literary structure of Galatians

Although the classification of opinions on Gal 5.13–6.10 given above may be a little over-schematic (scholars can and do combine a number of the various approaches mentioned), it demonstrates the great variety of interpretations that have been advanced and the continuing lack of consensus on these matters.

Given this state of affairs it could be suggested that the function of this section should be determined from its place in the literary structure of the letter. As we have seen, one of the greatest points of dispute is whether 5.13–6.10 should be treated in isolation from the rest of the letter; and so it is worth investigating whether a structural analysis of the letter could help solve this problem.

---

[60] See *Galatians*, 28–29, 163–170, 180–181, 187–192. G. Bornkamm, 'Die christliche Freiheit (Gal 5)', in *Das Ende des Gesetzes. Paulusstudien. Gesammelte Aufsätze* I, 5th edition, München 1966, 133–138 also notes a connection between the nomist disputes in Galatia and the 'works of the flesh'.

Almost all commentators provide some breakdown of the letter into its component parts and on many points there is universal agreement (e.g. on 6.11 as the beginning of an epilogue or postscript). However, there is considerable disagreement over the point that should be marked as the beginning of the exhortation: a few opt for 4.12, 4.21 or 4.31, while the majority are divided between 5.1 and 5.13.[61] While some stylistic criteria can be used (e.g. Paul's use of γάρ in 5.13 or οὖν in 5.1),[62] it soon emerges that decisions on this matter are based on prior conceptions of what constitutes 'exhortation' and what function the material in 5.13-6.10 is judged to have.[63] In other words, the structural outline offered by most scholars is a result of prior judgments on the function of this section and can have no independent value in deciding this question.

Nevertheless, some attempts have been made to provide a structural analysis from a literary or rhetorical point of view which could claim to offer a more independent judgment. J. Bligh, for instance, divided Galatians up into a complex series of major and minor chiastic sections, and on this basis concluded that the 'moral section' consists of 5.11-6.11.[64] But his artificial pattern of overlapping chiasms has been rightly dismissed as fanciful and it contributes nothing to our quest.[65]

---

[61] O. Merk gave a useful survey of opinions in 'Der Beginn der Paränese im Galaterbrief', *ZNW* 60 (1969) 83-104.

[62] See especially W. Nauck, 'Das οὖν-paräneticum', *ZNW* 49 (1958) 134-5.

[63] Thus Merk opts for 5.13 because he considers that only here does Paul really begin to discuss ethics, 'Beginn', 100-104; cf. among the commentators, Schlier, Lagrange, Becker and Mussner. Ebeling, however, argues that Paul's practical appeals begin at 5.1, *Truth of the Gospel*, 239-242; this view is also represented by Lightfoot, Burton, Guthrie and Bonnard, *L'Epître de Saint Paul aux Galates*, 2nd edition, Neuchâtel 1972.

[64] *Galatians in Greek*, Detroit 1966; cf. his commentary, *Galatians*, which reveals his view that the original Antioch discourse extends from 2.14 to 5.10!

[65] Note the trenchant criticisms by Betz in his review of Bligh's commentary in *JBL* 89 (1970) 126-7; C.K. Barrett also dismisses Bligh's thesis in 'The Allegory of Abraham, Sarah and Hagar in the Argument of Galatians', in *Rechtfertigung*, ed. J. Friedrich et al., Tübingen 1976, 3-5. J. Jeremias suggested a simpler chiastic structure, dividing the letter into two sections, 1.13-2.21 and 3.1-6.10, on the basis of 1.10-12, 'Chiasmus in den Paulusbriefen', *ZNW* 49 (1958) 152-3.

A more promising approach was pioneered by H.D. Betz. To the form-critical analysis of Galatians as a letter,[66] Betz added a new perspective by comparing Galatians with the rhetorical genre of a defence speech, thus proposing that it is a (rare) example of an 'apologetic letter'.[67] His analysis emphasized the unity and careful composition of the letter and made a number of valuable suggestions about its structure.[68] Unfortunately, however, his method of approach is able to contribute least to our understanding of the paraenetic section of the letter since, as he himself acknowledges, paraenesis plays only a marginal role in rhetoric.[69] He does, however, provide one noteworthy argument for the structural unity of 5.1-6.10 which, he suggests, is built on the threefold combination of indicative and imperative which heads each sub-section (5.1,13,25).[70]

Finally, we may note the attempt of B.N. Brinsmead to build on Betz's rhetorical analysis of the letter. Brinsmead maintains

[66] See J.L White, *The Form and Function of the Body of the Greek Letter*, Missoula 1972. N. Dahl undertook a detailed study of the epistolary structure of Galatians, based on a division between 'rebuke' (1.12-4.11) and 'request' (4.12-6.10) in an unpublished SBL Seminar Paper of 1973, 'Paul's Letter to the Galatians: epistolary genre, content and structure'.

[67] Betz, 'The Literary Composition and Function of Paul's Letter to the Galatians', *NTS* 21 (1974-5) 353-379 and his commentary, *Galatians*, 14-25. The only other example of an 'apologetic letter' cited is Plato, *Epistle* 7 (15).

[68] Betz's proposal has not, however, met with universal agreement by experts in this field. See especially D.E. Aune's review in *RSR* 7 (1981) 323-328, the critical remarks of G. Kennedy, *New Testament Interpretation through Rhetorical Criticism*, Chapel Hill 1984, 144-152, and the sweeping judgments of G. Lyons, *Pauline Autobiography. Towards a New Understanding*, Atlanta 1985, 112-119. It is striking that in his recent commentary, *2 Corinthians 8 and 9*, Philadelphia 1985, Betz detects a very similar structural pattern (exordium, narratio, propositio, probatio, peroratio) in letters of a very different rhetorical stamp (mostly deliberative). This indicates that the structure he proposes for Galatians is not specific to a forensic or apologetic style and is, perhaps, too general to be of much value.

[69] He terms 5.1-6.10 'exhortatio' or 'paraenesis' but admits that 'it is rather puzzling to see that parenesis plays only a marginal role in the ancient rhetorical handbooks, if not in rhetoric itself', *Galatians*, 254. Although H. Hübner defends Betz against some of his critics, he admits that his treatment of the paraenetic section is 'm.E. der schwächste Teil seiner Argumentation', 'Der Galaterbrief und das Verhältnis von antiker Rhetorik und Epistolographie', *TLZ* 109 (1984) 244.

[70] *Galatians*, 254-5.

that 5.13–6.10 can be understood within the rhetorical pattern as a 'refutatio', which picks up and answers the opponents' arguments.[71] On this basis he imagines he can reconstruct the opponents' 'ethical traditions' and he defines the purpose of this section very exactly as a polemical response to the ethics of the opponents. This striking proposal is, however, almost entirely arbitrary. Brinsmead provides no evidence for his assertion that these verses are a 'refutatio' and his argument works on the completely unfounded assumption that wherever Paul uses 'traditional' material he must be echoing the *opponents'* traditions.[72]

In all these three cases, then, what promised to be a relatively objective structural analysis of the letter has turned out to be of no value in our effort to determine the function of this section of the letter. It is clear that our questions can only be solved through careful exegesis and historical reconstruction.

Galatians and Pauline Ethics

Thus far we have restricted our focus to the paraenetic material in Gal 5.13–6.10 and the question of its function. Our discussion of the range of different theories advanced has indicated that, in inquiring why Paul dictated these paragraphs (if they are indeed his), we need to answer a number of subsidiary questions, such as: i) Is his exhortation here related to the argument of the earlier chapters concerning law and faith? ii) Is this section related to a concrete situation in the Galatian churches? iii) Who is Paul addressing in this exhortation and what problems, if any, does he have in view? iv) Is his main purpose in these verses to do with appeal, defence, explanation or polemic? These are among the questions that we hope to be able to answer by the end of our investigation.

---

[71] *Galatians*, 44, 53–4, 163–181.

[72] See Aune's devastating review òf Brinsmead's book in *CBQ* (1984) 145–7, concluding that his arguments are 'justified only by faith'!

But our interests range wider than this section or these questions alone. Paul's letter to the Galatians raises a whole range of questions concerning his ethics. Some of these relate specifically to 5.13–6.10 or particular verses within that section, while others arise out of the whole subject matter of the letter and the role of ethics and the law within Paul's theology. The following subjects are of particular relevance:

1. When Paul's exhortations in Galatians are placed alongside the Pauline and non-Pauline paraenesis elsewhere in the New Testament, as well as the contemporary ethical teaching in Jewish and Hellenistic circles, it has frequently been observed how much common and traditional material Paul uses. This phenomenon is most evident in the lists of virtues and vices which Paul offers (5.19–23) since both the inclusion of such lists and much of their content are well attested in other Christian and non-Christian sources.[73] Other features of Paul's paraenesis provide similar evidence: his citation of Lev 19.18 as a summary of the law in 5.14 and his use of Hellenistic-style 'sententiae' in 6.1–10 also suggest that his paraenesis is not an entirely original creation. The investigation of the traditional material in Pauline paraenesis has been most energetically pursued by Dibelius and his students; as we have already indicated, they contended that much early Christian ethical teaching was adopted more or less wholesale from contemporary tradition and had no significant connections with the theological insights which Paul, or others, were developing. In relation to Gal 6.1–10, the most thorough collection of 'parallels' from Hellenistic moral philosophy has been provided by H.D. Betz.[74] Our study of this material will there-

---

[73] A. Vögtle, *Die Tugend- und Lasterkataloge im Neuen Testament, exegetisch, religions- und formgeschichtlich untersucht,* Münster 1936; S. Wibbing, *Die Tugend- und Lasterkataloge im Neuen Testament und ihre Traditionsgeschichte unter besonderer Berücksichtigung der Qumran-Texte,* Berlin 1959.

[74] Betz, *Galatians,* ad loc.

fore contribute to a wide-ranging debate on Pauline ethics.[75]

2. The question of the source of Paul's ethics is also important for the study of their theological roots. The exhortation in Galatians, with its emphasis on freedom, the Spirit and belonging to Christ, has led many scholars to conclude that the roots of Paul's ethics lie not in his doctrine of justification by faith but in his 'Christ-mysticism' and in the experience of the gift of the Spirit. Thus A. Schweitzer confidently declared that 'there is no logical route from the righteousness by faith to a theory of ethics'; only Paul's mysticism could provide its rationale.[76] More recently, Sanders has also located the roots of Paul's ethics in 'participation in Christ' rather than concepts like 'justification' or 'covenant'.[77] Within the argument of Galatians, justification by faith features prominently in chapters 2-3, the Spirit is mentioned repeatedly from chapter 3 onwards and participation in Christ is ubiquitous. To explore how these themes relate to each other and how they are involved in Paul's concern for 'walking in the Spirit' will help to shed some light on the connections between Pauline theology and ethics.

3. Several verses in Gal 5-6 are classic examples of the Pauline combination of indicative and imperative. Paul urges the Galatians to stand firm in the freedom which Christ has given them (5.1), to resist the desires of the flesh which they have already crucified (5.16-18,24), and to walk in the Spirit in which they have life (5.25). Such phrases express what many consider to

---

[75] The debate concerns not only the content of Paul's ethics (see, e.g., O.L. Yarbrough, *Not Like the Gentiles. Marriage Rules in the Letters of Paul*, Atlanta 1985) but also such forms as the Haustafel (see, e.g., J.E. Crouch, *The Origin and Intention of the Colossian Haustafel*, Göttingen 1972). Cf. F.J. Ortkemper on Rom 12-13, *Leben aus dem Glauben. Christliche Grundhaltungen nach Römer 12-13*, Münster 1980).

[76] A. Schweitzer, *The Mysticism of Paul the Apostle*, E.T. 2nd edition, London 1953, 225; see the whole passage 219-226 and 293-333. J. Knox, *Chapters in a Life of Paul*, London 1954, 142-158 and L.E. Keck, 'Justification of the Ungodly and Ethics', in *Rechtfertigung*, ed. J. Friedrich et al, Tübingen 1976, 199-206, also doubt the ethical value of 'justification by faith'.

[77] *Paul and Palestinian Judaism*, 511-5.

be a fundamental paradox in Pauline ethics, the appeal to 'be what you are'. In a seminal essay in 1924 Bultmann emphasized the importance of this paradox as a key to understanding much else in Pauline theology,[78] and since then it has been the subject of intense discussion.[79] We may be able to shed some light on this matter by examining how Paul employs this indicative-imperative combination and what it reveals of the interplay of divine and human activity.

4. The dominant categories in Paul's ethics in Galatians are 'Spirit' and 'flesh'. Although this pair of terms is found very occasionally in the Old Testament and has some parallels in Qumranic and Hellenistic literature, Paul's special use of it in an ethical (rather than purely anthropological) context is particularly interesting. Our study may be able to contribute to the extensive discussion of Paul's understanding of σάρξ[80] by investigating this aspect of his usage.

5. Paul's contrast between being led by the Spirit and being under the law (5.18) has prompted many attempts to express the distinction between Pauline and 'legal' ethics. Some consider that Paul's ethics are essentially a matter of the internal working of the Spirit rather than the enforcement of legal rules ('the letter') from the outside.[81] Others stress the contrast between the 'fruit' of the Spirit and the 'works' of the law: this is taken to indicate that Pauline ethics are 'the natural outcome of a transformed nature rather than the laborious attempt to conform to an external

---

[78] 'Das Problem der Ethik bei Paulus', *ZNW* 23 (1924) 123-140; cf. his *Theology of the New Testament*, E.T. London 1952, I, 314-340.

[79] See for instance, H. Windisch, 'Das Problem des paulinischen Imperativs', *ZNW* 23 (1924) 265-81, and H. Schlier, *Galater*, 264-7; cf. G. Bornkamm, 'Baptism and New Life in Paul (Romans 6)', in *Early Christian Experience*, London 1969, 71-86 and E. Käsemann, 'The "Righteousness of God" in Paul', in *New Testament Questions*, 168-182. There is a useful survey of the discussion by W.D. Dennison, 'Indicative and Imperative: The Basic Structure of Pauline Ethics', *Calvin Theological Journal* 14 (1979) 55-78.

[80] See e.g. Bultmann, *Theology* I, 239-246; E. Brandenburger, *Fleisch und Geist. Paulus und die dualistische Weisheit*, Neukirchen-Vluyn 1968.

[81] Note the careful discussion of this point by S. Westerholm, ' "Letter" and "Spirit": the foundation of Pauline Ethics', *NTS* 30 (1984) 224-248.

code'.[82] Paul's talk of being led by the Spirit could suggest an automatic and spontaneous obedience; thus Betz remarks on Paul's 'almost naive confidence in the "Spirit"',[83] and Drane writes of Gal 5-6: 'Christians live on a new level of existence and so their actions will automatically follow from this new kind of existence'.[84] When Paul celebrates 'freedom' in Christ (5.1,13), does he mean freedom from all rules? Drane considers that 'the Jewish law with its specific precepts had gone forever, and Paul proposed to put in its place as the spring of moral action not a new set of rules, but Christ himself . . . Though he speaks of Christians serving one another in love (v 13, vi 1) such exhortations do not constitute moral rules in any sense whatever.'[85]

On the other hand, some consideration should be given to the fact that Paul does issue a detailed list of sins to be avoided (5.19-21) and gives a series of specific instructions in 5.26-6.10. Does this indicate, as W. Schrage maintains, that Paul's ethics do not just revolve around a single principle of love but have room for a range of individual moral rules as well?[86] W.D. Davies would go considerably further: he makes much of the fact that in 6.2 Paul talks of a 'law of Christ' and argues that Paul 'has turned out to be a catechist after the manner of a Rabbi.'[87] More recently there has been some discussion about whether Paul's ethics operate as 'law' and to what extent they are 'legal'.[88] While we

---

[82] T.W. Manson, 'Jesus, Paul, and the Law', in *Judaism and Christianity III. Law and Religion*, ed. E.I.J. Rosenthal, London 1938, 139.

[83] Betz, 'Spirit, Freedom and Law', 159.

[84] Drane, *Paul*, 53; cf. idem, 'Tradition, Law and Ethics in Pauline Theology', *NT* 16 (1974) 167-178 and Räisänen, *Paul and the Law*, 115.

[85] Drane, 'Tradition', 172; he intends to contrast this style of ethics with that to be found in 1 Cor. Cf. P. Richardson, *Paul's Ethic of Freedom*, Philadelphia 1979.

[86] W. Schrage, *Einzelgebote*; cf. his more recent book, *Ethik des Neuen Testaments*, Göttingen 1982, 180-185.

[87] W.D. Davies, *Paul and Rabbinic Judaism. Some Elements in Pauline Theology*, 4th edition, Philadelphia 1980, 129.

[88] E.P. Sanders, *Paul, The Law, and the Jewish People*, 105-114; R. Mohrlang, *Matthew and Paul. A Comparison of Ethical Perspectives*, Cambridge 1984, 35-42.

must acknowledge that Galatians may not be typical, our investigation may help to shed some light on this thorny issue in Pauline studies.

6. The coherence of Paul's statements on the law has been intensively discussed in recent years, especially in view of the contrasts between his varying negative and positive remarks about it. This question is obviously important in the discussion of Galatians. Paul's statements on the law appear to be consistently negative until 5.13, but there then follow comments about fulfilling the whole law (5.14) and fulfilling the law of Christ (6.2), although even in this passage Paul maintains that Spirit-led Christians are not under the law (5.18). As regards Pauline theology as a whole, there have been a number of studies proposing a radical development from an earlier negative to a later positive view of the law.[89] But verses like Gal 5.14 and 6.2 suggest that the tension is to be found even within the same letter (unless we take νόμος in these verses in a wholly different sense).[90] A number of attempts have been made to explain or resolve this tension in Paul's thought. Does he, at least implicitly, distinguish between a ritual and a moral law?[91] Do Paul's negative remarks relate to a legalistic misuse of the law (as a way of earning salvation or establishing one's own righteousness) and his positive remarks to its proper function (a 'third use' of the law, inasmuch as it contains God's demand)?[92] Or is Paul criticizing a Jewish nationalistic misunderstanding of the law, which fails to take account of its real priorities, viz. the faith and love which

---

[89] See especially U. Wilckens, 'Entwicklung' and H. Hübner, *Law in Paul's Thought*.

[90] Räisänen comments on the problems of theories of development, *Paul and the Law*, 8-9. Hübner has proposed a new way of understanding νόμος in Gal 5.14, 'Das ganze und das eine Gesetz. Zum Problemkreis Paulus und die Stoa', *KuD* 21 (1975) 239-256; cf. *Law in Paul's Thought*, 36-42.

[91] See C. Haufe, 'Die Stellung des Paulus zum Gesetz', *TLZ* 91 (1966) 171-178.

[92] Bultmann, *Theology* I, 341; C.E.B. Cranfield, 'St. Paul and the Law', in *New Testament Issues*, ed. R. Batey, London 1970, 148-172.

Christians now exercise?[93] Are Paul's negative and positive remarks given in response to different questions: does he say 'not by works of the law' in talking about *entry into* the church but 'keep the law' in discussing *behaviour within* it?[94] Or are Paul's contrasting statements just symptoms of his desperate attempts to win his argument and the self-contradictory conclusions to which he is drawn?[95]

7. A broader question touches on the subject matter of the whole letter: what is the meaning of the antithesis between works of the law and faith? The most common interpretation – strongly influenced by the Reformation theological tradition – takes this antithesis to represent a basic theological and existential contrast: between meriting salvation by good works and receiving it passively through faith as a gift.[96] One major problem for this interpretation is in coming to terms with Paul's specific comments about judgment on the basis of works (see e.g. Gal 5.21; 6.7-9);[97] another is whether either Jews or Christian

---

[93] In 'New Perspective' Dunn attempts to draw a distinction between 'works of the law' (circumcision, food laws and sabbath – 'the expression of a too narrowly nationalistic and racial conception of the covenant') and the law or law-keeping in general, 117-120. In 'Works of the Law', he explains his distinction more fully, in terms of two different attitudes to (or understandings of) the law: 'The law as fixing a particular social identity, as encouraging a sense of national superiority . . . that is what Paul is attacking . . . Divorced from that perspective, as the law understood in terms of faith rather than in terms of works, it can continue to serve in a positive role', 531; cf.538.

[94] Sanders, *Paul, The Law, and the Jewish People*, 4, 10, 83-4, 114, 143-5, 159.

[95] This is the position taken by H. Räisänen, 'Paul's Theological Difficulties with the Law', in *Studia Biblica 1978 III*, ed. E.A. Livingstone, Sheffield 1980, 301-320 and *Paul and the Law*. I have surveyed this issue among others in 'Paul and the Law: Observations on Some Recent Debates', *Themelios* 12 (1986) 5-15.

[96] See the survey of Lutheran views in Watson, *Paul, Judaism and the Gentiles*, chapter 1. The same perspective is also current in Reformed and Catholic exegesis: see e.g. C.E.B. Cranfield, 'St. Paul and the Law', and J.A. Fitzmyer, 'Paul and the Law', in *To Advance the Gospel. New Testament Studies*, New York 1981, 186-201.

[97] See W. Joest, *Gesetz und Freiheit. Das Problem des Tertius Usus Legis bei Luther und die neutestamentliche Paränese*, 3rd edition, Göttingen 1961. The problem has been discussed recently by K.P. Donfried, 'Justification and Last Judgment in Paul', *ZNW* 67 (1976) 90-110 and N.M. Watson,'Justified by faith; judged by works – an Antinomy?', *NTS* 29 (1983) 209-221.

'Judaizers' commonly held any such 'works-righteousness' theology.

As we noted above (pp.3-6) this whole interpretative tradition has come under fierce attack from Sanders, Watson and others, who maintain that Paul is not raising (or answering) any such generalized theological question. Sanders takes the contrast between 'works of the law' and 'faith' as restricted to the specific issue of how Gentiles *enter* the people of God. This suggests that Paul did not oppose 'works' as such or even 'the law' as such, but only the notion that Gentiles need to observe the whole Mosaic law (with all its distinctively Jewish customs) in order to enter the Christian community. Sanders' thesis also implies that 'the flat opposition between faith and the law comes only when he is discussing the requirement essential for membership in the people of God . . . When the topic was how people in that group should behave, he saw no opposition between faith and law'.[98] On this view judgment by works is no real anomaly and Paul's comments on fulfilling the law are readily explainable.[99] We may question, however, whether Sanders is right to posit such a sharp distinction between 'getting in' and 'staying in': we will need to investigate whether Galatians itself supports this distinction.[100]

Watson interprets the antithesis of 'faith' and 'works of the law' as essentially sociological rather than theological: 'For Paul, the term "works of the law" refers not to morality in general but to the practice of the law within the Jewish community; and the term "faith in Jesus Christ" refers not to a willingness to receive God's grace as a free gift and to renounce reliance on one's own achievements, but to the Christian confession of Jesus as the

---

[98] *Paul, The Law, and the Jewish People*, 114.

[99] See also U. Wilckens, 'Was heisst bei Paulus: "Aus Werken des Gesetzes wird kein Mensch gerecht"?', in *Rechtfertigung als Freiheit. Paulusstudien*, Neukirchen-Vluyn 1974, 77-109.

[100] See also the reply to Sanders by R.H. Gundry, 'Grace, Works and Staying Saved in Paul', *Biblica* 66 (1985) 1-38. Räisänen thinks that Paul has misrepresented Judaism, as if it were legalistic, 'Legalism and Salvation by the Law: Paul's Portrayal of the Jewish Religion as a Historical and Theological Problem', in *Die paulinische Literatur und Theologie*, ed. S. Pedersen, Århus 1980, 63-83.

Messiah and the social reorientation which this entails . . . The antithesis between faith and works merely asserts the separation of the church from the Jewish community; it does not provide a theoretical rationale for that separation'.[101] On this understanding, faith is not a passive attitude but the adoption of new Christian beliefs *and* practices: 'for Christian conduct is a vital constituent element of faith.'[102] Thus, this view can easily accommodate Paul's demand for Christian 'work' and his threat of judgment on Christians who are disobedient.[103] But we will have to enquire whether Watson's focus on the sociological context of the antithesis does sufficient justice to the theological issues which seem to surround and underlie it. Does the antithesis between 'faith' and 'works of the law', even when seen in its proper Jew-Gentile context, still express some far-reaching theological convictions?

In this chapter I have attempted to highlight some of the most important questions which arise in relation to Paul's ethics in Galatians. Many of these relate specifically to the function of Paul's paraenesis in 5.13-6.10, but others range more widely across the whole letter and a spectrum of ethical issues. It has become clear at various points that the only satisfactory approach to these questions is by means of a number of interrelated enquiries. In the first place, we need to gain the clearest possible understanding of the Galatian crisis in its historical context. This is essential if we are to discern what was at stake in the Galatian churches and how Paul's moral instruction might (or might not) be relevant to that situation (chapter 2). Secondly, we must assess

---

[101] *Paul, Judaism and the Gentiles*, 64-65. Watson argues the same point in connection with Phil 3 (78-9) and Romans (112-3, 119-121, 130, 134-5, 165); cf. his conclusion: 'It is therefore completely wrong to regard the phrase *sola gratia* as the key to Paul's theology; Paul does not believe that salvation is by grace alone. The view that he does so springs from a failure to recognise that the faith-works contrast is primarily sociological rather than theological in meaning. The faith-works contrast is only absolute as a contrast between the incompatible way of life practised by two different religious communities', 179.

[102] *Ibid.*, 65.

[103] See Watson's discussion of judgment by works in Romans 2 (115-6, 120).

Paul's response to the crisis, noting the major theological themes he develops and their relation (if any) to the exhortation at the end of the letter (chapter 3). Thirdly, we must focus considerable attention on 5.13–6.10 in particular, examining the style of these various statements, the specific issues they address and their function in relation to the Galatian crisis and the rest of the letter (chapters 4–6). On this basis we will be able to return to, and provide answers for, the range of problems outlined in this introductory chapter (chapter 7).

Chapter Two

The Galatians and the Demands of 'the Agitators'

The Nature of our Evidence

It is clear that Galatians is Paul's response to what he considered to be an alarming crisis in the Galatian churches; and, as we have just noted, the first step in understanding Paul's letter must be some attempt to reconstruct this Galatian crisis. But this historical task requires us to evaluate complex evidence, and at this point some observations on correct methodology are in order.

It will be necessary first to clarify what sort of reconstruction we require. There are many aspects of the crisis and many questions about those Paul calls 'the agitators'[1] which could be investigated, but not all will be of immediate relevance to our present enquiry. If we are to understand the issues at stake in Galatia and the way in which Paul's letter responds to them, we need to focus initially on three main questions: i) what were Paul's opponents advocating in the Galatian churches? ii) what

---

[1] οἱ ταράσσοντες ὑμᾶς (1.7); ὁ ταράσσων ὑμᾶς (5.10); οἱ ἀναστατοῦντες ὑμᾶς (5.12). They are usually termed 'Judaizers' but I have avoided the use of this term, chiefly in order to preserve the original sense of ἰουδαΐζειν: both in Galatians and elsewhere (Gal 2.14; Plutarch, Cic 7.5; LXX Esther 8.17; Josephus, Bell 2.454,463; Alexander Polyhistor, paraphrasing Theodotus in Eusebius, P.E. 9.22.5; Ignatius, Mag 10.3) it means to adopt Jewish customs or live like a Jew and never has the sense of encouraging others to become Jews. Thus the real 'Judaizers' are not Paul's opponents but the Gentiles in Antioch and Galatia. In referring to 'the agitators' or 'the opponents' I am conscious of using terms which reflect Paul's bias: they presumably understood their 'agitation' as beneficial correction and we cannot be entirely sure that they saw themselves as opposed to Paul (see Howard, Crisis, 7-11, 39,44). Thus some scholars prefer to use neutral terms such as 'the Teachers' (see Martyn, 'Law–Observant Mission') but we do not know whether they would have owned this title either. Paul's choice of terms for his opponents may echo the Old Testament references to those who 'trouble' Israel, Josh 6.18; 7.25; Judg 11.35; 1 Sam 14.29; cf. 1 Macc 3.5; 7.22 (I am grateful to Dr. R.P. Gordon for this suggestion).

arguments were they using to support their demands? iii) why were the Galatians willing to respond to them? The third question is obviously closely related to the second: the strength of the opponents' arguments will go a long way to explaining their success in persuading the Galatians. But it also invites analysis from another, more sociological, perspective since it concerns the social, as well as intellectual, factors that contribute to any such significant alteration of beliefs and behavioural patterns.

It is clear that our primary and decisive evidence for the Galatian crisis must be Paul's letter itself; but using this letter to reconstruct the situation it presupposes is by no means unproblematic and requires a carefully defined methodology. It may also be that some light can be shed on the Galatian crisis by studying historical parallels; but in this case we will need to take care that the evidence we adduce is truly 'parallel' to the events in the Galatian churches. We shall assess these two kinds of evidence in turn:

a) *Using Galatians.* If we are to use Galatians to reconstruct the Galatian crisis we must establish some criteria by which we may judge how to 'mirror-read' this letter. Many scholars have noted the difficulties inherent in this inevitably circular form of gathering evidence; some would go so far as to regard it as hopelessly speculative.[2] One of the problems we have to contend with is that Paul's response to the crisis, being so heavily polemical, inevitably delivers us a very partial and biased account of events. Given his obvious concern to wean the Galatians away from the influence of 'the agitators', we can hardly expect Paul to represent their views fully and fairly. We should never underestimate the distorting effect of polemic, and this may be

---

[2] See Lyons, *Pauline Autobiography*, 96ff. Using different, but equally appropriate imagery, M.D. Hooker describes this procedure for gaining evidence as 'an extremely difficult task, as prone to misinterpretation as the incidental overhearing of one end of a telephone conversation', 'Were there false teachers in Colossae?', in *Christ and Spirit in the New Testament*, ed. B. Lindars and S.S. Smalley, Cambridge 1973, 315. She does not, however, dismiss it as a hopeless task. I have discussed these methodological problems more fully in 'Mirror-Reading a Polemical Letter: Galatians as a Test Case', *JSNT* 31 (1987) 73-93.

particularly acute in Paul's descriptions of his opponents' motivation (5.7-12; 6.12-13).[3] It is likely that Paul has chosen to respond to only a few points in the opponents' message and that he has left out of account many issues on which he and they were entirely agreed. Thus our primary evidence is no neutral or comprehensive report; it needs to be handled with extreme caution.

Now, Paul must have known that his arguments would not be persuasive if he failed to address at least some of the basic facts of the crisis. At the very least, then, we would expect to find reflected in his letter what he considered to be the most important issues raised by his opponents and what he hoped would be recognized as salient points by the Galatians. Of course it is not impossible that Paul was misinformed about the crisis or misunderstood the message and purpose of his opponents; as we saw in the last chapter, this is an essential feature in the interpretation given by Schmithals and Marxsen. But the implications of this view are devastating: if our only solid evidence concerning the opponents is written under a major misapprehension about them, our search for the real opponents must be abortive. While we know nothing about Paul's sources of information, we know he had been to Galatia at least once (4.13), and the confidence with which he speaks about the Galatians' 'apostasy' probably indicates a reasonable amount of information.

However, great care is required in using Galatians as a 'mirror', for this can easily become an arbitrary exercise. There are dangers, for instance, if we allow ourselves to become unduly selective, focusing only on certain parts of the letter or certain types of remark (e.g., Paul's defensive statements).[4] Unless we have very good reasons to the contrary, we should take the whole letter as in some sense a response to the crisis brought about by the

[3] This is acknowledged and helpfully discussed by Mussner, *Galaterbrief*, 27-8 and Eckert, *Verkündigung*, 22-6, 234-6.

[4] J.B. Tyson only selects and investigates what he considers to be Paul's defensive remarks, 'Paul's Opponents in Galatia', *NT* 10 (1968) 241-254. Mussner, on the other hand, tries to identify the opponents' 'Schlagworte' and 'Einwände', *Galaterbrief*, 13. We have already noted (above p.17-8) how Schmithals bypasses most of Gal 3-4.

opponents, while we also need some criteria to judge which are the most revealing of Paul's statements. There are further dangers, however, if we rely overmuch on particular words and phrases which are taken to represent the very vocabulary of the opponents. Some scholars, for instance, latch onto Paul's mention of 'beginning' and 'completing' in 3.3 (ἐναρξάμενοι . . . ἐπιτελεῖσθε) and take this to reflect the opponents' theology of 'perfection'.[5] Others take Paul's mention of the στοιχεῖα τοῦ κόσμου (4.3,9), together with his reference to the Galatians' observance of the calendar (4.10), as an indication of the opponents' astrological syncretism; their observance of feasts is said to involve a mythical and cosmological conception of the law.[6] But in these and similar cases the argument depends on a fragile chain of assumptions: that we can tell where Paul echoes his opponents' language, that he knew the exact vocabulary they used, that he was willing to re-use it (ironically?), and that we can reconstruct the meaning which the opponents originally gave to it.[7]

[5] See, e.g., Oepke, Galater, 101; Jewett, 'Agitators', 206-7; Brinsmead, Galatians, 79-81. Because these terms can be used for the beginning and completion of a cultic act, Brinsmead concludes that they reflect 'a technical formula for progress in a religious mystery from a lower to a higher stage' (79) and so assumes that the opponents presented their law-programme as 'a completion of a mystery of which baptism is only an initiation' (191).

[6] Thus the opponents' theology is characterized as a Jewish Gnosis with Iranian influence, Wegenast, Tradition, 36-40; Schlier, Galater, 19-24. Cf. the description by G. Stählin: 'eine sektiererische judenchristliche Bewegung . . . die gnostisch gefärbt, aber doch in der Hauptsache gesetzlich bestimmt war', 'Galaterbrief', in RGG II, 1188; there are similar verdicts from Lührmann, Offenbarung, 69 and H. Koester, ΓΝΩΜΑΙ ΔΙΑΦΟΡΟΙ . The Origin and Nature of Diversification in the History of Early Christianity', HTR 58 (1965) 307-9. Reference to the angels' involvement in the giving of the law (3.19) has also been taken as a sign of Gnostic veneration of angel-powers.

[7] In the case of 3.3, the language Paul uses is probably entirely his own (Phil 1.6; 2 Cor 8.6, especially in the reading of B); and even if he has adopted it from his opponents, there is no need to assume they used it in the sense of a religious mystery as it is common vocabulary. See the justly cautious approach of Schlier, Galater, 123-4 and Betz, Galatians, 133-4. As for στοιχεῖα, it is admittedly an unusual term for Paul (elsewhere only in Col 2.8,20, where both authenticity and meaning are disputed); but it is not necessarily adopted from the opponents. Scholars continue to debate the meaning of the term (basic constituents? elemental

continued on p.40

39

Finally, we should note the danger of over-interpretation. Even though Galatians is a highly polemical letter we cannot assume that every statement Paul makes is a rebuttal of an equally vigorous counter-statement by his opponents. Not every denial by Paul need reflect an explicit assertion by the opponents; and not every command need reflect a deliberate effort by the Galatians (or the opponents) to flout that command. Thus Paul's statement in 5.11 ('If I, brethren, still preach circumcision, why am I still persecuted?') does not have to imply that he was being openly accused of preaching circumcision;[8] and 5.13 ('do not use your freedom as an opportunity for the flesh') does not necessarily indicate flagrant libertinism among the Galatians. Whether Paul's statements do imply such outright contrast (or whether they are intended merely to remind, to ward off potential misunderstanding, or to serve as rhetorical contrasts) can only be decided if a number of other criteria are brought into play. We need to note, for instance, the *tone* of his remarks (emphasis may

---

continued from p.39

teachings? astrological powers? angelic and spiritual forces?): see, for instance, the variety of conclusions reached by G. Delling, art. στοιχεῖον in *TDNT* VII, 670-687; A.J. Bandstra, *The Law and the Elements of the World*, Kampen 1964; E. Schweizer, 'Die "Elemente der Welt" Gal 4,3.9; Kol 2,8.20', in *Verborum Veritas*, ed. O. Böcher and K. Haacker, Wuppertal 1970, 245-259; W. Carr, *Angels and Principalities*, Cambridge 1981, 72-76. If it is hard enough to decide what Paul meant by the term, how much less can we reconstruct the opponents' meaning! It is interesting that Lührmann (see previous note) has recently argued that the terms used in 4.10 are not specifically 'gnostic' but equally applicable to all kinds of Judaism, 'Tage, Monate, Jahreszeiten, Jahre (Gal 4.10)', in *Werden und Wirken des Alten Testaments*, ed. R. Albertz et al., Göttingen 1980, 428-45. We are probably right to conclude with Vielhauer, 'Von einem Stoicheiakult in Galatien fehlt jede Spur', *Geschichte*, 117.

[8] It could be no more than a simple contrast between Paul and his opponents: they 'preach circumcision' – he used to but no longer does. One could even take this question as Paul's reply to a claim made by the intruders in Galatia who saw themselves as Paul's allies: we 'preach circumcision' and Paul really does too; see Howard, *Crisis*, 7-11 and P. Borgen, 'Observations on the theme "Paul and Philo"', in *Die paulinische Literatur und Theologie*, ed. S. Pedersen, Århus 1980, 85-102; cf. Betz, *Galatians*, 6: 'not everything that Paul denies is necessarily an accusation by his opposition and not everything that he accuses his opponents of doing or thinking represents their actual goals and intentions.'

indicate a real bone of contention), their *frequency* (repetition may signal an important issue), *clarity* (an ambiguous word or phrase is a poor foundation to build on), and *unfamiliarity* (an unfamiliar motif may reflect a special local problem responded to). If the application of these criteria across the whole letter provides a consistent and historically plausible result it can lead to valid conclusions, although some will be considerably more certain than others.[9] In this way our attempts to mirror-read Galatians need not be entirely 'arbitrary'.[10] It is unfortunate that the most recent attempt to mirror-read this letter, by Brinsmead, pays such scant attention to these methodological problems. While engaging in a 'dialogical' analysis of the letter, Brinsmead nowhere discusses by what criteria he judges that Paul's response sometimes employs the terms and traditions of his opponents, sometimes contradicts them and sometimes redefines or modifies them.[11] The speculative and implausible conclusions that Brinsmead reaches could make us deeply sceptical about the whole mirror-reading technique. In fact I think that it is a good deal more problematic than most scholars acknowledge, but, if we apply the criteria outlined above, it need not be regarded as wholly unworkable.

b) *Using historical parallels.* Since the evidence that we can derive from Galatians itself is entirely one-sided and can only be used with great caution, it is not surprising that attempts should be

[9] For further discussion see my article as in n.2 above.

[10] Lyons, *Pauline Autobiography*, 96: 'The "mirror reading" approach to the interpretation of Galatians may be challenged on several bases. It may be shown that the methodological presuppositions on which it rests are arbitrary, inconsistently applied and unworkable'. Lyons explains all Paul's antithetical constructions as a rhetorical device, 'often, if not always, examples of pleonastic tautology used in the interest of clarity' (110). But it is very doubtful if this is sufficient to explain, for instance, Paul's emphatic, repeated and explicit denials of the human/Jerusalem origin of his gospel in Gal 1-2.

[11] This is particularly disappointing after his acute criticisms of others, *Galatians*, 23-30. Paul's statements are often taken to reflect the opponents' vocabulary (e.g., in 3.3 and with terms like ζωή, ἐλευθερία etc.); elsewhere they indicate that the opponents had a different vocabulary (e.g., they emphasized spiritual circumcision and downplayed the cross, 87, 139-40); or again they pick up and modify the opponents' traditions (e.g., his theology of baptism is the 'dialogical counterpart' to their circumcision-sacramentalism, 139ff.).

made to illuminate the Galatian crisis with information gleaned from other sources. Obviously such information can only be valid evidence if it is shown to be 'parallel' to some degree with the Galatian situation as we know it from Galatians: in other words it can only be of secondary, not primary, importance. Nevertheless it could help to clarify what facts we can glean from Galatians itself.

One line of investigation here focuses on *the agitators*: can we find out more about these people from other sources and can we identify a movement to which they belong? Obviously we can only answer these questions if we have first established the identity of the agitators. From Paul's reference to 'another gospel' (1.6) we can assume that they were Christians, but it is rather more difficult to determine their racial and geographical origin. On the basis of the participle in 6.13 (οἱ περιτεμνόμενοι), a few scholars have maintained that Paul's opponents were judaizing Gentiles ('those who are getting themselves circumcised', cf. 5.3).[12] The majority, however, remain convinced that they were Jewish: they seem to be the object of Paul's attack in 4.30 ('cast out the slave woman and her son') and appear to have used sophisticated Scriptural arguments (see below). Thus many consider the participle in 6.13 to be in the middle voice ('those who go in for circumcision'),[13] and others take it as a reference to the Galatians,

[12] See especially J. Munck, *Paul and the Salvation of Mankind*, E.T. London 1959, 87-89, building on the work of E. Hirsch, 'Zwei Fragen zu Galater 6', *ZNW* 29 (1930) 192-7 and W. Michaelis, 'Judaistische Heidenchristen', *ZNW* 30 (1931) 83-89. The same conclusion is reached by Ropes, *Singular Problem*, 44-5 and A.E. Harvey, 'The Opposition to Paul', in *Studia Evangelica IV*, ed. F.L. Cross, Berlin 1968, 323ff., both, like Munck, explicitly reacting against the Tübingen hypothesis of Jewish-Christian emissaries from Jerusalem.

[13] See, e.g., O. Holtzmann, 'Zu Emanuel Hirsch, Zwei Fragen zu Galater 6', *ZNW* 30 (1931) 76-83; Schmithals, *Gnostics*, 26-28 and most commentators. Few, however, explain how the middle can have this meaning. Jewett takes it as a 'causative middle', 'Agitators', 202-3; but the grammars seem to indicate that a causative middle is reflexive where no object is indicated (see, e.g., *BDF* §317; A.T. Robertson, *A Grammar of the Greek New Testament in the Light of Historical Research*, New York 1919, 808-9). One should also note the textual variant περιτετμημένοι, read by P⁴⁶, B Ψ et al.; but this is undoubtedly the weaker reading, B. Metzger, *A Textual Commentary on the Greek New Testament*, London 1975, 598.

not the opponents.[14] As regards their geographical origin, the way Paul always refers to them in the third person (1.7; 3.1; 4.17; 5.7-12; 6.12-13) and the Galatians in the second (1.6,11; 3.1; 4.12ff.etc.) seems to indicate that they have come from outside the Galatian congregations.[15] But if so, where have they come from? It has often been argued – it was the cornerstone of F.C. Baur's thesis – that their origin was Jerusalem and that they were the same 'men from James' who had caused trouble in the church at Antioch (Gal 2.11-14). Watson, for instance, argues that the only reason Paul talks so much in Gal 2 about the previous disputes in Jerusalem and Antioch is that the Galatian crisis was a continuation of those controversies: the same problem has arisen in Galatia as in Antioch and it is natural to assume that the same people are responsible.[16]

If this identification could be established, one might hope it would give us a clearer picture of these agitators. We have a certain amount of information about Jewish Christianity in Jerusalem, not only from Paul (Gal 1-2) but also from Acts (see esp. Acts 15, 21); and Betz and Martyn have recently drawn in other information about Jewish Christianity from a later period, notably in the pseudo-Clementine literature.[17] Unfortunately, however, all this evidence is of doubtful value. The case for the Jerusalem origin of Paul's opponents is by no means compelling;[18] and even if it were, the evidence from Acts is somewhat

[14] Burton, *Galatians*, 351-4 although this requires a change of subject halfway through 6.13. The arguments for all these options are fully discussed by Howard, *Crisis*, 17-19 and P. Richardson, *Israel in the Apostolic Church*, Cambridge 1969, 84-9.

[15] Jewett, 'Agitators', 204. But it is possible that Paul deliberately distinguishes them in this way to drive a wedge between 'the agitators' and Galatian Christians who had not yet accepted circumcision.

[16] *Paul, Judaism and the Gentiles*, 59-61.

[17] Betz, *Galatians*, 9, 329-333; Martyn, 'Law-Observant Mission', referring to *The Ascents of James* and *The Preachings of Peter*.

[18] The fact that Paul sees a parallel between Antioch and Galatia need not mean that the same people are responsible for both events. It is equally possible that Jewish Christians came from Antioch to report on events there and Paul's relationship to the Jerusalem apostles. Moreover, although he specifically

43

suspect and the relevant sections in the pseudo-Clementine homilies are historically too distant to be of much value.[19] One could only appeal to such evidence with extreme caution and diffidence.

Some scholars think that Paul's Galatian opponents were also active in other churches of his and that information about them can be gleaned from his other letters, e.g., Colossians and the Corinthian correspondence. Thus Schmithals regards them as part of a general gnosticizing movement, and J. Gunther posits in all these churches 'common or similar Judaizing, ascetic, pneumatic, gnosticizing, syncretistic opponents'.[20] But in most cases the situations reflected in these other letters are not closely parallel to the Galatian crisis and thus cannot provide much illustrative material.[21]

---

continued from p.43

mentions 'the men from James' at Antioch (2.12), Paul seems slightly uncertain as to who is responsible for the events in Galatia (3.1; 5.10). Even if the agitators in Galatia had come from Jerusalem, it seems to me most unlikely that they were sent by James with the explicit purpose of making Paul's converts judaize, *pace* Watson, *Paul, Judaism and the Gentiles*, 49ff.: in that case Paul would hardly have been able to restrain his comments on James to mere ironical remarks about his reputation as one of the 'pillars' (2.2,6,9).

[19] Since *The Epistle of Peter to James* makes pointed reference to Paul's letter to the Galatians it is precarious evidence for what might have been said to bring about the Galatian crisis. On Betz's use of this literature, and especially his assumption that 2 Cor 6.14-7.1 reflects anti-Pauline polemic similar to that used by the agitators, see Lyons' criticisms, *Pauline Autobiography*, 98-105. Martyn suggests one needs both 'scientific control' and 'poetic fantasy' to be able to reconstruct the opponents' message ('Law-Observant Mission', 313); it would be safer to say that we must recognize different degrees of certainty in our conclusions.

[20] J.J. Gunther, *St. Paul's Opponents and their Background*, Leiden 1973, 9

[21] Gunther's thematic treatment blurs the contrast between the different situations reflected in Paul's letters. For instance, although Paul's opponents in Corinth were also Jewish (2 Cor 11.22) there is nothing to indicate that they propounded the same message as in Galatia. Although Colossians also refers to τὰ στοιχεῖα τοῦ κόσμου (2.8,20) and observance of days (2.16) it does not seem to be concerned with law or justification and its emphasis on Christology, asceticism and angel-worship suggests a rather different problem from that encountered in Galatia; see Vielhauer, *Geschichte*, 115-6. On Schmithals' thesis see Wilson's comment: 'there is in fact no reason whatsoever for assuming that Paul had to deal simply and solely throughout his career with one type of problem and one variety of opposition', 'Gnostics', 367.

Another way to shed light on the Galatian crisis would be to focus on *the Galatians* themselves: can we establish their historical and social context in order to explain their behaviour? Here, of course, we run up against the problem of ascertaining where these Galatians were living, and, if we locate them in 'North Galatia', our lack of historical evidence about this area.[22] However, we do know that the Galatians were Gentiles (they were not originally circumcised, 6.12, and they used to worship idols, 4.8-9); and the propaganda they were receiving was undoubtedly Jewish. This means that one relevant angle of approach would be to ask about the ways in which Gentiles were attracted to Judaism in this period. Although this question will only yield rather generalized evidence about proselytism in the Diaspora, it could still suggest ways of understanding the historical and social context of the Galatian crisis.[23] Of course, we will still need to take our primary bearings from the letter itself.

The Demand for Circumcision

Although many aspects of the Galatian crisis are unclear, there is at least one fact which is incontrovertible: the agitators in Galatia were demanding that Paul's converts should get circumcised. Strong evidence for this lies in Paul's unambiguous warning to the Galatians about the dangers of circumcision: 'I, Paul, say to you that if you are circumcised, Christ will be of no avail to you. I testify again to every man who gets circumcised that he is bound

[22] See above, chapter one nn.23-24. W.M. Ramsay, *A Historical Commentary on St. Paul's Epistle to the Galatians*, London 1900, made perhaps the most thoroughgoing attempt to relate archaeological finds to the exegesis of the letter; but he was working on the 'South Galatian' cities and even so often had to admit to an ignorance which has only partly been overcome in the years since his work.

[23] Of course we should not assume that Diaspora Judaism was all of a piece: it would be dangerous to assume, for instance, that the Alexandrian Philo is typical of all Diaspora Jews. Our knowledge of the Diaspora is still very sketchy, but improving slowly: see, e.g., the work by A.T. Kraabel on Sardis, 'Paganism and Judaism: The Sardis Evidence', in *Paganisme, Judaïsme, Christianisme. Influences et Affrontements dans le Monde Antique*, Paris 1978, 13-33.

45

to observe the whole law' (5.2-3). This is followed by an explicit statement about the intention of the opponents: 'Those who want to make a good showing in the flesh, they compel you to be circumcised, only so they may avoid persecution for the cross of Christ . . . they want you to be circumcised so they may boast in your flesh' (6.12-13). As we have noted, what Paul says about the motivation of the opponents in this highly polemical passage has to be taken with a pinch of salt; but we can presume that he is correct at least about the fact of their demand for circumcision. Indeed he clearly sees the situation in Galatia as analogous to the demand of the 'false brethren' for Titus' circumcision in Jerusalem (2.3-5). And at one point he goes so far as to wish their interest in circumcision would lead them to self-castration (5.12)!

The demand for circumcision is, then, a secure base from which to analyse the Galatian crisis. [24] But part of our concern is to discover as much as we can about how Paul's opponents were arguing their case and how they were achieving such success in Galatia. This is a particularly intriguing question in relation to circumcision since we know that this rite, although common among some eastern races, was generally treated with disdain in the Graeco-Roman world. Josephus complains that Apion 'derides the practice of circumcision'; Philo talks of circumcision as 'an object of ridicule among many people'; and several Roman writers bear out their testimony. [25] We have plenty of evidence which suggests that

---

[24] This topic is also taken as the starting-point by Eckert, *Verkündigung*, 31-71. In what follows, however, we will consider a wider range of possible interpretations of circumcision and give closer attention to primary sources.

[25] Josephus, *Apion* 2.137, τὴν τῶν αἰδοίων χλευάζει περιτομήν; Philo, *Spec Leg* 1.1, ἄρξομαι δ' ἀπὸ τοῦ γελωμένου παρὰ τοῖς πολλοῖς. For Roman opinion see, e.g., Tacitus, *Histories* 5.5, Petronius, frag.37 and Martial, *Epigrams* 8.82 (cited and discussed by M. Stern, *Greek and Latin Authors on Jews and Judaism*, 2 volumes, Jerusalem 1974, 1981). Jewish sensitivity on this matter is evidenced by the practice of 'epispasm' under Hellenistic pressure (1 Macc 1.15); and the Roman disdain can be seen in Hadrian's ban on circumcision, treating it as equivalent to castration (cf. Gal 5.12) or mutilation (cf. Phil 3.2), *Historia Augusta, Hadrian* 14.2 (discussed by Stern, *Authors* II, 619-21). Circumcision was apparently practised by at least some Egyptians, Arabs and other races (Herodotus, 2.104; Josephus, *Apion* 2.140-142) but seems to have been regarded by Romans as distinctively Jewish (Tacitus, *Histories* 5.5 'circumcidere genitalia instituerunt, ut diversitate noscantur').

46

circumcision was the most difficult hurdle for those who were attracted to Judaism and contemplated becoming proselytes.[26] How, then, did the agitators 'bewitch' (3.1), 'persuade' (5.7) or 'compel' (6.12) these Gentile Galatians to get circumcised?[27] As we have just noted, we can only answer this question from the letter itself and with judicious use of 'parallel' materials, especially from the Diaspora.[28] But first it is worth considering a number of proposals concerning the opponents' strategy.

i) Schmithals argues that, for the opponents in Galatia, circumcision was a Gnostic rite, taken over from Judaism but reinterpreted so that 'the act of circumcision portrayed the liberation of the pneuma-self from the prison of this body'.[29] He attempts to support this thesis by reference to the use of circumcision by the Ebionites, Elchasaites and Cerinthians, and by comparing the interpretation of circumcision in Col 2; but it has met with almost universal criticism. In the first place, Schmithals' use of the second-century 'Gnostic' movements is both arbitrary and anachronistic;[30] in each case our sources,

---

[26] Note the problem of finding for Drusilla a husband who was willing to be circumcised, Josephus, *Ant* 20.139. Metilius clearly impressed his captors by his willingness to judaize *and even* get circumcised (μεχρὶ περιτομῆς ἰουδαΐσειν, Josephus, *Bell* 2.454). Kuhn notes that of the 554 Jewish inscriptions found in Italy, only 8 refer to proselytes and 6 of these are women (so not required to be circumcised), art., προσήλυτος in *TDNT* VI, 732-3.

[27] It is difficult to know how to interpret Paul's reference to the opponents' use of compulsion (6.12). This was presumably no more physical than Peter's attempt to compel the Antioch Gentiles to judaize (2.14): in both cases the persuasion of arguments was probably backed up by activity which made the Gentiles feel excluded from the Christian community (2.12; 4.17); see further below, and Betz, *Galatians*, 315.

[28] Although we have several passages from Philo explaining circumcision, it is a great pity that Josephus apparently never completed his work in which he promised to explain the reason for circumcision (*Ant* 1.192,214; 4.198).

[29] *Gnostics*, 38.

[30] H.J. Schoeps has shown that the Ebionites were not Gnostic, *Jewish Christianity. Factional Disputes in the Early Church*, Philadelphia 1969, 121-130. Our evidence for the use of circumcision by the Elchasaites and Cerinthians mostly derives from Epiphanius, whose evidence is both late and unreliable (see A.F.J. Klijn and G.J. Reinink, *Patristic Evidence for Jewish-Christian Sects*, Leiden 1973, 63, 67-73). In any case, it is unlikely that any firm conclusions can be drawn by reading back second-century Gnostic systems into the Pauline era (Drane, *Paul*, 49-51; Eckert, *Verkündigung*, 64-71).

insofar as they are accurate and illuminating, show that the continued use of circumcision was an expression of 'Judaism' and not 'Gnosticism'.[31] Moreover, there is extremely little evidence for a positive evaluation of literal circumcision in any Gnostic movement.[32] Finally, it is clear that Paul's letter does not attack the use of circumcision because of its Gnostic associations – a fact which Schmithals acknowledges but dismisses on the assumption that the twentieth-century scholar can understand the Galatian situation better than Paul![33]

ii) Brinsmead has suggested that circumcision was presented to the Galatians as 'a powerful mystery initiation'. He argues that, since 'Judaism itself was presented to the Hellenistic world as a mystery', circumcision as the rite of initiation would be given 'a mystery-role' as 'a powerful sacrament'.[34] In this view he can claim some support from D. Georgi and E.R. Goodenough, who both emphasized the use made of the language and symbolism of the mysteries in the Diaspora synagogues.[35] On this general level it is true that mystery-language was sometimes used by

---

[31] Thus circumcision is associated with the OT Law; see e.g. Irenaeus, *Haer* 1.26.2 (Ebionites); Hippolytus, *Ref* 9.14.1 (Callistus).

[32] In the Gospel of Thomas logion 53 physical circumcision is dismissed as unprofitable, although it is better evaluated in the Gospel of Philip logion 123. Schmithals relies heavily on an unlikely 'gnostic' interpretation of Col 2.9-15, while he admits that the 'Gnostics' in Corinth had no use for circumcision since 'for Gnosticism . . . circumcision is an unnecessary action with only symbolic significance', *Gnostics*, 59 n.134. K. Grayston, 'The Opponents in Philippians 3', *ExT* 97 (1986-7) 170-172, argues that in Phil 3 Paul opposed 'a Gentile, semi-Gnostic group' who adopted circumcision 'out of semi-magical belief in ritual blood-shedding'. But none of the texts he cites reveals any such Christian 'magical' or 'Gnostic' interest in the rite before the second or third centuries A.D.

[33] *Gnostics*, 39: Paul 'is at a loss about the sense and reason in the practice of circumcision in Galatia'.

[34] *Galatians*, 145; see the whole section, 139-161; cf. Crownfield, 'Dual Galatians', 495.

[35] D. Georgi, *Kollekte*, 35-6 and *The Opponents of Paul in Second Corinthians*, Edinburgh 1987, 83-151, esp. 114-117; E.R. Goodenough, *By Light, Light. The Mystic Gospel of Hellenistic Judaism*, Amsterdam 1969 and *Jewish Symbols in the Graeco-Roman Period*, 13 volumes, New York 1953-1968. See also W.L. Knox, *St. Paul and the Church of the Gentiles*, Cambridge 1939, 27-54.

Hellenistic Jews, especially Philo.[36] But at no point do our sources give any clear indication of circumcision being interpreted as a rite of initiation into a mystery-cult.[37] In any case, Galatians itself gives no grounds for suggesting that the opponents advocated circumcision in these terms.[38]

iii) A more plausible suggestion has been put forward by Jewett. He writes: 'At first glance it may seem strange that a Hellenistic congregation would consider undergoing circumcision simply to enter the promised people of Israel. It may be, however, that the contact with their own Hellenistic aspirations was at the point of the promise of perfection which the Judaic tradition attached to circumcision'.[39] Certainly, he is able to appeal to rabbinic pronouncements on this point, based on Gen 17.1;[40] but it is damaging to his case that we never find this 'perfection' motif in the context of Hellenistic Jewish apologetic, where we would most expect it on Jewett's thesis. The only clue in Galatians indicating such an interpretation of circumcision is the use of ἐπιτελεῖσθε in 3.3; and we have already seen that it is precarious to build any theory on such an ambiguous word, especially since the rest of the letter does not seem to attempt to

---

[36] On Philo see Goodenough, *By Light, Light* and *An Introduction to Philo Judaeus*, Oxford 1962, 134-169. Josephus is not averse to comparing Judaism with τελεταί and μυστήρια (*Apion* 2.188-9). Juvenal also represents Judaism in mystery language (*Sat* 6.543 'arcanum in aureum'; 14.101-2 'servant ac metuunt ius, tradidit arcano quodcumque volumine Moyses') though it is not clear that Roman Jews would have used such language themselves. It is now generally agreed that Goodenough has overstated his case for a Dionysiac sacramentalism in Diaspora Jewish mysticism; see M. Smith, 'Goodenough's *Jewish Symbols* in Retrospect', *JBL* 86 (1967) 53-68.

[37] Brinsmead is clearly at a loss here; not even Philo interprets circumcision as a mystery-rite and Brinsmead can only gather a hotch-potch of unconvincing 'parallels', *Galatians*, 144-146.

[38] Brinsmead relies on reading ἐπιτελεῖσθε (3.3) as perfection in a mystery-initiation, and assumes that the opponents applied Paul's baptismal sacramentalism to circumcision; see the criticisms outlined above, pp.39-41.

[39] 'Agitators', 207.

[40] See, e.g., Gen Rabba 11.6; 46.1,4; M Nedarim 3.11 'despite all the religious duties which Abraham our father fulfilled, he was not called "perfect" until he was circumcised'. A similar tradition may underlie Jn 7.22-3.

counter any 'perfectionist' notions.[41] Thus we must conclude that Jewett's case, though interesting, is unproven.

iv) Borgen has also advanced an intriguing thesis. On the basis of 5.11 ('If I, brethren, still preach circumcision . . .') he suggests that the 'agitators' presented Paul as their ally: he had already preached circumcision to the Galatians because he had given instruction about the removal of the desires of the flesh (5.13-25) and this, according to some Jews of the time, was the real significance of circumcision. They could therefore represent bodily circumcision as the natural counterpart of Paul's preaching of ethical circumcision.[42] Once again, however, the evidence is too flimsy to bear the weight of this hypothesis. Besides the problems of mirror-reading a verse like 5.11, we cannot be confident that Paul's original preaching to the Galatians emphasized the removal of the passions of the flesh.[43] What is more, although 'circumcision of the heart' is a motif found in various strands of Judaism, the specific interpretation of circumcision as a cutting away of excess passion seems to be a special Philonic notion; it would be dangerous to assume that Philo's allegorical fantasies were an integral part of the agitators' theology.[44] Finally, we would still need to explain how they

---

[41] Contrast Colossians, which stresses the fulness of life in Christ probably in order to counter the desire for perfection through religious or ascetic observances.

[42] Borgen, 'Observations'; 'Paul Preaches Circumcision and Pleases Men', in *Paul and Paulinism*, ed. M.D. Hooker and S.G. Wilson, London 1982, 37-46; 'The Early Church and the Hellenistic Synagogue', *STh* 37 (1983) 55-78.

[43] Borgen appeals to Gal. 5.21, but that only tells us that Paul had previously warned about these vices, not that he had called them 'works of the flesh' or made a repeated appeal to counter 'the passion of the flesh'. Borgen also needs to assume that the agitators knew in what precise terms Paul had preached the gospel.

[44] The circumcision of the heart is mentioned in Lev 26.11; Deut 10.6; 30.6; Jer 4.4; 6.10; 9.25-6; Ezek 44.7,9; 1QS 5.5; 1QpHab 11.13. In his two extended discussions of the reasons for circumcision, *Spec Leg* 1.1-11 (cf. 1.304-5) and *Quaest Gen* 3.46-52, Philo mentions four explanations 'handed down from the old-time studies of divinely gifted men' (to prevent anthrax; to make the nation

continued on p.51

persuaded the Galatians to supplement their symbolic circumcision with the physical act – and here even Philo has to resort to the authority of Jewish traditions and the expectations of the Jewish community.[45]

v) This last point suggests that the 'persuasion' of the Galatians may have had as much to do with social pressures – their standing vis-à-vis the Jewish community – as with particular theological or symbolic interpretations of circumcision. Both Lütgert and Harvey have explained the Galatians' willingness to be circumcised in relation to the pressure exercised by local Jews. Lütgert, who pointed out 'wie fremdartig, unverständlich, ja widerwärtig den Heiden die Beschneidung war',[46] suggested that the local synagogue disapproved of their law-free life-style and pressurized them into becoming Jews through circumcision. In this way the Galatians would appease their opposition while also receiving protection from the state as a 'religio licita'.[47] What Lütgert fails to explain, however, is how or why such pressure would be exerted: what legal, social or moral authority would the

---

continued from p.50

more populous(!); to keep the body clean; to align the body with the mind) and then adds two of his own, clearly his special allegorical interpretations (the excision of excessive pleasure περιττῆς ἐκτομή . . . ἡδονῆς – a play on words; the correction of arrogance concerning our generative powers). He presents these last two as his own contribution, not as generally recognized Jewish interpretation of circumcision. Pace Borgen, Mig Abr 92 does not suggest otherwise: Philo does not say that his spiritual interpretation of circumcision was the same as that held by the allegorists he is attacking in this passage.

[45] Mig Abr 89-93 is particularly revealing: in arguing against those who abandon the literal practice in favour of the symbolic meaning of Jewish rites, Philo maintains that body and soul must be held together (93) but also that one should not incur the censure of others (presumably other Jews) or relax any of the customs fixed in Jewish traditions (μηδὲν τῶν ἐν τοῖς ἔθεσι λύειν, ἃ θεσπέσιοι καὶ μείζους ἄνδρες ἢ καθ' ἡμᾶς ὥρισαν, 90). See R.D. Hecht, 'The Exegetical Contexts of Philo's Interpretation of Circumcision' in Nourished with Peace, ed. F.E. Greenspahn et al., Chico 1984, 51-79.

[46] Gesetz und Geist, 98-9.

[47] Ibid., 94-106.

synagogue have had over these Gentiles?[48] Harvey provides some explanation of this by arguing that the Galatians were previously sympathetic to Judaism and used to attend the synagogue: having now lost the support of these Gentiles, the local Jews would do all they could to win them back and make their adherence permanent by obliging them to undergo circumcision.[49] However, there is no good evidence that the Galatian Christians were previously attached to the synagogues;[50] and if, as seems most likely, the agitators have come from outside Galatia, the pressure for conformity may have as much to do with Jewish Christianity and Jerusalem as with local synagogues.

If none of the various explanations we have discussed is satisfactory, they have at least made clear that to understand why the Galatians were willing to undergo circumcision we will have to enquire into both the theological arguments and the social factors involved.

a) *Theological arguments*

It is possible that we can identify at least one of the main themes used by the agitators to advocate circumcision. At 3.6 Paul

---

[48] The situation in the Diaspora was obviously rather different from Palestine, where, at times of nationalistic fervour, Jews could advocate forcible circumcision (1 Macc 2.46; Josephus, *Ant* 13.257-8, 318-9; *Bell* 2.454; *Vita* 112-3); see M. Hengel, *Die Zeloten. Untersuchungen zur jüdischen Freiheitsbewegung in der Zeit von Herodes I bis 70 n. Chr.*, Leiden 1961, 201-4. It is also unclear how the local Jews, if they were scandalized by the Galatians' antinomian behaviour, would have been appeased by circumcision. Further, G.F. Moore questions whether the special exceptions granted to Jews by the Romans would have applied to proselytes, *Judaism in the First Centuries of the Christian Era. The Age of the Tannaim*, 3 volumes, Cambridge, Mass. 1972-1930, I, 350-351.

[49] A.E. Harvey, 'Forty Strokes Save One: Social Aspects of Judaizing and Apostasy', in *Alternative Approaches to New Testament Study*, ed. A.E. Harvey, London 1985, 79-96, here at 86-88.

[50] Harvey appeals to Gal 4.9, but this does not indicate that the Galatians were rejoining the synagogue. In his review of Betz, *Galatians*, in *RSR* 7 (1981) 310-318, W.D. Davies also suggests that the Galatians were formerly Jewish sympathisers (or even proselytes), on the grounds that Paul's arguments in the letter presume familiarity with Jewish traditions: but this is easily explained by the fact that Paul was having to counter the arguments of his Jewish Christian opponents. Gal 3.1-5 and 4.8-9 make Davies' view extremely problematic.

suddenly introduces the figure of Abraham into his discussion with a quotation from Gen 15.6 (introduced only by καθώς). Abraham, and the discussion of the identity of the 'sons' or 'seed' of Abraham, dominate the argument of Gal 3.6-18, and then reappear at the end of the chapter ('If you are of Christ, then you are Abraham's seed', 3.29). Indeed, the Abraham story is invoked again in the extended allegory of 4.21-31, a passage whose use of scripture has often seemed to commentators even more forced and artificial than is usual for Paul. We may here refer to the criteria outlined above in discussing mirror-reading Galatians. The tone of these references to Abraham (i.e., their emphasis), their frequency, their clarity and their unfamiliarity all suggest, as many commentators have observed, that Paul's opponents in Galatia appealed to Abraham in their 'persuasion' of the Galatians; Paul is forced onto the defensive and has to match their scriptural exegesis with his own.[51] In particular, of course, they would have made use of Gen 17, where it is made very clear that the sign of the covenant, for both Abraham and his descendants, is circumcision: 'Every male among you shall be circumcised . . . So shall my covenant be in your flesh an everlasting covenant. Any uncircumcised male who is not circumcised in the flesh of his foreskin shall be cut off from his people; he has broken my covenant' (Gen 17.10-14).[52] Armed with such unambiguous texts the agitators could readily demonstrate that, to share in the Abrahamic covenant and the Abrahamic blessing (Gen 12.3; 18.18, etc.), the Galatians needed to be circumcised; indeed, such was the command of God in their Scriptures.

[51] See, e.g., Foerster, 'Abfassungszeit', 139, Martyn, 'Law-Observant Mission', 317-323, and especially Barrett, 'Allegory', who suggests that Paul has to respond to the opponents' use of the Sarah and Hagar stories and that at various points in Gal 3 Paul is using the same texts as his opponents. Although Paul also discusses Abraham themes in Rom 4 and 9, his treatment of them in Galatians is sufficiently peculiar to support the hypothesis that he is directly responding to his opponents at this point.

[52] On the opponents' use of Gen 17 see Burton, *Galatians*, 153-9, Duncan, *Galatians*, 87-8, Mussner, *Galaterbrief*, 216-7 and many other commentators. As Barrett notes: 'The adversaries did not act out of mere personal spite or jealousy; they held a serious theological position which they supported by detailed biblical arguments', 'Allegory', 15.

The explicit connection in the Genesis text between circumcision, Abraham and covenant ensured the frequent association of these themes in Jewish theology as can be seen in a wide range of Jewish literature, both from Palestine and from the Diaspora.[53] What is more, Abraham represented both the beginning and the foundation of Judaism, and this made him a key figure in the representation of Judaism to outsiders. In Diaspora Jewish literature he is frequently discussed from an apologetic perspective as the father of culture, philosophy and science.[54] But of particular relevance to the Galatian situation was his position as the first proselyte; indeed, on the basis of Gen 17.4-5 ('you shall be the father of many nations') he could probably be described as the father of proselytes who, by accepting circumcision, became his true descendants.[55] Thus the opponents could argue that the only way for the Galatians to secure their identity as members of God's people and recipients of his promises was by accepting

[53] See, e.g., Jub 15.9-35; Sirach 44.19-20; Theodotus, frag.5 (in Eusebius, *P.E.*9.22.7); 1 Macc 1.15, 60-63; and in rabbinic literature, M Aboth 3.11 (E.T. 3.12); b Sanhedrin 99a; b Yoma 85b; b Shabbath 135a (blood drawn at circumcision is covenant blood). Philo, *Quaest Gen* 3.46-52 and Josephus, *Ant* 1.192 both talk of circumcision in relation to Abraham on the basis of Gen 17 but neither makes much of the 'covenant' theme. In the NT see Acts 7.8 and Rom 4.9ff.

[54] Especially in Philo, Josephus, the fragments of Artapanus, Eupolemus and other Jewish apologists; the sources are discussed by Georgi, *Opponents*, 49-60 and S. Sandmel, *Philo's Place in Judaism. A Study of Conceptions of Abraham in Jewish Literature*, New York 1971. Brinsmead, *Galatians*, 111-114 probably overestimates the importance of these motifs in the Galatian context: they are certainly not reflected in Paul's letter.

[55] On Abraham as the first true proselyte see Jub 11.15-17; Apoc Abr 1-8; Josephus, *Ant* 1.154ff.; Philo, *Virt* 212ff.; Gen Rabba 46.2. Because some passages question whether the proselyte can claim the merit of 'the fathers' (e.g. M Bikkurim 1.4*j*, Drane, *Paul*, 28, 82 and Harvey, 'Opposition', 325-6 question whether it was possible to call proselytes 'sons of Abraham'. But here they are misled by the selectivity of Strack-Billerbeck (I, 119; III, 558). Other rabbinic passages make clear that Gen 17.4-5 could be interpreted to mean that Abraham was the father of proselytes (e.g. j Bikkurim 1.4; Tanchuma לך לך section 6); see J.G. Braude, *Jewish Proselyting in the First Five Centuries of the Common Era*, Providence, R.I. 1940, 99; B.J. Bamberger, *Proselytism in the Talmudic Period*, New York 1968, 67; D. Daube, *Ancient Jewish Law, Three Inaugural Lectures*, Leiden 1981, 9.

circumcision: their present half-way status was valueless.[56]

One of the closest parallels to the Galatian situation is the story of Izates, king of Adiabene, who, together with his mother Helena, was among the most important converts to Judaism in this period. Although there may be some distortion in the way Josephus recounts the events (*Ant* 20.17-96), his narrative at least reveals what he considers to be a plausible story. Helena and the king's wives were attracted towards Jewish worship (τὸν θεὸν σέβειν ὡς 'Ιουδαίοις πάτριον ἦν 20.34-5) by the propaganda of a Jewish merchant, Ananias, and others. Influenced by their example, Izates also wished to adopt Jewish customs, including circumcision, in order to make himself a genuine Jew (νομίζων τε μὴ ἂν εἶναι βεβαίως 'Ιουδαῖος, εἰ μὴ περιτέμοιτο, πράττειν ἦν ἕτοιμος 20.38). However, Helena and Ananias recognized that circumcision, as the unambiguous and unalterable sign of identification with Judaism and the Jewish nation, would alienate the people of Adiabene: they would not tolerate the rule of a Jew, devoted to the rites of another nation (20.39-42). Ananias, afraid lest the people hold him responsible for instructing the king in 'unseemly practices', argued that Izates could worship God without being circumcised – God would forgive his omission of circumcision in these dangerous political circumstances (20.41-2). Izates was content with this compromise until he was challenged by Eleazar, a Jew from Galilee with a reputation for strict observance of the law: he found Izates reading the law, and challenged him to do what it commanded, that is, to get himself circumcised (20.43-45). Izates readily agreed but then had to face the political consequences for abandoning his national traditions and committing himself to 'foreign practices' (20.47-48, 75-76, 81); Josephus records how

---

[56] Paul's warnings that the Galatians are turning *back* (4.9; 5.1) may indicate that the opponents represented their policy as a step *forward*; thus 3.3 may reflect the general tenor of their message, even if we cannot confidently identify here their exact vocabulary. Wilckens, 'Was heisst', suggests that they approached the Galatians as Jewish sympathisers 'die nun mit der Beschneidung den letzten, entscheidenden Schritt zum Eintritt in die Restgemeinde Israel . . . tun sollten', 87.

God preserved him despite various revolts by his nobles on this account (20.48, 75-91).

This story illustrates clearly how Scripture could be used to persuade Gentiles who were sympathetic to Judaism to accept circumcision. Paul's converts would have been taught by him to regard the Greek Old Testament as their Scripture (cf. 1 Cor 10.11; Rom 15.4). Thus when the agitators argued from the plain meaning of the Abraham stories in Genesis, they could well have used the same appeal that Josephus attributes to Eleazar: 'You ought not only to read the law but also, and even more, to do what is commanded in it. How long will you continue to be uncircumcised? If you have not yet read the law concerning this matter, read it now, so that you may know what an impiety it is that you commit' (Josephus, *Ant* 20.44-5).[57]

But the Izates story also demonstrates the social significance of circumcision. By accepting circumcision Izates was making an unalterable commitment to the beliefs and practices of Jews and was thus aligning himself with them socially and politically (much to the annoyance of his subjects). This suggests that we need to enquire into the social factors which would have contributed to the Galatians' willingness to be circumcised.

b) *Social factors*

From the evidence we have already adduced it appears that circumcision was one of the prime identity markers distinguishing Jews and those who wanted to identify themselves unambiguously with the Jewish people.[58] Although it is possible that in exceptional cases Gentiles could be regarded by Jews as proselytes without circumcision, it appears to have been generally recognized that circumcision was a necessary and decisive

---

[57] According to Gen Rabba 46.10, Izates and Monobazus were convicted by reading Gen 17, but this is probably only reasonable guesswork. M.D. Hooker, *Pauline Pieces*, London 1979, 73-4 emphasizes the influence of Scripture on the recently-converted Galatian Christians.

[58] See also Josephus' remark that the purpose of circumcision was to keep Abraham's people from being mixed with others, βουλόμενος τὸ ἀπ' αὐτοῦ γένος μένειν τοῖς ἄλλοις οὐ συμφυρόμενον, *Ant* 1.192.

requirement for adopting Jewish identity.[59] We have evidence that there were a considerable number of Gentiles attracted to Jewish practices and Jewish theology who probably also sometimes attended the synagogue (see below, pp.68-9). But to become a proselyte was a much more serious matter. What would induce Gentile men to accept the uncomfortable and unpopular act of circumcision and thereby declare themselves socially identified with the Jews? We know of some who did this under threat of their lives, and others who were prepared to pay this price for the sake of marrying a Jewess.[60] The Galatians clearly do not fall into these categories but are more like those who came under the influence of various 'significant others' (members of the family, admired teachers, etc.).[61] Juvenal reports that the sons of Jewish sympathisers soon get circumcised,[62] and the Adiabene royal family were clearly influenced by each other's examples and by teachers like Ananias and Eleazar. In

[59] N.J. McEleney, 'Conversion, Circumcision and the Law', NTS 20 (1973-4) 319-341 has gathered a number of scraps of evidence which could be taken to suggest that a proselyte need not always be circumcised; but his case has been well answered on each point by J. Nolland, 'Uncircumcised Proselytes?', JSJ 12 (1981) 173-194 (cf. Räisänen, Paul and the Law, 40-41). In Izates' case, even Ananias recognized that to omit circumcision was a fault requiring God's pardon (Ant 20.41-2).

[60] Under threat, Esther 8.17 and Josephus, Bell 2.454; cf. n.48 above. For marriage, Josephus, Ant 20.139,145.

[61] For a concise description of the role of 'significant others' in world-construction and world-maintenance, see P.L. Berger, The Social Reality of Religion, London 1967, chapter one: 'The world is built up in the consciousness of the individual by conversation with significant others (such as parents, teachers, "peers"). The world is maintained as subjective reality by the same sort of conversation, be it with the same or with new significant others (such as spouses, friends or associates). If such conversation is disrupted (the spouse dies, the friends disappear, or one comes to leave one's original social milieu), the world begins to totter, to lose its subjective plausibility. In other words, the subjective reality of the world hangs on the thin thread of conversation' (17). This model is clearly applicable to the Galatians who came under the influence of first Paul and then the agitators as successive 'significant others'. A fuller theoretical account is given in P.L. Berger and T. Luckmann, The Social Construction of Reality, London 1967, Part Three.

[62] Juvenal, Sat 14.99: the sons of Sabbath-observing fathers 'mox et praeputia ponunt'.

the case of the Galatians, the agitators became these 'significant others' whose approval and acceptance soon came to matter much more than Paul's (4.16-20).

In order to understand the Galatians' action, we should recall the precariousness of their social position as Christians. As Christian converts they had abandoned the worship of pagan deities (4.8-11) and this conversion would have involved not only massive cognitive readjustments but also social dislocation. To dissociate oneself from the worship of family and community deities would entail a serious disruption in one's relationships with family, friends, fellow club members, business associates and civic authorities.[63] Although the wealthy few in Corinth appear to have been able to avoid this social disruption, it seems to have been a common experience for most early Christian communities and is taken for granted as the case in Galatia (among other regions of Asia Minor) when Christians there are addressed in 1 Peter: it is assumed here that the Christians were being socially ostracized (1 Pet 2.12,15,18-20; 3.1,13-16; 4.3-5,12-16),[64] and the author does his best to offset this disadvantage with pastoral encouragement.[65] Paul's presence in Galatia and his creation of Christian communities there had helped to establish a social identity for these Christians; the lavish attention they bestowed on Paul (4.12-15) is probably a measure of their dependence on him. His departure from Galatia must then have underlined their social insecurity. They could not now share in their national and ancestral religious practices, but neither were

---

[63] A.D. Nock, *Conversion. The Old and New in Religion from Alexander the Great to Augustine of Hippo*, Oxford 1933, 156: 'the ever-present loss of social amenities, club life and festivals'.

[64] Gal 3.4 τοσαῦτα ἐπάθετε could provide evidence for a similar phenomenon in Galatia, but it is not clear whether Paul refers here to great persecution (Lightfoot, *Galatians*, 134) or great experiences of the Spirit (Schlier, *Galater*, 124; Betz, *Galatians*, 134). Certainly Roman writers are universally negative towards the anti-social 'superstitio' which characterized Christians: Tacitus, *Annals* 15.44.2-8; Suetonius, *Nero* 16; Pliny, *Ep* 10.96.1-10.

[65] See J.H. Elliott, *A Home for the Homeless. A Sociological Exegesis of I Peter, Its Situation and Strategy*, London 1982. However, I am unpersuaded by his contention that the addressees were πάροικοι in the literal, legal sense of 'resident aliens' or 'country-dwellers'.

they members (or even attenders) of the Jewish synagogues although they had the same Scriptures and much the same theology as those synagogues. If they lived in the towns of North Galatia they were geographically somewhat remote and may have been unaware of the existence of similar Pauline churches elsewhere.

With such a precarious social identity we can understand how the Galatians were impressed by the agitators' message. These Jewish Christians had the same faith in Christ but were themselves circumcised. Since Paul discusses Jerusalem and 'the pillars' at such length (1.18-2.10; 4.25-26) it is likely that his opponents, whether or not they themselves came from Jerusalem, had impressed on the Galatians the fact that the pillars of the church, in the place which the Christian movement recognized to be its true origin and authority, were also circumcised Jews preaching the gospel to other Jews.[66] They could argue, therefore, with some justification, that to belong to the Christian movement involved Jewish identity, and for Gentiles like the Galatians that necessitated circumcision. They may even have argued that Paul, himself a circumcised Jew, normally circumcised his converts but had left them in Galatia with an inadequate initiation.[67] And it is possible that they reinforced this aspect of the Galatians' inadequate status by deliberately refusing to eat with them, or withdrawing from them at the Lord's supper (ἐκκλεῖσαι ὑμᾶς θέλουσιν, ἵνα αὐτοὺς ζηλοῦτε, 4.17; cf. 2.11-14).[68]

---

[66] Paul's irony in 2.2,6,9 is most easily explained as his reaction to his opponents' over-evaluation of these 'pillars'; 'Jerusalem is our mother' (4.26) may be an echo of their teaching.

[67] This would be one way of mirror-reading Gal 5.11 and 1.10 (he 'pleases men' by omitting to insist on circumcision in Galatia). They could have described the Galatians' baptism as the first part of proselyte initiation without its completion in circumcision. On Jewish proselyte baptism at this time see Epictetus, Diss 2.9.20-21.

[68] On 4.17 see Schlier, Galater, 212. For the social impact of Jewish exclusiveness in the Diaspora see Josephus, Apion 2.210 and Juvenal, Sat 14.96-104. The latter passage makes clear how this could induce those who desired acceptance to become fully initiated by becoming proselytes.

By accepting circumcision the Galatians would also regularize their position in relation to the rest of Galatian society. Although Jews may not have been popular, at least the Jewish religion had a long-established pedigree; it was not a suspicious novelty like the Christian movement.[69] By becoming proselytes the Galatians could hope to identify themselves with the local synagogues and thus hold at least a more understandable and recognizable place in society.[70] The adjustments required for this move were minor compared to their Christian conversion: the resocialization was a relatively straightforward matter.[71]

These social factors are not all easily teased out of Paul's letter, since Paul focuses so much on the theological issues. But we have sufficient hints in the letter and sufficient knowledge of the social implications of proselytism to support the suggestions outlined above. Together with the agitators' theological propaganda, they go a long way towards explaining the Galatians' willingness to be circumcised.

Observance of the Law

Although circumcision was without doubt an important issue in the Galatian crisis, it is not so clear at first sight what significance was given to the law. Scholars continue to debate whether the agitators demanded obedience to the law as a whole or whether they were prepared to allow the Galatians to be selective or

---

[69] Nock, *Conversion*, 161-3, 202-11. Judaism was tolerated in the Roman world largely because it was a national and ancestral religion.

[70] Proselytes seem to have been made welcome in Diaspora synagogues: Philo refers to Moses' requirement that they be given 'special friendship and more than ordinary good-will', *Spec Leg* 1.52 (cf. Lev 19.33-34). The Galatians would thus be welcomed into a community renowned for its cohesiveness, Cicero, *pro Flacco* 66; Tacitus, *Histories* 5.5; Josephus, *Apion* 2.283.

[71] In sociologists' terms, a secondary rather than a primary socialization. The ease with which a fundamental conversion can be supplemented by less drastic additions is well illustrated in Apuleius, *Metamorphoses* 11: Lucius' initiation into the Isis mysteries is soon followed by an initiation into the Osiris cult.

superficial in their observance of it. The uncertainty on this matter arises out of three passages in Paul's letter:

i) Although Paul talks frequently about 'the law' or 'the works of the law' he mentions remarkably few of the actual practicalities of law-observance. Indeed, apart from circumcision, we have only his complaint in 4.10: ἡμέρας παρατηρεῖσθε καὶ μῆνας καὶ καιροὺς καὶ ἐνιαυτούς. Moreover, this phrase refers to calendar observance in very general terms; it does not explicitly mention Jewish sabbaths and festivals (contrast Col 2.16), but only 'days', 'months', 'seasons' and 'years'.

ii) In 5.3 Paul issues a solemn warning to the Galatians about the implications of their circumcision: μαρτύρομαι δὲ πάλιν παντὶ ἀνθρώπῳ περιτεμνομένῳ ὅτι ὀφειλέτης ἐστὶν ὅλον τὸν νόμον ποιῆσαι. That he has to make this statement at all could suggest that the Galatians were unaware of their obligations to the law; or, if the emphasis lies on the *whole* law to be kept (ὅλον τὸν νόμον), it could indicate that their commitment to the law was only partial.

iii) In 6.13 Paul affirms: οὐδὲ γὰρ οἱ περιτεμνόμενοι αὐτοὶ νόμον φυλάσσουσιν. This polemical statement could be taken to mean that the agitators ('those who go in for circumcision') and/or the Galatians ('those who get circumcised' – see above p.42) were not interested or not sincere in their observation of the law.

We have already noted some of the ways in which these verses have been used in reconstructing the Galatian crisis. The general terms Paul uses for calendrical observance in 4.10, combined with his reference in 4.9 to the Galatians' return to their service of τὰ ἀσθενῆ καὶ πτωχὰ στοιχεῖα have led some scholars to propose that the agitators were not presenting their demand for festival-keeping in 'orthodox' Jewish terms but with a concern for astrology and the cosmic/gnostic significance of certain days.[72] Schmithals argues on the basis of 5.3 and 6.13 that the

---

[72] See above n.6. Because such lists are common in apocalyptic Jewish literature (e.g., Jub 1.14; 6.34-8; 1 Enoch 72-82), Schlier regards 4.10 as an indication of the

agitators were not interested in law observance at all; in fact 6.13 should be taken at face value and 'obviously means a renunciation of the law in principle'.[73] Less extreme hypotheses have also been put forward. Jewett, for instance, suggests that the agitators had a subtle policy: they 'tactfully did not mention that circumcision imposed the obligation to obey the entire range of the law (Gal v.3)'. They were only concerned for 'quick and observable results' and 'it was more important to them that the Galatians be circumcised and begin to keep the festivals than that they do so for proper reasons'.[74] Others have also taken these verses to indicate that the opponents were insincere, or selective, in their demand for observance of the law.[75]

However, we should also note the evidence which points in a contrary direction. For instance, we must take account of the fact that in 4.21 Paul addresses the Galatians, λέγετέ μοι, οἱ ὑπὸ νόμον θέλοντες εἶναι, τὸν νόμον οὐκ ἀκούετε; this address and the allegory which follows it would be completely valueless if none of the Galatians was seriously concerned to listen to and submit to the law. Indeed the allegory concludes with an appeal not to submit again to 'the yoke of slavery' (ζυγῷ δουλείας, 5.1); and since this almost certainly alludes to the

---

continued from p.61

opponents' 'apocryphal' Judaism, *Galater*, 203-7. Schmithals takes 4.9-10 to represent a gnosticizing tendency, *Gnostics*, 44, and Jewett concludes that 'the cultic calendar was presented to the Galatians on a basis which was far from orthodox', 'Agitators', 208.

[73] *Gnostics*, 33 wrongly claiming support from Lightfoot and Schlier. In n.51 he goes so far as to take these verses to indicate 'a well-defined libertine tendency', a conclusion which he appears to retract in 'Judaisten', 55. Cf. Marxsen, *Introduction*, 53-5.

[74] 'Agitators', 207-8; cf. Sanders, *Paul, The Law, and the Jewish People*, 29.

[75] See, e.g., Crownfield, 'Singular Problem', 500, Brinsmead, *Galatians*, 64-5,119, Lightfoot, *Galatians*, 219, Bonnard, *Galates*, 129, Schlier, *Galater*, 231-2, 281, Mussner, *Galaterbrief*, 347-8. Hirsch, 'Zwei Fragen', 194 talks of the Galatians' 'bungling' in their attempt to observe the law.

Jewish notion of 'the yoke of the law',[76] it would be quite pointless if the Galatians were not interested in observing the law.

But it is not only this one passage which supports such a conclusion. If we are to take the whole of Paul's letter as a serious reply to the Galatian crisis we cannot overlook the sustained polemic, from 2.15 onwards, against the works of the law, justification by the law and submission to the law. We cannot, with Schmithals, dismiss most of Gal 3-4 as traditional material derived from Paul's debate with Jews,[77] since the arguments concerning faith, law and Spirit are explicitly related to the Galatian crisis (3.1-5; 4.4-7, 21). Paul's emphatic, repeated and unambiguous attempts to limit the significance of the law, to drive a wedge between the law and the Abrahamic promises and to contrast the law with faith in Christ point (in accordance with our mirror-reading criteria) to the significance of the law in the Galatian dispute and in the message of the agitators. Otherwise we would have to conclude that the core of Paul's argument in this letter was entirely misdirected; and that is a conclusion to which we should only be driven as a last resort.[78]

However, we should still attempt to explain those verses which cause difficulties for this reconstruction. As regards 4.10, it appears that the reason why Paul highlights the Galatians' calendar observance, out of all the manifold 'works of the law', is because he sees here a point of direct comparison with their former pagan worship. Both pagan and Jewish religion involve

---

[76] The rabbinic expression 'the yoke of the Torah' (M Aboth 3.5; b Sanhedrin 94b etc.) has its roots in the OT conception of the yoke of God (Jer 2.20; 5.5; Ps 2.3) which Sirach interpreted as the yoke of wisdom (Sir 51.26). See K. Rengstorf, art. ζυγός, in *TDNT* II, 900-1 and M. Maher, ' "Take my yoke upon you" (Matt XI.29)', *NTS* 22 (1975-6) 97-103.

[77] *Gnostics*, 41-2, further elaborated in 'Judaisten', 49-50.

[78] In 'Judaisten', 43-53 Schmithals argues that, although neither the opponents nor the Galatians were concerned with the law, Paul saw commitment to the law as the implication of their circumcision and so laboured to persuade them that the law was incompatible with their Christian faith. But this leaves Paul urging the Galatians not to do the works of the law (3.1-5) although he knows they have no intention of doing them anyway! It seems extremely unlikely that Paul would waste his time with such irrelevant arguments in this critical situation.

observing certain sacred 'days' and Paul deliberately chooses such general terms as 'days', 'months' and 'seasons' in order to emphasize the similarities between these two forms of religion: hence he can score a useful polemical point by describing their new Jewish practice as a regression to their former way of life. Nothing in this verse indicates that the Galatians' law-observance was partial or 'unorthodox'.

When interpreting 5.3 we must recall our methodological caution in mirror-reading Paul's assertions (above p38-41). We should not necessarily assume that his warning about the implications of circumcision implies that the agitators, or the Galatians, consciously denied or downplayed the need for law-observance. It could be, rather, that Paul intended to hammer home a fact concerning which the Galatians were not wholly ignorant but only somewhat naïve: they were prepared to submit to the law, but they needed to face realistically the implications of observing the *whole* law.[79] This interpretation is supported by the way this verse follows so closely on the appeal of 4.21 to 'those who desire to be under the law', and the probability that it is intended to pick up the emphasis on 'all things written in the book of the law' in 3.10;[80] as Kümmel writes, 'In 5.3 Paul did not make known to the Galatians a new fact, but only wanted to remind them anew of a known fact which they had not sufficiently taken into consideration'.[81]

Finally, the heavily polemical context of 6.13 should make us

---

[79] Vielhauer rightly notes that Paul's stress is on ὅλον, 'Gesetzesdienst und Stoicheiadienst im Galaterbrief', in *Rechtfertigung*, ed. J. Friedrich et al., Tübingen 1976, 545. The question of becoming a 'debtor' (ὀφειλέτης) may add to the point but is probably not of major significance, pace Howard, *Crisis*, 16.

[80] 3.10 is probably the verse in Paul's mind when he writes μαρτύρομαι δὲ πάλιν, Watson, *Paul, Judaism and the Gentiles*, 71 and those cited in his n.109. Some editors of Paul's text (D* F G et al.) were clearly uncertain what πάλιν referred to and left it out. It is quite unnecessary to take 4.21 and 5.3 as directed to two different groups in the Galatian churches, Drane, *Paul*, 47-8, 82-3.

[81] *Introduction*, 300; cf. Eckert, *Verkündigung*, 41-2 and Betz, *Galatians*, 259-61. Jewett's thesis is seriously inconsistent: he takes 5.3 to indicate that the agitators did not mention the need to observe the whole law (207), but still maintains that they thought that obedience to the entire law was necessary for salvation and

extremely hesitant to take this verse at face value.[82] Paul's statement that the agitators advocate circumcision only for self-protection and self-glorification and not for the sake of the law is clearly intended to undermine their credibility and to shock the Galatians. It is difficult to know what evidence Paul would have adduced if he had been pressed to support this statement; perhaps his old Pharisaic standards were more exacting than theirs (1.14), or perhaps he thought of his opponents as in the same position as Peter, making themselves transgressors of the law by associating with Gentiles while also claiming to uphold the law (2.18).[83] In any case, Paul's snide remark that they do not really keep the law does not disprove but rather, paradoxically, confirms our impression from the rest of the letter that the agitators expected the Galatians to observe the law in conjunction with their circumcision. Thus, although the evidence is more ambiguous than in the case of circumcision, it is highly probable that law-observance was an important ingredient in the agitators' demands.

a) *The agitators' arguments*
It is also possible to make some suggestions about the way the agitators argued their case. We have already noted that Paul expends considerable effort in Gal 3 arguing for a distinction between Abraham and the law: the Abrahamic blessing belongs to those ἐκ πίστεως, not those ἐξ ἔργων νόμου (3.6-10) and the covenant sealed with Abraham cannot be annulled by the law which came 430 years later (3.15-17); the Abrahamic promises

---

continued from p.64
would follow in due course (201-2). He takes their circumcising campaign as arising from Zealot pressure in Palestine (204-6), but it is not clear how Zealots would be pleased by proselytes who had only a minimal commitment to the law.

[82] As Schmithals insists it must, 'Judaisten' 53-54: the agitators were not interested in the law but only wanted to avoid the anger of the synagogue by circumcising their converts. Apparently the synagogue Jews were expected not to notice that these agitators and their converts rejected the law!

[83] Howard, *Crisis*, 15-16; Sanders, *Paul, The Law, and the Jewish People*, 23. Some take 6.13 as Paul's adoption of a traditional polemic against Jewish law-observance (cf. Acts 7.53; Mt 23.3; Rom 2.17ff.;8.3), Eckert, *Verkündigung*, 32-5, Betz, *Galatians*, 316. See also Barrett, *Freedom and Obligation*, 87.

and the law are to be clearly distinguished (3.18-22). All of this suggests that the opponents used Abraham in their arguments for the law as well as for circumcision and tended to associate the law with the Abrahamic covenant-promises. In fact that is no more than one would expect from those steeped in the Jewish tradition. On the basis of Gen 26.5 ('Abraham obeyed my voice and kept my charge, my commandments, my statutes and my laws') and similar verses concerning Abraham's obedience, it was assumed in Jewish traditions of many kinds that Abraham had kept the law even before its promulgation on Sinai.[84] Moreover, the terms 'covenant' and 'law' were frequently welded together in Jewish thought. The association begins with the Sinai narratives and is prevalent throughout the Old Testament.[85] It was obvious to Jews of all kinds that their covenant obligations were laid out in the law.[86] Thus if the Galatians were urged to be circumcised in order to enter the covenant (Gen 17), it was natural to associate law-observance with their new covenant status.

It is possible that we can detect some other Scriptural arguments used by the agitators, although our evidence in these cases is less strong. In the densely-packed verses, 3.10-12, Paul advances a complex argument from Scripture. Two of his quotations seem somewhat artificially introduced since their *prima facie* meaning seems to run counter to the thrust of his argument.

---

[84] See, e.g., Jub 15.1-2; 16.20ff; Sir 44.20; CD 3.2; 2 Baruch 57.1-3; Philo, *Abr* 3-6,60-62,276; M Kiddushin 4.14; b Yoma 28b.

[85] The tables of the law given on Sinai are the tables of the covenant, Ex 34.28; Deut 4.13; 9.9 etc. To transgress the law is to break the covenant, Deut 17.2; 2 Kings 17.15; 18.12; Hos 8.1. See further H.J. Schoeps, *Paul. The Theology of the Apostle in the Light of Jewish Religious History*, London 1961, 213-6.

[86] A. Jaubert concludes her study, *La Notion d'Alliance dans le Judaïsme aux Abords de l'Ère Chrétienne*, Paris 1963, with the observation: 'la Loi . . . est inséparable de toute les catégories de l'Alliance juive', 457. At Qumran it is clear that those who enter the 'covenant of grace' have 'freely devoted themselves to the observance of God's precepts', 1QS 1.7. For the law as the 'yoke of the covenant' in rabbinic literature see A.Büchler, *Studies in Sin and Atonement in the Rabbinic Literature of the First Century*, London 1928, 1-118 and Sanders, *Paul and Palestinian Judaism*, 84-238.

In 3.10 he quotes Deut 27.26 which pronounces a curse on those who do not abide by everything written in the book of the law; but somehow Paul manages to turn this curse against those who *do* the works of the law. And in 3.12 the promise about law-observance in Lev 18.5 ('he who does these things will live by them') is quoted only when it has already been ruled out of court by the previous quotation from Hab 2.4. In the scholarly debate on Paul's logic in these verses it has sometimes been suggested that Paul is struggling to re-use quotations first employed by his opponents.[87] Certainly such verses would have been ready ammunition in their assault on the Galatians. In these and many other places Scripture unambiguously declares a blessing on those who keep the law and a curse on those who neglect to do so; if the Galatians took their Scriptures seriously they were doubtless urged to do what they say in this matter.[88]

It might also be instructive to compare the ways in which Jews presented and commended the law in the Diaspora. The most extensive extant apology for the law is Josephus' work *Contra Apionem*, but many similar points are made by Philo and by other Hellenistic Jews. In these works the Jewish law is praised because of its extreme antiquity, and it is often claimed that other nations were taught by Moses or borrowed many of his ideas in their legislation.[89] Indeed it is claimed, especially by Philo, that the Jewish law is in fact a universal law, a law of nature which

---

[87] For the debate on Paul's puzzling logic here see H. Hübner, *Law in Paul's Thought*, 36–42; N.A. Dahl, 'Contradictions in Scripture', in *Studies in Paul. Theology for the Early Christian Mission*, Minneapolis 1977, 159–177; Dunn, 'Works of the Law'. For the suggestion that Paul is turning back on his opponents Scriptures they had themselves used see Barrett, 'Allegory', 6–7 and Watson, *Paul, Judaism and the Gentiles*, 71.

[88] Given Paul's attempt to distinguish between the Spirit and the law in 3.1–5 and 4.4–6, it is possible that his opponents argued for their conjunction; after all, God's promise in Ezek 36.27 is 'I will put my Spirit within you and cause you to walk in my statutes and be careful to observe my ordinances'.

[89] See, e.g., Josephus, *Apion*, 2.154–6,168,256–7,279–81; Aristobulus in Eusebius, *P.E.* 8.10.4; 13.12.1,4 (Pythagorus, Plato, Socrates and Orpheus borrowed from Moses); Artapanus in *P.E.* 9.27.4–6; Eupolemus in *P.E.* 9.26.1.

corresponds to the order God has created in the world and the reason he has implanted in men.[90] Josephus proudly records the widespread admiration with which Gentiles regard the law: 'as God permeates the universe, so the Law has found its way among all mankind . . . Indeed, were we not ourselves aware of the excellence of our laws, assuredly we would have been compelled to pride ourselves upon them by the multitude of their admirers' (*Apion* 2.284, 286). Probably the most effective way of commending the law, however, was to highlight the ways in which it produced those qualities generally regarded as virtues in the Hellenistic world. Thus Josephus repeatedly emphasizes how the law is the epitome of ἀρέτη: it promotes εὐσεβεία, κοινωνία, φιλανθρωπία, δικαιοσύνη, σωφροσύνη and many other similar virtues.[91] In common with other Jewish apologists, he also emphasizes these qualities in narrating the lives of Jewish heroes.[92] It thus appears that Paul's opponents could have drawn on a powerful battery of arguments to commend the law to the Galatian Christians.

b) *The Galatians' willingness to accede*

That those Galatians who were willing to be circumcised should also be prepared to observe other requirements of the law is, in fact, quite understandable. We know that there were many Gentiles attracted to Jewish customs and to the Diaspora synagogues at this time. Josephus' boast about the 'multitude of admirers' was by no means unfounded: he and others provide plenty of evidence that 'the masses have long since shown a keen desire to adopt our religious observances' (he mentions partic-

---

[90] This is ubiquitous in Philo's work; see the discussion by Goodenough, *By Light, Light*, 48-94. Cf. Aristobulus' attempt to show that the sabbath is a cosmic law of nature in Eusebius, *P.E.* 13.12.9-16.

[91] *Apion* 2.146,170-171,211-4,283-4,291-5. Cf. 4 Macc, Ps.-Phocylides, Testaments of the 12 Patriarchs, Ep Arist, the Jewish Sibyllines etc.

[92] E.g., *Ant* 1.18-24 (Moses), 155 (Abraham), 222 (Isaac); 2.40ff., 140ff. (Joseph) etc.; cf. Ps-Eupolemus in Eusebius *P.E.* 9.17.2-9 (Abraham); Philo, *Abr; Mos* etc.

ularly the Sabbath, fasts, lighting of lamps and food-regulations, *Apion* 2.282).[93] Although it is a matter of some dispute whether such Gentiles were everywhere given the technical title 'God-fearers', the reports of such Gentile 'judaizing' tendencies by neutral or even hostile observers puts their existence beyond doubt.[94] Thus by beginning to observe the law, even in its most distinctively Jewish aspects, the Galatians were following a path which many of their contemporaries would have understood (and which some other Gentile Christians also trod subsequently).[95]

But the Galatians would have had much more reason than most Gentiles to observe the law. If, as we have argued, their adoption of circumcision signalled their desire to identify, as proselytes, with the Jewish nation and Jewish Christianity, they must have understood it to include a commitment to the demands of the law. Our Jewish sources make clear that circumcision/proselytism necessarily involved adopting the customs of the Jews: 'the

[93] Apart from the general comments in *Apion* 2.123,209-10,261,280-6 and *Ant* 3.217 (cf. Philo, *Mos* 2.17-25), Josephus mentions Jewish sympathisers in Damascus (*Bell* 2.560), Antioch (*Bell* 7.45), throughout Syria (*Bell* 2.463) and in Rome (*Ant* 18.82). Several Roman authors comment on the popularity of Jewish customs among non-Jews in Rome; see, e.g., Juvenal, *Sat* 14.96-106; Horace, *Sat* I 9.67-72; Suetonius, *Domitian* 12.2; Dio Cassius 37.17.1; 57.18.5; 67.14.1-2. Cf. the evidence for Pisidia and Greek cities in Acts 13.16,26,43,50; 16.14; 17.4; 18.7. Josephus no doubt exaggerates in claiming that Gentiles observed Jewish practices in every nation and city (*Apion* 2.282), but the scattered evidence we have certainly suggests a widespread tendency.

[94] On the slightly ambiguous evidence in Acts see K. Lake, 'Proselytes and God-Fearers', in *The Beginnings of Christianity, Part I. The Acts of the Apostles*, volume 5: *Additional Notes*, ed. K. Lake and H.J. Cadbury, London 1933, 74-96. A.T. Kraabel, 'The Disappearance of the "God-Fearers"', *Numen* 28 (1981) 113-126 has argued that both the existence and the title of 'God-fearers' are a Lukan invention; but others have shown that the evidence for the existence of Gentile sympathisers of Judaism is irrefutable and that they were at least sometimes called θεοσεβεῖς, E. Schürer – G. Vermes – F. Millar, *The History of the Jewish People in the Age of Jesus Christ (175 B.C.–A.D. 135)*, volume 3, Edinburgh 1986, 150-176; T.M. Finn, 'The God-fearers Reconsidered', *CBQ* 47 (1985) 75-84. I am informed that J. Reynolds has now published a conclusive inscription from Aphrodisias which mentions Gentile 'God-fearers', in a recent *Supplement to the Proceedings of the Cambridge Philological Society*, Cambridge 1987.

[95] See, e.g., Col 2; Ignatius, *Mag* 8-10; *Philad* 6; Tertullian, *Ad Nat* I 13.3-4.

proselyte takes upon him all the words of the law'.[96] In these conditions it is difficult to imagine how the Galatians would have hoped to win the acceptance of the agitators, the Jewish Christians in Jerusalem or the local synagogues without accepting the obligation of keeping the law.

But there is one other important aspect of their situation we have yet to consider. If Gentiles were attracted to the Jewish law this was probably at least partly because of the detailed instruction it contained for the conduct of ordinary life. As F. Millar comments, 'no religion entirely lacks this; but in Judaism it is much more definite and more comprehensive than in the ancient religions'.[97] The traditional customs of the Jews had an air of antiquity and authority about them but they could also help to direct the pattern of the whole of life; as Josephus remarks, 'Religion governs all our actions and occupations and speech; none of these things did our lawgiver leave unexamined or indeterminate' (*Apion* 2.171). By contrast, the Galatians must have felt themselves in a somewhat precarious and uncertain position. We cannot be certain what moral instruction Paul had left with them; in 5.21 he indicates that he had warned them about a list of vices but we do not know how extensive or practical his instructions had been. At various points in his letters he refers to patterns or traditions of teaching (1 Thess 4.1-2,6,11; 1 Cor 4.17; 11.2; Rom 6.17); but these were flexible oral traditions without the fixity of authoritative written texts.[98] Paul clearly expected

---

[96] Sifra Kedoshim pereq 8.3 (E.T. in Moore, *Jüdaism*, I 331) the passage continues, 'The authorities say, if a proselyte takes upon himself to obey all the words of the Law except one single commandment, he is not received'. The rabbinic description of the reception of a proselyte by circumcision and immersion includes the recitation of representative 'weighty' and 'light' commandments in order to make clear the candidate's new obligations (b Yebamoth 47a-b). Josephus also assumes that circumcision involves adopting the customs of Jews, *Ant* 13.257-8; 20.145-6. See Braude, *Jewish Proselyting*, 8.

[97] Schürer-Vermes-Millar, *History of the Jewish People*, III, 155.

[98] It used to be held that Paul and other New Testament writers drew on a fixed code of ethics used in a catechism, A. Seeberg, *Der Katechismus der Urchristentheit*, Leipzig 1903; P. Carrington, *The Primitive Christian Catechism*, Cambridge 1940. But this is an hypothesis rarely supported nowadays.

his converts to be 'taught by God' (1 Thess 4.9) or 'led by the Spirit' (Gal 5.18; Rom 8.14). If his experience at Corinth is anything to go by, it appears that he tended to underestimate the needs of his Gentile converts for basic moral instruction: he is clearly surprised that the Corinthians did not share his moral assumptions.[99] So long as Paul was present, he was at hand to give moral guidance. But in his absence, and without an established tradition of Christian ethics and experience, his advice to 'walk in the Spirit' must have appeared distinctly unsatisfactory. With no law to distinguish right from wrong, and no rituals to deal with transgressions and provide reassurance, their security and self-confidence were somewhat shaky. As Betz comments with only a little exaggeration, 'under these circumstances, their daily life came to be a dance on a tightrope!'[100]

Another factor contributing to their uncertainty in this area may have been the onset of divisions and disputes in the Galatian churches. Such difficulties seem to be indicated by Paul's warning in 5.15 against 'biting and devouring one another', and there is further evidence in 5.26 and in Paul's emphasis on social sins in his list of 'the works of the flesh' (discussed further in chapter five below). Although we cannot tell what caused these disputes (they were probably exacerbated by 'the agitators'), they must have helped to unsettle the Galatians and to reinforce their uncertainty about themselves and their patterns of behaviour. How were they to tell who was right or wrong in such disputes and how could they fix the boundaries of acceptable belief and behaviour?[101]

---

[99] J.C. Hurd, *The Origin of I Corinthians*, London 1965, shows how Paul's initial preaching of the gospel could be understood in almost libertinistic terms.

[100] *Galatians*, 9; cf. *idem*, 'Defense', 107 and 'Spirit', 155. Ebeling comments: 'Liberation of the Gentile Galatians from bondage to the elemental spirits of the universe brought a deep sense of relief, but it could also bring a no less deep sense of insecurity as to where to find a firm anchor for life, in the face of such totally unaccustomed freedom', *Truth of the Gospel*, 251.

[101] Berger notes: 'The reality of the Christian world depends upon the presence of social structures within which this reality is taken for granted . . . When this plausibility structure loses its intactness or continuity, the Christian world begins to totter and its reality ceases to impose itself as self-evident truth', *The Social Reality of Religion*, 47.

In such circumstances the agitators' proposals must have seemed specially attractive. The introduction of Jewish rites and ceremonies provided a means whereby the Galatians could constantly reinforce their identity as the people of God. Just as the Jewish purity rules would be an effective means of maintaining their separate status in Galatian society, so observing the regulations on prayers, festivals and Sabbaths would be a constant reminder of their new status. The importance of such rituals as a reinforcement of a religious world-view is well recognized by sociologists of religion.[102] The 'works of the law' would perform a crucial social function in preserving the Galatian Christian communities.[103]

In the same way the moral directives in the law must have been most welcome to the Galatians. As Betz notes, 'they needed concrete help, and the opponents of Paul could provide it. Entering into the Sinai covenant and obedience to the Torah would provide them with the means to deal with human failure and misconduct'.[104] It would also provide positive instruction for so many areas of their ordinary lives. Paul had, after all, left them with these authoritative documents; now with Jewish Christian interpreters to guide them, it was natural for the Galatians to seek in the law the clear and comprehensive moral directives which they needed.

---

[102] See, e.g., Berger and Luckmann, *Social Construction of Reality*, 174-6; M. Douglas, *Purity and Danger*, London 1966, 114-139; H. Mol, *Identity and the Sacred*, Oxford 1976, 233-245.

[103] R. Heiligenthal rightly emphasizes that 'es sich bei den "Gesetzeswerken" im Galaterbrief um Zeichen der Gruppenzugehörigkeit handelt', 'Soziologische Implikationen der paulinischen Rechtfertigungslehre im Galaterbrief am Beispiel der "Werke des Gesetzes"', *Kairos* 26 (1984) 38-53, at 41. Cf. Meeks' comment: 'The Pauline school rejected circumcision and purity rules, thus giving up one of the most effective ways by which the Jewish community maintained its identity over against the pagan society in which it lived. This was the practical issue at dispute between Paul and his opponents in Galatia', 'Toward a Social Description of Pauline Christianity', in *Approaches to Ancient Judaism, II*, ed. W.S. Green, Missoula 1980, 33.

[104] *Galatians*, 273; cf. Ebeling, *Truth of the Gospel*, 251: 'The vertigo that could result from freedom understandably made them vulnerable to an offer to fill the void by means of the Jewish Torah'.

Conclusion

Our investigation of the Galatian crisis has had to progress slowly and cautiously. We have noted the difficulty of using the evidence of Paul's own letter and the problems in supplementing this from other sources; and we have had to appraise the strengths and weaknesses of a number of different reconstructions of the crisis. In carefully sifting our historical evidence, we have focused particularly on circumcision and observance of the law and have investigated the significance of these not simply as theological symbols but as activities with important social implications. The issues at stake in the Galatian crisis were *the identity* of these Galatian Christians and their *appropriate patterns of behaviour*: should they regularize and confirm their place among God's people by getting circumcised and becoming proselytes? And should they adopt the ritual and ethical norms of the Jewish people? Our investigation has demonstrated how attractive and reasonable the agitators' proposals in these matters appeared.

It is important to note the specific social context in which this dispute takes place. As far as the agitators are concerned, the issues are not abstract or generalized, on the level of 'what must man do to be saved?' Rather, they concern a specific historical anomaly, that Gentiles who claim to belong to God's people have not yet adopted the identity and norms of Jews. We must not lose sight of these particular issues when we come to discuss Paul's response to the crisis; for, while it is quite possible for Paul to make generalized theological observations on the basis of a particular problem, we should always approach his arguments first in the light of their immediate historical contexts.

Finally we may note that our analysis of circumcision and law-observance has highlighted the dual aspect of the Galatian crisis: it raised questions concerning both identity and behavioural patterns. These two cannot, of course, be separated. The Galatians' more secure identity as proselytes would involve a whole range of duties, while the practice of those duties would in turn confirm their status in the people of God. The categories I have adopted, 'identity' and 'behavioural patterns', arise out of our study of the social implications of circumcision and law-observance. They are similar to E.P. Sanders' talk of 'getting in' and 'staying in'. But while Sanders and others discuss Galatians almost exclusively under the heading of 'getting in', this chapter has demonstrated that behavioural patterns/staying in are as much a part of the debate as identity/getting in.[105] In other words, the question of ethics is an important ingredient of the Galatian crisis.

---

[105] Gundry, 'Grace', 8-9 rightly takes issue with Sanders on this point and insists that the letter is as much about 'staying in'.

Chapter Three

Paul's Response in the Main Body of the Letter

By investigating the chief demands of 'the agitators' and their attractiveness to the Galatians we have been able to gain a clearer conception of the main issues in dispute in Galatia. This should now enable us to analyse Paul's response to the crisis and assess its effectiveness. We have noted at several points the persuasiveness of the agitators' arguments: on many issues they had Scripture, tradition and logic on their side. Clearly Paul was faced with a formidable task if he was to counteract their message; but, equally clearly, what was at stake in this crisis was his whole presentation of the gospel and his own identity as apostle to the Gentiles.

Our investigation of the crisis has highlighted the twin notions of *identity* and *behavioural patterns*, and we shall examine Paul's response with these topics particularly in mind. Since our prime concern in this study is with Paul's ethics, we might be tempted to jump straightaway to his ethical instructions at the end of the letter. But further reflection would caution us against adopting too narrow an approach at this point. Since identity and behavioural patterns are so closely interlinked in the Galatian crisis, we should not expect that Paul could deal with them in watertight compartments. Thus our study requires at least a brief investigation of the main body of the letter where questions of identity (e.g., 'who are the children of Abraham?') are explicitly raised. Our study of these passages will be concerned to unearth how Paul counters the agitators' arguments and how his very different notions of Christian identity are linked with his alternative strategy for Christian behaviour.

The Antioch Episode and Justification by Faith

Our present concern with Paul's response to the agitators' demands means that we can leave on one side most of Paul's autobiographical narrative in Gal 1-2. Although he is probably responding here to charges or insinuations which concern *his* identity as apostle to the Gentiles, most of this section does not have a direct bearing on what the agitators proposed for *the Galatians*.[1] However, at the end of this narrative (2.11-21) Paul recounts the incident of his disagreement with Peter at Antioch over the question of eating with Gentiles. Although this event is probably recorded last in the series chiefly because it occurred last,[2] it also serves an important purpose as a bridge between the more historical and the more theological sections of the epistle. It acts as a transition in two ways. First, the issue involved in the Antioch dispute is the fundamental equality of Jew and Gentile and the mistake of forcing Gentiles to 'judaize' – an issue that is also at the heart of the Galatian crisis from Paul's perspective. And secondly, it provides an occasion for Paul to say how he argued (or would have liked to argue) with Peter (vv.14b-21), using phrases which dovetail with the rest of the letter. Indeed, it has often been remarked that what Paul records of his statement to Peter sounds as if it were addressed to the Galatian agitators. Clearly this is an opportunity for Paul to set out some of the main themes of his forthcoming argument.[3]

---

[1] For an analysis of Paul's strategy in this section see J.D.G. Dunn, 'The Relationship between Paul and Jerusalem according to Galatians 1 and 2', *NTS* 28 (1982) 461-478. B.R. Gaventa, 'Galatians 1 and 2: Autobiography as Paradigm', *NT* 28 (1986) 309-326, considers that Paul presents himself in these chapters as a paradigm for the Galatians (cf. 4.12); but this can only be true to a very limited extent since most of what Paul recounts is wholly unlike the Galatians' experience.

[2] This still seems to be the most likely explanation, despite Lüdemann's recent arguments to the contrary, *Paul*, 57-9, 75-7.

[3] According to Betz's rhetorical analysis, 2.15-21 functions as the 'propositio' setting out the issues to be discussed in the following 'probatio', *Galatians*, 18-19, 113-114. The initial address to Peter is clear in vv.14-15 and should be borne in mind also for the interpretation of vv.17-18; but the discussion of justification by faith, crucifixion with Christ and life by faith is also programmatic for the rest of the letter. On this 'double audience' see J.D.G. Dunn, 'Incident', 6 and n.116.

Paul's rebuke of Peter initially concerns a matter of behaviour – he withdrew from table-fellowship with Gentile Christians because of the Jewish food-laws. But in Paul's view this had major theological implications concerning 'the truth of the gospel' (v.14) and raised acutely the question of the identity of Jews and Gentiles in Christ (vv.14-16). The behaviour of Peter and the rest of the Jewish Christians is condemned because it is inconsistent (up to this point Peter himself was not 'living like a Jew').[4] More serious, however, is the fact that Peter, by withdrawing from Gentile fellowship, is in effect compelling Gentiles to 'judaize', that is, to adopt the laws and customs of their Jewish-Christian brethren.[5] To Paul this betokens a wholly mistaken understanding of the identity of Jewish and Gentile believers and demonstrates that Peter and the others are 'not walking straight in line with the truth of the gospel' (οὐκ ὀρθοποδοῦσιν πρὸς τὴν ἀλήθειαν τοῦ εὐαγγελίου, 2.14).[6]

This charge requires that Paul set out what is 'the truth of the gospel', in particular as it affects Jews and Gentiles. Hence in vv.15-21 he spells out some of the basic facts of the gospel, beginning with statements easily accepted by Peter and other Jewish believers in Christ.

Although they were Jews by birth and not 'Gentile sinners' (ἐξ ἐθνῶν ἁμαρτωλοί),[7] they knew that a man is not justified ἐξ

---

[4] Dunn, 'Incident', discusses how much of the law (e.g. a 'Noachian' code?) the Gentile Christians in Antioch were already observing. But it is clear that neither they nor Peter were living as Jews should (ἐθνικῶς καὶ οὐχὶ Ἰουδαϊκῶς ζῆς, v.14) and this suggests an obvious neglect of some of the purity-rules in the law.

[5] On ἰουδαΐζειν, see above, chapter 2, n.1.

[6] Although the exact sense of the NT hapax ὀρθοποδεῖν is not clear, the most probable interpretation of the verse appears to be 'they were not on the right road towards the truth of the gospel' (so Mussner, Galaterbrief, 144; G.D. Kilpatrick, 'Gal 2.14 ὀρθοποδοῦσιν', in Neutestamentliche Studien für R. Bultmann, ed. W. Eltester, Berlin 1957, 269-274). Peter and the rest had swerved from the right path. This is substantially the same as 'not walking in line with/according to' the truth of the gospel (Bruce, Galatians, 132; Betz, Galatians, 110-111).

[7] The identification of 'Gentiles' and 'sinners' was a standard Jewish axiom: see, e.g., 1 Sam 15.18; LXX Ps 9.18; Ps Sol 2.1-2; 17.25; Jub 23.23-4; 24.28 (cf. the

continued on p.78

ἔργων νόμου but by faith in Jesus Christ (2.15-16).[8] The repeated statements of the contrast between 'faith in Christ' and 'works of the law' in 2.16 emphasize the way that justification by faith in Christ modifies the standard Jewish distinction between 'Jews' and 'Gentile sinners'.[9] The immediate context of the Antioch dispute makes clear that 'works of the law' are equivalent to 'living like a Jew', and Paul's point is that this distinctively Jewish pattern of behaviour is not an essential feature of justification, either for Jews or for anyone else (ἄνθρωπος . . . πᾶσα σάρξ). In fact, v.17 goes on to show that Jewish believers may need to abandon their previous distinction from 'Gentile sinners': in 'seeking to be justified in Christ', we Jews may be found to be sinners ourselves (εὑρέθημεν καὶ αὐτοὶ ἁμαρτωλοί, echoing

---

continued from p.77

corollary in 22.16: do not eat with them); 4 Ezra 3.28-36; Mt 5.47 with Lk 6.32; Mt 26.45 with Lk 18.32; K. Rengstorf, art. ἁμαρτωλός, *TDNT* I, 324-6. Dunn, 'Incident', 27-8, suggests that 'Gentile sinners' may have been a pejorative slogan used by 'the men from James'. Neitzel's attempt to reconstrue the verse ('we Jews by birth and not Gentiles, sinners', 'Zur Interpretation von Galater 2,11-21', *TQ* 163 (1983) 15-39, 131-149) must be judged unconvincing since it leaves ἁμαρτωλοί hanging awkwardly and unexplained at the end of the clause.

[8] At least in one clause, Paul talks explicitly of faith *in* Christ (εἰς Χριστὸν Ἰησοῦν ἐπιστεύσαμεν , 2.16). But it remains disputed whether the other clauses in the same verse (διὰ πίστεως Ἰησοῦ Χριστοῦ and ἐκ πίστεως Χριστοῦ) mean the same 'faith in Christ' or refer to 'the faithfulness of Christ'. See Hays, *Faith of Jesus Christ*, 139-191 as the most recent exponent of the latter view. However, Hays fails to explain the relationship between Christ's faithfulness to God and the Christian's faith in (or 'towards') Christ; and he is forced to take Abraham's faith as a prototype of Christ's faithfulness, despite the clear link between the Galatians' and Abraham's faith in the καθώς connecting 3.5 and 3.6. Although the obedience of Christ plays an important part in Rom 5 and Phil 2, there is no convincing evidence that is to be understood in Galatians under the cryptic reference to πίστις Χριστοῦ. That phrase is better taken as a convenient shorthand for 'faith in Christ' (cf. 3.22,26).

[9] Since the textual evidence relating to δέ at the beginning of 2.16 is rather evenly balanced (omitted by P⁴⁶ A; read by ℵ B C D*) it would be unwise to build much on either reading (see Hübner's attack on Dunn on this score, 'Was heisst bei Paulus', 126ff.). But we can still tell from the content of 2.16 (Jew and Gentile alike cannot be justified by works of the law) that it modifies the typically Jewish perspective of 2.15 (Jews are distinct from and superior to 'Gentile sinners').

ἐξ ἐθνῶν ἁμαρτωλοί in v.15). The Antioch episode is a good example of how this happens: there the gospel demanded that Jewish believers should eat with and live like Gentiles (ἐθνικῶς ζῆς v.14), even though from the perspective of the law they would be judged as 'sinners'.[10]

But if this is a correct understanding of the gospel, there are important objections to be answered and consequences to be drawn. In the first place, the observation that faith in Christ may require Jews to live like Gentile 'sinners' raises the urgent question whether Christ then acts as a 'servant of sin' (ἆρα Χριστὸς ἁμαρτίας διάκονος; v.17).[11] It is possible that this question was raised in the Antioch dispute: did Paul really think that belonging to Christ should lead Jewish believers into sinful disregard of the law?[12] Inasmuch as such a question reflects more widespread fears concerning the antinomian implications of Paul's teaching (cf. Rom 3.8; 6.1; Acts 21.21), it is important enough for Paul to frame a careful response. The suggestion that Christ promotes or encourages sin is met by an emphatic denial (μὴ γένοιτο) followed by what appears to be a counter-charge (2.18): it is only

---

[10] See Burton, *Galatians*, 129-30; Mussner, *Galaterbrief*, 176-7; Howard, *Crisis*, 43-4; R. Kieffer, *Foi et Justification à Antioche. Interpretation d'un Conflit (Ga 2.14-21)*, Paris 1982, 53-57. Some interpreters consider that 'we Jews' are found to be sinners in recognizing the need for salvation in Christ, G. Klein, 'Individualgeschichte und Weltgeschichte bei Paulus. Eine Interpretation ihres Verhältnisses im Galaterbrief', *Ev Th* 24 (1964), 126-165; J. Lambrecht, 'The Line of Thought in Gal.2.14b-21', *NTS* 24 (1977-8) 484-495. But this cannot adequately explain how it could then be charged that Christ 'serves' or 'promotes' sin (v.17c).

[11] It is uncertain whether ἆρα should be accepted ἄρα or ἆρα (which probably occurs nowhere else in Paul). But in either case it almost certainly introduces a question since the phrase is matched by μὴ γένοιτο which in almost every other case is used by Paul to answer a question (Gal 6.14 is the only exception). Thus most exegetes take the phrase as a question although a few demur (Borse, *Galater*, 114-5; C.F.D. Moule, *An Idiom Book of New Testament Greek*, Cambridge 1959, 196; R. Bultmann, 'Zur Auslegung von Galater 2,15-18', in *Exegetica*, Tübingen 1967, 394-9).

[12] See T. Zahn, *Der Brief des Paulus an die Galater*, Leipzig 1905, 128; Betz, *Galatians*, 120. H. Feld even suggests it is intended to be a quotation of Peter's very words in the dispute, '"Christus Diener der Sünde". Zum Ausgang des Streites zwischen Petrus und Paulus'. *TQ* 153 (1973) 119-131.

by rebuilding the demands of the law (as Peter and the others did at Antioch) that one would make oneself a 'transgressor' (παραβάτης) in eating with Gentiles.[13] In fact, Christ does not promote sin because to be justified in Christ means to be crucified with him (2.19) and that means 'to die to the law through the law' (ἐγὼ γὰρ διὰ νόμου νόμῳ ἀπέθανον).[14] For those who have 'died to the law' its moral requirements setting out the Jewish way of life can no longer be the true criterion which distinguishes righteous from sinful behaviour. The fact that Jews abandon the law for the sake of table-fellowship with Gentiles is 'sin' from a Jewish perspective but not for one who has died to the law; hence although Jewish Christians are technically 'sinners' in eating with Gentiles, it cannot be said that Christ has promoted sin in any

---

[13] It is still disputed what role 2.18 plays in Paul's argument. However I consider it most likely that a) γὰρ connects it to v.17 with an implied ellipsis: 'By no means; in fact the case stands quite the opposite, for . . .' cf. 3.21; Rom 9.14-15; 11.1 and Lightfoot, *Galatians*, 117. Lambrecht posits too sharp a break at this point ('Line of Thought', 491-3) which is rightly modified by Kieffer, *Foi et Justification*, 60-61. b) Paul's use of the first person singular is probably a literary-stylistic device which tactfully avoids a direct attack on Peter although his action is here alluded to (see Schlier, *Galater*, 96-7; R.C. Tannehill, *Dying and Rising with Christ. A Study in Pauline Theology*, Berlin 1967, 56-7). It also anticipates his use of 'I' in vv.19-20 thus setting out the alternatives – rebuilding the law or dying to it – which he faces as a Jewish believer in Christ. c) The action described in this verse is the rebuilding of the law and the structures of the 'old' Israel (see C.K. Barrett, 'Paul and the "Pillar" Apostles', in *Studia Paulina*, ed. J.N. Sevenster and W.C. van Unnik, Haarlem 1953, 1-19, at 18). It would constitute the Christian a transgressor of the law (παραβάτης) not because it is impossible to live under the law without sinning (*pace* Schlier, *Galater*, 97; W. Mundle, 'Zur Auslegung von Gal 2,17-18', *ZNW* 23 (1924) 152-3), nor because he would thereby sin against the gospel (*pace* Duncan, *Galatians*, 69; Neitzel, 'Interpretation', 131-7) but because it would condemn his previous relaxation of the law in the interests of Gentile-Christian fellowship (see Oepke, *Galater*, 61; Becker, *Galater*, 30; Mussner, *Galaterbrief*, 178-9; Räisänen, *Paul and the Law*, 259). The excision of this verse as a gloss (Schmithals, 'Judaisten', 41-3) is a desperate and unwarranted expedient.

[14] We will explore further at the end of this chapter the significance of the cross as a symbol of a radical break with the past. The significance of 'dying to the law' (cf. Rom 7.1-4; on the unusual dative see Tannehill, *Dying and Rising*, 18) is that the law is no longer valid for a dead man: 'as soon as a man is dead, he is free from the obligation of the commands' (R. Johanan in b Shabbath 30a, based on Ps 88.6). Paul's talk of dying to the law *through the law* seems to be deliberately paradoxical but remains somewhat enigmatic. The context suggests the thought is not that of

continued on p.81

absolute sense.[15] For the truth of the gospel, according to which Jews as well as Gentiles are justified by faith in Christ, establishes a new pattern and standard of life. Jewish believers no longer live simply Ἰουδαϊκῶς (2.14). In a series of statements about his 'life' (2.19-20) which clearly echo his comment on Peter's life (2.14),[16] Paul asserts that he lives to God (ἵνα θεῷ ζήσω) only inasmuch as his life is taken over by Christ (ζῶ δὲ οὐκέτι ἐγώ, ζῇ δὲ ἐν ἐμοὶ Χριστός) and is now characterized not by law but by faith: ὃ δὲ νῦν ζῶ ἐν σαρκί, ἐν πίστει ζῶ τῇ τοῦ υἱοῦ τοῦ θεοῦ . . .

It must be admitted that this is not the only possible interpretation of these densely-packed verses; at some points Paul's thought is so compressed as to be somewhat obscure.[17] Nevertheless, several points relevant to our enquiry emerge with sufficient clarity:

i) Paul's argument with Peter in these verses concerns the identity of Jewish believers in Christ. He is clearly attempting to redefine that identity in ways which contradict some standard Jewish assumptions but are based on what he calls 'the truth of the

---

continued from p.80

the law revealing or inciting sin (Burton, *Galatians*, 132-3; Bruce, *Galatians*, 143-4) but of the role of the law in the crucifixion of Christ and hence those crucified with him (Tannehill, *Dying and Rising*, 58-9). The phrase may therefore point forward to 3.13 and the curse-verdict on Christ crucified (so Schlier, *Galater*, 99-101; A. van Dülmen, *Die Theologie des Gesetzes bei Paulus*, Stuttgart 1968, 25-6; F-J. Ortkemper, *Das Kreuz in der Verkündigung des Apostels Paulus*, Stuttgart 1968, 22).

[15] See Burton, *Galatians*, 125-6; Räisänen, *Paul and the Law*, 76 n.173.

[16] The emphatic use of ἐγώ in vv.19-20 probably implies more than a personal confession on Paul's part; it is an indication that Paul 'takes seriously the situation of salvation history which must be expressed in his life, and has taken a way which Peter and the rest must also tread' (E. Stauffer, art. ἐγώ in *TDNT* II, 357; cf. Kieffer, *Foi et Justification*, 67).

[17] For other interpretations which differ to some degree from‧that given here see the articles listed in the notes above, together with V. Hasler, 'Glaube und Existenz. Hermeneutische Erwägungen zu Gal.2, 15-21', *ThZ* 25 (1969) 241-51; W.G. Kümmel, ' "Individualgeschichte" und "Weltgeschichte" in Gal 2.15-21', in *Christ and Spirit in the New Testament*, ed. B. Lindars and S.S.‧Smalley, Cambridge 1973, 157-173. Kieffer's detailed exposition, *Foi et Justification*, 13-80, is very close to that represented here.

gospel' and focus particularly on the cross.

ii) Within this context, what Paul terms 'the works of the law' appear to be those activities which express Jewish identity, what Paul calls ζῆν Ἰουδαϊκῶς (2.14). This link between doing the works of the law and Jewish identity is precisely what we would expect from our analysis of the agitators' demands: both for them and for Paul doing what the law demands is a sign of adopting the Jewish way of life. This means that when Paul polemicizes against 'works of the law' he is not attacking 'works' as such in an attempt to divorce 'believing' from 'doing': the butt of his attack in this letter is 'the works *of the law*', that is, maintaining a Jewish life-style.[18] As Watson comments: 'The faith-works antithesis is not an antithesis between faith and morality-in-general, but an antithesis between life as a Christian, with its distinctive beliefs and practices, and life as a Jew'.[19]

iii) Thus, part and parcel of his redefinition of Jewish-Christian identity is Paul's redefinition of appropriate patterns of behaviour. The Antioch dispute begins with the eminently practical issue of eating-habits and we have seen that a central aspect of the debate is the definition of 'sin' and whether behaviour which ignores the law is always and at all costs to be avoided. Paul's conclusion sketches the outline of a new way of life, not based on law but shaped by Christ and conducted 'in

---

[18] The popular conception has been that 'works of the law' represent legalism (see, e.g., D.P. Fuller, 'Paul and "the Works of the Law"', *Westminster Theological Journal* 38 (1975-6) 28-42). But E. Lohmeyer rightly argued that the phrase is a purely neutral description of Torah-observance (*Probleme paulinischer Theologie*, Darmstadt 1954, 31-74) and several scholars have recently insisted that Paul attacks the performance of these works not because they encourage self-righteousness but because they are bound up with Jewish national identity and hence exclude Gentiles: so J.B. Tyson, ' "Works of the Law" in Galatians', *JBL* 92 (1973) 423-32; Dunn, 'New Perspective' and 'Works of the Law'; Sanders, *Paul, The Law, and the Jewish People*. Since Paul talks in this context of 'dying to the law', it is impossible to take 'works of the law' as referring to only a few notably distinctive activities, *pace* Dunn, 'New Perspective'; cf. J. Blank's reply to Wilckens in 'Warum sagt Paulus: "Aus Werken des Gesetzes wird niemand gerecht"?', in *Evangelisch-Katholischer Kommentar zum Neuen Testament, Vorarbeiten Heft I*, Zürich 1969, 79-95.

[19] *Paul, Judaism and the Gentiles*, 65.

faith'. Thus faith emerges as the key factor both in identity ('we are justified by faith in Christ') and in behaviour ('the life I now live I live by faith'): it embraces both the indicative and the imperative and determines how the Christian who believes the gospel should 'walk straight in line' with its truth.[20]

Thus even at this early stage it can be seen how Paul's letter to the Galatians addresses *both* the issue of identity *and* that of behavioural patterns – issues which we saw to be intimately connected in the Galatian crisis. Of course, thus far, in repeating (with suitable modifications) his response to Peter, Paul has been chiefly concerned with the identity and life-style of *Jewish-Christians*. This has at least one important negative implication for Gentiles: they do not need to adopt a Jewish identity and life-style in order to be justified believers in Christ. The more positive aspect of 'the truth of the gospel' – what believing in Christ does imply about Gentile-Christian identity and behaviour – is the subject of the following arguments in Gal 3-4, where Paul unequivocally addresses the Galatian situation.

The Spirit in the Galatian Churches

It is surely significant that the main argument of the letter (what Betz identifies as the 'probatio') begins with an appeal to the Galatians' experience of the Spirit (3.1-5). The weight that Paul puts on this point is evident in his suggestion that it constitutes a knock-down proof for his case: τοῦτο μόνον θέλω μαθεῖν ἀφ' ὑμῶν (3.2). In fact, of course, he does not treat this point as sufficient since he goes on to present a series of complex scriptural arguments (3.6ff.); but it is still important enough to rank first in his chain of argumentation (as well as reappearing in 4.6-7).

Although Paul's initial rebuke of the Galatians (3.1) picks up the theme of the crucifixion from the previous verse (2.21) his

---

[20] See J.A. Ziesler, *The Meaning of Righteousness in Paul. A Linguistic and Theological Enquiry*, Cambridge 1972, 165: 'As faith is indivisible, there is no distinction of that faith which is a response to God's action in Christ (i.e. justifying faith) from that which is the Christian's continuing life.'

real emphasis here lies not on the content of the preaching but on its experiential result: the Galatians received the Spirit. The way Paul describes this experience makes clear the assumption that the Spirit is the gift of God (τὸ πνεῦμα ἐλάβετε 3.2; ὁ ἐπιχορηγῶν ὑμῖν τὸ πνεῦμα 3.5; the point is explicit in 4.6). The significance of the fact that God supplies the Spirit to non-proselyte Gentiles is clarified when it is seen in the light of two apparently common assumptions of Jewish theology. i) Given that Gentiles were 'sinners' and the Spirit was 'holy', it was taken for granted that the Spirit would not be given to non-Jews and, indeed, was only to be expected in the context of law-observance.[21] ii) In many strands of Judaism it was not expected that God would pour out his Spirit in any general way until the dawn of a new age, when, in line with Ezek 37, it would signify the revitalization of Israel.[22] These two notions are typically combined in the eschatological prophecy of Jubilees 1: 'And I shall create for them a holy spirit, and I shall purify them so that they will not turn away from following me from that day and forever. And their souls will cleave to me and to all my commandments. And they will do my commandments. And I shall be a father to them, and they will be sons to me. And they will all be called "sons of the living God"' (1.23-25).

In line with this eschatology, and in common with other early Christians, Paul interpreted the experience of the Spirit as the fulfilment of the promise (3.14) and the inauguration of 'the fulness of time' (Gal 4.4-6; cf. Rom 8.23; Acts 2.15-21). Like the author of Jubilees, he takes the Spirit's presence as proof that its recipients are 'sons' of God; for Paul, their Spirit-inspired 'Abba'-

[21] See Ezek 36.22 and the discussion of rabbinic texts by D. Hill, *Greek Words and Hebrew Meanings*, Cambridge 1967, 220-232. See especially Num Rabba 20.1 (idolatrous Gentiles are too unclean to receive the holy gift) and Mekilta Beshallah 7, lines 133-138 (obedience to the law is an essential condition for receiving the Spirit).

[22] Besides Ezek 37.1-14, see Ezek 39.29; Joel 3.1 (MT); Is 32.9-20; 44.1-5; Enoch 61.11; M Sota 9.15 (end); Gen Rabba 26.6. These and other texts are discussed by W.D. Davies, *Paul and Rabbinic Judaism*, 202ff. The special emphasis on the 'Spirit' in the Qumran hymns is probably a symptom of the eschatological fervour of the community.

prayer demonstrates their filial relationship (4.6).[23] In this sense the presence of the Spirit is palpable evidence for their identity as members of the people of God. But it is essential for Paul's argument that in one crucial respect the Galatians' experience contradicted normal Jewish expectations: they did not receive the Spirit ἐξ ἔργων νόμου (3.2,5). The fact that their experience of the Spirit in the past (3.2) and the present (3.5) was not dependent on law-observance is the fundamental point here. Exactly how they *did* receive the Spirit is rather unclear, being cryptically summarized as ἐξ ἀκοῆς πίστεως.[24] Probably the crucial word in this expression is πίστις, for this can lead directly into the argument from Gen 15.6 about Abraham's faith (3.6ff). In any case, by appealing to their experience of the Spirit, Paul clearly intends to assure the Galatians that, without becoming proselytes, they are nonetheless fully-approved members of the family of God.[25]

But as in 2.14-21 the careful definition of identity has immediate implications for behaviour. If this is the way the Galatians began, and the way that God continues to work miracles in their midst, it is also the way that they should continue to live. This is the clear implication of Paul's ironic question in 3.3: ἐναρξάμενοι πνεύματι νῦν σαρκι ἐπιτελεῖσθε; It is important to observe the categories Paul adopts here. The Spirit, the determining factor of the Galatians' Christian identity, is appealed to as their only appropriate standard of behaviour. And, as a neat contrast to πνεῦμα, Paul seizes on σάρξ, apparently

---

[23] On the dispute about whether to take ὅτι in 4.6 in a declarative or causal sense see, besides the commentators, Lull, *Spirit in Galatia*, 105-119. In either case the Spirit demonstrates the Galatians' status as sons; cf. Rom 8.14-17.

[24] The four main options for interpreting this phrase are well set out by Hays, *Faith of Jesus Christ*, 143-9. Since πίστις is anarthrous (contrast 1.23) and is clearly intended to match Abraham's experience in 3.6, it is almost certainly to be understood as 'faith' (not 'the faith'/'the gospel', as in Betz, *Galatians*, 128). But whether the whole phrase should be taken as 'hearing accompanied by faith' or 'the message that evokes faith' (or other variants of these two options) is impossible to determine.

[25] In this respect Paul's theological logic exactly matches that of the author of Acts 10.44-8; 11.15-18; 15.7-11.

including within that term what he has just called ἔργα νόμου.[26] Thus, in setting out the choice before the Galatians, Paul employs a dualism which will be basic to his later description of two alternative patterns of behaviour (5.13-6.10).

The Abrahamic Family Redefined

In chapter 2 we noted at a number of points the significance of the Abrahamic traditions in the Galatian crisis and the ways in which the opponents could have used Scriptural and current Jewish traditions about Abraham to argue their case. In his response, Paul discusses Abraham in a variety of contexts, and the number of his different attempts at reinterpretation indicates his special concern to appropriate the Abrahamic promises for his presentation of the gospel. In his discussion of the Antioch dispute, Paul took what was common between himself and Peter (justification by faith in Christ) to show that it entailed quite different practical results from those Peter demonstrated. In his rebuke of the Galatians, he appealed to their own experience of the Spirit to support his understanding of how they should live. And similarly in this case, Paul seizes on the Abrahamic traditions which were so central to the Galatian debate; and his tactic is so to interpret them in the light of Christ that he can counter his opponents' propaganda and support his own understanding of Christian identity and behaviour. We may observe his redefining technique at six points:[27]

---

[26] Although some commentators restrict the reference of σαρκί here to circumcision (e.g., Burton, *Galatians*, 148; Duncan, *Galatians*, 81; Betz, *Galatians*, 133-4), others insist, more plausibly, that the term is broad enough and vague enough to include pursuing ἔργα νόμου in general; see, e.g., Bonnard, *Galates*, 63; Schlier, *Galater*, 123; Bruce, *Galatians*, 149.

[27] In this connection see C.K. Barrett, *From First Adam to Last. A Study in Pauline Theology*, London 1962, 33-45 and *Freedom and Obligation*, 22-29. C. Dietzfelbinger, *Paulus und das Alte Testament*, München 1961, demonstrates how Paul reads the Christian gospel into the Abraham story. See also K. Berger, 'Abraham in den paulinischen Hauptbriefen', *Münchener Theologische Zeitschrift* 17 (1966) 47-89.

i) Paul broaches the subject of Abraham abruptly in 3.6 with a sudden quotation of Gen 15.6 (introduced only by καθώς). Clearly he chooses this text because of the emphasis it places on Abraham's faith and its association with δικαιοσύνη (cf. Gal 2.15-17).[28] But in contrast to many Jewish interpretations, Paul declines to connect this verse with Abraham's merit, his observance of the law or even his obedience when tested;[29] the sole essential feature of Abraham's response to God was his faith. This enables Paul to 'demonstrate' (γινώσκετε ἄρα 3.7) that the sons of Abraham are characterized not by circumcision (οἱ ἐκ περιτομῆς 2.12) but by faith (οἱ ἐκ πίστεως 3.7,9). In fact, Paul carefully omits any mention of Abraham's circumcision;[30] even a 'spiritual' interpretation of circumcision (cf. Phil 3.3; Rom 2.25-9) might be open to misunderstanding in this context. Thus while appealing to Abraham Paul entirely bypasses the Gen 17 text on circumcision in order to underline the sole criterion of faith; and by 'faith' he clearly understands what has been 'revealed' as 'faith in Christ' (3.22-3).[31]

ii) This selective use of the Genesis narrative is followed by a citation in 3.8 which combines the promises of Gen 12.3 and

---

[28] Elsewhere in the LXX πίστις and δίκαιος/δικαιοσύνη are found together only in Hab 2.4 (see Gal 3.11), 1 Sam 26.23 and Jer 49.5. Gen 15.6 will prove important for Paul's argument again in Rom 4.3.

[29] Cf. 1 Macc 2.52; Mekilta Beshallah 7, lines 139ff. For other rabbinic references see Mussner, *Galaterbrief*, 218; Sandmel, *Philo's Place*, 81-2; Strack-Billerbeck III, 200-201. See above pp.65-6 for Abraham as observer of the Torah. It is noticeable that although 1 Macc 2.52 and Sir 44.20 also call Abraham πιστός (cf. Gal 3.9), they use the adjective in the sense of 'faithful to the will of God' rather than Paul's 'believing'. Paul's use of Gen 15.6 also contrasts with Jas 2.18-24, although, as we shall see, Paul is nonetheless concerned to see faith 'at work' (Gal 5.6).

[30] Contrast Romans 4, where both faith and circumcision are under discussion but Paul shows that faith was the earlier and decisive feature in Abraham's δικαιοσύνη. Clearly the same approach would have been disadvantageous for Paul in addressing the Galatian crisis; the Galatians could reply that they were simply following Abraham's example, adding circumcision to their faith! See Burton, *Galatians*, 155-9; Bruce, *Galatians*, 154-5; A.T. Hanson, *Studies in Paul's Technique and Theology*, London 1974, 69.

[31] Again, contrast Romans 4. Here in Galatians Paul does not attempt to demonstrate any clear correspondence between Abrahamic and Christian faith, nor does he clarify how Abraham could believe before faith 'came' (3.23).

18.18.[32] Again the context in which Paul cites the text determines his interpretation: the blessing promised through Abraham to 'all the nations' is regarded as a prophecy (προϊδοῦσα) and an anticipation of the gospel (προευηγγελίσατο) – that is, for Paul, the gospel to the Gentiles (1.16; 2.8-9). In Paul's hands, the text indicates not how many idolaters would find blessing as proselytes, but how God will justify the Gentiles ἐκ πίστεως even while they remain ἔθνη – that is, uncircumcised and, technically, sinners (2.15).[33] In this light, the Abrahamic promises already legitimated Paul's law-free mission to the Gentiles.

iii) Despite his considerable ingenuity in adapting the Genesis text to his purposes, even Paul could not find a text which connected Abraham with a central aspect of Christian identity – the Spirit. We have just noted the importance of the Spirit in Paul's argument and we may here observe how he endeavours to associate it with the Abrahamic motif even though he has no text to cite in his support. We have already noted one way of linking the two themes: the transition from 3.5 to 3.6 is established through the common motif of 'faith', so that the Galatians' experience of the Spirit is treated as parallel to (καθώς) Abraham's receipt of righteousness. Another example occurs in 3.14 where the blessing of Abraham which reaches the Gentiles is matched with the receipt of the promised Spirit through faith. It is not immediately obvious what logic links these two parallel ἵνα-clauses,[34] but the mention of 'promise' (τὴν ἐπαγγελίαν τοῦ πνεύματος) clearly establishes a connection with the following

---

[32] Πᾶσαι αἱ φυλαὶ τῆς γῆς in LXX Gen 12.3 (cf. Gen 28.14; Acts 3.25) is replaced by πάντα τὰ ἔθνη from LXX Gen 18.18 (cf. Gen 22.18; 26.4).

[33] Paul's semi-technical use of ἔθνη in 2.14-15 (see above) suggests that it was important for him to change the text of LXX Gen 12.3 in order to include precisely this term.

[34] It is generally agreed that the two clauses are co-ordinate rather than sequential, while the second may be intended to clarify the first, Schlier, Galater, 140; Bruce, Galatians, 167. The theological connection between 'the blessing of Abraham' and 'the promise of the Spirit' is discussed by B. Byrne, 'Sons of God' – 'Seed of Abraham'. A Study of the Idea of the Sonship of God of All Christians in Paul, Rome 1979, 156-7 and S.K. Williams, 'Justification and the Spirit in Galatians', JSNT 29 (1987) 91-100.

references to the Abrahamic promises.[35] Finally, in the midst of the 'allegory', Paul throws in a reference to Isaac's birth κατὰ πνεῦμα (4.29; parallel to δι' ἐπαγγελίας, 4.23). This reference to the Spirit is also left unexplained but it helps to reinforce the impression that the true Abrahamic family is characterized by the Spirit as well as by faith.

iv) In his argument up till 3.14 Paul has 'proved' that the blessings of the Abrahamic family are open to Gentiles and are associated with faith and the Spirit. Only in 3.13-14 has Christ entered the scene as the one whose cursed death enabled the blessing to reach Gentiles ἐν Χριστῷ 'Ιησοῦ (3.14). It is possible that this phrase is meant to echo the Genesis texts quoted in 3.8 which declared blessing to the Gentiles ἐν σοί (Abraham). If so, this implicit association between Abraham and Christ is then made unmistakably clear in 3.16.[36] Here Paul seizes on the collective singular, σπέρμα, mentioned in the promises to Abraham and his 'seed' (Gen 13.15; 17.8, etc.); against its more normal meaning (and his normal usage, Rom 4.18; 9.7; 11.1 etc.), he draws out the implications of its singular number to refer to one man ὅς ἐστιν Χριστός (cf. 3.19). It is widely acknowledged that Paul's technique here reflects a rabbinic mode of exegesis;[37] but his treatment of the noun is not without its parallels in the LXX (see Gen 4.25; 21.13; 2 Sam 7.12) and may even echo a Jewish 'messianic' interpretation of the Abrahamic and Davidic seed.[38] In any case, this identification of 'the seed' as

---

[35] The alternative reading τὴν εὐλογίαν τοῦ πνεύματος P⁴⁶ D* F G etc. is probably an assimilation to εὐλογία in the first part of the verse, Metzger, *Textual Commentary*, 594.

[36] See A.J.M. Wedderburn, 'Some Observations on Paul's Use of the Phrases "in Christ" and "with Christ"', *JSNT* 25 (1985) 83-97. J.C. Beker, *Paul the Apostle. The Triumph of God in Life and Thought*, Philadelphia 1980, 50-51 notes that in Gal 3 Christ is merely the 'enabler' of the promise until 3.16 where he becomes 'the sole content of the promise'.

[37] See esp. D. Daube, *The New Testament and Rabbinic Judaism*, London 1956, 438-44.

[38] See O. Betz, 'Die heilsgeschichtliche Rolle Israels bei Paulus', *Theologische Beiträge* 9 (1978) 1-21, at 11-12; M. Wilcox, 'The Promise of the "Seed" in the New

continued on p.90

Christ enables Paul to affirm that all the blessings of the Abrahamic family are available only through Christ. Abrahamic faith is now discussed as faith in Christ (3.22-9); the Gentiles are saved by being baptised into Christ (3.26-9); and the Spirit is now described as the Spirit of God's Son (4.6). It is only those who belong to Christ who can truly be called Abraham's seed in the corporate sense (3.29).[39]

v) This discussion of the seed is embedded in an argument which constitutes a sustained attempt to draw a clear distinction between the Abrahamic promises and the Mosaic law (3.15ff.). Paul here counters the common fusion of these two entities which was one factor that had led the Galatians to assume that their entry into the Abrahamic covenant involved their obligation to the law. He uses a variety of arguments to insist that the two must be clearly differentiated. The law was given 430 years later (cf. Ex 12.40) and cannot alter or overrule the διαθήκη previously established by God (3.15-17).[40] Abraham's inheritance was dependent solely on promise – it did not spring from the law (3.18; cf. Rom 4.13-14). The law was intended to operate only until 'the seed' came to inherit the blessings (3.19, 23ff.); in

---

continued from p. 89

Testament and the Targumim', *JSNT* 5 (1979) 2-20. For further discussion of Paul's technique here see R.N. Longenecker, *Biblical Exegesis in the Apostolic Period*, Grand Rapids 1975, 123-4 and E.E. Ellis, *Paul's Use of the Old Testament*, Edinburgh 1957, 70-73.

[39] See Barrett, *Freedom and Obligation*, 38: 'Of course Paul knows that "seed" is a collective noun, but it was necessary for him first to break down the old collectivity of race in order to establish the new collectivity which is coming into · being, in an inconceivable unity, with and in Christ.'

[40] There is still some uncertainty concerning the precise legal practice envisaged here. The most plausible interpretation may be that of E. Bammel, 'Gottes ΔΙΑΘΗΚΗ (Gal III.15-17) und das jüdische Rechtsdenken', *NTS* 6 (1959-60) 313-9, who refers to the מתנת בריא in rabbinic law; but his argument has recently been criticized by Räisänen, *Paul and the Law*, 129. Paul appears to be exploiting the dual meaning of διαθήκη – both 'covenant' (3.17, the LXX translation for ברית) and human 'will' or 'testament' (3.15); see the discussion in Burton, *Galatians*, 500-5 and Byrne, *'Sons of God'*, 158, n.84.

contrast to the direct address of God's promise, it was given through angels and by a mediator (3.19-20).[41] Finally the law and the promises, while not in contradiction, were not intended for the same function: the receipt of righteousness is possible through faith, not through the law (3.21-5). Paul thus amasses a whole catena of proofs to demonstrate the separate and unique validity of the Abrahamic promises; they are independent of the law and cannot be made contingent on law-observance.

vi) Paul's final attempt to redefine the Abrahamic traditions is found in the 'allegory' of 4.21-31. This is his most extensive and most polemical use of the Abraham story which so overturns the natural reading of the Sarah and Hagar events that standard Jewish notions are completely reversed. Such a 'tour de force', accompanied by strange and even arbitrary exegesis, is probably best explained as Paul's reply to his opponents' use of this very story.[42] It mirrors Paul's tactic evidenced throughout this epistle, where he attempts to show that the Galatians' attraction to circumcision and the law will achieve the very opposite of their intentions.[43] Once again the question concerns the true family of Abraham. According to Paul's 'allegorical' interpretation,[44] the Sarah-Isaac line of descent embraces not Jews but those (Jews and Gentiles) who are freed by Christ, while Hagar and Ishmael represent the slavery of those under the law. Paul reaches such a

---

[41] Without entering into the many complexities of these verses, it is worth nothing Paul's remarkable attempt to distance God from the law through the intermediary angels; however he does not quite deny that God is the ultimate author of the law, pace Hübner, Law in Paul's Thought, 26-7 (the E.T. at the top of p.27 mistakenly prints διά for ὑπό).

[42] So Drane, Paul, 43-4 and Barrett, 'Allegory', 8-16. This would explain why Paul includes this scriptural argument which many commentators have regarded as quite superfluous (e.g., Burton, Galatians, 251 'an afterthought').

[43] This repeated reversal of values renders implausible L. Gaston's plea that it is unthinkable for Paul to refer to unbelieving Jews as 'Ishmael', 'Israel's Enemies in Pauline Theology', NTS 28 (1982) 400-423. His attempt to reinterpret the passage is distorted by an apologetic concern to clear Paul of the charge of 'anti-Semitism'.

[44] Commentators continue to debate whether Paul's technique is really 'allegory' or 'typology'; see Hanson, Studies, 91-103.

startling conclusion by a variety of means,[45] but the course of his argument is determined by the construction of a list of opposites representing the characteristics of two covenants (δύο διαθῆκαι 4.24). Here, rather than playing Abraham off against Moses, the Abrahamic story is itself divided into two. Sarah and Hagar represent two covenants,[46] the basis of two very different family identities. One is associated with promise, inheritance, Spirit and the Jerusalem above: this is Sarah's line, the family of freedom and therefore to be identified as those 'freed' by Christ. The other is descended from Hagar, a family of slavery and thus to be interpreted as those under the 'slavery' of the law. By this cunning use of word-associations Paul reaches his triumphant conclusion that Abraham's legitimate heirs are those who enjoy freedom in Christ (4.31-5.1).

All this elaborate argumentation about the Abrahamic family serves the purpose of persuading the Galatians that their identity as children of Abraham is secure on the basis of their faith in Christ. In countering the agitators' emphasis on law and circumcision, Paul has attempted to prove that Gentiles who believe in Christ and receive the Spirit and freedom 'in Christ' are the true heirs of the Abrahamic promises, as was foreseen by Scripture itself. But what are the practical implications of their status in the Abrahamic family? Although Paul hints at these in Gal 3-4 in his positive references to the Spirit and faith and the negative remarks about the law, the practical aspects of their position as 'sons of Abraham' are more clearly spelled out in

---

[45] These include an enigmatic identification of Sinai and Hagar (4.25, see Mussner, *Galaterbrief*, 322-5), an appeal to Is 54.1 by 'gezerah shawah' (4.27, see Barrett, 'Allegory', 11-12, with reference to the exegetical method 'kemin homer') and a reference to Jewish persecution of Christians (4.29).

[46] In this context it would clearly be impossible to refer to these two covenants as 'old' and 'new' (contrast 2 Cor 3). The two women to whom they correspond were contemporary and Paul is concerned to distinguish the 'legitimate' from the 'illegitimate' covenant heirs (see Richardson, *Israel*, 99-101). The old/new language of Jer 31 would hardly fit Galatians anyway, since the Abrahamic covenant was older than the Mosaic. Although he is aware of this, E. Grässer still confusingly discusses Gal 3-4 using the terminology of 'old' and 'new' covenants, *Der Alte Bund im Neuen*, Tübingen 1985, 56-77.

5.1-6. These verses build on the 'allegory' of 4.21-31 in setting before the Galatians the stark alternatives of the two ways of life associated with the two covenants. They can choose the 'covenant' of circumcision, with its obligation to observe the whole law (5.3) and so take upon themselves the yoke of slavery (5.1); but they should realize that such a course of action will mean that Christ is of no benefit to them (5.2), since they will be cut off from him and fall from grace (5.4). On the other hand, they may choose the 'true' Abrahamic covenant in its line of descent through Isaac. In this case they will enjoy the benefits of freedom, of Christ and of God's grace. Paul sums up those benefits in 5.5: 'we' (who believe in Christ) are characterized by the gift of the Spirit (πνεύματι)[47] and are marked by faith (ἐκ πίστεως); and on those grounds we have a sure hope and eager expectation of righteousness (ἐλπίδα δικαιοσύνης ἀπεκδεχόμεθα). These are the distinguishing marks of the true Abrahamic covenant as it is fulfilled in Christ, as the whole of Gal 3-4 has set out to prove. Thus Paul can sum up his argument in 5.6: in Christ neither circumcision nor uncircumcision are significant status-indicators (οὔτε περιτομή τι ἰσχύει οὔτε ἀκροβυστία):[48] all that counts is faith working through love (ἀλλὰ πίστις δι᾽ ἀγάπης ἐνεργουμένη).[49]

This formulation in 5.6 is particularly significant for two reasons:

i) In summing up the arguments of the earlier parts of the letter on the equality of Jew and Gentile in Christ (2.14-21; 3.13-14, 26-29 etc.) it focuses particularly on the mark of circumcision, the

---

[47] The role of this dative in the sentence is unclear. Betz notes that it is a 'theological abbreviation' placed first as 'the primary datum of Christian existence', Galatians, 262.

[48] The verb ἰσχύει suggests Paul's concern to dismiss the validity of these signs as marks of covenant membership (or the lack of it); Schlier, Galater, 234, Betz, Galatians, 262-3. The context shows that circumcision would have a disastrous effect on the Galatians if they were to accord it such validity.

[49] The long dispute on the voice of the participle (middle – 'faith operative through love'; passive – 'faith set in motion by love') is now almost universally settled in favour of the middle; see esp. the discussion by Mussner, Galaterbrief, 353-4.

pivotal issue in the Galatian crisis. By dismissing its significance, Paul is undermining the agitators' main argument 'on the inadequacy of the Galatians' present status. This is far more radical than Ananias' political expediency in allowing Izates special exemption from circumcision. It is a far-reaching redefinition of the identity-markers of the people of God: what is decisive now is being in Christ, possessing the Spirit and having a faith which works through love.

ii) It is equally significant that this definition of identity has an active emphasis – faith must work through love. Although the true Abrahamic family are free from the yoke of the law, they are not free from the obligation to *work* – to turn their faith into loving behaviour. Once again it is clear that Paul is not at all concerned in this letter to attack 'works' as such, only works of *the law*. And once again it is apparent that Paul's redefinition of Christian identity inevitably includes a concern for the practical aspects of Christian behaviour.

Each of these three sections we have studied represents Paul's attempt to counteract the 'persuasion' of his opponents. Where they had emphasized Jewish identity, proselyte status, the Abrahamic covenant of circumcision and the requirement of law-observance, Paul argues for a new understanding of identity, based on faith in Christ and the gift of the Spirit, and a new pattern of obligation that involves freedom from the works of the law and a commitment to continue in the Spirit, letting faith work itself out in love. In each section we have noted the close relationship between Paul's definition of Christian identity and his outline description of Christian behavioural patterns. Two phrases in the letter sum up this relationship particularly clearly. At 2.14 Paul accuses Peter and the rest of not 'walking in accordance with the truth of the gospel' and at 5.7 he asks the Galatians who has prevented them from 'obeying the truth' (τίς ὑμᾶς ἐνέκοψεν [τῇ] ἀληθείᾳ μὴ πείθεσθαι;). Clearly the 'truth' that Paul expounds in the course of Gal 2-4 is not to be given merely intellectual assent: it is meant to be 'obeyed' and to determine the pattern of their 'walk'.

We are entitled to ask, however, whether Paul's arguments constitute an effective response to the Galatian crisis. To some extent one might suspect that his subtle linguistic tricks merely baffled the Galatians. His deft redefinition of 'sinners' and 'transgressors' in the Antioch dispute, his sudden emphasis on the singular number of σπέρμα (equally suddenly forgotten in 3.29), and his startling association of disparate objects in the 'allegory' were possibly even harder for the Galatians to comprehend than they are for us. It is difficult to tell what they would have thought of Paul's selective use of Scripture and his somewhat strained exegesis of his key verses. We do not know how familiar they were with Scripture and it is possible that they were simply bemused by his impressive exegetical dexterity. One suspects that the arguments which carried most weight were those which appealed to their own experience – the references to their receipt of the Spirit (3.1-5) and their initial relationship with Paul (4.12-20). But one also suspects that the agitators, who had all the advantages of personal presence in Galatia, would have had little difficulty in countering most of Paul's points.

We should press this question of 'effectiveness' particularly in relation to Paul's descriptions of appropriate behaviour. In the last chapter we noted the Galatians' attraction to the law and suggested that one reason for this attraction was its provision of practical instruction for daily living. In his letter up until 5.12, Paul has presented many reasons why the Galatians should not practise the works of the law and he has, as we have seen, provided broad descriptions of the Christian life as 'living by faith' (2.19-20), continuing in the Spirit (3.1-5) and making faith work through love (5.1-6). But these definitions of Christian behaviour, while demonstrating in general terms how to 'obey the truth', do not yet meet the more practical requirements of the Galatians. Thus we may observe that the passages we have studied so far prepare the way for the ethical instruction which follows in 5.13-6.10, but also that Paul's argument would have been seriously deficient without some attempt to define how to continue in the Spirit or how to make faith work through love. In due course we will need to assess how effectively Paul achieves his aims even in 5.13–6.10, but for the time being we may conclude that *the main body of the letter both points towards and renders necessary the ethical instruction at the end.*

Continuity and Discontinuity

Before we launch into a detailed study of Paul's moral exhortation, we should note the theological framework within which his discussion proceeds. His handling of the Abraham theme indicates his concern to show that his gospel is *continuous with* these Jewish traditions, but at the same time he emphasizes the *new* situation brought about by the cross (death to the law) and the gift of the Spirit. Since this combination of continuity and discontinuity could have a bearing on the way he presents his ethics (e.g., in what respect they are continuous with or distinct from Jewish moral traditions) it is worth a brief investigation at this point.

It is clearly crucial to his argument to be able to 'prove' that the Galatians are legitimate 'sons of Abraham' (since they share his faith) and that the promises to Abraham are in a direct line of continuity with the 'faith' and 'blessing' of Gentile Christians; he can even claim that these promises 'preached the gospel in advance' (προευηγγελίσατο 3.8). But at the same time he can say that faith 'came' or 'was revealed' only with the coming of Christ (3.23–5) and that the gospel was only 'revealed' to him in his call-experience (1.15–16). In a similar vein, when discussing the theme of sonship in 4.1–7, Paul begins his analogy with reference to a son and heir in his minority who waits for the προθεσμία of his father. But as the analogy continues and climaxes in 'the fulness of time', it becomes clear that the process is not nearly so straightforwardly continuous but in fact has to be described as the *change of status* from slavery to sonship, with the granting of adoption (υἱοθεσία, v.5).[50] In this mixed analogy, where the son

---

[50] The lexica and most of the commentators agree that υἱοθεσία means 'adoption as sons' or 'the status of sonship arising out of adoption', see *BAG* s.v.; Burton, *Galatians*, 220–1; Bruce, *Galatians*, 197–8. In either case the idea does not accord exactly with 4.1–2 which concerns a son waiting to receive his inheritance.

reaching maturity becomes the slave receiving freedom and adoption, one can see encapsulated the combination of continuity and discontinuity in Paul's perspective on Israel's history.[51]

Another illustration of this tension is Paul's treatment of the 'covenant' theme. On the one hand, he makes use of 'covenant' language, insisting on the permanent validity of the Abrahamic covenant established 430 years before the law (3.17) and represented by Sarah and her line of descent (4.21ff.). On the other hand, he has to rid the term of its usual associations with circumcision, law and the election of Israel and fill it with new content like faith in Christ and the gift of the Spirit. One cannot conclude that Paul has simply adopted Jewish covenant notions *or* that he has rejected them altogether; his radical interpretation defies any such univocal conclusion.[52]

Abraham, sonship and covenant are just three examples of Paul's hermeneutical activity in Galatians, where Jewish terminology and Scripture itself are selected in order to be remoulded and redefined in the light of Christian faith. But perhaps the most striking example of this occurs at the very end of the letter where Paul pronounces a blessing on 'all who will walk

[51] In 4.1-7 it is not always clear who 'we' (vv.3,5) and 'you' (plural v.6; singular v.7) refer to. 4.1-5, which talks of children under authority (cf. 3.24-5 under the law's custody) and the redemption of οἱ ὑπὸ νόμον is most naturally taken to refer to Israel; but the way the passage continues in vv.6-11 (Gentiles who were also once under τὰ στοιχεῖα are now becoming sons) makes it possible to read the whole passage as referring to Jews and Gentiles alike. See Betz, *Galatians*, 204-5, Mussner, *Galaterbrief*, 268, Byrne, *'Sons of God'*, 176-8 and the extended discussion by Howard, *Crisis*, 66-82.

[52] Sanders rightly argues (against Davies) that Paul's theology is not simply a revamped version of 'covenantal nomism', *Paul and Palestinian Judaism*, 511-5; but he probably goes too far in asserting that 'Paul in fact explicitly denies that the Jewish covenant can be effective for salvation, thus consciously denying the basis of Judaism' (551). It would be better to say that Paul attacks the traditional understanding of the covenant in radically redefining its terms (thus Sanders himself in *Paul, The Law, and the Jewish People*, 46 and 'Jesus, Paul and Judaism', in *ANRW* II 25:1, 434). T.J. Deidun grossly overstates his case in finding 'new covenant' motifs everywhere in Paul, *New Covenant Morality in Paul*, Rome 1981. Hooker may be nearer the truth in discerning in Paul a fundamental 'covenantal' pattern ('divine election and promise lead to human acceptance and response') to be distinguished from 'covenantal nomism', 'Paul and "Covenantal Nomism"', in *Paul and Paulinism*, ed. M.D. Hooker and S.G. Wilson, London 1982, 47-56.

by this rule' (the κανών of 6.15): εἰρήνη ἐπ' αὐτοὺς καὶ ἔλεος καὶ ἐπὶ τὸν Ἰσραὴλ τοῦ θεοῦ (6.16). The strange syntax of this blessing may indicate that it is an adaptation of a Jewish blessing[53] but, given the context of the letter as a whole, it is probable that Paul here (the only occasion in his extant letters) reapplies the very title 'Israel' to those (Gentiles as well as Jews) who believe in Christ.[54] If even the name 'Israel' can be so redefined, clearly nothing can be regarded as exempt: all of Israel's traditions can be taken up and reinterpreted in a new light.

From a sociological point of view one could explain this combination of continuity and discontinuity in terms of sectarian ideology. Any sect in the process of breaking away from the parent religion will endeavour to justify its existence as the sole legitimate heir of the religious tradition while also introducing a host of reinterpretations which define its difference from the rest of the religious community.[55] In this respect, as has often been pointed out, Paul's methods of Scriptural exegesis are closely analogous to those employed at Qumran, since both groups were sectarian movements with their roots in Jewish traditions.[56] In

[53] There are similar traditional petitions in the Kaddish and the Shemoneh Esre; the 19th Benediction (date uncertain) ends, 'bestow peace, happiness and blessing, grace and loving-kindness and mercy upon us and upon all Israel, your people'; see Richardson, *Israel*, 78-84.

[54] On this controversial verse, see, beside the commentaries, Richardson, *Israel*, 74-84, G. Lüdemann, *Paulus und das Judentum*, München 1983, 27-30, and the debate between G. Schrenk, 'Was bedeutet "Israel Gottes"?', *Judaica* 5 (1949) 81-94; 'Der Segenswunsch nach der Kampfepistel', *Judaica* 6 (1950) 170-190 and N.A. Dahl, 'Der Name Israel: Zur Auslegung von Gal.6,16', *Judaica* 6 (1950) 161-170. Although Schrenk takes 'Israel of God' to refer to Jewish Christians only (cf. Richardson – all those as yet unbelieving in Israel who will finally be saved), Dahl puts up a convincing case for the majority view that *all* Christians are intended. He shows that a) the context in Galatians indicates that all those in Christ inherit Israel's privileges and titles, and b) elsewhere Paul distinguishes between a 'true' and 'false' Israel (Rom 2.29; 9.6; Phil 3.2-3; 1 Cor 10.18; Gal 4.21-31). To this may be added the observation that Paul frequently uses the parallel phrase 'the church of God' (Gal 1.13; 1 Cor 1.2; 10.32 etc.).

[55] See Watson, *Paul, Judaism and the Gentiles*, 38-48 for examples from Qumran, the Johannine community and Paul.

[56] F.F. Bruce, *Biblical Exegesis in the Qumran Texts*, London/Grand Rapids 1959.

Paul's letters, as in the Qumran documents, one finds a plethora of Jewish texts and themes taken over into a new context and given radically new meanings. The antitheses developed on the basis of these new meanings reinforce the sect's separation from the parent body. But what does a theological analysis of this phenomenon reveal? One important clue to the theological currents at work in Paul's letter comes from the context of his final blessing. The κανών referred to in 6.16 is the principle enunciated in the previous verse: οὔτε περιτομή τί ἐστιν οὔτε ἀκροβυστία ἀλλὰ καινὴ κτίσις. References to 'new creation' sometimes mean little more than 'a new beginning in life',[57] but since this one comes immediately after a reference to the crucifixion of the κόσμος (6.14) we are entitled to enquire whether this dualistic and 'cosmic' language reflects the influence of apocalyptic theology. Rereading the letter with this question in mind we can observe how two rather different notions of history seem to run side by side. On the one hand, Paul can talk of epochs of history, of purposes and promises and of the arrival of the time of fulfilment (3.15-4.7), all of which suggests a linear development of time marked by progression. But he can also describe the present time as 'the present evil age' (1.4) from which one needs to be 'rescued', and he depicts salvation in Christ as the total antithesis to the slavery of the law, flesh and world; from this perspective the Christ-event is not the completion of world-history but its total reversal. In other words, the theology of Galatians is characterized by a combination of 'salvation-history' and 'apocalyptic'.

The use of these terms in relation to Galatians is not unproblematic: their applicability depends on some controversial decisions about their definition. If 'salvation-history' (Heilsgeschichte) is taken to represent the description of God's saving purposes through an historical sequence of events, then at

---

[57] E.g. in rabbinic discussion of proselytes, Gen Rabba 39.14; b Yebamoth 48b; E. Sjöberg, 'Wiedergeburt und Neuschöpfung im palästinischen Judentum', *STh* 4 (1950) 44-85.

least some of Gal 3-4 with its concern for the historical relationships between Abraham, the law and Christ must come into this category.[58] Unfortunately, the term 'apocalyptic' can be employed in a bewildering variety of ways: it can be used to define a particular genre of literature (or form of revelation – e.g. through visions), or a particular type of eschatology, or a particular mode of thought (and in each case one could well ask how well circumscribed each 'particular' entity is).[59] By focusing on such formal characteristics as visions, one might conclude, with C. Rowland, that there is very little 'apocalyptic' material in Paul's letters;[60] and by limiting our interest to the near-expectation of the end we would have to agree with J.C. Beker that Galatians is an exception which does not match the other apocalyptic Pauline letters.[61] However, if we are concerned with a *mode of thought* bearing apocalyptic characteristics we are entitled to investigate passages which do not necessarily mention visions or an imminent eschaton. And although different scholars define them differently, we can with reasonable safety follow W. Meeks' list of typical apocalyptic characteristics:

1. Secrets have been revealed to the author or prophet.
2. These secrets have to do with a cosmic transformation that will happen very soon. Time moves toward that climax, which separates 'this age' from 'the age to come'.
3. Central among the events to happen 'at the end of days' is judgment: the rectification of the world order, the separation

---

[58] See O. Cullmann, *Salvation in History*, London 1967, especially the definition of salvation-history, 74–78. On the whole issue see U. Luz, *Das Geschichtsverständnis des Paulus*, München 1968.

[59] For recent influential attempts to define 'apocalyptic' see J. Collins (ed.), *Apocalypse: The Morphology of a Genre*, *Semeia* 14 (1979) and articles by L. Hartman, E.P. Sanders and others in D. Hellholm (ed.), *Apocalypticism in the Mediterranean World and the Near East*, Tübingen 1983.

[60] C. Rowland, *The Open Heaven. A Study of Apocalyptic in Judaism and Early Christianity*, London 1982.

[61] Beker, *Paul the Apostle*, 58: 'Galatians threatens to undo what I have posited as the coherent core of Pauline thought, the apocalyptic co-ordinates of the Christ-event that focus on the imminent, cosmic triumph of God'.

of the good from the wicked, and assigning the appropriate reward or punishment.

4. Consequently the apocalyptic universe is characterized by three corresponding dualities: (a) the cosmic duality heaven/ earth, (b) the temporal duality this age/the age to come, and (c) a social duality: the sons of light/the sons of darkness, the righteous/the unrighteous, the elect/the world.[62]

Although he eschews any prior definition of 'apocalyptic', J.L. Martyn is clearly dependent on some such list of characteristics when he analyses Galatians and finds it shot through with 'apocalyptic antinomies'.[63] There is reference in Galatians to the revelation (ἀποκάλυψις) of Jesus Christ which Paul himself received (1.12,16), but of special significance is the way Paul describes the coming of Christ as the awaited revelation of faith (εἰς τὴν μέλλουσαν πίστιν ἀποκαλυφθῆναι, 3.23). This alerts us to the fact that at least some of the 'apocalyptic' events usually expected in the future are here regarded by Paul as past or present: hence he can say that the cosmos has already been crucified (6.14), that the καινὴ κτίσις has begun (6.15) and that Christians are now being rescued from 'the present evil age' (1.4). The final judgment which is still eagerly awaited (5.5), with its reward and punishment (6.5-10), is nonetheless partly anticipated in the justification of those who believe, so that the apocalyptic 'dualities' (Meeks) or 'antinomies' (Martyn) are vividly portrayed in the present time: in the battle between 'Spirit' and 'flesh', and in the contrasts between 'slavery' and 'freedom', the realm of Christ and the influence of the στοιχεῖα τοῦ κόσμου. As Martyn rightly insists, these battles are not part of the original creation or inherent in the cosmos: they are triggered off by an apocalyptic event, the coming of Christ and the dawn of the new creation.[64]

---

[62] W. Meeks, 'Social Functions of Apocalyptic Language in Pauline Christianity', in D. Hellholm (ed.), *Apocalypticism*, 687-705, here at 689.

[63] J.L. Martyn, 'Apocalyptic Antinomies in Paul's Letter to the Galatians', *NTS* 31 (1985) 410-424; Martyn appears to use 'antinomy' to mean 'contrast' or 'conflict'.

[64] 'Apocalyptic Antinomies', 416-421.

From this perspective, then, Galatians can be seen to contain elements of 'apocalyptic' theology.

However, we should note here several points which clarify or qualify the role of 'apocalyptic' thought in this letter. *In the first place*, we should observe that apocalyptic language of the end of the cosmos and the birth of a new creation is not here applied in any physical sense (contrast Rom 8.18ff.): it signifies rather a reordering of social relationships in which the 'old world' of social division between 'circumcised' and 'uncircumcised' is abolished and a new social entity is created.[65] Paul's statement that the κόσμος was crucified *to me* (ἐμοί, 6.15), demonstrates that this event is primarily conceived in anthropological rather than physical terms. But Paul's ἐμοί should not lead us to conclude that his statement only bears reference to an individual's self-understanding, since the following verses show that he is concerned with the *community* of those who will 'walk' by the canon of the new creation.[66] In other words, Paul appears to be employing apocalyptic motifs to describe a new pattern of existence created by the Christ-event, a pattern which overthrows Jewish traditions and establishes a new community of Jew and Gentile in Christ.

Secondly, as Martyn notes, the emphasis on the crucifixion in 6.14 'reflects the fact that through the whole of Galatians the focus of Paul's apocalyptic lies not on Christ's parousia, but rather on his death'.[67] It is the cross of Christ which marks the 'death' of the 'old' world and is the 'stumbling-block' to the old patterns of

---

[65] P.S. Minear, 'The Crucified World: The Enigma of Galatians 6,14', in *Theologia Crucis – Signum Crucis*, ed. C. Andresen and G. Klein, Tübingen 1979, 395-407.

[66] See the important conclusion of J. Baumgarten, *Paulus und die Apokalyptik*, Neukirchen-Vluyn 1975, 227-243: entering into the famous debate between Bultmann and Käsemann on the role of apocalyptic in Paul, Baumgarten concludes that Paul tends to interpret cosmological motifs in anthropological terms, but that his anthropology is not individualistic but tempered by ecclesiology.

[67] 'Apocalyptic Antinomies', 420.

thought and behaviour (2.19-21; 3.1, 13-14; 5.11; 6.12-14).[68] Indeed it is remarkable that the resurrection of Christ, which elsewhere in Paul is the prime example of an apocalyptic event (note esp. 1 Cor 15), is almost entirely absent in Galatians (1.1 is the only reference). The Spirit stands in the place of the resurrection as the token of the dawn of the new age, but the emphasis on the cross underlines the negative thrust of the letter: the old era of life under the law is *past*. The cross demonstrates to the Galatians in the starkest possible terms that in Christ they have *died to* the old patterns of existence.[69] And since they must have known that the preaching of the cross was strange and abhorrent to their Gentile and Jewish contemporaries, Paul's emphasis on it as the distinguishing mark of the gospel they believed (3.1) serves to highlight their social distinction from those outside the church. As Meeks has pointed out, 'The novelty of the proclamation, violating or at least transcending expectations based either on reason or on Jewish traditions (1 Cor 1.18-25), permits it to serve as a warrant for innovation . . . the unexpected, almost unthinkable fact that the Messiah had died a death cursed by the Law entailed a sharp break in the way the people of God would henceforth be constituted and bounded'.[70]

Thirdly, while considering the function of this apocalyptic

---

[68] In relation to the law, the 'offence' of the cross may be specially heightened by the fact that, as one crucified, Christ came under the curse of the law (Gal 3.13-14): this clarifies the *choice* that must be made between faith in Christ and commitment to the law (in its verdict on Christ). Although it is difficult to ascertain if this train of thought was significant in Paul's previous persecution of Christians and subsequent conversion (see the discussion by Räisänen, *Paul and the Law*, 249-251), it probably plays a (subsidiary) role in the argument of Gal 3 (see M.D. Hooker, 'Interchange in Christ', *JTS* n.s. 22 (1971) 349-361).

[69] On Paul's unusual use of datives in this connection see C.F.D. Moule, 'Death "to sin", "to law" and "to the world": A Note on Certain Datives', in *Mélanges Bibliques*, ed. A. Descamps and A. de Halleux, Gembloux 1970, 367-375.

[70] W. Meeks, 'The Social Context of Pauline Theology', *Int* 36 (1982) 266-277, here at 273-4; cf. his *First Urban Christians*, 168-9, 175-7. I am not, however, persuaded by Meeks' correlation of Paul's paradoxical message with the high status-inconsistency of many of Paul's prominent converts.

language, we should note its effect in setting before the Galatians the clearest possible alternatives. In their present position they must have been conscious of a range of possible patterns of existence – their old way of life as Gentiles, the Pauline pattern of their original conversion and the life-style advocated by the agitators; they may also have been conscious that it was possible to observe the law to varying degrees. Paul, however, reduces their choice to *two* and his use of apocalyptic motifs, with their sharp contrasts, enables him to present his choice in the simplest and starkest terms: either freedom or slavery, either God or the στοιχεῖα, either Christ or the whole law, either the Spirit or the flesh.[71]

Finally, we should return to our observation that Galatians combines apocalyptic motifs with a salvation-historical outlook. Within a consistent apocalyptic framework the past and present are all part of the 'evil age' from which one awaits redemption, and righteousness is only to be found in the coming 'new creation'. In Galatians, however, such radical antitheses are presented side by side with elements of continuity and purposeful history: Abraham was himself justified by faith, the Scriptural promises now reach their fulfilment, the child is coming to his maturity. From one perspective, all of the past has been slavery under 'the elements of the world', while from another it has provided examples, precedents and prophecies of the gospel. To some extent this combination of factors is present in many forms of Jewish apocalyptic: even in Daniel and the Qumran documents there are faithful witnesses, Scriptural promises and historical progressions that prepare the way for the apocalyptic event.[72] But it is important to remain aware of this duality within Paul's

---

[71] On the effect of this apocalyptic dualism in lumping everything outwith the church into the same category see Meeks, *First Urban Christians*, 183ff.

[72] See, e.g., Dan 9.15-16, 24-27; CD 1.1-4.12; 1QpHab.

theology as well, lest we interpret him too one-sidedly and relax the tension which these two factors create.[73]

In this chapter we have reviewed some of the themes of the main body of Galatians with a number of purposes in mind. We have tried to analyse some ways in which Paul counters his opponents' propaganda, we have examined the links he creates between 'identity' and 'patterns of behaviour', and we have investigated the theological framework in which the whole letter is written. Our study has highlighted how Gal 2-4 point towards and require the moral instruction at the end of the letter. We are now in a position to study 5.13-6.10 in detail since we can now determine if (or how) this passage meets the requirements of the Galatian situation and fits into the train of thought of the earlier parts of the letter. We have completed two of the tasks in our agenda at the end of chapter one; the third, a careful study of 5.13-6.10 with a view to its purpose and style, can now begin.

---

[73] In *Paul the Apostle*, Beker remarks: 'The history of Israel is for Paul not simply the old age of darkness; he softens the dualism between the ages by interpreting Israel's history in a typological light' (150); 'apocalyptic dualism is tempered by the salvation-history understanding of Israel's place in God's saving design for his creation' (181). The correct way to express this creative mix of apocalyptic and salvation-history is at the heart of the passionate debate between Käsemann and Stendahl on justification by faith: see Stendahl, *Paul Among Jews and Gentiles*, 78-96 and 129-132 and Käsemann, 'Justification and Salvation History in the Epistle to the Romans', in *Perspectives on Paul*, London 1971, 60-78.

Chapter Four

The Sufficiency of the Spirit

In our reconstruction of the Galatian crisis we noted the dual challenge presented by the agitators to the Galatians: i) why were the Galatian Christians in such an anomalous position, claiming to be heirs of Israel's privileges yet uncircumcised? and ii) why were they not obeying the will of God as it was laid down in the law? As we observed in connection with this latter challenge, one of the attractions in the agitators' proposals for law-observance may have been the security of a written and authoritative code of law; in comparison, Paul's ethical policy may have appeared dangerously ill-defined. How could the Galatians be sure that 'walking in the Spirit' would provide them with sufficient moral safeguards? Would it help them solve their practical problems? Would it match the moral standard required by God in his law? These are some of the concerns which must have played a part in the Galatian crisis and to which some response from Paul was required.

It is important to note what a difficult task Paul faces here – indeed how difficult he has made it for himself. In his attempt to break the spell of the Galatians' attraction to the law he has depicted it as a form of *slavery* (2.4-5; 4.1-11; 4.21-5.1) and hence emphasized the freedom of those in Christ. But to talk of 'freedom', of being 'redeemed from the law', of 'dying to the law' could have the effect of unsettling the Galatians, reinforcing the sense of moral insecurity which had been one factor driving them into the arms of the agitators. In the course of his discussion of the law, Paul had described its role as that of a παιδαγωγός (3.24-5) –

the child-minder who restrains and disciplines the child until he or she reaches maturity.[1] This analogy was ideal for his argument since it illustrated both the restrictive effect of the law and its temporary role.[2] But the triumphant declaration that 'with the coming of faith we are no longer under a παιδαγωγός' (3.25) could prove as threatening to the Galatians as it was liberating to Paul. The restraining effect of the law – how it countered 'the evil impulse', guarded God's people from straying into sin and provided a 'fence' around them – was proudly claimed as one of the glories of the law in both Diaspora and Rabbinic Judaism.[3] Paul's claim that this 'protective custody' had come to an end could therefore be interpreted by the agitators as both dangerous and irresponsible.

---

[1] On the role of the παιδαγωγός in Greek and Roman society see E. Schuppe, art. παιδαγωγός, PW 18, 2375-2385 and S. Bonner, *Education in Ancient Rome. From the Elder Cato to the Younger Pliny*, London 1977, 38-46. The best recent survey of primary sources is by N.H. Young, *'Paidagogos: The Social Setting of a Pauline Metaphor'*, NT 29 (1987) 150-176.

[2] On the place of this analogy in Gal 3 see J.S. Callaway, 'Paul's Letter to the Galatians and Plato's *Lysis*', *JBL* 67 (1948) 353-5; R.N. Longenecker, 'The Pedagogical Nature of the Law in Galatians 3.19-4.7', *Journal of the Evangelical Theological Society* 25 (1982) 53-61; D.J. Lull, ' "The Law was our Pedagogue": A Study in Galatians 3.19-25', *JBL* 105 (1986) 481-498. Lull argues that Paul's use of this image portrays a positive role for the law in disciplining and restraining Israel and that this supports the interpretation of παραβάσεων χάριν in 3.19 as 'in order to deal with transgressions' rather than 'to generate or provoke transgressions'. However, whether you viewed the restraining influence of the παιδαγωγός as good or bad depended on whether you were the parent employing him or the child under his care! Paul's emphasis is on release from this restriction, but the agitators, using different analogies, would no doubt regard such 'freedom' as a dangerous thing (see below). Lull's interpretation of 3.19 depends on the highly contestable assumption that Paul's view of the law's function is consistent throughout this section.

[3] For the Diaspora see, e.g., Josephus, *Ant* 4.210-11; 16.43; *Apion* 2.174: 'for all this our leader made the law the standard and rule, that we might live under it as under a father and master, and be guilty of no sin through wilfulness or ignorance'; on the law as a 'fence' around Israel, Ep Arist 139, 142. For the rabbis and the 'evil impulse' (yeser hara') see, e.g., b Berakoth 5a; b Kiddushin 30b: 'My children, I created the Evil Desire, but I [also] created the Torah as its antidote [lit. spices]; if you occupy yourself with the Torah you shall not be delivered into its hand . . . ' (E.T. Soncino edition, 146). Although, to my knowledge, no Jewish text expressly compares the law to a παιδαγωγός (perhaps because the law could not be thought of in a merely *temporary* role), Philo praises the παιδαγωγός since

continued on p.108

In our discussion of the Antioch dispute we noted that Paul himself was aware of such objections to his theology. To disregard the prohibition of the law and to become like Gentile 'sinners' in the name of Christ could be represented as making Christ a 'servant of sin' (ἁμαρτίας διάκονος, 2.17).[4] To rebut this charge with a μὴ γένοιτο and a counter-accusation (2.18) was one thing: it was quite another to show how living by faith and walking by the Spirit really constituted 'living to God' (2.19) and doing his will.

In this chapter we will explore a number of indications that Paul framed his final exhortations in 5.13-6.10 with these problems in mind. Whether or not he is here responding to direct criticism from his opponents,[5] he seems to be aware of some of the anxieties which arose in connection with his prescription for ethics. Our task here is to investigate how he defends his policy and explains the sufficiency of the Spirit for moral behaviour.

Freedom in the Slavery of Love: 5.13

Paul's exhortation begins with another resounding declaration of freedom – in fact freedom was the *purpose* of their calling (ὑμεῖς

---

continued from p.107

παιδαγωγοῦ . . . πάροντος οὐκ ἂν ὁ ἀγόμενος ἁμάρτοι, *Mut* 217 and elsewhere describes παιδαγωγοί and νόμοι as having a parallel role in training, *Mig* 116; cf. 4 Macc 1.17 ἡ τοῦ νόμου παιδεία.
[4] See above pp.77-81. In Pseudo-Clementine Homilies 17.13-19 (E. Hennecke, *New Testament Apocrypha*, ed. W. Schneemelcher, E.T. ed. R.McL. Wilson, London 1965, II, 122-3), we find a Jewish-Christian presentation of Peter's reply to Paul at Antioch, accusing him of lawlessness. Indeed, Paul's statements on circumcision continue to invite Jewish attacks on his 'antinomian teachings', S.B. Hoenig, 'Circumcision: The Covenant of Abraham', *JQR* n.s. 53 (1962-3) 322-334, at 323.
[5] Watson, *Paul, Judaism and the Gentiles*, 147 suggests that they accused Paul of 'gratifying the desire of the flesh'. Martyn, 'Apocalyptic Antinomics', 416, claims that the 'teachers' understood the law to be the antidote to the evil-impulse and that they used the term σάρξ to speak of this impulse. J. Markus, 'The Evil Inclination in the Letters of Paul', *Irish Biblical Studies* 8 (1986) 8-20 goes so far as to claim ἐπιθυμία σαρκός as a translation of the Hebrew יצר בשׂר in 1QH 10.23. There is, in fact, no evidence that the 'flesh' language derives from the agitators.

γὰρ ἐπ' ἐλευθερίᾳ ἐκλήθητε, ἀδελφοί, 5.13). This declaration clearly echoes that of 5.1 but also stands in striking contrast to it: whereas 5.1 naturally interpreted freedom as resisting the 'yoke of slavery' (ζυγὸν δουλείας), 5.13 introduces a paradox: the Galatians are to use their freedom *in slavery* to one another through love (διὰ τῆς ἀγάπης δουλεύετε ἀλλήλοις). There can be no doubt that Paul has consciously created a paradox here, since he represents this δουλεία not as the antithesis of freedom but as its necessary outworking.[6] Indeed the phrase 'be slaves to one another' is itself somewhat paradoxical since slavery is a hierarchical social structure, not a relationship of mutual self-sacrifice.[7]

But such phrases demonstrate more than Paul's love of paradox. They show his intention to make clear that the 'freedom' he advocates has stringent moral obligations built into it – not the obligations of the law but the obligation of love. The reference to love seems designed to echo the statement a few verses earlier about 'faith working through love' (5.6). Although a Christian understanding of Abrahamic faith is not connected with circumcision, it *is* linked with love; and love, expressed in mutual service, is an essential practical consequence of freedom. Thus faith and freedom are by no means morally bankrupt.

But this verse also contains a reference to a possible misuse of freedom: μόνον μὴ τὴν ἐλευθερίαν εἰς ἀφορμὴν τῇ σαρκί. It is important to note the term Paul uses for the danger to be avoided: σάρξ. In our analysis of 2.15-21 we saw that a central aspect of Paul's response to the Antioch event was his attempt to relativize the law's definition of 'sin'; although to eat with Gentiles was 'sin' from the law's perspective, such standards did not apply to those who had 'died to the law'. This whole debate, and the charge that Christ promoted 'sin', made it difficult for

---

[6] See Oepke, *Galater*, 169; Schlier, *Galater*, 243-4; cf. Rom 6.18-23.

[7] The Stoic paradox – that even a slave can be free (to live according to nature or reason) – is quite different from Paul's emphasis on the obligations of freedom, which could be seen as a variant of the Jewish notion that God's people are freed in order to serve him (Ex 4.23; 19.4-6; 20.1-6; Lev 25.42). On Paul's use of this theme see, e.g., F. Mussner, *Theologie der Freiheit nach Paulus*, Freiburg 1976.

Paul to keep using such vocabulary as ἁμαρτία: his Galatian audience, like the Jewish–Christians at Antioch, would all too readily hear in it its standard association with disobedience to the law. This is probably one reason why Paul's ethical instructions in Galatians are not based on a contrast between δικαιοσύνη and ἁμαρτία, but on one between πνεῦμα and σάρξ. Paul does not warn against giving an opportunity to 'sin', but giving an opportunity to 'the flesh'.

But if σάρξ does not have the precise connotations of disobedience to the law, what connotations does it have? Although it is widely recognized today that σάρξ is an extremely complex and slippery word in Paul's vocabulary, it is remarkable that the modern translations and the recent commentators immediately assume that Paul is referring here to 'libertinism' or antinomian 'licence'.[8] In fact none of the occurrences of this term up to this point in the letter could bear that meaning (1.16; 2.16,20; 3.3; 4.13–14,23,29) and even the list of 'works of the flesh' in 5.19-21 does not fit neatly into the category 'libertinism' (see below, chapter 5). We shall have to investigate later the various nuances in Paul's use of this term σάρξ (see below, chapter 6), but for the present we may suggest that the terminology he uses is deliberately selected in order to redefine the moral categories of Christian behaviour.

Thus, already in 5.13, we have indications that Paul wants to show how Christian faith and freedom do have far–reaching moral implications, even if they do not exactly fit the categories of the law.

Dealing with the Flesh: 5.16-18, 24-25

Paul describes what is evil and threatens the moral life as 'the flesh' (5.13). Whether the agitators or the Galatians were already

---

[8] NEB 'the lower nature'; NIV 'the sinful nature'; GNB 'your physical desires'; JB 'self-indulgence'; Bruce, *Galatians*, 240 'libertinism', 'unrestrained licence'; Schlier, *Galater*, 242-3 'Antinomismus'; Mussner, *Galaterbrief*, 358 'das libertinistische Missverständnis'. Betz, *Galatians*, 275 refers rather more ambiguously to 'flagrant misconduct'.

familiar with this description of the moral threat is difficult to determine,[9] but in any case we have just noted one good reason for Paul's use of this term: it does not have the legal connotations of ἁμαρτία. But now he goes on to show how the moral life he advocates can deal with this threat and provide adequate safeguards against it. If he is not proposing that the Galatians keep the law to guard them from 'sin', what will counteract 'the flesh'? The answer Paul offers is, of course, the Spirit. Thus there emerges another reason for Paul's choice of the 'flesh' category: by building on his earlier dualism of 'flesh' and 'Spirit' (3.3; 4.29) Paul can present his moral solution as 'the Spirit', that is, in terms that the Galatians will immediately recognize as the *continuation* of the way they began their lives in Christ (3.1-5).

Gal 5.16 constitutes an appeal that the Galatians should continue as they began (λέγω δέ, πνεύματι περιπατεῖτε) and a confident statement that this will ensure that they do not fulfil the desire of the flesh (καὶ ἐπιθυμίαν σαρκὸς οὐ μὴ τελέσητε). This resounding confidence is striking (οὐ μή with aorist subjunctive expresses 'the most definite form of negation regarding a future event').[10] Paul could hardly have used any simpler or more direct way of expressing his assurance in the moral safeguard he proposes. But such a statement needs some explanation. Why does 'walking in the Spirit' exclude the 'desire of the flesh'? Why are these incompatible? An explanation is provided in the next verse (introduced by γάρ)[11] which describes the *conflict* between flesh and Spirit: ἡ γὰρ σὰρξ ἐπιθυμεῖ (picking up ἐπιθυμίαν

---

[9] Betz assumes that the Galatians are conscious of having problems with 'the flesh', *Galatians*, 8-9 and Martyn considers that the agitators advocated the law as the solution to 'the flesh', 'Apocalyptic Antinomies', 416. 5.21 indicates that Paul had earlier warned the Galatians about a list of vices but we do not know if he had identified them as 'works of the flesh' (none of his other lists of vices are so introduced).

[10] BDF, section 365; cf. E. de W. Burton, *Syntax of the Moods and Tenses in New Testament Greek*, Edinburgh 1894, section 172. It is most unlikely that this construction expresses a prohibition (RSV; Bonnard, *Galater*, 112 n.1), since it is found thus in the NT only in Mt 13.14; Acts 28.26, both citing LXX Is 6.9.

[11] Burton, *Galatians*, 300; Schlier, *Galater*, 248. There is certainly no indication that 5.17 should be read as a *contrast* to 5.16.

σαρκός from 5.16) κατὰ τοῦ πνεύματος, τὸ δὲ πνεῦμα κατὰ τῆς σαρκός (5.17). These two clauses are then further explained (again, γάρ) in terms of the warfare between the flesh and Spirit: ταῦτα γὰρ ἀλλήλοις ἀντίκειται. Such mutual opposition clearly implies mutual exclusion and thus satisfactorily explains why the Galatians' walk in the Spirit will not fulfil the desire of the flesh (5.16). But this also means that their 'freedom' in the Spirit should not be taken to mean freedom to live however they like. Warfare excludes some options and necessitates others. If they walk in the Spirit they are caught up into this conflict, which means that they are not free to do whatever they want – ἵνα μὴ ἃ ἐὰν θέλητε ταῦτα ποιῆτε (5.17). Such conflict ensures that their freedom is not absolute, for their walk in the Spirit will set them against the flesh and thus define the moral choices they must make.

This exegesis of the last clause in 5.17 (ἵνα μὴ ἃ ἐὰν θέλητε ταῦτα ποιῆτε) departs from the common lines of interpretation. In fact this clause is generally acknowledged to be one of the most difficult in the whole letter. It contains two related conundra: i) whether ἵνα should be taken in a telic (purpose) or ecbatic (result) sense; and ii) the identity of the 'wants' (ἃ ἐὰν θέλητε) which are being forestalled. The first problem is not soluble on purely grammatical grounds since ἵνα can bear either meaning in the New Testament, reflecting the 'Semitic mind' which Moule describes as 'notoriously unwilling to draw a sharp dividing line between purpose and consequence'.[12] Only the context can determine this, together with the second, issue.

The various solutions offered in explanation of this clause have been on three main lines:

---

[12] *Idiom Book*, 142; *BDF*, section 391; *BAG* s.v. II 2. Most commentators take ἵνα as ecbatic (Lightfoot, Lagrange, Oepke, Bonnard, Ridderbos, Betz etc.) while some insist on a telic sense (e.g. Burton, Sieffert, Schlier, Mussner).

a) v 17 expresses the conflict of flesh and Spirit which results in the flesh frustrating the Spirit-inspired wishes of the believer.[13] The strongest argument for this interpretation is the supposed parallel with Rom 7.14-25 (and, perhaps, the widespread Christian experience of frustrated good intentions). In most important respects, however, this verse is quite different from Rom 7,[14] and this interpretation would not only put 5.17 in sharp contrast to the confidence of 5.16 but it would also wholly undermine Paul's purpose in this passage; if he is admitting here that the flesh continually defeats the Spirit's wishes, Paul is hardly providing a good reason to 'walk in the Spirit'! Unless we judge Paul to be wholly unaware that he is destroying his own case, we must accept that the context rules this interpretation out.[15]

b) v 17 expresses the conflict of flesh and Spirit as two forces which equally frustrate each other (ecbatic ἵνα) or attempt to do so (telic ἵνα).[16] This interpretation takes good account of Paul's phrase 'whatever you desire' (ἃ ἐὰν θέλητε) and emphasizes the statement of mutual opposition (ταῦτα γὰρ ἀλλήλοις

---

[13] R.A. Cole, *The Epistle of Paul to the Galatians*, London 1965, 158; Lightfoot, *Galatians*, 207; H.N. Ridderbos, *The Epistle to the Galatians*, E.T.Grand Rapids 1956, 203-4; Borse, *Galater*, 195-6; P. Althaus, ' "Das ihr nicht tut, was ihr wollt". Zur Auslegung von Gal.5,17', *TLZ* 76 (1951) 15-18; J.D.G. Dunn, 'Rom.7, 14-25 in the Theology of Paul', *ThZ* 31 (1975) 257-273, at 267-8.

[14] For a good summary of the differences between these two passages see R.H. Gundry, 'The Moral Frustration of Paul before his Conversion: Sexual Lust in Romans 7.7-25', in *Pauline Studies*, ed. D.A. Hagner and M.J. Harris, Exeter 1980, 228-245, at 238-9.

[15] I can only presume that this interpretation has arisen under the impression that Paul is providing here a disinterested description of the Christian life. But if the thesis of this chapter is correct, this is not so: Paul is attempting to defend and commend his understanding of morality and the sufficiency of walking in the Spirit.

[16] C.J. Ellicott, *A Critical and Grammatical Commentary on St. Paul's Epistle to the Galatians*, London 1859, 115; Burton, *Galatians*, 300-302; Oepke, *Galater*, 174-5; Schlier, *Galater*, 249-50; Mussner, *Galaterbrief*, 377-8; Betz, *Galatians*, 279-281. Of these Oepke and Betz take ἵνα in an ecbatic sense, and the rest seem to presume that the intentions of the two forces are carried out anyway.

ἀντίκειται) in the middle of the verse. But it falls foul of the same problem as the previous interpretation. To admit that there is a 'stalemate' between flesh and Spirit does not fit either the confident statement of 5.16 or Paul's need to show the sufficiency of the Spirit.[17] Most who follow this line admit that this verse describes an immature or unsatisfactory Christian state, but Paul himself provides no such disclaimer.[18] Only if the ἵνα clause is taken as an expression of intent alone (i.e. in a purely telic sense) could it be made to fit the context,[19] but even then we could expect some further statement to show how the Spirit's intent is successful, while the intent of the flesh is not. 5.18 does not seem to serve this requirement.

c) v 17 expresses the conflict of flesh and Spirit as having the purpose (or result) of frustrating the fleshly desires.[20] This has the great advantage of fitting the context well, supporting and illustrating the confident statement of 5.16. Its problems lie in accommodating the central clause ('these are opposed *to each other*')[21] and explaining why 'whatever you want' should be taken as 'what the flesh desires'.

---

[17] Mussner, *Galaterbrief*, 377-8, attempts to interpret this stalemate in a positive sense: the two forces cancel each other out and thus leave the Christian with real freedom of will. But this conclusion (i.e. you can now do what you want) is the very opposite of Paul's concluding phrase!

[18] Elliott (115) describes this as 'the earlier and more imperfect stages of a Christian course' and Oepke (174-5) takes 5.17 as 'eine unwürdige Willensknechtung' which is far from normal and is intended to contrast with the full submission to the Spirit referred to in 5.18; but this puts excessive weight on the δέ at the beginning of 5.18 and treats 5.17 as a digression between 5.16 and 5.18. Betz rightly notes the incompatibility of this verse with its context if interpreted along these lines; but he holds to the interpretation and regards it as a relic of a 'pre-Pauline' anthropology. Bruce, *Galatians*, 245 cautiously concurs.

[19] This seems to be the position advocated by E. Schweizer, art. πνεῦμα in *TDNT VI*, 429 and D. Wenham, 'The Christian Life: A Life of Tension?', in *Pauline Studies*, ed. D.A. Hagner and M.J. Harris, Exeter 1980, 80-94, at 83.

[20] This interpretation can be traced back to Chrysostom, but has fewer modern adherents: Duncan, *Galatians*, 166-8 and Jewett, *Paul's Anthropological Terms*, 106-7.

[21] Duncan (167-8) in effect takes this as a parenthesis so that the final clause follows from the Spirit's opposition to the flesh.

Our own solution, briefly stated above, does not follow any of these interpretations exactly, but draws on the strong points of each. The context of this whole section (5.13–6.10), and 5.16 in particular, strongly suggests that Paul is concerned to prove that the Spirit provides sufficient moral direction and protection against 'the flesh'. The Galatians have indeed been called to freedom (5.13) but the Spirit ensures that this is not a *carte blanche* for 'doing whatever you want' (ἃ ἐὰν θέλητε; cf. 1 Cor 6.12: πάντα μοι ἔξεστιν ἀλλά . . .). The flesh would certainly exploit this absolute freedom (5.13) but the Spirit provides a counteracting force which motivates and directs them to *exclude* the flesh. In other words, the Galatians are not in the dangerous position of being free to 'do whatever you want' because, as they walk in the Spirit, they are caught up into a warfare which determines their moral choices. The warfare imagery is invoked not to indicate that the two sides are evenly balanced[22] but to show the Galatians that they are already committed *to* some forms of activity (the Spirit) and *against* others (the flesh). The Galatians need have no fear that Paul's talk of 'freedom' and 'following the Spirit' will leave them without moral direction in a structureless existence 'doing whatever they want'. The warfare between flesh and Spirit ensures that this is not the case: ταῦτα γὰρ ἀλλήλοις ἀντίκειται ἵνα μὴ ἃ ἐὰν θέλητε ταῦτα ποιῆτε.[23]

The advantage of this interpretation is that it fits the context of 5.13–16 well, takes all the various ingredients of 5.17 seriously *and* provides a good explanation for the following verse: εἰ δὲ

---

[22] *Pace*, e.g., H.A.W. Meyer, *The Epistle to the Galatians*, E.T. Edinburgh 1884, 307-9; Burton, *Galatians*, 302; Mussner, *Galaterbrief*, 377-8.

[23] This interpretation would fit either a telic or an ecbatic rendering of ἵνα since it seems to be assumed that the purpose is achieved. If it is read as a purpose-clause, the question, 'Whose purpose is it?' (Oepke, *Galater*, 174-5) may be wrongly put: it does not express the purpose of any 'person' or 'force' (Spirit/flesh/both forces) but of a 'state of affairs' – the fact that these two are opposed to each other, the warfare between them. If Paul was pressed to say whose purpose was expressed in this state of affairs, I suppose he would answer, 'God's'. I am indebted to a remark by Watson, *Paul, Judaism and the Gentiles*, 107 for setting me off on the train of thought leading to this interpretation.

πνεύματι ἄγεσθε, οὐκ ἐστὲ ὑπὸ νόμον (5.18). If walking in the Spirit means being involved in the war against the flesh it provides clear directions for life: it means being *led* (i.e., directed) by the Spirit. And what seems at first to be a sudden intrusion of 'the law' now falls into place: Christians are no longer 'under the law', that is, under its restraining, disciplining and directing influence (cf. ὑπὸ παιδαγωγόν, 3.23-5)[24] because the Spirit provides all the necessary guidance in the fight against the flesh. They do not need the law to marshal their behaviour: in the Spirit-led battle against the flesh they have all the direction they need.[25]

This passage raises a number of other questions which we must leave on one side for the moment: Does Paul envisage 'flesh' and 'Spirit' as two impulses at work in man or two powers that influence him 'from outside'?[26] Since the Spirit is contrasted with both 'flesh' and 'the law', is there some association between these two entities?[27] We will return to these questions in chapter six

---

[24] ὑπὸ νόμον clearly recalls the material in 3.23-4.5, designating the restraining and restricting power of the law. There is nothing to indicate any overtones of condemnation (Ridderbos, *Galatians*, 204) or legalistic self-righteousness (Burton, *Galatians*, 302-3; Schlier, *Galater*, 250): neither would fit the description of Christ himself being ὑπὸ νόμον(4.4).

[25] Duncan, *Galatians*, 169 rightly glosses the verse: 'If you know the life of the Spirit with its safeguards, you neither require nor recognize the safeguards of the Law'. Cf. Betz, *Galatians*, 281. Lull, *Spirit in Galatia*, 114, 117ff., suggests that ἄγεσθε here is intended to echo the παιδαγωγός directly. The verbal connection is probably too remote, but the conceptual link – the direction of the law and the direction of the Spirit – is certainly present.

[26] Most commentators recognize that πνεῦμα here is not a human spirit but the Spirit of God (exceptions are Lagrange, *Galates*, 147; O'Neill, *Recovery*, 68) which is why I use a capital 'S' throughout. But it is still possible to think of the Spirit as forming an internal impulse (like the rabbinic 'good inclination') or as an external power (like the Spirit or Prince of Light in 1QS 3-4). The 'flesh' is even more enigmatic; is it a bodily ingredient, a human orientation or a superhuman 'power'?

[27] Martyn, 'Apocalyptic Antinomies', 416 correctly notes how 'the law' and 'the flesh', which one would expect to be opposites, are here lumped together in a new opposition to the Spirit. Whether this shows that 'the Law proves to be an ally of the Flesh' is not immediately clear, but their association (cf. 3.3) is certainly intriguing.

and can rest content for now with our conclusion on the purpose of this brief passage. Paul here demonstrates that the threat of 'the flesh' can be repulsed by the Spirit; that walking in the Spirit involves warfare and so does not leave the Christian to do whatever he wants, but excludes the fleshly option; and that in this way the Spirit provides all the necessary moral direction without requiring submission to the control of the law.

Having described the sufficiency of the Spirit in defeating the flesh Paul now proceeds to spell out their various characteristics in two famous lists (5.19-23). We will return to these in due course but will concentrate here on the further statement he makes about dealing with the flesh in 5.24-5. Were it not for its familiarity, 5.24 would surely strike us as a most extraordinary remark: οἱ δὲ τοῦ Χριστοῦ ['Ιησοῦ] τὴν σάρκα ἐσταύρωσαν σὺν τοῖς παθήμασιν καὶ ταῖς ἐπιθυμίαις.[28] One notable feature of this statement is that Christians are described not as the objects but as the *agents* of this crucifixion. The verb is obviously chosen because of its association with the crucifixion of Christ,[29] but it is not that Christians *have been crucified* with Christ as in 2.19 and 6.14, but that *they themselves have crucified* the flesh. The choice of an active voice lays the emphasis on the action and responsibility of Christian believers. Whether or not Paul intends to allude here to baptism is difficult to determine.[30] What is important to note is that he describes this event as the achievement of those who 'belong to Christ': for this implies that to return to the flesh would be to renounce what they themselves have done (not just what has been done to them).

---

[28] Since some texts omit 'Ιησοῦ (P[46] D F G et al.), both Nestle-Aland[26] and UBS[3] put it in square brackets.

[29] Betz, *Galatians*, 289-90, considers a passage in Philo, *Som* 2.213 to be 'a remarkably close parallel to Paul's teaching at this point'. But they have little in common beyond the reference to crucifixion, since Philo is describing the helpless state of the passion-loving mind (νοῦς) under the judgment of God.

[30] It is much discussed in the commentaries: see esp. Schlier, *Galater*, 263-4 and H. Weder, *Das Kreuz Jesu bei Paulus*, Göttingen 1981, 198-201. The parallel in Rom 6.1-6 does refer explicitly to baptism.

The other interesting feature of this verse is that it proclaims the death of the flesh not as a duty or a hope but as a past event.[31] The language of death clearly leads on into the following verse which gives, by contrast, a statement about life: εἰ ζῶμεν πνεύματι, πνεύματι καὶ στοιχῶμεν (5.25). This is closely parallel to 2.19-20 and 6.14-15 where references to past death and crucifixion are immediately followed by statements about present life and new creation; the only difference is that in 5.24-5 the death of the *flesh* gives way to the life of the *Spirit*.

These two points together give the statement in 5.24 a peculiar force which supports and secures Paul's earlier remarks in 5.16-18. Can life in Christ supply a sufficient safeguard against 'evil', defined as 'the flesh'? The answer is here again a resounding 'yes', because to belong to Christ means to destroy the flesh. Christ is far from being a 'servant of sin' (2.17), for those who belong to him do not encourage but *kill* the flesh. And it is not just the case that the Spirit opposes the flesh as opposing forces in a *battle* (5.17); from another perspective it can be said that the Spirit is a new form of life which follows after the *death* of the flesh.

Again a number of questions arise from this statement and its relationship with 5.16-18. If the flesh has been crucified, why is it still a force to be reckoned with? If it has died 'with its passions and desires',[32] why does its 'desire' still tempt the Christian and threaten the Spirit? (5.16-17)? What is 'the flesh' here spoken of as being crucified? Is it an aspect (or part) of the individual (cf. 2.19, 'I have been crucified') or an aspect of 'the world' (cf. 6.14, 'the world has been crucified to me')? How is the 'death' and 'life' spoken of in 5.24-5 related to the apocalyptic theme of 'new creation' in 6.14-15?

---

[31] Duncan, *Galatians*, 176 recognizes that Paul refers to a 'an act consummated at a definite moment in time' but errs in thinking that 'the act of crucifixion is to be distinguished from the death to which it is the prelude'. 'To be crucified' and 'to die' are (understandably) synonyms in 2.19.

[32] The distinction between παθήματα and ἐπιθυμίαι is unclear, since Paul's only other use of the former in the sense of 'passion' has an active sense (Rom 7.5); see Burton, *Galatians*, 299-300, 320-321.

Like the questions we have noted in relation to 5.16-18, these will have to be held over until they can receive a thorough investigation (in chapter six). For the present we may simply note the function of these statements in Paul's argument. In 5.24-5 Paul describes belonging to Christ as entailing a shift in the pattern of existence as decisive as moving from 'death' to 'life', a change which creates the sharpest possible break with 'the flesh'. Since their life is now determined by the Spirit who adequately rebuffs the desire of the flesh and determines their conduct in the warfare, the Galatians can have the utmost confidence in following Paul's proposal of 'walking in the Spirit': this (and this alone) will ensure victory over the moral threat and it will direct their moral choices without requiring them to have recourse to the law.[33]

The Fruit against which there is no Law: 5.22-3

Although we have now considered one of Paul's references to the law in this section (in 5.18), the other occurrences of νόμος (5.14,23; 6.2) must not be left out of account. As will become apparent shortly, 5.14 and 6.2 are best taken together and need some considerable discussion, so it will be convenient to begin with 5.23.

Paul's phrase κατὰ τῶν τοιούτων οὐκ ἔστιν νόμος (5.23) comes at the end of a list of 'virtues' entitled ὁ καρπὸς τοῦ πνεύματος. Before considering the reference to the law, it is worth enquiring whether there is any particular significance in his choice of this title. Elsewhere in the Pauline corpus fruit metaphors recur (e.g. Rom 1.13; 6.21-2; 7.4-5; 15.28; Phil 1.11,22; 4.17; Col 1.6,10; Eph 5.9-11) and commentators have seen in Paul's reference to 'fruit' (in contrast to τὰ ἔργα τῆς σαρκός 5.19) an allusion to the natural or spontaneous quality of

---

[33] Cf. Betz, 'Defense', 111: 'Thus Paul shows that also his ethics, based upon the Spirit, is [sic] "reasonable" and can solve the problems the Galatians are having with regard to the "flesh".'

Christian behaviour,[34] the notion of growth of character,[35] or an emphasis on such virtues being *given* by God/the Spirit.[36] It should be noted, however, that Paul can use the metaphor of 'fruit' or 'harvest' for both good and bad activities (Rom 6.21-2; 7.4-5; cf. sowing and reaping in relation to flesh as well as Spirit, Gal 6.7-8) so it is not clear that there is anything specifically Christian about 'bearing fruit' as such.[37] It is also important to observe that we cannot absolutize the notion of *gift*: if love and goodness are part of the fruit of the Spirit, they are also the subject of Paul's exhortation, since he urges the Galatians to *work at* such things (5.6,13; 6.4, 9-10).[38]

Several commentators have compared this verse with the fruit metaphors in the gospel-tradition (e.g. Mt 3.7-10; 7.15-20; Mk 12.1-12; Lk 13.6-9; Jn 15.1-6),[39] but since these passages are dependent on the use of this theme in the Old Testament,[40] it

---

[34] See e.g. Cole, *Galatians*, 167; Burton, *Galatians*, 313; Oepke, *Galater*, 180. Ebeling, *Truth of the Gospel*, 256 contrasts 'the world of technology' (works) and 'the world of nature' (fruit).

[35] Duncan, *Galatians*, 173; Guthrie, *Galatians*, 148; cf. E. Schweizer, 'Traditional Ethical Patterns in the Pauline and Post-Pauline Letters and their Development', in *Text and Interpretation*, ed. E. Best and R.McL. Wilson, Cambridge 1979, 195-209, at 198.

[36] Schlier, *Galater*, 255-6; Mussner, *Galaterbrief*, 385; Deidun, *New Covenant Morality*, 81: 'The καρπός image evokes the inner dynamism of the Spirit and the "passivity" of the Christian: the "fruit" is not the product of the Christian's labouring, but the effect of another's activity. The Christian receives it as gift.' It is also frequently remarked that the singular καρπός , contrasting with the plural ἔργα, signifies the harmony and unity of these qualities; Duncan, *Galatians*, 174; Ridderbos, *Galatians*, 207; Schrage, *Einzelgebote*, 54-6.

[37] E. Kamlah, *Die Form der katalogischen Paränese im Neuen Testament*, Tübingen 1964, 181-2 takes καρπός to mean simply 'sign' or 'characteristic'. Betz, *Galatians*, 286, interprets the term as 'benefits' and draws attention to the Stoic notion of the virtues as 'the fruits of the soul'.

[38] Thus, rightly, Betz, *Galatians*, 287: 'the "fruit of the Spirit" presupposes man's active involvement (cf. 5:25).' Schlier, *Galater*, 255-6 and Deidun, *New Covenant Morality*, 118-9 suggest that Paul avoided the term ἔργα because of a link with the 'works-righteousness' of the law. But Paul suffers no embarrassment in talking of Christian works (Gal 6.4,10; 2 Cor 9.8; 1 Thess 1.3).

[39] Lightfoot, *Galatians*, 209; Oepke, *Galater*, 180.

[40] See W. Telford, *The Barren Temple and the Withered Tree*, Sheffield 1980, on the cursing of the fig-tree in Mk 11.

may be that Paul's metaphor can be illuminated from Jewish tradition. In the Old Testament, Israel is frequently described as a fruit-bearing tree[41] and in several prophetic passages – most notably the 'song of the vineyard' in Is 5 – she is criticized for failing to bear the fruit (i.e. moral behaviour) expected of her.[42] In eschatological prophecies there are many promises concerning Israel's future fruitfulness, in both literal and metaphorical terms,[43] and in at least two passages, Is 32.15-16 and Joel 2.18-32, this is explicitly connected with the Spirit.

We may presume that Paul was familiar with this imagery both from the Old Testament and from subsequent Jewish traditions;[44] it is also possible that he was aware of the re-use of these images in the developing gospel-tradition.[45] Paul's reference to the 'fruit of the Spirit' may therefore be intended to evoke the prophetic statements on Israel and the promise for her future: such fruit is what God has always demanded of his people and what was promised for the 'age to come'. Now, in 'the fulness of time' (Gal 4.4) as 'the Spirit is poured out from on high' (Is 32.15), the people of God are able to produce the 'fruit' which was expected of them. By choosing a word with these rich associations, Paul is able to provide his appeal with further support: if the Galatians will only continue to walk in the Spirit, they will

---

[41] A vine/vineyard: Ps 80.8-18; Is 5.1-7; 27.2-6; Jer 2.21; 12.10; Ezek 15.1-8; 17.1-10; 19.10-14; Hos 10.1; an olive tree: Jer 11.16; Hos 14.6. Fruitfulness (in progeny) is an important theme of the Genesis narrative, both as a command to mankind (Gen 1.28; 9.1,7) and as a promise to Abraham and his family (Gen 17.2,6,20; 22.17; 28.3-4, etc.). This language is probably echoed in Col 1.6,10; see E. Lohse, *Colossians and Philemon*, E.T. Philadelphia 1971, 20, and N.T. Wright, *Colossians and Philemon*, Leicester 1986, 53.

[42] Is 5.1-7; Jer 2.21; 8.13; 24.8-10; Mic 7.1ff.

[43] Is 27.2-6; 37.30-32; Jer 31.27-8; 32.41; Ezek 17.22-4; Hos 14.5-8; Joel 2.18ff.; Amos 9.13-15.

[44] See e.g. Jub 16.26; 1QS 8.20; 1 Enoch 93.2-10; 4 Ezra 5.23-4 etc. In a few texts the 'fruit' is defined more specifically as works of the law: 4 Ezra 9.31-2; 2 Baruch 32.1; Gen Rabba 30.6; b Sotah 46a.

[45] H. Riesenfeld, *The Gospel Tradition*, E.T. Oxford 1970, 190-199.

actually produce the sort of behaviour which God requires.[46]

If this point is made allusively through the reference to ὁ καρπὸς τοῦ πνεύματος it is spelled out rather more clearly, although in a negative form, at the end of the list: κατὰ τῶν τοιούτων οὐκ ἔστιν νόμος. This phrase is usually translated 'against such things there is no law' and explained as a deliberate understatement: 'the mild assertion that there is no law against such things has the effect of an emphatic assertion that these things fully meet the requirements of the law (cf. v.14)'.[47] But several scholars have considered that, if the phrase is given this interpretation, it is so obvious as to be 'trivial' or entirely 'superfluous'.[48] Why should Paul need to point out that there is no law against 'love, joy, peace' etc.?

One way of alleviating this problem might be to take τῶν τοιούτων as masculine rather than neuter so that the phrase reads 'there is no law against such people'.[49] This might then relate to 5.18 where Paul insists that those led by the Spirit are not 'under the law': no law can condemn people who exhibit these qualities (cf. Rom 8.1).[50] However, the context suggests that the neuter is

[46] Since Paul refers to the 'blessing of Abraham' (3.14), it may be relevant to note that that blessing reads 'El Shaddai bless you and make you fruitful and multiply you' (Gen 28.3-4). If this is coming true literally through the inclusion of Gentiles (Gal 4.27), it is also being fulfilled in a metaphorical sense, through the 'fruit of the Spirit'.

[47] Burton, *Galatians*, 318; R. Bring, *Commentary on Galatians*, E.T. Philadelphia 1961, 267-8; Mussner, *Galaterbrief*, 389: 'Der Satz klingt leicht ironisch und spricht eigentlich eine Selbstverständlichkeit aus.'

[48] Oepke, *Galater*, 183 ('der triviale Satz'); Hofmann ('mehr als überflüssig') cited in Schlier, *Galater*, 262; Zahn, *Galater*, 266. H. Sahlin, 'Emendationsvorschläge zum griechischen Text des Neuen Testaments III', *NT* 25 (1938) 73-88 considers that its reading 'merkwürdig blass und nichtsagend' but his emendation of the passage, omitting the whole list of the fruit of the Spirit and reading κατὰ τῶν τοιούτων ἔστιν νόμος after the works of the flesh, is wholly implausible (82-3).

[49] Duncan, *Galatians*, 175 (following Moffatt's translation); Cole, *Galatians*, 169; Ridderbos, *Galatians*, 208; Oepke, *Galater*, 183; the plural number does not, of course, match the singular καρπός.

[50] However, see above n.24 on ὑπὸ νόμον in 5.18. Those who take 5.23 to mean 'there is no law (required) to restrain such people' (Lightfoot, *Galatians*, 210; Duncan, *Galatians*, 175-6, etc.) can appeal to 1 Tim 1.9 but have to stretch the meaning of κατά here considerably.

the better interpretation[51] and, even if the masculine is preferred, we still need to explain why Paul should feel it necessary to make such a remark.

Another way of solving the problem is adopted in the NEB translation and seems to be implicit in the remarks of several commentators on this phrase: 'there is no law *dealing with* such things as these'.[52] This depends on taking κατά to mean 'concerning' and is usually interpreted in the sense that these moral qualities are in a sphere wholly distinct from law, a sphere in which rules and regulations are irrelevant.[53] This interpretation is not impossible but it requires taking κατά in a sense very unusual in the New Testament,[54] and it leaves Paul apparently contradicting his own remark in 5.14. When he has just cited the love-command from the law (5.14), it is difficult to see how he could say that there is no law dealing with love etc.[55]

---

[51] It appears to operate as a neat parallel to τὰ τοιαῦτα in 5.21, Burton, *Galatians*, 319; Schlier, *Galater*, 262-3 and most commentators. Since such qualities can only be displayed in the lives of individuals there is ultimately little difference between the two readings of the gender.

[52] This is strongly supported by G.M. Styler, 'The Basis of Obligation in Paul's Christology and Ethics', in *Christ and Spirit in the New Testament*, ed. B. Lindars and S.S. Smalley, Cambridge 1973, 175-187 at 179 n.11; he regards the usual translation as 'at best a massive understatement: as a piece of irony it is unconvincing.'

[53] See, e.g., Bruce, *Galatians*, 255; Borse, *Galater*, 205; Deidun, *New Covenant Morality*, 118: Paul intends 'to remind the Galatians that "agape" . . . belongs to a sphere in which the Law is simply irrelevant.' Oepke, *Galater*, 183 and Schlier, *Galater*, 263 refer more generally to the end of the 'power' of the law.

[54] Its only other possible occurrences in this sense in the NT are Jn 19.11, Acts 25.3 and 1 Cor 15.15; but see *BAG* s.v. 1.2.b. However there is a remarkable parallel in Aristotle, *Pol* 3.8 (1284a 13), speaking of entirely virtuous men: κατὰ τῶν τοιούτων οὐκ ἔστι νόμος, αὐτοὶ γάρ εἰσι νόμος . . . (apparently first noted as a parallel to Gal 5,23' by E. Bäumlein, 'Ueber Galat. 5,23', *Theologische Studien und Kritiken*, 1862, 551-3 and later independently discovered by J.D. Robb, 'Galatians V. 23. An Explanation', *ExT* 56 (1944-5) 279-80). But as Bruce notes (255-6), 'Paul probably does not quote directly and consciously from Aristotle' since the affinity between the two phrases in their respective contexts is 'rather remote'.

[55] Although it may be true to say that law cannot *enforce* such qualities as love (Bruce, 255) or that law provides demands without enabling people 'to act with ethical responsibility' (Betz, 289), it is not at all clear how all this can be read into Paul's simple statement in this verse. We shall consider at the end of our investigation in what sense Paul's ethics here are (or are not) 'legal'.

It would probably be better, then, to keep the usual translation and to enquire whether such a phrase is really as superfluous as it is sometimes made out to be. In fact, given the note of defence we have found in other parts of this section, it could be regarded as entirely fitting. When the Galatians are worried that Paul's interpretation of Christ and of the Spirit will lead them into 'sin', he can claim that the Spirit leads to such utterly unobjectionable behaviour as 'goodness', 'peace' and 'self-control'; no law (certainly not the Mosaic law) could be cited against those qualities. But here we must note the selectivity Paul employs, for his point can only stand so long as he leaves out of account the eating of 'unclean food' and the disregard of Jewish festivals and circumcision which he also regards as the necessary consequence of the Spirit's work in his Gentile churches. A law, the Mosaic law, could certainly be cited against such behaviour! As far as it goes, Paul's statement is entirely correct and must have been calculated to have some persuasive force in inducing the Galatians to entrust themselves to the leading of the Spirit. But from an objective standpoint we should be aware that such a 'positive' remark about the relationship of the Spirit to law (and Mosaic law in particular) can only be made if certain topics, on which Paul clashed with the law, are left on one side.

At this point an interesting comparison can be made with the use of virtue-lists in Hellenistic Judaism. One of the reasons for citing such lists was an apologetic desire to show that what the law required was exactly in line with the virtues prized in the Hellenistic world, even the four 'cardinal virtues' φρόνησις, ἀνδρεία, σωφροσύνη and δικαιοσύνη.[56] In this sense the virtue-lists were 'bridge-building' exercises which often omitted, toned down or reinterpreted the specifically Jewish features of the

---

[56] See esp. Sap Sol 8.7; 4 Macc 1.19; Philo, Ebr 23; Josephus, Apion 2.170-171 in relation to the four cardinal virtues. For other virtue-lists see, e.g., Josephus, Apion 2.145-6, 211-4, 283, 291-5; Philo, Op Mundi 73; Virt 181-2 (the virtues of proselytes); Sacr 27.

Torah.[57] Paul is also using his virtue-list as a bridge – in his case building back, as it were, to the law from a list of qualities which, while they do not include the most common Platonic or Stoic terms, would be generally recognized as the description of a noble life. If Diaspora Jews used virtue-lists to commend the law as compatible with a highly moral way of life, Paul uses such a list to commend the morality of life in the Spirit as compatible with the law. His distinctive stance emerges of course when one observes the context of the letter as a whole, for there were probably few Jews in the Diaspora who would accept that, so long as one practised love, kindness and self-control, it did not matter if one failed to observe Jewish rites and food regulations.[58] But Paul knew as well as his fellow Jews how useful a generalized list of virtues could be in explaining and defending one's moral policies, and he exploits this possibility in 5.22-3.

Fulfilling the Law (of Christ): 5.14 and 6.2

Although Paul's statement about freedom and slavery in 5.13 should alert us to his love of paradox, we are still somewhat taken aback to find him support his appeal for love with a straight-forward reference to the *law*: ὁ γὰρ πᾶς νόμος ἐν ἑνὶ λόγῳ πεπλήρωται, ἐν τῷ· ἀγαπήσεις τὸν πλησίον σου ὡς σεαυτόν (5.14). After so many chapters in which the law has been viewed in a negative light – Paul has talked of 'the curse of the law', 'the yoke of slavery', of its era coming to an end and of Christians 'dying' to it – it is startling to find it introduced in a positive argument for love. If, as Watson notes, Paul's 'characteristic view

---

[57] Note, for instance, the omission of many Jewish customs in Ps-Phocylides; the reinterpretation of Jewish food-laws as examples of δικαιοσύνη in Ep Arist 128-171; and Josephus' explanation of Jewish tenacity in observing the Mosaic laws as φρόνησις and καρτερία (= ἀνδρεία), *Apion* 2.183, 283.

[58] Philo castigates the 'allegorists' in Alexandria for taking this line (*Mig* 89-93) but we have little other evidence for such a self-consciously 'liberal' or 'secularized' trend in the Diaspora.

in Galatians is to concede possession of the law to the Jewish community',[59] why does he mention it here in an appeal for Christian love? And since a few verses later Paul can still talk of Christians not being 'under the law' (οὐκ ἐστὲ ὑπὸ νόμον, 5.18), what can he possibly mean by *fulfilling* the law in loving one's neighbour? This verse has been described as 'the most unexpected development of Paul's thought in this letter'.[60] Is it irreconcilable with the rest of the letter and to be dismissed as an example of Paul's self-contradictory views on the law?[61] Or is it a 'necessary nuance' in Paul's presentation of his case?[62]

Our problems with Paul's statement in 5.14 are actually compounded by a remark he makes a few verses later: ἀλλήλων τὰ βάρη βαστάζετε καὶ οὕτως ἀναπληρώσετε τὸν νόμον τοῦ Χριστοῦ (6.2). The reference to 'fulfilling the law' suggests some connection with 5.14, but Paul's talk of a 'law of Christ' is doubly astonishing: not only is 'law' here a positive entity but it is conjoined with Christ, despite the fact that 'Christ' and 'law' have stood in the strongest possible contrast throughout the letter (2.16-21; 3.23-6; 4.1-7; 5.1-6). We will start our investigation with this, the hardest verse, before returning to 5.14 and the meaning of 'fulfilling the law'.

1. The Law of Christ
The explanation of this phrase is described by Betz as 'one of the most crucial problems in the whole letter'.[63] Paul's expression – ὁ νόμος τοῦ Χριστοῦ – has only one parallel elsewhere in his letters, and that is the equally puzzling reference in 1 Cor 9.21 to his being ἔννομος Χριστοῦ. The context shows that Paul uses

[59] Watson, *Paul, Judaism and the Gentiles*, 71.
[60] G. Shaw, *The Cost of Authority. Manipulation and Freedom in the New Testament*, London 1983, 50. Hübner has described the anomaly of 5.14 most fully in 'Das ganze und das eine Gesetz'.
[61] See esp. Räisänen, 'Difficulties' and *Paul and the Law*.
[62] S. Westerholm, 'On Fulfilling the Whole Law (Gal.5:14)', *SEÅ* 51-2 (1986-7) 229-237, at 231.
[63] Betz, *Galatians*, 299.

ἔννομος Χριστοῦ to describe a position which is neither ὑπὸ νόμον nor ἄνομος θεοῦ (9.20-21) and it indicates his ability to coin phrases which exploit the flexibility of the Greek language but whose meaning is not altogether easy to define. We should bear this verbal dexterity in mind when interpreting Gal 6.2 as well.

A variety of attempts have been made to explain 'the law of Christ' which we may discuss under four heads:

a) It has been suggested that ὁ νόμος τοῦ Χριστοῦ should be translated 'the law of the Messiah' and taken to reflect a rabbinic notion that in the new age the Messiah would reinterpret or repromulgate the law. The most thorough exponent of this view is W.D. Davies,[64] who adduces a string of Old Testament and rabbinic statements to the effect that, in the Age to come, the law will be modified, renewed, freshly expounded or even replaced by a new law.[65] However, the evidence that this would be known as 'the law of the Messiah' is extremely thin. Davies can gather only five possible references (Eccles Rabba 11.8; Song Rabba 2.13,4; Targum on Is 12.3 and on Song 5.10; Yalkut Is 26.2)[66] and himself admits that 'the evidence that we have been able to adduce in favour of a new Messianic Torah . . . is not impressive . . . The result of our survey is not in any sense decisive'.[67]

---

[64] *Torah in the Messianic Age and/or the Age to Come*, Philadelphia 1952, revised and expanded in *The Setting of the Sermon on the Mount*, Cambridge 1963, 109-190.

[65] In the OT: Is 2.1-5; 42.2-4; Jer 31.31-4; in rabbinic literature: Lev Rabba 9.7; 13.3; Midrash to Ps 146.7; b Sanhedrin 51b; b Shabbath 151b. A. Schweitzer, *Mysticism*, 187-93 and L. Baeck, 'The Faith of Paul', *JJS* 3 (1952) 93-110, cited these and other texts as evidence for the notion that the law would come to an end in the Messianic age. Schoeps, *Paul*, 168-75 argues that 'a specifically widespread opinion in rabbinic literature is that in the Messianic era the old Torah will cease altogether with the evil impulse, but that God will give a new Torah through the Messiah' (172).

[66] Hebrew texts and translations in Davies, *Setting*, 172-9.

[67] *Setting*, 188. Cf. Strack-Billerbeck III, 577 and IV, 1-3 where the editors insist that such evidence as there is for a Messianic Torah suggests only a new

continued on p.128

Given this diffidence by its prime exponent, it is not surprising
that most scholars doubt the relevance of these rabbinic passages
to the texts which Davies seeks to explain (Mt 5-7; Gal 6.2). The
paucity of evidence for this rabbinic notion, its ambiguity and late
date (it is possibly influenced by Christian language) make it too
indirect and too inconclusive to be of much value in explaining
Paul's phrase.[68]

b) Whether or not one accepts the influence of a rabbinic notion
of a 'Messianic Torah', it could be held that Paul thought of the
teaching of Jesus as a Christian law and alluded to it with this
phrase in Gal 6.2. On this point Davies is confident: 'Paul must
have regarded Jesus in the light of a new Moses, and . . . he
recognized in the words of Christ a νόμος τοῦ Χριστοῦ which
formed for him the basis for a new kind of Christian Halakah'.[69]
Davies considered Paul's mind to be 'permeated with Jesus'
sayings' which are echoed throughout Paul's ethical teaching
(notably in Rom 12-13; 1 Thess 4-5; Col 3). C.H. Dodd eventually supported a similar position on the basis of the ἔννομος
Χριστοῦ phrase in 1 Cor 9.21 (taken to refer to the commands of

continued from p.127

interpretation of the old. P. Stuhlmacher's thesis that Paul has in mind a Zion-
Torah mentioned in some prophetic texts (*Versöhnung, Gesetz und Gerechtigkeit.
Aufsätze zur biblischen Theologie*, Göttingen 1981, 168-75; cf. O. Hofius, 'Das
Gesetz des Mose und das Gesetz Christi', *ZTK* 80 (1983) 262-286) is rightly
dismissed by Räisänen, *Paul and the Law*, 239-45; it is built on the flimsiest of
evidence.

[68] Although Davies has received some support, e.g. from J. Jervell, 'Die
offenbarte und die verborgene Tora. Zur Vorstellung über die neue Tora im
Rabbinismus', *STh* 25 (1971) 90-108, his evidence has been disputed or discounted
by E. Bammel, 'νόμος Χριστοῦ', in *Studia Evangelica III*, ed. F.L. Cross, Berlin
1964, 120-128; P. Schäfer, 'Die Torah der messianischen Zeit', *ZNW* 65 (1974)
27-42; and R. Banks, *Jesus and the Law in the Synoptic Tradition*, Cambridge 1975,
65-81.

[69] *Paul and Rabbinic Judaism*, 144; cf. *Setting*, 341-66 for a fuller and slightly
modified statement of his case.

Christ in 1 Cor 7.10 and 9.14).[70] Dodd considered Paul's instructions in Gal 6.1-5 to be a reapplication of Jesus' teaching in Mt 23.4 and 18.15-16 so that Paul's reference to fulfilling the law of Christ 'connotes the intention to carry out . . . the precepts which Jesus Christ was believed to have given to his disciples, and which they handed down in the Church'.[71]

Such an interpretation, however, encounters both methodological and theological problems. It is notoriously difficult to establish where Paul is alluding to or dependent on the teaching of Jesus. Estimates of such allusions range from 8 to well over 1000[72] and such objective criteria as can be applied do not provide sufficient support for Dodd's thesis on Gal 6.1-5.[73] Moreover, even if Paul drew extensively on the teaching of Jesus it is most

---

[70] In *The Bible and the Greeks*, London 1935, 37 Dodd denied that Gal 6.2 could mean the 'Torah of Jesus', but his perspective had changed somewhat by the time he wrote *Gospel and Law. The Relation of Faith and Ethics in Early Christianity*, Cambridge 1951, 64-83 and 'Ἔννομος Χριστοῦ', originally published in 1953, reprinted in *More New Testament Studies*, Manchester 1968, 134-148.

[71] 'Ἔννομος Χριστοῦ', 147. Dodd's position is supported in general by R.N. Longenecker, *Paul: Apostle of Liberty*, New York 1964, 183-190.

[72] V.P. Furnish, *Theology and Ethics in Paul*, Nashville 1968, 51-66 found 8 allusions and was critical of Davies' excessive enthusiasm in spotting parallels to Jesus' teaching; Davies, who detected 25 such parallels (*Paul and Rabbinic Judaism*, 136-142) accused Furnish of pursuing too mathematical an approach (146 n.1). It was A. Resch, *Der Paulinismus und die Logia Jesu in ihrem gegenseitigen Verhältnis untersucht*, Leipzig 1904, who found more than 1000 allusions, 28 of them in Gal 5-6. His vast overstatement of the case has made scholars very wary of supposed allusions; but the debate has been given fresh impetus by D.L. Dungan, *The Sayings of Jesus in the Churches of Paul*, Oxford 1971 and D.C. Allison, 'The Pauline Epistles and the Synoptic Gospels: the Pattern of the Parallels', *NTS* 28 (1982) 1-32.

[73] The following factors would strengthen the case for an allusion: a) notable congruence of vocabulary; b) similar context of thought; c) dissimilarity to common pagan or Jewish terms/ideas; d) a reason for harking back to Jesus' teaching; e) a cluster of such allusions. In the light of these criteria, Dodd's case appears rather weak: βάρη and φορτίον (Gal 6.2,5) are terms also found in Mt 11.30 and 23.4 but the context is very different, while the general resemblance of Gal 6.1-2 to Mt 18.15-16 is too vague to bear much weight. Brinsmead's attempt to support and expand Dodd's case, *Galatians*, 174-6, 182-5, is unconvincing. On Gal 5.14 see below.

unlikely that he would have treated it as a code of precepts or described it as a 'law of Christ'. Whatever authority such teaching may have held, Jesus did not function for Paul as a rabbi or as a 'second Moses'.[74] Indeed the very fact that he usually merely *alludes* to such teaching puts it in an entirely different category from an authoritative collection of rules.[75]

c) Recently some scholars have speculated that the origin of the phrase 'the law of Christ' lies with Paul's Galatian opponents and that Paul is adopting their terminology in his argument against them. Georgi was apparently the first to suggest this thesis,[76] which has since found a number of supporters.[77] Given the agitators' commitment to the law as (Jewish) Christians, we can well imagine that such language would not be out of character; but, within the limits of our ability to 'mirror-read' the text (see above pp.37-41), 'imagination' is about all we have to go on here. Since Paul himself can use a similar phrase in 1 Cor 9.21, it does not seem inconceivable that he should coin such paradoxical terminology himself; and, in fact, it is probably easier to believe this than that he has taken the risk of employing a phrase which the Galatians would have heard used in a very unPauline sense. In

---

[74] Furnish, *Theology*, 59-66; Sanders, *Paul and Palestinian Judaism*, 511-5. The later descriptions of Christianity as a new covenant with a new law (e.g. Barnabas 2.6; 21.8; Ignatius, *Mag* 2.1) may allude to Gal 6.2 but are more influenced by the theology of Matthew or James than that of Paul.

[75] Cf. the incisive critique of Dodd by Räisänen, *Paul and the Law*, 77-82. It is noticeable that Davies modifies his position somewhat in a more recent essay, 'The Moral Teaching of the Early Church', in *The Use of the Old Testament in the New and Other Essays*, ed. J.M. Efird, Durham N.C. 1972, 310-332: he now considers there are only 8 'clear parallels' with Jesus' teaching and states that, with 'the law of Christ', 'the reference is *in part at least* to the teaching of Jesus' (327, my emphasis); he does not indicate what else it might refer to.

[76] According to Betz, *Galatians*, 300 n.71; I can find no indication of authorship in the text he cites. Previously J. Weiss had suggested this was a pre-Pauline phrase, *Earliest Christianity. A History of the Period AD 30-150*, E.T. Gloucester, Mass. 1970,II, 554; cf. G. Friedrich, 'Das Gesetz des Glaubens Röm 3,27', *ThZ* 10 (1954) 401-417, at 407-8 and M. Hengel, *Between Jesus and Paul. Studies in the Earliest History of Christianity*, E.T. London 1983, 151 n.137.

[77] D.A. Stoike, *'The law of Christ': A Study of Paul's Use of the Expression in Galatians 6:2*, Th.D. dissertation, Claremont 1971; Betz, *Galatians*, 300-1; Brinsmead, *Galatians*, 163-185.

any case, we still have to decide what Paul himself meant by 'fulfilling the law of Christ'.[78]

d) It is possible to take νόμος in Paul's phrase ὁ νόμος τοῦ Χριστοῦ in the extended sense of 'norm' or 'principle'. On this view, Paul is not talking of the Mosaic law or a new law promulgated by Christ but is describing, with a conscious word-play, the 'principle' that controls the Christian life.[79] In this case it is usually considered that Paul is deliberately echoing his statement in 5.14, so the principle he enjoins is the rule of love.[80]

These four approaches represent the wide diversity of opinions on this verse. It is possible that no simple formula will fully explain Paul's meaning, but the following exegetical observations may provide the best available solution:

i) It is important to establish first the close connection between 6.2 and 5.13-14. This is acknowledged by most commentators and is apparent in the parallel references to mutual obligation (δουλεύετε ἀλλήλοις 5.13; ἀλλήλων τὰ βάρη βαστάζετε 6.2) and the repetition of verbs from the root πληροῦν (πεπλήρωται 5.14; ἀναπληρώσετε 6.2). Indeed the theme of mutual obligation is in each case, more specifically, mutual *service*, since the bearing of burdens is a slave's task.[81] Thus whether Paul has in mind the specific βάρη of moral failure (6.1) or, more generally, the

---

[78] Wilckens, who regards this hypothesis as 'nicht unmöglich', suggests that the agitators used this phrase in the course of condemning sinful fellow-Christians and that Paul picks it up to interpret it 'entgegen solchem Missbrauch in seinem wahren Sinn', 'Entwicklung', 176; but this still leaves us with the problem of what Paul considered to be its 'true sense'.

[79] Räisänen, *Paul and the Law*, 80: '*Nomos* is being used in a loose sense, almost metaphorically'; Eckert, *Verkündigung*, 160-161; van Dülmen, *Theologie des Gesetzes*, 66-8; Burton, *Galatians*, 329; Guthrie, *Galatians*, 152-3; Bruce, *Galatians*, 261. R.B. Hays, 'Christology and Ethics in Galatians: The law of Christ', *CBQ* 49 (1987) 268-290 glosses νόμος as 'a regulative principle or structure of existence' (276). The parallels usually cited for this extended sense of νόμος are Rom 3.27; 7.21 and 8.2 (ὁ νόμος τοῦ πνεύματος τῆς ζωῆς ἐν Χριστῷ Ἰησοῦ).

[80] Luther, *Galatians*, 539: 'The law of Christ is the law of love'. Cf. Ellicott, *Galatians*, 125; Mussner, *Galaterbrief*, 399.

[81] Cf. Aristophanes' comic use of the slave's burden-bearing task in the opening scene of *Frogs*, where Xanthias struggles with Dionysus' heavy luggage. In 1 Cor 9.19-21, being ἔννομος Χριστοῦ is related to being a *slave* to all.

manifold spiritual and physical burdens of everyday life,[82] what he enjoins in this verse is 'serving one another through love' (5.13). Thus the following phrase 'and so you will fulfil the law of Christ'[83] must be interpreted with reference to the statement in 5.14 about the fulfilment of the whole law through the love-command.

ii) Given this close parallel between these two passages, the following conclusion seems reasonable: since 'the whole law' fulfilled by love in 5.14 is the Mosaic law (see further below), we should take Paul's reference to 'fulfilling the law of Christ' as *another reference to fulfilling the Mosaic law*, while this is now qualified with the genitive τοῦ Χριστοῦ. This, of course, raises the crucial question: why should 'fulfilling the law *of Christ*' (6.2) be parallel to 'fulfilling the law through love' (5.14)?

a) The most obvious answer would be that, like others in the early church, Paul regarded the love-command in Lev 19.18 as the text Jesus used to summarize the law.[84] Unfortunately, this is one of those cases of a plausible but unprovable allusion to Jesus'

---

[82] Ridderbos, *Galatians*, 213 and Mussner, *Galaterbrief*, 399 are among those who restrict the reference of 'burdens' to the moral weaknesses of 6.1; but the parallels in Rom 15.1 and 1 Cor 12.26 should probably make us interpret the term more generally, so Burton, *Galatians*, 329; Betz, *Galatians*, 299. In any case, J.G. Strelan, 'Burden-Bearing and the Law of Christ: A Re-examination of Galatians 6.2', *JBL* 94 (1975) 266-276, does not carry conviction with his argument that Paul here refers to the burden of financial support for Jerusalem; see, in reply, E.M. Young, ' "Fulfil the Law of Christ". An Examination of Galatians 6.2', *Studia Biblica et Theologica* 7 (1977) 31-42.

[83] It is hard to be sure if the better text is *future indicative* ἀναπληρώσετε (so Metzger, *Textual Commentary*, 598, Lightfoot, Betz, Mussner et al. on the basis of P[46] [ἀποπληρώσετε] B F G and most ancient versions) or *aorist imperative* ἀναπληρώσατε (so Burton, Borse et al. following ℵ A C D etc.). The former reading probably has the edge.

[84] Jesus' use of Lev 19.18 to summarize the law is attested in several strands of the synoptic tradition (Mk 12.31=Mt 22.39; Lk 10.27; Mt 19.19; cf. Mt 7.12); these witness to 'the strong conviction in the early Church that Jesus summarised the moral law by citing Lev. xix 18', H. Montefiore, 'Thou shalt Love thy Neighbour as Thyself', *NT* 5 (1962) 157-170, at 158.

teaching, since Paul does not make explicit his dependence on Jesus and could have seized on this well-known summary of the law quite independently.[85] But it remains quite possible that Jesus' emphasis on this command was already familiar in Christian paraenesis and is consciously echoed here by Paul: hence to fulfil the law through love would be to fulfil the law τοῦ Χριστοῦ (as taught by Christ).

b) There are also explicit connections in Paul's letters between 'love' and 'Christ' through the example of Christ in his death.[86] Indeed, earlier in this letter he had described Christ as 'the Son of God who loved me and gave himself for me' (2.20).[87] There is also an interesting parallel to Gal 6.2 in Rom 15.1-3 where Paul appeals to the strong to bear with (βαστάζειν) others' weaknesses, not to please themselves but to please their neighbours (τῷ πλησίον echoing the love-command ἀγαπήσεις τὸν πλησίον, 13.9); the reason given is the example of Christ – καὶ γὰρ ὁ Χριστὸς οὐχ ἑαυτῷ ἤρεσεν (15.3). Thus to fulfil the law through love would be to fulfil it in a Christ-like way (just as love is a prime characteristic of those 'in Christ', Gal 5.6,22), and this again might justify the genitive τοῦ Χριστοῦ.[88]

This suggests that when Paul talks of 'fulfilling the law of Christ' he means 'fulfilling the law in the way exemplified (and

---

[85] On other Jewish uses of Lev 19.18 and the golden Rule see below pp.135-6.

[86] The importance of the example of Christ for the interpretation of this verse is emphasized by H. Schürmann, ' "Das Gesetz des Christus" Gal 6,2. Jesu Verhalten und Wort als letztgültige sittliche Norm nach Paulus', in *Neues Testament und Kirche*, ed. J. Gnilka, Freiburg 1974, 282-300, and by Hays, 'Christology and Ethics'.

[87] Cf. Rom 5.8; 8.37-9; 2 Cor 5.14-15 and note also Eph 5.2, 25.

[88] Schürmann, 'Gesetz des Christus', 289-90 overstates his case by drawing a parallel between Christians' mutual burden-bearing (Gal 6.1-2) and Christ's sin-bearing (he appeals to Is 53), although Hofius, 'Gesetz', 282-3 supports him. Hays, 'Christology and Ethics', also blunts the force of his argument by referring in general terms to Christ's 'faithfulness' and 'obedience', without demonstrating their relationship to 'love'.

taught?) by Christ', i.e. fulfilling it through love. He is not alluding to a new code called 'the law of the Messiah' and, although he may be conscious of the love-command as a special emphasis in Christ's teaching, he is not referring to a new collection of rules based on Jesus' words. Rather, νόμος here, as in 5.14, refers to the Mosaic law (not just a 'norm' or 'regulative principle'),[89] only now it is qualified by the genitive τοῦ Χριστοῦ. This genitive should not be taken in the sense of a law promulgated by Christ[90] but in the looser sense of the law *redefined through Christ*.[91] In the case of nouns which accompany νόμος, Paul often exploits the flexibility of the Greek genitive so that each phrase requires careful exegesis.[92] Moreover, as Moule remarks, 'a genitive like "of Christ" must often be interpreted largely by the context and the probabilities'.[93] In this case the context (especially the link with 5.13-14) suggests that Paul is referring to fulfilling the (Mosaic) law τοῦ Χριστοῦ, and the probabilities are that this τοῦ Χριστοῦ means 'the law in its relationship to Christ', that is, 'the law as redefined and fulfilled by Christ in love'.

---

[89] This is not to deny that Paul can use νόμος to mean 'principle' (probably in Rom 3.27 and 8.2); but the important similarities between Gal 5.14 and 6.2 necessitate taking νόμος in both cases as a reference to the (Mosaic) law. Cf. Sanders, *Paul, The Law, and the Jewish People*, 97-8.

[90] *Contra* Burton, *Galatians*, 329; Duncan, *Galatians*, 181; Bligh, *Galatians*, 473.

[91] Cf. Wilckens, 'Entwicklung', 175: 'das Gesetz in seiner Bestimmtheit durch Christus'. On a more general level Schrage remarks: 'Einerseits ist das alttestamentliche Ethos auch für den Christen eine authoritative Instanz, anderseits aber gewinnt diese Instanz ihre Verbindlichkeit doch erst von der Beziehung zu Christus her. Das alttestamentliche Gesetz muss – pointiert formuliert – erst zum Gesetz Christi werden (vgl. Gal 5:14 mit 6:2), bevor es zur Norm christlichen Lebens werden kann', *Einzelgebote*, 237-8.

[92] Note the different uses of the genitive in νόμος θεοῦ (Rom 7.22,25); νόμος Μωϋσέως (1 Cor 9.9); νόμος τοῦ ἀνδρός (Rom 7.2); νόμος τῆς ἁμαρτίας (Rom 7.23,25) and νόμος τοῦ πνεύματος (Rom 8.2).

[93] C.F.D. Moule, ' "Fulness" and "Fill" in the New Testament', *SJT* 4 (1951) 79-86, here at 82. Col 2.11, ἡ περιτομὴ τοῦ Χριστοῦ, is another case in point.

This interpretation highlights the subtlety of Paul's genitival construction νόμος τοῦ Χριστὸς and we will have to consider in due course what purpose is served by this attempt to redefine νόμος. But our analysis also demands some consideration of the meaning of 'fulfilling the law' since this phrase is found, with slight variations, in both 5.14 and 6.2. This problem will now occupy our attention.

2. Fulfilling the Law

We have seen that Gal 5.14 and 6.2 are bound together by a common reference to the fulfilment of the law: in 5.14 the whole law is fulfilled (πεπλήρωται) in one command (the love-command) and in 6.2 those who bear burdens will fulfil (ἀναπληρώσετε) 'the law of Christ'. The problem of comprehending such phrases is well illustrated by the particular anomaly contained in Paul's statement in 5.14.

When he cites Lev 19.18 as the 'one word' (i.e. command) in which the whole law (ὁ πᾶς νόμος) is fulfilled, Paul may appear to be proceeding in a way quite analogous to other Jewish traditions. The saying attributed to his contemporary Hillel (its authenticity is disputed) immediately springs to mind: 'What is hateful to you, do not do to your neighbour. That is the whole law; everything else is commentary. Go and learn it' (b Shabbath 31a). Another 'parallel' comes from a slightly later period, from Rabbi Akiba, who cites 'Thou shalt love thy neighbour as thyself' as the 'great principle' (כלל גדול) in the law (Gen Rabba 24.7).[94] There are also a number of statements in rabbinic literature which describe a certain practice as the fulfilment of the whole law.[95] However, even if the rabbis would have felt

---

[94] For other rabbinic texts using this command see Strack–Billerbeck I, 363-4. In the Testaments of the 12 Patriarchs, love of God and love of neighbour are commands used to summarize the law (Test Iss 5.2; Dan 5.3).

[95] See the texts collected by H.W.M. van de Sandt, 'An Explanation of Rom.8,4a', Bijdragen. Tijdschrift voor Filosofie en Theologie 37 (1976) 361-378, at 373 (I am grateful to Dr. J.A. Ziesler for referring me to this article). The closest in

comfortable with all of the *ingredients* of Paul's statement in 5.14, they would have registered strong objections to the *context* in which he made it. For, while urging that the love-command is the fulfilment of the law, Paul also instructs the Galatians that they should not take on the yoke of the law (5.1), that they do not live under it (5.18) and that they must on no account get circumcised (5.3-4). Indeed, he even warns them about the disaster that will ensue if, through circumcision, they become indebted to keep the whole law (ὀφειλέτης ἐστὶν ὅλον τὸν νόμον ποιῆσαι 5.3). At this point, then, the parallel with the rabbis breaks down, for they never intended their summarizing statements to mean that other parts of the law should be wilfully ignored![96] Paul is not using Lev 19.18 as a summary which *includes* all the rest of the commands of the law; he does not consider that everything else in the law is commentary on it, to be learned and obeyed. And this suggests that, when he writes ὁ πᾶς νόμος ἐν ἑνὶ λόγῳ πεπλήρωται, he is *either* not referring to the Mosaic law at all, *or* using the verb 'fulfilled' in a rather different sense from the otherwise similar statements in rabbinic texts.

Hans Hübner has taken the first of these options by focusing attention on the linguistic distinction between ὅλος ὁ νόμος in 5.3 and ὁ πᾶς νόμος in 5.14.[97] The former he regards as a reference to the Mosaic law with emphasis on its quantitative measurement. But the latter, with its unusual attributive place-

---

continued from p.135

content to Gal 5.14 is Mek Vayassa on Ex 15.26: 'This teaches that if one is honest in his business dealings and the spirit of his fellow creatures takes delight in him, it is accounted to him as though he had fulfilled the whole Torah'.

[96] See Moore, *Judaism* II, 83-88; Sanders, *Paul and Palestinian Judaism*, 112-4; *idem*, 'On the Question of Fulfilling the Law in Paul and Rabbinic Judaism', in *Donum Gentilicium*, ed. E. Bammel et al., Oxford 1978, 103-126, esp. 112-117.

[97] Hübner's case is set out in detail in 'Das ganze and das eine Gesetz'. The main points are repeated in *Law in Paul's Thought*, 36-41, and their theological implications drawn out in 'Identitätsverlust und paulinische Theologie. Anmerkungen zum Galaterbrief', *KuD* 24 (1978) 181-193.

ment of πᾶς, emphasizes totality and does not refer to the Mosaic law; it is an ironic expression, playing on the Jewish understanding of 'the whole law' but really referring to a quite different identity: 'Thus the whole Law of Moses simply is not identical with the Law "as a whole" which holds good for Christians'.[98]

However, Hübner's case, ingenious as it is, cannot stand. Since νόμος has meant 'the Mosaic law' all the way up till this point in Galatians and continues to bear this reference four verses later in 5.18, and since 5.14 itself contains a quotation from the Mosaic law (Lev 19.18 is one of the λόγοι contained in the νόμος), it is extremely unlikely that ὁ πᾶς νόμος can mean anything other than the whole Mosaic law. Moreover the parallel in Rom 13.8-10 is an unmistakable reference to Mosaic law and the subtle distinction Hübner maintains between that passage and Gal 5.14 does not carry conviction.[99]

But if Hübner's option is a dead-end, can Paul's 'fulfilment' language shed any light on our problem? Many years ago Burton noted that 'the precise meaning of this sentence [5.14] turns in no small part on the meaning of πεπλήρωται', adding that it has been subject to 'diverse interpretations'.[100] Although some of the older commentaries and several recent translations take πληρόω here to mean 'sum up',[101] no parallels can be adduced with this

---

[98] *Law in Paul's Thought*, 37; Hübner describes this as Paul 'linguistically hitting below the belt in his fight against the Jewish understanding of the Law'.

[99] *Law in Paul's Thought*, 37, 83-88. Similar criticisms of Hübner's thesis are voiced by Sanders, *Paul, The Law and the Jewish People*, 96-7, Räisänen, *Paul and the Law*, 27 n.72, and by U. Luz in his review of Hübner's book in *ThZ* (1979) 121-3.

[100] *Galatians*, 294.

[101] Burton cites Weizsäcker and Stapfer as supporters of the interpretation 'sum up'; it is adopted by Moffatt, NEB, NIV, JB and GNB. Mussner, *Galaterbrief*, 370 takes 'Aufgipfelung' (summation) as part of the meaning here, appealing to Rom 13.8-10; but that passage shows a distinction between ἀνακεφαλαιόω and πληρόω.

meaning, while the use of the verb elsewhere in Paul requires the meaning 'fulfil' or 'fully accomplish' (Rom 8.4; 13.8-10).[102] Hence Paul's statement that the law is fulfilled in one command must be taken as an ellipsis for 'fulfilled in the practice of this one command'.[103]

But here we must observe some striking linguistic data. In the LXX πληϱοῦν is never used in relation to the law (nor is its equivalent מלא in the Hebrew Bible) although a variety of other terms are employed.[104] In other Greek Jewish literature also, πληϱοῦν is never found with νόμος, although it is used very occasionally with objects such as ἐντολή.[105] In rabbinic literature, where מלא is no longer in currency, statements about fulfilling the law usually employ some form of the verb קום , but this does not have the same resonance as the verb πληϱοῦν, with its implication of 'fulness' and 'completion'.[106] Thus, when he talks of the law being fulfilled (πεπλήϱωται) or of Christians who fulfil (ἀναπληϱώσετε) the law of Christ, Paul is using vocabulary unprecedented in the Jewish tradition.

---

[102] Cf. Rom 15.19 (fully preaching the gospel of Christ), 2 Cor 10.6 (obedience is complete), Col 4.17 (fulfil a ministry). *BAG*, πηλϱόω 3, prefers to translate Gal 5.14 'the whole law has found its full expression in a single word', because of the past tense used. But the perfect can be explained otherwise ('the law stands fulfilled/fully accomplished') and *BAG* can cite no explanatory parallel for its interpretation. The suffix in ἀναπληϱόω (6.2) adds little if anything: it also means 'fully accomplish' (not 'fill up what is lacking', *pace* Meyer, *Galatians*, 323-4).

[103] So Lightfoot, *Galatians*, 205; Burton, *Galatians*, 295.

[104] In the Hebrew Bible the standard terms for observing the law;, with their normal LXX equivalents, are:שׁמר (φυλάσσω/τηϱέω); עשׂה (ποιέω); שׁמע (ἀκούω); קום (ἱστάνω/ἐμμένω); see E. Hatch and H. A. Redpath, *A Concordance to the Septuagint and the Other Greek Versions of the Old Testament (including the Apocryphal Books)*, Oxford 1897. The references to 'fulfilling the word of the Lord' always relate to prophecies, e.g. 1 Kings 2.27; 2 Chron 36.21.

[105] Test Naph 8.7 (ἐντολαὶ νόμου . . . πληϱοῦνται); 1 Macc 2.55 (λόγον πληϱῶσαι); Philo, *Praem* 83 (πληϱῶσαι τοὺς λόγους); Sib Or 3.246 (πληϱοῦντες . . . θεοῦ φάτιν, ἔννομον ὕμνον). Josephus uses ἀναπληϱοῦν for completing a contract, *Ant* 8.58. For use in secular Greek see *LSJ* and *MM* s.v. Among the Apostolic Fathers note Barn 21.8 and Polycarp, *Phil* 3.3 (with ἐντολή).

[106] See van de Sandt, 'An Explanation of Rom. 8,4a', 364-375.

It is also important to note that Paul uses a variety of terms for Jewish observance of the law (e.g. φυλάσσω, ποιέω, πράσσω) but never in this connection employs πληρόω.[107] The four occasions on which he uses (ἀνα-) πληρόω in relation to the law all concern *Christians* (Rom 8.4; 13.8; Gal 5.14; 6.2; cf. Rom 13.10 πλήρωμα νόμου) and this verb-root could be said to be his favourite vocabulary in describing the Christian relationship to the law.[108] Thus we may suggest that the key to Gal 5.14 (and 6.2) lies in Paul's distinctive use of unusual vocabulary (πληροῦν) and that the contrast with 5.3 lies not in the description of the law (ὅλος ὁ νόμος – ὁ πᾶς νόμος) but in the different verbs used (ποιεῖν – πληροῦν). This point has been observed by H.D. Betz and S. Westerholm[109] but it remains for us to draw out the implications of Paul's choice of terminology.

i) The verb πληροῦν, whose semantic field is dominated by notions of 'filling' and 'completion', implies the total realization and accomplishment of the law's demand and dovetails neatly with Paul's argument earlier in the letter that God's purposes and promises had reached their fulfilment in Christ (ὅτε δὲ ἦλθεν τὸ πλήρωμα τοῦ χρόνου, 4.4). In discussing fulfilment language in the New Testament in general, Moule has noted both the remarkable frequency of this language (compared to Jewish texts) and the conviction it expresses of the final consummation of God's will and plan.[110] Indeed this has often been noted in relation to Mt 5.17 (the only non-Pauline New Testament text referring to fulfilment of the *law*) where Matthew's language echoes his convictions on the fulfilment of Scripture in general and prophecy in

---

[107] The details are as follows: φυλάσσω (Gal 6.13; Rom 2.26); ποιέω (Gal 3.10,12; 5.3; cf. Rom 2.13,14); ἐμμένω (Gal 3.10); πράσσω (Rom 2.25); τελέω (Rom 2.27); δουλεύω (Rom 7.25); ὑποτάσσομαι (Rom 8.7).

[108] But Paul does use ἱστάνω in Rom 3.31 and describes Christian duty as τήρησις ἐντολῶν θεοῦ (1 Cor 7.19). It is just possible that Rom 2.13-14, 26-27 refer to Gentile Christians.

[109] See Betz, *Galatians*, 275; Westerholm, 'On Fulfilling the Whole Law'.

[110] C.F.D. Moule, 'Fulfilment-Words in the New Testament: Use and Abuse', *NTS* 14 (1967-8) 293-320.

particular.[111] The significance of Paul's use of this verb in relation to the law has less often been recognized. But there is no reason to doubt that he also uses it to describe the total realization of God's will in line with the eschatological fulness of time in the coming of Christ.[112]

ii) We may also suggest that Paul chose this vocabulary partly because of its *ambiguity*! To say that 'the whole law is fulfilled in one command' leaves unclear the status of the rest of the commandments. To describe the law as 'summed up' in the love-command would give the impression that all of it is to be obeyed (as an expression of love), while to say that it has been 'reduced' to the love-command would involve an explicit renunciation of the rest of the law, perhaps more than Paul is willing to concede at this point in his argument. 'Fulfilment' conveys a stronger impression of satisfying the law's demands without the exactitude implicit in such terms as 'doing' or 'keeping' the law.[113] In this way Paul is able to make a strong argument in favour of his concern for love (it fulfils the law [of Christ]) at the same time as he urges the Galatians not to observe some of the law's requirements. Thus Räisänen is right to observe that Paul's 'looseness of speech' makes it possible for him 'to impress his Christian readers on the emotional level' (28), although he does not note that this is particularly the case with regard to

---

[111] The meaning of πληρῶσαι in Mt 5.17 is fully discussed by H. Ljungman, *Das Gesetz erfüllen. Matth. 5:17ff. und 3.15 untersucht*, Lund 1954; see also J.P. Meier, *Law and History in Matthew's Gospel. A Redactional Study of Mt. 5:17-48*, Rome 1976, 73-81, Banks, *Jesus and the Law*, 208-213, and U. Luz, 'Die Erfüllung des Gesetzes bei Matthäus (Mt.5.17-20)', *ZTK* 75 (1978) 398-435. It is not impossible that Paul has derived his vocabulary from this, or a similar, saying; but this depends, of course, on whether it is authentic to Jesus (or a very early addition to the Jesus tradition) or a Matthean creation.

[112] See J.C. Fenton, 'Paul and Mark', in *Studies in the Gospels*, ed. D.E. Nincham, Oxford 1955, 89-112, showing how time, Scripture and law are all 'fulfilled' in Paul (92-3).

[113] The ambiguity of Matthew's πληρῶσαι is also often noted; see Räisänen, *Paul and the Law*, 87-8 and M.D. Goulder, *Midrash and Lection in Matthew*, London 1974, 261-2, who suggests that Matthew uses this term as a 'smokescreen' to hide his vacillating conception of Jesus as one who both deepened and abrogated the law's demands.

πληροῦν.[114] Westerholm, who does note the significance of this verb, rightly concludes: 'For Paul it is important to say that Christians "fulfil" the whole law, and thus to claim that their conduct (and theirs alone) fully satisfies the "real" purport of the law in its entirety, while allowing the ambiguity of the term to blunt the force of the objection that certain individual requirements . . . have not been "done".'[115]

We may sum up our conclusions on these verses as follows. In both 5.14 and 6.2 νόμος refers to the Mosaic law and in both verses Paul uses a specialized and somewhat unusual verb, 'to fulfil', in relation to the law. In both cases he sees this fulfilment coming about through love or mutual service, and in 6.2 (no mere 'afterthought')[116] he defines this fulfilment of the law with the genitive τοῦ Χριστοῦ, meaning 'the law as it is redefined through Christ'.

What function do such statements have in Paul's argument? They seem to indicate that, for all his talk of 'dying to the law', Paul is still concerned to show how the moral standards of the law are taken up into and fully realized in the life of the Spirit. In this sense these statements are, as Sanders notes, a 'debating device' as Paul outflanks his opponents by arguing that his ethical path is the real way to fulfil the law.[117] Given the Galatians' attraction to the law, it would have been dangerous to dismiss the significance of the law altogether, but the positive statements Paul makes here

---

[114] Räisänen correctly notes Paul's need to affirm that the law is fulfilled, *Paul and the Law*, 67-8, 71, 82-3, 201, 265; but he fails to see the particular significance of πληροῦν. None of his arguments against Betz's distinction between ποιεῖν and πληροῦν (63-4 n.104) carries conviction (e.g. his appeals to minor textual variants prove nothing about Paul's usage). Most commentators take ποιεῖν and πληροῦν as synonymous, Schlier, *Galater*, 245, Mussner, *Galaterbrief*, 370; cf. Hübner, *Law in Paul's Thought*, 49 n.81.

[115] 'On Fulfilling the Whole Law', 235.

[116] *Pace* Räisänen, *Paul and the Law*, 79: 'the idea of a νόμος τοῦ Χριστοῦ is introduced almost as an afterthought when Paul is no longer discussing the problem of the Torah at all'.

[117] *Paul, The Law and the Jewish People*, 97; the case is strengthened by a comparison with the argument about wisdom in 1 Cor 1-3.

about the law are hedged about with sufficient ambiguity to prevent the impression of reinstating the law (cf. 2.18): Christians do not 'observe' the law, they 'fulfil' it, and they fulfil it through the one love-command and as it is redefined as 'the law of Christ'. The 'looseness of speech' here may be the only way Paul can establish his point without wholly compromising his statements elsewhere about the passing of the era of the law. In this case, *even in relation to the law* there are elements of 'continuity' alongside the sharp discontinuity of the 'new creation'.

Finally we should note that these two references to 'fulfilling the law' are not issued as commands but as indicative statements.[118] Paul does not instruct the Galatians to fulfil the law but assures them that if they love (or bear one another's burdens) they will, in fact, fulfil the law (of Christ).[119] In this way Paul is careful not to present the law as the basis or motivation for love. Elsewhere he will show that love springs from faith (5.6) or from the Spirit (5.22). Thus these statements about the law could not be interpreted as representing a new form of bondage to it but function rather as an assurance that its demands are met by those whose directive power is the Spirit.[120]

Conclusion

We have now investigated a number of key passages in Paul's description of ethics which demonstrate the defensive strategies he employs in order to commend his understanding of Christian morality to the Galatians. We have seen Paul reaffirm Christian

---

[118] In the case of 6.2 this depends on which textual reading one adopts; see above n.83.

[119] Although 5.14 is introduced by γάϱ it does not provide the motivation for love but a demonstration of its effect; cf. Betz, *Galatians*, 275: 'in loving, the Torah is always fulfilled also, but such a statement is made in retrospect'.

[120] Westerholm, 'On Fulfilling the Whole Law', 235: ' "fulfilling" the law is, for Paul, the result of Christian living, the norms of which are stated in quite different terms'. He rightly draws parallels with Rom 8.4 and 13.8-10 and concludes, 'Paul never speaks of the law's fulfilment in prescribing Christian conduct, but only while describing its results' (237).

freedom (5.13a) but define it in terms of the slavery of love (5.13b) and clarify how the warfare between flesh and Spirit ensures that it is not an absolute freedom (5.17b). We have noted the importance of the Spirit-flesh dualism which enables Paul to define the moral threat as 'flesh' (not 'sin') and then to show how this threat has been dealt with through 'crucifixion' (5.24) and can be continually repulsed by the power of the Spirit (5.16-17). This amounts to saying that the Spirit will provide both moral safeguards and moral directives which render the law superfluous (5.18). But walking in the Spirit is more than just an adequate alternative to the law. It also leads to precisely the sort of behaviour which God requires of his people (the 'fruit') and which entirely matches up to the values of the law (5.22-3). Indeed this point is made even more explicit in Paul's references to fulfilling the law (of Christ): here Paul insists that through love (5.14) or mutual burden-bearing (6.2) they will actually fulfil the requirement of the whole Mosaic law, fulfilling it, indeed, as it is redefined and refocused through Christ (6.2).

All of this indicates that we will fail to grasp the significance of the way Paul expresses his moral instruction if we do not see it in the context of his debate with the Galatians. These verses are not an independent or dispassionate account of Christian ethics tacked on to the end of an argumentative letter, but a continuation and completion of the argument. Paul devises his exhortation in such a way as to commend his moral opinions and defend them against accusations of lawlessness or inadequacy. Like any good competitive salesman, Paul distinguishes his policy from the one advocated by his opponents (the threat is 'flesh' not sin; led by the Spirit you are not under the law) while also claiming that it reaches the same goal (bearing fruit; fulfilling the law) by a better means. To a certain extent this last point can only be achieved through employing a certain measure of ambiguity: by a selection of the unobjectionable features of life in the Spirit (5.22-3), by the use of the ambiguous verb 'to fulfil' (less exact than 'observe' or 'do') in relation to the law, and by suggesting a Christian redefinition of that law with the genitive 'of Christ' (6.2). But ambiguity is the price Paul has to pay for his attempt to claim the law in support of his own proposals for Christian morality.

In providing a rationale for the various references to the law in this section, our analysis suggests that Paul is not involved in thoughtless self-contradiction concerning the law – although the ambiguities he resorts to do cover over a certain tension in his attitude to the law. This tension includes the same combination of continuity and discontinuity with Jewish tradition as we saw in relation to Paul's whole theology in this letter. Although, in line with Paul's apocalyptic perspective, the Christian life is lived in the Spirit, not under the law (which is part of the past era), yet from the perspective of salvation-history and the 'fulfilment' of God's purposes in Christ, it can be said that Christian love 'fulfils' the whole law. Thus Paul's more 'positive' references to the law in 5.13ff. are not wholly irreconcilable with the earlier parts of the letter, especially since they do not reinstate the law in a 'third use' as a code to be observed, but merely state that by walking in the Spirit through love the Galatians will in fact fulfil its demand.

Given sufficient space (i.e. another book!) we could follow through these same points in relation to Paul's other major discussion of the law in Romans. Despite the many differences between these two letters, we also find in Romans the combination of statements about dying to the law (7.1-6) with others about fulfilling it (8.4; 13.8-10; cf. 3.31); and again the fulfilment language serves to protect Paul from implying the necessity of detailed observance of its commands since, as a matter of fact, some of his specific instructions (e.g. in 14.1-6) contradict the rules of the law. When he describes Christ as the τέλος νόμου (10.4) Paul may again be exploiting the ambiguity of a term, since τέλος can mean both 'termination' and 'goal'.[121] As in Galatians, this ambiguity arises from a deep-seated tension in Paul's theological perspective which combines the apocalyptic dualism of the Adam-Christ typology (5.12-21) with a conviction

---

[121] See the recent book by R. Badenas, *Christ, the End of the Law. Romans 10:4 in Pauline Perspective,* Sheffield 1985 and my review in *JTS* 38 (1987) 170-173.

that God's covenant promises to Israel are irrevocable (chs. 9-11). Perhaps we may conclude that in each letter Paul is not only fighting to establish a difficult argument but also himself struggling to rethink and re-express the obligations of God's people in the light of the constancy of God and the radically new events of the resurrection and the inclusion of Gentiles by faith.[122]

---

[122] In the final chapter I will explore the implications of these points more fully in comparison with current scholarship on Paul and the law.

Chapter Five

The Practical Value of the Spirit

In the verses which we have studied thus far, mostly in 5.13-25, we have noted a defensive and argumentative purpose in Paul's remarks: he is concerned to show that the Spirit provides moral direction, overcomes moral dangers ('the flesh') and produces the sort of behaviour which fulfils the demand of the whole law. All of this is entirely necessary if he is to assure the Galatians that they can 'live to God' without submitting to the 'yoke' of the law. But these verses have not given much in the way of practical moral instruction. It was suggested above (pp. 68-71) that the Galatians were attracted to the law partly because it provided a comprehensive code of behaviour. In our survey of the main themes in the body of Paul's letter we have noted his concern to link identity to behaviour, to describe the truth of the gospel *and* to urge the Galatians to obey it. But his outline descriptions of the Christian life – living by faith, continuing in the Spirit, faith working through love – remained on an extremely general level. And even in 5.13-25 the only detailed instructions Paul has provided have been the lists of 'works of the flesh' and 'fruit of the Spirit'. His remark in 5.21 ('I warn you, as I warned you before, that those who do such things shall not inherit the kingdom of God') suggests that the Galatians were already familiar with at least some of the contents of one of these lists. But we could well understand if they wanted to know how such abstract qualities as 'peace' and 'goodness' were to be displayed in practice. It therefore seems worthwhile to enquire whether the rest of Paul's exhortation (5.26-6.10) goes any way to provide the Galatians with a clearer idea of what it means to 'walk in the Spirit'.

146

It is interesting to observe that Gal 5.26–6.10 are verses often largely or wholly neglected in discussions of the letter, although a few particularly noticeable remarks ('the law of Christ', 6.2; sowing to the Spirit or the flesh, 6.7-8) tend to receive attention. One reason for this is that there is continuing uncertainty about the relevance of these various maxims for the Galatian churches in their present crisis. Is this passage a collection of independent instructions randomly thrown together and dealing with general matters of Christian morality? Or is it carefully constructed to meet particular needs in the Galatian churches? Or is its true character somewhere between these two extremes? Two problems are intertwined here – the problem of *structure* and the problem of *relevance* – and it will be best to consider each in turn.

The Problems of Paul's Collection of Maxims

(a) The first problem concerns the internal *structure* of this part of Paul's letter, a matter which has rarely been given thorough investigation. Many scholars assume that we have here a random collection of titbits of moral advice. O'Neill, who, as we saw in chapter one, regards the whole section (5.13–6.10) as an interpolation, goes so far as to say that 'there is no connection between one admonition and the next, except sometimes a similarity of subject or a catch-phrase; the collector is not pursuing a connected argument'. He thus divides 5.13–6.10 into 'fifteen separate pieces of advice, each stylistically distinct, and distinct in thought, from its neighbour'.[1] As we noted in chapter one (pp. 10-12), Dibelius reaches a similar conclusion on the basis of his generic analysis of 'paraenesis' which contains, by definition, 'groups of sayings very diverse in content, lacking any particular order'.[2] Indeed he discusses Gal 6.1-10 as an example of

---

[1] O'Neill, *Recovery*, 67; cf. 71: 'There is no inner idea running through the collection, although each saying shares the family likeness'.

[2] Dibelius, *James*, 3.

'paraenesis' held together only by the use of artificial catchwords (Stichwörter): he cites βαστάζετε . . . βαστάσει (6.2-5), θερίσει . . . θερίσομεν (6.8-9) and καιρῷ . . . καιρόν (6.9-10). In his view 'one saying is attached to another *simply* because a word or cognate of the same stem appears in both sayings'.[3]

Although most commentators do not endorse Dibelius' generic analysis, Schlier speaks for many when he describes these verses as 'a series of examples which hang together only loosely'.[4] He is not alone in refraining from the attempt to subdivide 5.25-6.10 into component subsections;[5] but other commentators divide the material in 6.1-10 into two parts, some making a break between vv.5 and 6,[6] others between vv.6 and 7.[7] There is also a variety of opinions as to where to mark the beginning of this section of maxims, with 5.25, 5.26 and 6.1 all possible candidates.[8] Most of these judgments are simply stated without argument. The most thorough and self-conscious structural analysis of this passage appears in Betz's commentary but he never explains the criteria by which he subdivides 5.25-6.10 into 11 subsections.[9] In commenting on these verses he treats them as a collection of 'sententiae' arranged 'seriatim' but 'not without organization and structure'; 'the sequence is neither unco-ordinated nor overly systematized; some connection is provided by language and inner logic'.[10] Unfortunately, Betz never discusses what 'inner logic' he discerns here.

[3] *James*, 6, my emphasis.

[4] Schlier, *Galater*, 269: 'eine Reihe von Beispielen, die nur lose miteinander zusammenhängen'.

[5] Cf. Duncan, *Galatians*, 178; Bruce, *Galatians*, 58.

[6] E.g., Lightfoot, *Galatians*, 67; Burton, *Galatians*, 325,334; Meyer, *Galatians*, 320; Ridderbos, *Galatians*, 10, 216-7.

[7] E.g., Lagrange, *Galates*, 155,159; Oepke, *Galater*, 166. Mussner, *Galaterbrief*, 10,402-3 divides the section into three: 5.26-6.5; 6.6; 6.7-10.

[8] For 5.25 are Duncan, Oepke, Schlier, Lührmann, Becker, Betz; for 5.26, Ridderbos, Bonnard, Mussner; for 6.1, Lightfoot, Ellicott, Lagrange, Bruce.

[9] Betz, *Galatians*, 23: one of these 'sections' seems to be merely the address 'brothers', which Betz mistakenly lists as '6.1b'.

[10] *Galatians*, 291-2.

It must be acknowledged, of course, that the attempt to break Paul's letters down into neatly-defined sections is a somewhat artificial procedure. Paul himself does not provide headings and subdivisions (much less chapters and verses!) and we have no right to expect that his thought should be neatly packaged into self-contained units. Gradual transitions, digressions and repetitions are, in fact, entirely characteristic features of his writing.[11] But this means that, if we encounter a part of Paul's letter without an obvious logical sequence, we need not conclude that his various statements are entirely random. Only a study of their content will reveal what, if any, inner connections exist.

At this point it will be simplest to set out my proposed structural analysis of these verses which will be given fuller justification in the exegesis that follows. I take 5.25-26 as the 'heading' for the maxims that follow, with the reference to 'walking by the Spirit' both rounding off the previous discussion of flesh and Spirit and introducing the new collection of instructions.[12] Within this collection we may distinguish the various maxims on thematic grounds: some emphasize the Galatians' corporate responsibilities to one another (A) while others concern the individual's accountability before God (B). The 'structure' of this collection would then appear to be a loose interweaving of these two themes:

5.25-6 The Heading – appeal and prohibition
6.1a   Responsibility to correct a sinning church-member (A)
6.1b   Accountability – 'look to yourself' (B)
6.2   Responsibility to bear the burdens of one another (A)

---

[11] See N.A. Dahl, 'The Missionary Theology in the Epistle to the Romans', in *Studies in Paul*, Minneapolis 1977, 70-94: 'In order to follow the flow of thought in the Pauline letters, one should pay more attention to thematic statements, gradual transitions and "ring compositions" than to the division into chapter and verse or to headings and systematized outlines supplied by modern translations and commentaries'(79).

[12] Cf. Eckert, *Verkündigung*, 142 on 5.25: 'Der Vers kann als Zusammenfassung der bisherigen Erörterungen, zugleich aber auch als Motto über die folgenden Ermahnungen verstanden werden'.

6.3-5   Accountability – 'test your own work, bear your own load'
         (B)
6.6   Responsibility to support those who teach (A)
6.7-8   Accountability – 'how you sow will be how you reap'
         (B)
6.9-10   Responsibility to do good to all men, especially Christians
         (A)

The exegesis that follows will be based on this thematic analysis without suggesting that this is the only way that the text can be understood. Although it is based on an eight-part division, it should be clear that this analysis by no means represents an atomistic understanding of the text. Rather, it aims to highlight its internal connections in the interweaving of the two complementary themes.[13]

(b) The second problem is the *relevance* of these various maxims to the situation of the Galatian churches.[14] The great diversity of opinion on this matter has already been noted in relation to the whole 'paraenetic' section of this letter (see chapter one).

On the one hand, Dibelius denied that these moral maxims were devised or assembled with a view to the concrete problems of the Galatian churches. A number of commentators would concur with his judgment, at least with regard to some of the maxims in 6.1-10;[15] Bonnard can describe them as 'un ensemble indivisible de préceptes moraux courants dans les Églises du premier siècle'.[16]

On the other hand, several scholars have insisted that one 'cannot explain why a supposedly unprovoked exhortation appears in this heated letter in which everything else written seems to be directly called forth by the specific disturbance in

---

[13] Ebeling, *Truth of the Gospel*, 260 notes that 'the passage repeatedly considers the relationship of individuals to themselves and to others from the perspective of their mutual involvement'.

[14] Eckert, *Verkündigung*, 132 considers that 'das Kardinalproblem der Paränese des Galaterbriefes' is 'die Frage nach dem Grad ihrer Situationsbezogenheit'.

[15] See above p. 11 n.31.

[16] Bonnard, *Galates*, 126; cf. Burton, *Galatians*, 334 on 6.6-10: 'the apostle . . . adds exhortations having to do with the general moral and religious life of the churches'.

Galatia'.[17] This has led to a number of attempts to relate some or all of these maxims to particular features of the Galatian crisis. Lütgert and Ropes saw prime evidence here for their 'second-front' – self-styled pneumatics (οἱ πνευματικοί, 6.1) who prided themselves on their possession of the Spirit (6.3-5), despised the local teachers (6.6), arrogantly provoking other Christians (5.26) and engaging in bitter hostility with the 'nomists' in the Galatian churches (5.15, 26).[18] Schmithals took most of the same texts as evidence for Gnostics: their 'emphatic self-assertion' as 'pneumatics' is evidenced in 6.1, while 5.25 bears witness to their failure to associate Spirit-possession with spiritual conduct. Schmithals even describes 'the works of the flesh' as 'typically Gnostic manners of conduct' and considers that 'Gnostic pneumatics are splendidly described by the characterization in Gal. 5.26'.[19] A modified version of the same view is presented by Jewett, who finds in 5.25-6.10 evidence for the Galatians' 'typical Hellenistic misunderstanding about the Spirit', where enthusiasm led to the blurring of ethical distinctions, the 'scornful rejection of the impending future judgment' (6.5-10) and a proud self-centredness (5.26; 6.3-4) which dispensed with teachers (6.6).[20] Other interpreters see evidence in 6.1 for a charismatically-endowed 'spiritual' élite (Barrett)[21] or the sort of 'flagrant misconduct' which provoked the Galatians' search for a means to deal with transgressions (Betz).[22] A few find in 6.6-10 an allusive appeal for the Galatians to remedy their tardiness in contributing to Paul's collection for Jerusalem.[23]

---

[17] L.W. Hurtado, 'The Jerusalem Collection and the Book of Galatians', *JSNT* 5 (1979) 46-62 at 54; cf. Ropes, *Singular Problem*, 22: 'nor is mere general advice to be expected in this epistle, with its manifest definiteness of purpose'.

[18] Lütgert, *Gesetz und Geist*, 9-21; Ropes, *Singular Problem*, 25, 42.

[19] Schmithals, *Gnostics*, 46-49, 52-53.

[20] Jewett, 'Agitators', 209-212.

[21] Barrett, *Freedom and Obligation*, 78-9.

[22] Betz, *Galatians*, 295-6.

[23] Lightfoot, *Galatians*, 55,216; Hurtado, 'Jerusalem Collection'; Borse, *Standort*, 37-8,145.

Some of these attempts to find 'relevance' for these maxims must be judged as an over-enthusiastic misuse of 'mirror-reading' (see above pp.37-41). In several cases, for instance, everything hinges on taking Paul's ὑμεῖς οἱ πνευματικοί (6.1) as an ironic echo of the Galatians' self-designation. There may be good reason to take such a phrase as ironic in 1 Corinthians (2.13; 3.1; 12.1; 14.37 etc.), but the evidence in Galatians suggests that Paul could here describe all his converts as 'spiritual' without any intended irony (3.2-5; 5.25).[24] We should also be wary of assertions that mutual provocation and envy (5.26) must apply to Gnostics: experience proves that they do not have a monopoly on these vices! Nor need Paul's references to future judgment imply that the Galatians consciously and scornfully rejected the notion; preachers have always found this motif a valuable sanction even (or especially?) for people who already recognize its seriousness.

The only safe method of procedure here is a cautious use of the mirror-reading criteria outlined in chapter two, with careful attention to the content and emphases of the text. As we have already noted, many of the maxims concern community-life, and at two points in this section Paul makes pointed remarks about community disputes. The most emphatic of these is in 5.15 where he warns the Galatians: 'if you bite and devour one another, beware lest you be consumed by one another'. This warning appears to be more than a merely hypothetical contrast to the love and mutual service enjoined in 5.13-14,[25] and its seriousness is underlined by the subsequent warning in 5.26 about vanity, mutual provocation and envy. In between these two verses comes Paul's list of 'the works of the flesh'. Extensive research on such vice-lists has shown that it would be foolhardy to take them in any simple way as a direct reflection of the sins of the person or

---

[24] Betz, *Galatians*, 296-7; Burton, *Galatians*, 327; Mussner, *Galaterbrief*, 398.

[25] The syntax – εἰ + present indicative – indicates a real and present state; see *BDF*, section 372 and Schlier, *Galater*, 246: 'Es handelt sich um faktische Vorgänge in den galatischen Gemeinden'. Betz's observation, *Galatians*, 277, that Paul's language here is hyperbolic does not justify his reading of the verse as hypothetical.

community addressed.[26] The form and many of the contents are purely traditional and Paul himself admits here that he is echoing an earlier (baptismal?) catalogue.[27] Nonetheless, there may be some significance in the weighting of the vices enumerated and it is therefore important to note that, although the list begins and ends with vices typical in Jewish polemic against Gentiles,[28] its centre consists of a block of eight vices (ἔχθραι, ἔρις, ζῆλος, θυμοί, ἐριθεῖαι, διχοστασίαι, αἱρέσεις, φθόνοι) which relate to the problems of community dissension.[29] While some of these terms are paralleled in other Pauline vice-lists, others are unique to this passage and their heavy concentration suggests that Paul has deliberately emphasized these features of fleshly conduct.[30] When this evidence is taken together with the direct warnings against hostility and envy in 5.15 and 5.26 (where φθονοῦντες echoes φθόνοι in the vice-list), it can be seen that all the relevant mirror-reading criteria (tone, frequency, clarity, unfamiliarity) point towards a situation of discord in the Galatian churches.

---

[26] See especially Vögtle, Tugend- und Lasterkataloge and Wibbing, Tugend- und Lasterkataloge; note also B.S. Easton, 'New Testament Ethical Lists', *JBL* 51 (1932) 1-12 and E. Schweizer, 'Gottesgerechtigkeit und Lasterkataloge bei Paulus (inkl. Kol und Eph)', in Rechtfertigung, ed. J. Friedrich et al., Tübingen 1976, 461-477. This counts against Schmithals' attempt to take all these vices as a reflection of Galatian Gnosticism, *Gnostics*, 52-3.

[27] See Betz, *Galatians*, 281, 284-5 drawing attention to the formula 'inherit the kingdom of God' which may indicate a pre-Pauline catechetical tradition (cf. 1 Cor 6.9-11); cf. G.E. Cannon, *The Use of Traditional Materials in Colossians*, Macon, Georgia 1983, 51-94.

[28] See Wibbing, Tugend- und Lasterkataloge, 86-88. There is no reason to regard these vices as especially Gnostic (Schmithals, *Gnostics*, 52), Celtic (Lightfoot, *Galatians*, 13) or 'South Galatian' (Ramsay, *Galatians*, 446-454)!

[29] Although some MSS add φόνοι after φθόνοι (A C D F G etc; cf. Rom 1.29), it is best omitted (pace Borse, Galater, 200-201); see Metzger, Textual Commentary, 597-8.

[30] ἔρις and ζῆλος are also found together in 1 Cor 3.3 and Rom 13.13 and are combined with θυμοί and ἐριθεῖαι in 2 Cor 12.20. ἔχθραι, διχοστασίαι and αἱρέσεις are used nowhere else in vice-lists and are not common Pauline terms. The list in 2 Cor 12.20 which shows a similar concentration on community strife clearly reflects special problems in the Corinthian church.

This conclusion, which is also held by a wide range of scholars,[31] still leaves open the question of the relationship between the agitators' activities and the dissension in the Galatian churches. It is often assumed that the agitators' presence caused friction between those Galatians who were persuaded by their message and those who were not, and this may receive some support from Paul's description of the agitators as 'those who unsettle you' (οἱ ἀναστατοῦντες ὑμᾶς 5.12).[32] But it is also possible, as was suggested in chapter two, that the disunity of the Galatian churches was one of the causes contributing to the agitators' success: a divided church is more susceptible to the offer of a new identity and a new code of behaviour. These two possibilities are not, of course, mutually exclusive, and the relationship between community-dissension and the desire to become proselytes may be complex. As with the relation between party-spirit and wisdom in the Corinthian church (1 Cor 1-4), it is hard to distinguish between cause and effect.

For our present purposes it is only necessary to note that there is sufficient evidence for communal strife in the Galatian churches and that this may well be the best context in which to understand the various maxims gathered in 5.25-6.10. We must be careful not to draw conclusions too quickly from their form of expression: some scholars seem to have decided in advance that these maxims are of *universal* application (i.e. are not specifically for Galatia)

---

[31] On the specific relevance of the central section of the vice-list and the discord in the Galatian churches see, e.g., Vögtle, *Tugend- und Lasterkataloge*, 30; Easton, 'Ethical Lists', 5-6; Wibbing, *Tugend- und Lasterkataloge*, 91, 95-7; Schweizer, 'Gottesgerechtigkeit', 466-7; Furnish, *Theology and Ethics*, 84-6; Ebeling, *Truth of the Gospel*, 258; and, among the commentators, Bruce, *Galatians*, 250; Bonnard, *Galates*, 113; Lagrange, *Galates*, 149; Mussner, *Galaterbrief*, 383. For a contrary opinion see Becker, *Galater*, 73 and Borse, *Galater*, 193, 207.

[32] Burton, *Galatians*, 297; Mussner, *Galaterbrief*, 373-4; Bornkamm, 'Freiheit', 134-5. It is probably impossible to pinpoint more exactly the nature of such strife (see Oepke, *Galater*, 186) and it is certainly unnecessary to conclude that there were two clearly-defined opposing parties (nomists and 'pneumatics', Lütgert, *Gesetz und Geist*, 9-21).

because many of them are framed in *general* terms.[33] In fact the mixture of general exhortations and specific instructions defies any such neat categorization; only careful exegesis can determine the role these various maxims are intended to play.

The Maxims in 5.25-6.10

i) 5.25-26 The heading – appeal and prohibition

5.25 neatly expresses the familiar Pauline combination of indicative and imperative, set out in chiastic order to emphasize the centrality of the Spirit: εἰ ζῶμεν πνεύματι, πνεύματι καὶ στοιχῶμεν. The Spirit who is the source of the Galatians' life in Christ (3.1-5; 4.4-6) must also be their standard of obedience. Instead of περιπατεῖν (5.16), Paul uses here the unusual term στοιχεῖν, whose particular nuance – to 'walk in line' – seems to indicate that the Spirit is an order or rule to which the Galatians should align themselves.[34] This suggests that Paul is concerned that the Spirit be applied to concrete moral behaviour and that this phrase, as well as rounding off the discussion of flesh and Spirit in 5.13-24, opens the new section of more specific moral instruction. As Betz has noted, Paul's indicative-imperative statements in this chapter may be strategically placed (5.1,13,25) to open up new phases of his instruction.[35] These factors make it appropriate to consider 5.25 as the 'introduction' or 'heading' which establishes the purpose of the following remarks: they spell out more exactly what it means to 'walk in the Spirit' and, as we shall see,

---

[33] Mussner, who follows Dibelius in his assessment of this passage, remarks that 5.26-6.6 are 'allgemeine Ermahnungen, wie die Formulierung in der 1. Person Plural erkennen lässt', *Galaterbrief,* 396, n.1. Meyer, *Galatians,* 320 and Guthrie, *Galatians,* 154 take 6.6-10 as 'general exhortation'.

[34] From the military use (marching in ordered rows) Oepke, *Galater,* 186 interprets its sense here as 'der Marschorder des Geistes folgen'. It is used again in this letter in 6.16.

[35] Betz, *Galatians,* 254-5,294; cf. Ebeling, *Truth of the Gospel,* 241-2.

often do so by drawing directly on the virtues listed as the 'fruit of the Spirit'.

Closely linked with 5.25 in (subjunctive) mood, but acting as the negative foil to its positive exhortation, the following verse issues a prohibition: μὴ γινώμεθα κενόδοξοι, ἀλλήλους προκαλούμενοι, ἀλλήλοις φθονοῦντες. As we have just noted, this verse, together with 5.15 and the emphasis on social sins in 'the works of the flesh', is a clear indication of the social disharmony threatening the Galatian churches. It is precisely this vanity, provocation and envy which mark the breakdown of community life in the Galatian churches. Since Paul gives us no more precise information, it is precarious to attempt to reconstruct exactly who was provoking and envying whom.[36] It is quite clear, however, that Paul is especially concerned with the destructive effects of such provocation and envy for which he considers the root to be vanity or pride, κενοδοξία.[37] Such behaviour stands in the sharpest possible contrast to the 'peace' and 'self-control' listed as the fruit of the Spirit; it is clearly incompatible with walking in the Spirit.

ii) 6.1a Responsibility to correct a sinning church-member

After warning against the dangers of pride and provocation, Paul immediately gives specific instructions about one instance in the life of the congregation which would most naturally give rise to

---

[36] Duncan, *Galatians*, 179 considers that the Jewish-Christians may be provoking their envious Gentile brethren, while Burton, *Galatians*, 323 suggests that the law-abiding Galatians are made envious of the liberty of less scrupulous Christians.

[37] See Oepke on κενόδοξος in *TDNT* III, 662: 'One who is able or who tries to establish an unfounded opinion (κενὴ δόξα), one who talks big, who is boastful and vainglorious'.

these faults -- the occasion of the lapse of a fellow-Christian into sin.[38] In the phrase ἐὰν καὶ προλημφθῇ ἄνθρωπος ἔν τινι παραπτώματι, the meaning of προλημφθῇ is rather uncertain: it could refer to being unexpectedly overtaken by sin, or to being found in sin by another Christian.[39] In either case Paul is more concerned with how to deal with the problem than with the παράπτωμα itself.[40] The event should not be made an occasion for self-righteous condemnation of the sinner, which would only provoke or crush him. Rather, it is an opportunity for spiritual people to display the fruit of the Spirit: ὑμεῖς οἱ πνευματικοὶ καταρτίζετε τὸν τοιοῦτον ἐν πνεύματι πραΰτητος. Paul addresses the Galatians as πνευματικοί since all have received the Spirit (3.2,5)[41] and so he can appeal to them to show a consistent 'spiritual' attitude. πνευματικοί expresses the indicative (cf. εἰ ζῶμεν πνεύματι 5.25) which grounds and necessitates the imperative, καταρτίζετε ἐν πνεύματι πραΰτητος (cf. πνεύματι στοιχῶμεν 5.25). Paul is manifestly applying the basic principle of 5.25 and appealing for the exercise of meekness-and-gentleness (πραΰτης) which is one of the features of the Spirit's fruit (5.23). The Galatians' manner of life in the community, including their treatment of offenders, must be an outworking of their obedience to the Spirit.

[38] Although Paul uses the general term ἄνθρωπος, he seems to be referring to a member of the Christian community. Some have argued that 6.1 opens a new section because of the direct address ἀδελφοί. But this alone is not conclusive: elsewhere in Galatians ἀδελφοί sometimes stands at the head of a section (1.11; 3.15; 4.12; 5.13), but it is also sometimes embedded in the midst of an argument (4.28,31; 5.11). Here it seems that it draws attention to a specific danger illustrating the importance of the injunctions in 5.25-26.

[39] The former is advocated by G. Delling, art. λαμβάνω κτλ, in TDNT IV, 14-15; the latter by Schlier, Galater, 270 and most commentators. Since ἐν can be instrumental or local, both interpretations seem equally possible.

[40] Betz, Galatians, 296 acknowledges this and thus undercuts his own thesis, based on this verse, that Paul is concerned by 'flagrant misconduct' in the Galatian churches.

[41] On the apparent absence of irony here see above, p.152.

iii) 6.1b Accountability – 'look to yourself'

The balance of motifs in this whole section between public responsibility and personal accountability is finely exposed here in the way Paul suddenly shifts from a second person *plural* command to correct *another* (καταρτίζετε τὸν τοιοῦτον) to a second person *singular* command to look to *oneself* (σκοπῶν σεαυτόν).[42] Paul stresses that each individual must be on his guard, particularly, perhaps, those most involved in the work of correction. Self-examination is necessary μὴ καὶ σὺ πειρασθῇς; it arises from the humble recognition that one is just as vulnerable to that sin committed as the brother who is at fault. Thus Paul immediately counters the danger that his instruction may be taken up by self-righteous moral watch-dogs of the community; rather, acknowledgement of one's own vulnerability must exclude all κενοδοξία (5.26). The two parts of 6.1 are bound together, not only by the way they neatly balance each other, but also by the implications of acting ἐν πνεύματι πραΰτητος; for πραΰτης represents both gentleness in dealing with others (1a) and humility in recognition of one's own weakness before God (1b).[43] Thus Paul spells out an application of πρατης in both its aspects and demonstrates its importance for maintaining loving relationships in the community.

iv) 6.2 Responsibility to bear the burdens of one another

The recognition that each member is as liable to fall as any other leads Paul to stress the mutual work of burden-bearing (ἀλλήλων

---

[42] Burton rightly points out that this use of second person singular 'serves to make the exhortation more pointed', *Galatians*, 328; it does so precisely by applying it to each individual.

[43] See F. Hauck and S. Schulz, art. πραΰς, in *TDNT* VI, 645-51 and C. Spicq, 'Bénignité, Mansuétude, Douceur, Clémence', *RB* 54 (1947) 321-339. In secular Greek the noun usually means 'gentleness', while in the LXX, where it often translates עני etc., it includes the notion of humility before God; both nuances are evident here.

is emphatic as first word). He resumes here the theme of v.1a, the support of fellow-Christians, while the focus probably broadens to include any kind of physical, moral or spiritual burden (βάρη).[44] As we saw in the last chapter, this verse echoes Paul's injunction in 5.13-14 to serve one another through a neighbourly love which fulfils the law. In other words, burden-bearing depends on the love (ἀγάπη) which should be the chief characteristic of the Christian community (cf. 5.6). Thus, at least implicitly, Paul is again drawing on the qualities listed as the fruit of the Spirit in 5.22-23; here he shows how the prime virtue, ἀγάπη, is worked out in mutual support. The contrast with 5.26 is pointed up by the way ἀλλήλων echoes the ἀλλήλους . . . ἀλλήλοις of that verse: by walking in the Spirit, the Galatians will fulfil the law of Christ and transform their present mutual provocation into mutual loving support.

v) 6.3-5 Accountability – 'test your own work, bear your own load'

In this cluster of verses Paul's focus returns to the individual member of the community and his self-understanding (εἰ δοκεῖ τις . . . δοκιμαζέτω ἕκαστος . . . ἕκαστος . . . βαστάσει vv.3-vv.3-5). One could sum up their content in terms of self-deceit (v.3), self-testing (v.4) and personal accountability (v.5). Thematically they belong closely together.[45] To reckon yourself to be something when you are nothing (v.3) is precisely the error of vanity which Paul had warned about in the introduction (κενόδοξοι 5.26; cf. δοκεῖ 6.3). Paul's point is probably not that everybody is worth nothing, so that every self-opinion is false;[46] rather, he warns the Galatians (with perhaps a side-glance at the

---

[44] See above, p.132 n.82.

[45] There are also a number of linguistic links (e.g. in uses of ἑαυτός and ἕκαστος).

[46] Pace, e.g., Oepke, Galater, 189; Schlier, Galater, 273; Mussner, Galaterbrief, 400. Hübner, Law in Paul's Thought, 103ff. rightly insists that, according to 6.4, some self-opinion is justified.

Jerusalem apostles, 2.6,9) that it is dangerously easy to overestimate one's own importance and so delude oneself.[47]

Verse 4, then, follows a natural sequence in urging each man to test his own work: ἕκαστος and ἑαυτοῦ stress individual responsibility in this respect. Such self-scrutiny is a favourite theme in Paul's challenge to his churches.[48] The second part of the verse – καὶ τότε εἰς ἑαυτὸν μόνον τὸ καύχημα ἕξει καὶ οὐκ εἰς τὸν ἕτερον – is not easy to interpret. It is usually translated in some such way as 'and then his reason to boast will be in himself alone and not in his neighbour'.[49] This translation takes εἰς to mean 'with reference to' or 'with regard to' and the standard interpretation, given by most commentators, is that Paul is allowing boasting on the basis of one's own work but not by comparison with others. Although this makes reasonable sense in the context and takes καύχημα in its usual sense of 'ground for boasting', it is not unproblematic since it is not easy to see how the two εἰς-clauses match each other.[50] Indeed, a strong case can be made for understanding εἰς in terms of 'direction' and translating the phrase 'and then he will direct his boast to himself alone and not to his neighbour'.[51] If this is correct, the point of

---

[47] φρεναπατᾶν ıs apparently a verb coined here by Paul. Lightfoot comments: 'it brings out the idea of subjective fancies and thus enforces the previous δοκεῖ', *Galatians*, 213. For the possible link with Paul's ironic remarks about οἱ δοκοῦντες εἶναί τι (2.6) see Barrett, *Freedom and Obligation*, 80–81.

[48] Rom 14.22; 1 Cor 3.10-15; 11.28; 2 Cor 13.5; 1 Thess 5.21 etc.

[49] RSV; similarly in AV, NIV, Moffatt.

[50] If the first (εἰς ἑαυτόν) is taken as (boasting) 'in oneself', what would it mean to boast 'in another' (εἰς τὸν ἕτερον)? Alternatively, if the second clause is taken as 'in comparison with another', what can it mean to boast 'in comparison with oneself? The NEB translation, 'then he can measure his achievement by comparing himself with himself and not with anyone else' is the best one can do in this line, but requires a lot to be read into εἰς ἑαυτόν. Hübner's attempt to solve this problem (*Law in Paul's Thought*, 107: comparing one's own work with the demand made on the Christian [5.14]) is even more complex.

[51] This interpretation is rarely canvassed in the major commentaries, although I have noted it in H. Lietzmann, *Die Briefe des Apostels Paulus. 1. Die Vier Hauptbriefe*, Tübingen 1910, 260 ('so behalte er den Ruhm für sich und spiele sich nicht andern gegenüber auf') and Borse, *Galater*, 211. Bruce, *Galatians*, 259, gives a similar translation but no explanation in the commentary on 6.4. For boasting 'in' an achievement or person Paul uses the prepositions ἐν, ἐπί or ὑπέρ. Of the

continued on p.161

Paul's injunction is to minimize rivalry (5.26) and to encourage self-control (see again 5.23 ἐγκράτεια): after testing one's own work one must not flaunt it before others but keep one's boast to oneself.

It is interesting to note that Paul is entirely positive about the work (ἔργον)which must be tested and even acknowledges that it is right to boast about one's work within proper limits.[52] If Paul polemicizes against ἔργα νόμου that is clearly not just because they are something 'worked': even faith works through love (5.6 πίστις δι' ἀγάπης ἐνεργουμένη). Whether the singular ἔργον is significant (in distinction from the plural ἔργα νόμου) we shall have to consider in due course in the light of the whole perspective of these ethical instructions. Here τὸ ἔργον ἑαυτοῦ seems to refer to the basic character of a person's existence,[53] and it is almost certainly this personal achievement which Paul has in mind when he warns the Galatians ἕκαστος γὰρ τὸ ἴδιον φορτίον βαστάσει (6.5). This verse neatly sums up what Paul has been saying about personal accountability;[54] the

---

continued from p.160

occasions when he uses εἰς (cf. 2 Cor 10.13,15,16; 11.10) at least one other probably has the meaning 'boasting to someone': 2 Cor 8.24 τὴν οὖν ἔνδειξιν τῆς ἀγάπης ὑμῶν καὶ ἡμῶν καυχήσεως ὑπὲρ ὑμῶν εἰς αὐτοὺς ἐνδεικνύμενοι εἰς πρόσωπον τῶν ἐκκλησιῶν (see C.K. Barrett, *The Second Epistle to the Corinthians*, London 1973, 230). Cf. Rom 4.2 ἔχει καύχημα ἀλλ' οὐ πρὸς θεόν.

[52] The difficulty of most commentators, who approach these verses with the prior assumption that 'boasting in works' is incompatible with Pauline theology, is well evidenced in Schlier, *Galater*, 274, Mussner, *Galaterbrief*, 401 and E. Synofzik, *Die Gerichts- und Vergeltungsaussagen bei Paulus*, Göttingen 1977, 44. Hübner, *Law in Paul's Thought*, 105-8 rightly underlines Paul's positive view here. The response to Hübner by G. Klein, 'Werkruhm und Christusruhm im Galaterbrief und die Frage nach einer Entwicklung des Paulus', in *Studien zum Text und zur Ethik des Neuen Testaments*, ed. W. Schrage, Berlin 1986, 196-211 is not ultimately convincing, although his interpretation of εἰς ἑαυτόν . . . εἰς τὸν ἕτερόν (208-9, appealing to Phil 2.16) comes quite close to that advocated here.

[53] Hübner, *Law in Paul's Thought*, 104: 'the basic "set" of his existence in so far as this finds expression in activity'.

[54] γάρ indicates the ground for both the previous verses and is not, *pace* Betz, *Galatians*, 303, 'simply marking the addition of a similar statement'.

burden (φορτίον) to be borne seems to represent the weight not of suffering or sin but of responsibility before God.[55] The sentiment initially appears to be in contradiction to 6.2 which it echoes (βαστάζετε . . . βαστάσει); but the two verses fit well alongside each other because, as we have begun to demonstrate, this whole section is composed of the interweaving of two complementary themes – mutual responsibility and personal accountability.[56] While supporting and correcting others, the individual believer must look to himself, test himself and bear his own responsibility. It is possible, though not certain, that the future tense (βαστάσει) looks particularly to the final judgment.[57]

vi) 6.6 Responsibility to support those who teach

Many commentators are puzzled by this verse. The reference to those who teach and those who are taught the word appears suddenly without any contextual connections and seems to refer to specific details of community life for no obvious reason. 'The subject is new, having no direct relation to the topic of the epistle as a whole', declares Burton, while Mussner refers to the way that Paul 'schaltet . . . überraschenderweise in V 6 eine eigenartige Mahnung ein'.[58] However, at least part of the difficulty is solved

[55] So most commentators (Mussner, *Galaterbrief*, 401-2 excepted). Cf. φορτίον in the sense of duty/responsibility in Epictetus, *Diss* 2.9.22 (cited by Betz ad loc.).
[56] Burton comments: 'The paradoxical antithesis to v.2a is doubtless conscious and intentional . . . It is the man who knows he has a burden of his own that is willing to bear his fellow's burden', *Galatians*, 334.
[57] Cf. 5.10 ὁ δὲ ταράσσων ὑμᾶς βαστάσει τὸ κρίμα. An eschatological reference is supported by Mussner, Bonnard, Bruce and Schlier, but denied by Betz ('the future tense is gnomic . . . not eschatological', *Galatians*, 304). There is an interesting parallel in 4 Ezra 7.104-5.
[58] Burton, *Galatians*, 335; Mussner, *Galaterbrief*, 402. Bonnard considers that all attempts to integrate this saying into the context 'sont aujourd'hui abandonnés', *Galates*, 125.

when it is seen how the two themes of individual and corporate responsibility interweave throughout this passage. Just as the command to restore others is balanced by the need to look to oneself (v.1), so the emphasis on bearing one's own burden (v.5) must be balanced by the acknowledgment that there are those in the congregation who need particular support (v.6). In this way δέ could signal a mild contrast to the previous verse, while the thought-content echoes and amplifies that of 6.2: the κοινωνία that should abound in the Christian congregation (as it operated also between Paul and the Jerusalem apostles, 2.9) is an expression of bearing one another's burdens. The fact that Paul singles out those who 'teach the word' need not imply any particular scandalous abuse of the Galatians' teachers;[59] as those who were most responsible for the spiritual welfare of the congregations and obviously in need of their support, it is natural that here, as elsewhere in discussing Christian community life, Paul's attention should focus on the teachers.[60] That the student should share his goods with his teacher (κοινωνείτω . . . ἐν πᾶσιν ἀγαθοῖς) is, once again, a practical application of the fruit of the Spirit: the Galatians are to walk in the Spirit by exercising ἀγαθωσύνη (cf. 5.22).[61] The love and goodness of life in the Spirit find an extremely practical expression in the support of the teachers with 'all good things'.

---

[59] See above pp.151-2. Eckert, *Verkündigung*, 146-7 suggests that the agitators would be particularly hostile to the teachers as those who remained most faithful to Paul. There is nothing to justify Hurtado's suggestion that ὁ κατηχῶν τὸν λόγον refers to the Jerusalem church, 'Jerusalem Collection', 54-5.

[60] Cf. Paul's discussion of the support of Christian workers in 1 Cor 9; 2 Cor 11.7-11; 1 Thess 2.7-10; Phil 4.10-11, and the logion of Christ echoed in Mt 10.10; Lk 10.7; 1 Cor 9.14; 1 Tim 5.18. What makes this verse distinctive is that the teachers appear to be resident among the Galatian Christians while deriving at least some of their livelihood from the support of the churches. Unfortunately we cannot tell how many were in this category or how widespread this practice had become.

[61] Most commentators take τὰ ἀγαθά as material goods, but Oepke, who takes κοινωνείτω in the sense 'let him receive in fellowship', has to interpret it as spiritual blessings (students do not usually receive *material* benefits from their teachers!), *Galater*, 192-3 (cf. Meyer, *Galatians*, 327-331). But elsewhere κοινωνεῖν clearly means the fellowship of giving (Rom 12.13; cf. Barn 19.8), while Oepke's reading makes Paul's comment largely pointless.

vii) 6.7-8 Accountability – 'how you sow will be how you reap'

Paul now offers a final statement on the personal accountability of each person (ἄνθρωπος v.7) before God. It opens with an appeal to the Galatians not to let themselves be deceived (μὴ πλανᾶσθε); they must face reality, since the God who watches over oaths (1.20) and shows no partiality (2.6) is not mocked (οὐ μυκτερίζεται).[62] Paul illustrates the justice of God's dealings with mankind by appealing to a well-known illustration: 'what a man sows, that will he also reap'. This agricultural proverb was apparently familiar in most ancient cultures and is common in both Jewish and early Christian writings.[63] Here Paul adapts it to his own purposes: in v.8 he changes the image slightly from the seed sown (ὃ ἐὰν σπείρῃ) to the soil into which it is sown (ὁ σπείρων εἰς τὴν σάρκα . . . εἰς τὸ πνεῦμα), and applies it to the antithesis of flesh and Spirit which he has employed throughout this letter (cf. 3.3; 4.29; 5.13ff.).

This final reference to flesh/Spirit sums up Paul's exhortation, and, indeed, the message of the whole letter. To sow to one's own flesh (εἰς τὴν σάρκα ἑαυτοῦ) is to indulge in pride, envy and other 'works of the flesh' which Paul has highlighted; and it includes, on a broader scale, any activity which remains bound to a purely human way of life (see below, chapter six).[64] All one can

---

[62] Although the language here is strong, there is no indication (pace Jewett, 'Agitators', 211-2) that the Galatians were wilfully or consciously rejecting the notion of divine judgment.

[63] In Greek and Latin literature, see, e.g., Plato, Phdr 260d; Demosthenes, Cor 159; Cicero, Orat, 2.65; Plautus, Mer 71. In the OT, Job 4.8; Ps 126.5; Prov 22.8; Hos 8.7 etc. In Philo, Conf 21,152; Mut 268-9; Som 2.76 etc.; cf. Test Levi 13.6; 4 Ezra 4.28ff. In the NT, Lk 19.21-2; Jn 4.35-6; 1 Cor 9.11; 2 Cor 9.6.

[64] Oepke, Galater, 195 explains the use of ἑαυτοῦ here as 'um die enge, egozentrische Beziehung zwischen Mensch und Fleisch zum Ausdruck zu bringen'; but see below pp.203-12. On the analogy of the use of the sowing-reaping theme in relation to generosity in 2 Cor 9.6, Lightfoot, Galatians, 13-14,55,216, Burton, Galatians, 339-40 and Borse, Galater, 214-6 take these verses as giving incentive specifically for the liberality envisaged in 6.6. But the proverb is too common, and the categories 'flesh' and 'Spirit' too broad, to restrict the reference in this way.

expect to reap from that way of life is 'destruction' (φθορά).[65] But
to sow to the Spirit is to walk in line with the Spirit's directions: it
is to put into practice 'the fruit of the Spirit' (the one agricultural
metaphor recalls the other) and to apply it to the community in
the ways in which Paul has been urging. The result that one can
expect to reap from the Spirit is 'eternal life' (ζωὴ αἰώνιος; cf.
5.25 εἰ ζῶμεν πνεύματι . . .). The choice of sowing to Spirit or
flesh is the choice of a person's basic direction in life. Paul can
admit only these two possibilities which signify, for him, the
choice between obeying and disobeying the truth.

viii) 6.9-10 Responsibility to do good to all unfailingly

This final couplet returns to the theme of mutual responsibility
expressed in two synonymous clauses: τὸ καλὸν ποιοῦντες . . .
ἐργαζώμεθα τὸ ἀγαθόν. The hortatory subjunctive here sums up
the section in the same mood as it began (5.25-6), while linguistic
links tie these two verses to what preceded (θερίσει v.8,
θερίσομεν v.9) and to each other (καιρῷ v.9, καιρόν v.10). In
fact these verses make clear what has been implicit throughout,
that one's individual accountability is partly concerned with how
one fulfils one's responsibilities to others: a man sows to the Spirit
(and reaps the happy consequence) precisely by doing good to all.
Thus the two themes, though distinct, are not mutually exclusive
but complement and explicate each other; and Paul's use of catch-
words here is by no means artificial but represents a fundamental
connection of thought. Paul urges the Galatians to do good,
conscious that they may not only be deceived (vv.3,7) but also
grow weary (ἐγκακεῖν) and become faint (ἐκλύειν).[66] He

---

[65] Cf. the association of σάρξ and θάνατος in Rom 8.6, 13. The reaping
metaphor and the future tense suggest the final judgment (Hos 6.11; Joel 4.13; 4
Ezra 4.26-32; Mt 13.39; Rev 14.14-20 etc.).

[66] The two verbs are almost synonymous but may , perhaps, be distinguished
as losing heart (ἐγκακεῖν) and losing strength (ἐκλύειν), Lightfoot, *Galatians*,
217. On the textual variants in 6.9-10 see Barrett, *Freedom and Obligation*, 117
n.66.

encourages them to persevere since only those who do so will reap their reward 'in due time' (καιρῷ . . . ἰδίῳ v.9).[67] Such perseverance requires all the patience which comes from the fruit of the Spirit (μακροθυμία 5.22) as the Galatians wait for the 'due time'. This eschatological perspective leads on to a concluding appeal (ἄρα οὖν) to do good to all men 'while we have opportunity' (ὡς καιρὸν ἔχομεν). Once again the 'goodness' (ἀγαθωσύνη) of the fruit of the Spirit is applied in doing good (τὸ ἀγαθόν) to all. The verbs here make clear that such fruit is not simply received, but involves work and activity (ποιοῦντες v.9, ἐργαζώμεθα v.10) which correspond to the ἔργον that must be tested (v.4). The scope of this beneficence is universal – 'to all' – but the final clause (μάλιστα δὲ πρὸς τοὺς οἰκείους τῆς πίστεως) signifies the priority of the Christian community. Although the universalism of the initial statement is not thereby revoked,[68] this final clause is a revealing indication of the restricted scope of Paul's exhortation. Throughout this passage his prime concern has been with relationships and responsibilities within the churches, in the household bound together by their faith in Christ (οἱ οἰκεῖοι τῆς πίστεως).[69] It is here that particular problems appear to have arisen and this therefore constitutes a crucial test whether the Galatians will continue to walk in the Spirit.

[67] καιρός may be especially appropriate as it is often used for the time of harvest (Mt 13.30; Mk 11.13; Acts 14.17) as well as for the end of history (Mk 13.33; 1 Thess 5.1; 1 Cor 4.5; 7.29; Rev 1.3 etc.).

[68] Betz, *Galatians*, 311: 'It is not intended to revoke the preceding high-flying universalism, but to direct the attention of the readers to the concrete historical reality of the Christian community'. Contrast Montefiore, 'Thou Shalt Love', 161-3.

[69] For the church as a household cf. 1 Cor 3.9-17; 2 Cor 6.14-16; Eph 2.19-22. The frequency of this metaphor undermines Hurtado's attempt to read οἰκεῖοι τῆς πίστεως as a specific reference to the Jerusalem church, 'Jerusalem Collection', 53-57.

The Purpose of These Maxims

Our analysis of these verses inevitably leads to the conclusion that they are no mere appendix added to the letter by way of conventional moral advice. Rather, they represent Paul's desire to give concrete instructions, to spell out for the Galatians in practical terms what it means to 'walk in the Spirit'. Many of these maxims function as practical illustrations of the ingredients of 'the fruit of the Spirit' – e.g. πραΰτης (6.1), ἀγάπη (6.2), ἐγκράτεια (5.26; 6.4), μακροθυμία (6.9-10) and ἀγαθωσύνη (6.6,10) – and thus serve to 'earth' these abstract qualities in detailed moral instruction.[70] Throughout Paul endeavours to remind the Galatians of their accountability to God and their responsibilities to one another and he is especially concerned with the problems of pride and dissension in the Galatian churches which threaten to destroy them altogether. He appeals to them to sow to the Spirit having shown that only the fruit of the Spirit can counteract and overcome these problems in their midst.

The exegesis just propounded helps to corroborate the solutions suggested above to the problems of structure and relevance. These verses are not structured in a series of logical steps, but neither are they a purely random collection of remarks. Following on the introductory exhortation and warning in 5.25-6, they develop the two main themes of personal accountability and corporate responsibility which constantly balance each other throughout this section. They are held together by more than just catch-words, and even verses like 6.6 can be seen to be integrated with the whole pattern. We can also safely conclude that these various maxims are by no means irrelevant to the Galatian churches but are intended to meet their general problems of strife and division. We cannot take every detail in the list of vices as a reflection of a flagrant error in Galatia or relate each remark to a

---

[70] On Paul's ability to give concrete application of his general ethical exhortations see Schrage, *Einzelgebote*, 61-64.

particular or immediate crisis. There is therefore no solid evidence for 'Gnostic', 'libertine' or 'Hellenistic' tendencies among the Galatian Christians. Rather, the issues which Paul picks out – the restoration of a sinning brother, the dangers of boasting, the need to support teachers – are prime examples of situations where communal strife can break out. The general form of expression of some of the maxims (5.26; 6.2; 6.5; 6.7-10) does not preclude them from being applied, as here, to the particular problems of the Galatian churches, while the specific form of others (6.1; 6.3-4; 6.6) need not imply reference to an immediate scandalous incident.[71] Only by a careful observation of Paul's emphasis – the points to which he returns and on which he lays most stress – can we see the issues that lie behind these maxims, viz. Paul's overriding concern for the unity and harmony of the Galatian churches which he believes to be under a most serious threat. By discussing these problems under the rubric of 'walking in the Spirit' Paul is able to present to the Galatians the same choice of flesh or Spirit which he has forced upon them throughout the letter.

There is also another respect in which these exhortations cohere well with the rest of the letter. As we noted in chapter three, Paul's objection to the 'works of the law' was on the grounds that these represented the imposition of Jewish cultural standards on Gentile believers. His vision of the Christian community is one in which there is no 'Jew' or 'Gentile', for all are one in Christ (3.28). He disapproved of Peter's withdrawal from table-fellowship (2.12) and the agitators' exclusion of the Galatians (4.17) since both caused strife and division within the Christian fellowship. Thus in providing instructions for the new community, in which old social and cultural barriers are overcome, he naturally emphasizes the bonds of love and fellowship which should bind them together. If the truth of the gospel concerns unity in Christ,

---

[71] See O.M.T. O'Donovan, 'The Possibility of a Biblical Ethic', *TSF Bulletin* 67 (1973) 15-23 on the distinction between 'universal'/'particular' as relating to the *audience in view* in any ethical statement and 'general'/'specific' as describing its *mode of expression*.

it must be obeyed in mutual burden-bearing and the commitment to serve one another in love. Just as the paraenesis in Romans climaxes with the appeal (to Jewish and Gentile Christians) to 'welcome one another, as Christ has welcomed you' (Rom 15.7), so Paul in Galatians closes his argument for justification by faith with the vision of a 'household of faith' committed to doing good to all (6.10).

These observations, however, give rise to another important question: to what extent do these maxims provide the Galatians with sufficient moral instruction? At least two factors are involved in this question of 'sufficiency' – the *scope* of Paul's instructions and their *style*.

As regards scope, it is clear that Paul has touched on only a few moral issues here. There are a host of other matters which the Galatians might well have wanted precise instruction about but which are not even broached in these brief exhortations. If the Galatians were looking for anything like a comprehensive code of behaviour, they would surely have been disappointed with this! It appears that Paul prefers to discuss in detail only those matters which he knows to be problematic in the Galatian churches – the in-fighting that threatens to destroy them altogether (5.15). It may be that he hopes that once the churches are restored to harmony they will together be able to discern the will of God under the leading of the Spirit (cf. Phil 2.1-5; 1 Thess 5.12-22). Or perhaps he is confident that the 'teachers' (6.6) will be able to provide further moral guidance.

The style of Paul's instruction is, as we have noted, a mixture of catalogues of vices and virtues, general exhortations and specific examples. Again, if the Galatians were hoping for codifiable rules and regulations, they would not have been well satisfied by what Paul offers. To be sure, Paul does give some detailed commands, as for instance in 6.1 and 6.6.[72] But even these community rules are incapable of casuistic application for there is still a considerable

---

[72] Drane's remark that 'such exhortations do not constitute moral rules in any sense whatever' (see above p.30) appears somewhat exaggerated.

latitude of interpretation in such phrases as 'a spirit of gentleness' or 'with all good things'.

Thus if, as we have suggested, one reason for Paul's exhortation in 5.13–6.10 is to provide a clearer description of morality under the leading of the Spirit, we must conclude that it still falls short of what the Galatians may have been looking for in the Mosaic law. This indeed highlights the precariousness of Paul's position with regard to ethics: he appears to be unwilling (or unable) to provide his Gentile converts with the detailed moral advice they often required. In the final chapter we will consider this problem more fully.

The Significance of 'Parallels'

The verses in Gal 5–6 which we have been studying in this chapter are a valuable 'test-case' for another important aspect of Paul's ethics: the extent to which he 'borrows' material from contemporary Jewish or Hellenistic ethical traditions. This question has received special attention from H.D. Betz in his commentary on these verses, where he has drawn on his extensive knowledge of Hellenistic moral and philosophical literature. It will be convenient, therefore, to discuss this question with particular reference to Betz's thorough work on the matter.

It is Betz's conviction that Paul's instructions in these verses both conform to and draw from contemporary popular philosophy to a notable degree. In commenting on the catalogue in 5.19–23 he remarks that, with the exception of ἀγάπη, 'all concepts are common in Hellenistic philosophy' (281); 'the individual concepts are not in any way specifically "Christian", but represent the conventional morality of the time' (282). Much the same can be said of the maxims or 'sententiae' in 5.25–6.10: 'With regard to the content of the *sententiae*, there is little that is specifically Christian . . . The Christian is addressed as an educated and responsible person. He is expected to do no more than what would be expected of any other educated person in the Hellenistic culture of the time. In a rather conspicuous way Paul conforms to the ethical thought of his contemporaries' (292).

Such general statements are backed up with detailed evidence relating to practically every clause in these verses. Although 'extensive research has not turned up *verbatim* parallels' (291), Betz adduces a host of quotations and references which he considers to be analogous to Paul's maxims. Many of Paul's terms, for instance, are said to derive from Hellenistic philosophy or the diatribe literature. ἐγκράτεια (5.23) 'was a central concept of Hellenistic ethics' (288), the term κενόδοξος (5.26) 'is well-known from Hellenistic philosophy' (294); καταρτίζειν (6.1) is 'another highly significant concept from Hellenistic philosophy' (297), and σκοπῶν (6.1) and τὸ καλὸν ποιεῖν (6.9) derive from the same source (298, 309). But the parallels go much further than mere vocabulary. On frequent occasions Betz cites sentiments from contemporary Hellenistic literature similar to Paul's maxims and thus notes that the content of his instructions 'does not transcend similar maxims in Hellenistic literature' (298, on 6.1). He considers that 'the anthropological tradition in which Paul stands goes back to early Greek thought' (301, on 6.3), or even that Paul's maxim (in 6.4) 'contains, implicitly as well as explicitly, a number of ethical doctrines which are shared by Greek philosophers and the Apostle' (302).

On a few occasions Betz notes that the language of these maxims 'must . . . be understood in the context of Pauline theology' (297, cf. 302) and he remarks on some basic differences between Paul and Hellenistic philosophy: for Paul, the ground of boasting (6.3) 'is divine grace, and not reason, as it is for the philosophers' (303), and self-sufficiency (6.5) comes not through philosophy but from 'the Christian faith and the guidance of the Spirit' (304). But even in this case Betz still considers that Paul shares the 'Hellenistic concept of "self-sufficiency"' (304). His verdict on 6.6 is therefore typical of his whole approach: 'the content is not specifically Christian, but can be understood on the basis of its parallels in Hellenistic diatribe literature. The Christian meaning, therefore, is secondary and must be concluded on the basis of the present context' (305).

At first sight Betz's case seems persuasive and his evidence, listed in copious footnotes, quite overwhelming. He has an expertise in this area as great as any other living New Testament scholar. On closer inspection, however, many of his statements turn out to be insufficiently supported by the evidence he adduces. His discussion is sometimes based on the unwarranted assumption that 'terms' and 'concepts' are identical, i.e., that concepts are not only expressed by, but also to be equated with, particular units of vocabulary. This is especially misleading when such vocabulary units are discussed in isolation from the network of sentences in which they appear. This type of analysis leads Betz into such confusing statements as that 'the concept of "goodness" (ἀγαθωσύνη) represents a late development in the Greek language; it may come from Hellenistic Judaism' (288, the footnote refers to the first uses of the *term* in the LXX).[73] A similar confusion must lie behind Betz's quite remarkable statement on τὸ καλὸν ποιεῖν in 6.9: 'the language comes from Hellenistic philosophy' (309). But this vocabulary is surely about the most common in all Greek literature! And this remark by Betz also highlights another major problem in his discussion: he is constantly comparing Paul with an extremely generalized entity called 'diatribe literature' or 'Hellenistic philosophy'. This can apparently include everything from Plato to Marcus Aurelius, taking in such strange bedfellows as Epicurus, Aristotle and Philo on the way! It is quite baffling to see how Betz can lump all these multifarious sources together as a uniform yardstick against which to measure Paul, when elsewhere he (quite rightly) draws careful distinctions between Paul's own letters![74]

However, the validity of Betz's detailed comments can only be tested fairly in each individual case. Taking an example almost at random, we might consider his remarks on Gal 6.1b, ὑμεῖς οἱ πνευματικοὶ καταρτίζετε τὸν τοιοῦτον ἐν πνεύματι

---

[73] For a devastating critique of the constant confusion between 'term' and 'concept' in *TDNT* see J. Barr, *The Semantics of Biblical Language*, Oxford 1961, chapter 8.

[74] See, e.g, *Galatians*, 141 (on 3.7), 165 (on 3.19) and 176: 'we must be very careful not to simply harmonize Galatians with Romans'.

πραΰτητος, σκοπῶν σεαυτὸν μὴ καὶ σὺ πειρασθῇς. Betz describes καταρτίζειν as 'another highly significant concept from Hellenistic philosophy, where it describes the work of the philosopher-"psychotherapist" and educator' (297). He cites in support a phrase from Plutarch, *Cato Minor* 65.5 where philosophers are urged to persuade an obstinate man to save his life and so restore him to what is best for him (καταρτίσαι πρὸς τὸ συμφέρον). This is all very well as an isolated example of a similar use of καταρτίζειν (although in Plutarch it is restoring a man from his folly, not, as in Paul, from his 'transgression'), but the claim that this is a 'highly significant concept from Hellenistic philosophy' needs considerably more support than this. In his footnote (43) Betz refers to a number of texts from Plutarch, Epictetus, Philo, the letter of Aristeas, Lucian and Pliny. These various authors hardly represent a unitary philosophical perspective, and the texts here cited are in fact a remarkable hotchpotch. Some use a term from the καταρτίζειν root, but in two of these (Plutarch, *Alex* 7.1; *Them* 2.5-6) it means 'training' not 'restoration', and in one it is used for massaging the body (Epictetus, *Diss* 3.20.10 – compared to the good effect of being reviled by an opponent). None of the other texts uses καταρτίζειν or any cognate of it. This in itself would not be a problem had not Betz given the impression that the *term* was significant. If in fact he means the *concept* 'restoration', he could have dispensed with his references to texts using καταρτίζειν (which, as we have just seen, are hardly relevant anyway) and concentrated on the remarks in 'Hellenistic philosophy' about restoring fellow human beings. In fact he does have one good example of this (Lucian, *Demonax* 7) but other references concern leniency in judgment on others (Pliny, *Ep* 8.22.1; Ep Arist 191) which is hardly the same as restoration. Moreover, two other texts cited are not even remotely analogous to Paul's statement (Epictetus *Diss* 4.9.16 – if you will it, you can reform yourself; Ep Arist 281 – a good general saves the lives of his soldiers)! In other words this lengthy and initially impressive note contains remarkably little to support Betz's sweeping statement about the Hellenistic character of Paul's ethics.

In a further comment on Gal 6.1, Betz *contrasts* Paul's language and theological context with the 'analogous regulation' at Qumran (297). The footnote at this point (45) curiously begins with references from Aboth (hardly relevant to Qumran!) and then lists a number of passages from the Scrolls, one of which is actually much closer to Paul than anything from Betz's 'Hellenistic philosophy'. The Community's regulation states that 'they shall rebuke one another in truth, humility, and charity . . . let no man accuse his companion before the Congregation without having first admonished him in the presence of witnesses' (1QS 5.24–6.1). Since, like Gal 6, this is set within a community context (it does not concern a philosopher in relation to the rest of humanity) and since the rule echoes the list of virtues in 1QS 4, just as ἐν πνεύματι πραΰτητος echoes πραΰτης in Gal 5.23, this is actually quite a close parallel to Paul's instruction and perhaps of greater importance than any of the philosophical texts.

Finally, in his comment on the last part of 6.1, Betz writes that 'the term σκοπέω . . . has its background in Hellenistic philosophy' (298). I confess that I find this statement completely baffling. σκοπέω is common in Greek from the fifth century B.C. (Pindar, the tragedians etc.) and the texts from Epictetus and Philo which Betz cites in his footnote (52) contain perfectly ordinary examples of the verb (meaning 'mark' or 'consider') without any specialized philosophical sense; moreover, none of them mirrors Paul's phrase σκοπῶν σεαυτόν. Betz considers that this phrase 'comes from the Socratic tradition', citing the famous Delphic maxim γνῶθι σεαυτόν ('know yourself'). He concludes that 'Paul must have taken the maxim from the tradition of popular philosophy' (298). Once again an examination of Betz's alleged 'parallels' (in footnotes 54–55) shows the fragility of his supporting evidence.

Betz's treatment of this verse (and, perhaps, many others) thus borders on what Sandmel drew attention to as 'parallelomania'.[75]

---

[75] S. Sandmel, 'Parallelomania', *JBL* 81 (1962) 1–13; Sandmel defines his term as 'that extravagance among scholars which first overdoes the supposed similarity in passages and then proceeds to describe source and derivation as if implying literary connection flowing in an inevitable or predetermined direction' (1).

This is not to suggest that we should not look for 'parallels' or 'analogies' between Paul's statements and other earlier or contemporary writers, but that we must be wary of that *extravagance* which finds parallels where none exist, makes much of quite insignificant parallels, or fails to take into account the broader context in which apparently similar statements occur.[76] In this last respect Betz's work is especially disappointing since, despite occasional references to the Pauline 'context', he fails to clarify the differences in theological and anthropological perspective between Paul and, for instance, the Stoics (among whom one could also distinguish between Seneca, Epictetus, Marcus Aurelius, etc.). In relation to Paul's statement on 'self-examination' (6.4), Betz lists a number of 'ethical doctrines' which Paul has in common with 'Greek philosophers' (*sic*, 302). All that these amount to, however, is that a man should examine himself, his own life and work, and not compare himself with others (but see above pp.160-1 for an alternative translation for the end of Gal 6.4). It is hard to see what significance lies in this commonsensical notion, which could be just as much at home in Jewish wisdom literature as in 'Hellenistic philosophy'.[77] What *is* significant, however, is that such an instruction on the lips of, say, Epictetus would signify something very different from Paul's meaning in this context. The Stoic Epictetus examines himself in order to discern his essential rational nature and to measure his behaviour by it (Betz even cites a text which illustrates this),[78] while Paul tests his work to see if it is of value before God and will stand his scrutiny at the judgment.[79] Moreover the Stoic's self-examination is at the heart of his philosophy since he defines 'the good' in individualistic terms, as what is under his own control,[80] while Paul encourages this self-testing in the context of

---

[76] Sandmel, 'Parallelomania', 1-7; cf. T.L. Donaldson, 'Parallels: Use, Misuse and Limitations', *EQ* 55 (1983) 193-210.

[77] See, e.g., Prov 4.26; Sir 10.28; 18.20; 37.27.

[78] *Diss* 4.7.40, cited by Betz, 302 n.91 where he rightly notes that what is to be scrutinized is τὸ ἡγεμονικόν, i.e. reason (λόγος); cf. *Diss* 2.8.1-8; 2.11.1ff. and many other passages.

[79] On 6.3-5 see above pp.159-162; cf. 1 Cor 3.10-15; 9.24-27; 11.27-32.

[80] Epictetus, *Diss* 1.1; 1.12; 1.22.9ff. etc.

a community in which each member's 'work' is to support and even suffer with his fellow believers.[81] In other words, whether he derives this maxim from Stoicism or not, the really significant features of Paul's use of it are worlds apart from the 'ethical doctrine' of a Greek philosopher like Epictetus.[82]

It thus appears that the business of detecting and assessing significant 'parallels' between Pauline ethics and contemporary Jewish or Hellenistic literature is considerably more complex than Betz's treatment suggests. Of course it would be absurd to claim that Paul operated in a vacuum, totally uninfluenced by his Jewish upbringing or his social environment in the Jewish Diaspora and Graeco-Roman world. He inevitably borrowed many ethical (as well as theological) traditions; indeed on some points it would have been almost impossible to say anything *entirely* new! The really interesting questions do not concern who else said the same as Paul but how Paul uses the traditions he inherits and what meaning they acquire within his social and theological context.[83] There is, of course, a danger here of letting theological evaluations colour one's judgments: it is possible to be improperly concerned to prove Paul's uniqueness or moral superiority in relation to his surrounding culture.[84] One may suspect the influence of Bultmannian theology on Betz's judgments when he simultaneously asserts that there is no new Christian *content* in Paul's ethics, but that his *general conception* of ethics is specifically Christian, differing from both Jewish

[81] See above pp. 158-9 on the balance between personal accountability and responsibility for others, even bearing their burdens (6.2).

[82] Hays, 'Christology and Ethics', 283-288 draws a similar contrast between Paul and the Stoics in relation to 6.2.

[83] The methodological issues here are discussed by J.K Riches and A. Millar, 'Conceptual Change in the Synoptic Tradition', in *Alternative Approaches to New Testament Study*, ed. A.E. Harvey, London 1985, 37-60; they demonstrate effectively in relation to 'the kingdom of God' how the meaning of Jesus' use of this phrase must be determined not just by its antecedents or contemporary analogies but by the network of ideas and activities with which it is linked.

[84] This apologetic concern is occasionally present, for instance, in W. Barclay, *Flesh and Spirit*, London 1962 (e.g. on love, 66-8) and is more noticeable in J.N. Sevenster, *Paul and Seneca*, Leiden 1961.

'legalism' and the Hellenistic concern for ethical ideals.[85] Probably every scholar has his own theological prejudices in this matter. But our awareness of the different *social contexts* in which Paul and his contemporaries lived should help us to attain a more dispassionate view of the matter. If, for instance, Paul's communal context helps to explain his emphasis on *love*, it also demonstrates why, given the 'sectarian' setting of his churches, the priority is put on love for the 'household of faith' (Gal 6.10). It would be an extremely complex and inevitably subjective judgment to declare whether this was a 'better' or 'worse' ethic than Stoic individualism, especially since this latter was often combined with a concern for all humans as fellow rational beings and 'children of God'.[86] In any case, such value judgments should not distract us from our primary task of understanding how Paul's ethics took their particular shape within his social context and religious/philosophical environment.

---

[85] See Betz, *Galatians*, 286, 292-3; Bultmann, 'Das Problem der Ethik', 138-9; *Theology* I, 314-7; cf. Hays, 'Christology and Ethics', 270.

[86] See, e.g., Epictetus, *Diss* 1.3.1; 1.9.1-9; 1.13 (attitude to slaves); 1.18 (pity for erring mankind). This emphasis is particularly noticeable in Marcus Aurelius, *Meditations*.

Chapter Six

Flesh and Spirit

We have now studied all the contents of Gal 5.13–6.10 in some detail and a number of suggestions have been put forward to explain the purpose of these various statements within Paul's overall argument. However, one important matter still remains: we have yet to consider the meaning of the Spirit-flesh dualism which dominates this section. A number of facts require attention, some of which we have already noted in passing:

i) Paul uses the Spirit-flesh dualism here as the framework within which to present his moral instructions; he contrasts 'the desire of the flesh' with the leading of the Spirit, and constructs corresponding vice and virtue lists, 'the works of the flesh' and 'the fruit of the Spirit'. 'Flesh' and 'Spirit' thus designate two alternative ways of life and imply distinct ethical practices. Such use of this dualism is almost unique in the Pauline corpus. Although σάρξ and πνεῦμα are used elsewhere as anthropological terms or in relation to humankind ('all flesh') and the Spirit of God, the Spirit-flesh dualism is remarkably rare in an *ethical* context. It occurs three times as an *anthropological* contrast (1 Cor 5.5; 2 Cor 7.1; Col 2.5), and twice in (pre-Pauline?) formulae about Christ (Rom 1.3-4; 1 Tim 3.16); on two other occasions it is used in a contrast between Jewish privileges (especially circumcision) and Christian life 'in the Spirit' (Rom 2.28-9; Phil 3.3-4). But, apart from Gal 5-6, it is absent from all the detailed ethical sections in Paul and the only other passage where the ethical dimensions of this dualism are portrayed is Rom 7-8. There we find a contrast between those who walk κατὰ σάρκα and those who walk κατὰ πνεῦμα (Rom 8.4-14; cf. 7.5-6) although the moral characteristics of these two ways of life are not spelt out in any detail (nor is the dualism used in Rom 12-15). Thus one question which will concern us is the reason for Paul's application of this multivalent dualism to his *moral* instructions in Galatians.

ii) We have already noted the fact that the Spirit-flesh dualism does not appear for the first time in Galatians in 5.13-6.10. Its two previous occurrences in 3.3 and 4.29 not only serve to hold the various sections of the letter together but also show that the Spirit-flesh dualism is applicable to the contrast between faith and law as well as to ethics. When in 3.3 Paul sets before the Galatians the ironic question ἐναρξάμενοι πνεύματι νῦν σαρκὶ ἐπιτελεῖσθε; the context shows that σάρξ includes reference to 'the works of the law'.[1] Similarly, in the course of the allegory in 4.21-31, Paul contrasts Ishmael's birth κατὰ σάρκα (4.23,29) with Isaac's κατὰ πνεῦμα (4.29; cf. δι' ἐπαγγελίας 4.23). Although the contrast may have arisen out of the supernatural circumstances of Isaac's birth,[2] the allegory gives it a broader application: just as Isaac (ὁ κατὰ πνεῦμα) stands for those who enjoy freedom in Christ, Ishmael (ὁ κατὰ σάρκα γεννηθείς) represents unbelieving Jews under the slavery of the law who now as then (οὕτως καὶ νῦν 4.29) 'persecute' the true descendants of Abraham (cf. 5.11; 6.12). Thus the slavery of the law is here somehow subsumed under the category κατὰ σάρκα, just as the works of the law are involved in σάρξ in 3.3. Meanwhile, the end of the letter shows an even more explicit connection between the law and flesh, through circumcision. Paul accuses his opponents in 6.12 of wanting εὐπροσωπῆσαι ἐν σαρκί – a phrase which is clarified in the following verse, where the desire to have the Galatians circumcised is explained as ἵνα ἐν τῇ ὑμετέρᾳ σαρκὶ καυχήσωνται (6.13). The circumcised flesh of the Galatian 'converts' is thus one obvious link in the connection between law and flesh.

Again it is worth comparing these facts with other Pauline letters. As we have just noted, the Spirit-flesh dualism is used

---

[1] See above, chapter 3 n.26.
[2] Schlier, *Galater*, 217; Bruce, *Galatians*, 217.

twice elsewhere in a contrast between 'Jews' and 'Christians' (regarded as 'true Jews'). In Phil 3.3ff. those who serve πνεύματι θεοῦ and boast in Christ Jesus are contrasted with those who put confidence ἐν σαρκί, of which one good example would be the Jew who, like Paul himself, could point to his circumcision, his Jewish descent and his law–observance. In Rom 2.28-9 περιτομὴ ἐν σαρκί is contrasted with περιτομὴ καρδίας which is then glossed as ἐν πνεύματι οὐ γράμματι.[3] This again illustrates the connection between circumcision and flesh (cf. Col 2.11,13; Eph 2.11) which derives from its description in Gen 17 as 'the covenant in your flesh'.[4] When it comes to Rom 7-8, however, Paul seems to be more careful to distinguish the law from 'the flesh': although life ἐν τῇ σαρκί involved the arousal of 'sinful passions' through the law (7.5) and although the law could be described as 'weak through the flesh' (8.3), Paul specifically designates the law itself as πνευματικός (7.14, in contrast to ἐγὼ σάρκινος). Thus the hostility of 'the mind of the flesh' towards God can be seen in its refusal to submit to the law of God (8.7).

This attempt in Rom 7-8 to distinguish law from flesh (at least in principle) is part of an argument for the integrity of the law, that it is truly holy and righteous (Rom 7.12, 16). By contrast, to have acknowledged the law as πνευματικός in Galatians would have utterly destroyed Paul's whole argument (see especially 3.2-5)! This may indicate that there are polemical reasons for Paul's loose association of law and flesh in Galatians (as also in Phil 3). At the same time we must note that Paul's extraordinary double use of the Spirit-flesh dualism in Galatians is unique. In Phil 3 it is used in a theological contrast between faith and law but not in an ethical dualism, while in Rom 7-8 its ethical dimension is

---

[3] In 7.5-6 the πνεῦμα-γράμμα contrast is absorbed into the dualism of πνεῦμα-σάρξ. Contrast 2 Cor 3.3-6 where the benefit of the Spirit is in its writing ἐν πλαξὶν καρδίαις σαρκίναις!

[4] Gen 17.11,13,14,23-25; cf. Ezek 44.7,9; Lev 12.3. The LXX adds references to σάρξ in the context of circumcision in Gen 34.24; Jer 9.25. In later Jewish literature see Sir 44.20; Jdt 14.10; Jub 15.13-33; 4 Ezra 1.31. In some rabbinic texts – b Shebuoth 13a; b Sanhedrin 99a – circumcision is referred to as the 'covenant of flesh'.

clear but the law is distinguished from the flesh side of the dualism. Only in Galatians do we find πνεῦμα-σάρξ being applied *both* to the theological distinction between 'faith in Christ' and 'submission to the law' (3.3; 4.29) *and* to the ethical distinction between 'the fruit of the Spirit' and 'the works of the flesh' (5.13-6.10). We must therefore investigate how Paul can use it in both these senses and what this double possibility implies for our understanding of such phrases as 'giving opportunity to the flesh' (5.13).

iii)In both uses of this dualism in Galatians flesh is obviously a negative category: it would be a bad thing to 'complete in the flesh' or to 'sow to the flesh', while those like Ishmael 'born according to the flesh' persecute the true children of Abraham. It is one of the puzzles of Galatians, as indeed of all Paul's letters, that the same term σάρξ, which can have such negative connotations, can also be used in a variety of expressions with what appear to be quite innocent meanings. For all his derogatory remarks about flesh, Paul does not see any contradiction between living 'by faith' and living ἐν σαρκί in Gal 2.20 (cf. Phlm 16 and Phil 1.22,24 in contrast to Phil 3.3-4). 2 Cor 10.2-4 suggests a distinction between living ἐν σαρκί (acceptable, or at least inevitable) and living κατὰ σάρκα (unacceptable), but in Rom 8.4-9 the two prepositional phrases appear to be identical and equally negative. This bewildering variety of uses forces us to inquire just what Paul means by σάρξ and why, in certain contexts at least, it acquires such negative connotations.

iv) Finally, a number of related questions concern the relationship of 'flesh' and 'Spirit' to the believer. To say that those who belong to Christ Jesus have crucified the flesh (5.24) would seem to suggest that Christians no longer have any relationship with the flesh. Yet previously Paul had warned the Galatians that they could succumb to its desires (5.13,16) and later he talks of the danger of their sowing to the flesh (6.8). Similarly, it might appear from Paul's statements about receiving the Spirit and being directed by the Spirit (3.2-5; 4.6; 5.18) that the Christian's relationship to the Spirit was purely passive: yet Paul still urges the Galatians to walk by the Spirit and to sow to the Spirit (5.25;

181

6.8). These are in fact the familiar signs of the interaction of indicative and imperative in Pauline ethics. The Galatians have crucified the flesh (indicative) but are still urged to resist it (imperative); they have been given the gift of the Spirit and its fruit, yet still need to work to bring its benefits into their lives. Only a clearer understanding of 'the flesh' and 'the Spirit' and how they relate to the human agent can clarify the sense of these striking indicative-imperative combinations.

The meaning of Paul's term σάρξ and the πνεῦμα-σάρξ dualism has been heavily disputed in the last century of Pauline scholarship and it is obviously impossible to embark here on a full investigation of the matter or to give anything like a proper history of research on the problem.[5] Nonetheless, it will be helpful to draw the outlines of some common trends of interpretation and to assess the strengths and weaknesses of various current opinions. Two main concerns have dominated discussion of this issue: i) comparison of Paul's anthropology with Jewish and Hellenistic thought; and ii) theological analysis of Paul's own statements. We will consider each in turn.

Comparative Study

Through the work of F.C Baur and his followers, nineteenth-century New Testament theology was heavily influenced by the idealist tradition, which tended to interpret πνεῦμα in Paul as 'the principle of consciousness' forming the link between man and God, as opposed to 'flesh', which was 'anything merely

---

[5] There have been a number of monographs specifically on 'flesh', the most recent being A. Sand, *Der Begriff 'Fleisch' in den paulinischen Hauptbriefen*, Regensburg 1967 and E. Brandenburger, *Fleisch und Geist*, Neukirchen-Vluyn 1968. The best history of research is given by Jewett, *Paul's Anthropological Terms*, 49-95; cf. also Sand, *Fleisch*, 3-121 and O. Kuss, *Der Römerbrief*, Regensburg 1963, 521-529.

outward, sensuous and material'.[6] However, this tradition was absorbed into, and finally shattered by, the 'history of religions' studies at the end of the nineteenth century (die religions-geschichtliche Schule)[7] whose endeavour – to compare the New Testament with contemporary Jewish and Hellenistic thought-worlds – is still an essential ingredient of New Testament studies today. H. Lüdemann set the agenda for many decades of discussion of Pauline anthropology by his sharply-defined antithesis between Paul's 'Jewish' notion of flesh (man as a whole in his weakness) and his (latterly more dominant) 'Hellenistic' conception, in which flesh is devalued as material substance.[8] Although few have been able to accept that Paul was quite as schizophrenic as Lüdemann suggested, many subsequent studies have assumed a fundamental distinction between 'Jewish' and 'Hellenistic' perspectives on 'the flesh', arguing either that Paul was significantly influenced by his Hellenistic environment on this point or that his use of σάρξ remains thoroughly Hebraic, free from the taint of Hellenistic anthropological dualism.[9]

---

[6] Baur, *Paul* II, 126-128. Cf. Lightfoot, *Galatians*, 206 on the link between law and flesh: 'they both move in the same element, in the sphere of outward and material things'. There are still echoes of this tradition in Bultmann (see below) and in comments like that of Ridderbos: 'Paul brings the law and the flesh into relationship with each other here [Gal 3.3] because the law has its bearing upon all sorts of physical conditions and activities', *Galatians*, 114. This analysis may be more applicable to Hebrews (see 7.15 ἐντολὴ σαρκίνη and 9.10 δικαιώματα σαρκός) where the visible/invisible contrast is important.

[7] Jewett, *Paul's Anthropological Terms*, 61-2 rightly notes the effect of the studies of H. Gunkel and others which overturned the idealist notion of πνεῦμα.

[8] H. Lüdemann, *Die Anthropologie des Apostels Paulus und ihre Stellung innerhalb seiner Heilslehre*, Kiel 1872. Paul's argument in Romans is divided into Jewish (Rom 1-4) and Hellenistic (Rom 5-8) sections.

[9] Decisive Hellenistic influence on Paul's anthropology was claimed by, e.g., O. Pfleiderer, *Paulinism. A Contribution to the History of Primitive Christian Theology*, E.T. London 1877; W. Morgan, *The Religion and Theology of Paul*, Edinburgh 1917. See the critique by A. Schweitzer, *Paul and His Interpreters*, E.T. London 1912, 66-77. Among those arguing for a wholly 'Hebraic' Paul were H.W. Robinson, *The Christian Doctrine of Man*, Edinburgh 1911 and many of those influenced by the Biblical Theology movement, such as J.A.T. Robinson,

continued on p.184

In recent decades we have learned to be much more cautious about making generalized contrasts between 'Jewish' and 'Hellenistic' thought-worlds. By the first century A.D. social and political events had brought about, in some places and in certain styles of literature, a fruitful interpenetration of these two cultures.[10] Some forms of 'Judaism' were much more 'hellenized' than others, so that we must distinguish between several types of 'Jewish' anthropology, some more 'dualistic' than others.[11] There are also many pitfalls inherent in the process of hunting for 'parallels': superficial similarities in the use of a term like σάρξ can mask substantial differences of emphasis or cause us to overlook vastly different theological and philosophical perspectives. As we saw at the end of the last chapter, the identification and evaluation of 'parallels' is a much more complex process than many of its enthusiastic practitioners recognize![12]

Probably the two most significant parallels drawn with Paul in the use of 'flesh' and the Spirit-flesh dualism are the writings of Philo and the Qumran literature. A brief study of these will help to highlight both the problems and the benefits of such comparative study.

---

continued from p.183

The Body. A Study in Pauline Theology, London 1952 and W.D. Stacey, *The Pauline View of Man in relation to its Judaic and Hellenistic Background*, London 1956. Cf. Davies, *Paul and Rabbinic Judaism*, 17ff.. Sand, *Fleisch*, continues the same tradition.

[10] See the classic study by M. Hengel, *Judaism and Hellenism. Studies in their Encounter in Palestine during the Early Hellenistic Period*, E.T. London 1974.

[11] Within Jewish literature, for instance, we clearly need to distinguish between various strands in the Old Testament, as well as between apocalyptic, rabbinic and Hellenized-wisdom literature. It is one of the weaknesses of R. Gundry's work, *'Soma' in Biblical Theology with Emphasis on Pauline Anthropology*, Cambridge 1976, that he does not sufficiently distinguish the various kinds of 'anthropological duality' he discusses. In relation to Paul see S. Laeuchli, 'Monism and Dualism in the Pauline Anthropology', *Biblical Research* 3 (1958) 15-27.

[12] See above pp.170-7.

a) *Philo.* Although Philo's use of πνεῦμα and σάρξ has often been noted in comparison with Paul,[13] it is E. Brandenburger who has made the most extensive study of these parallels in arguing that the two writers, both representative of Hellenistic Judaism, share a remarkably similar perspective.[14] In the course of a lengthy discussion of a wide range of texts in Philo and Paul, Brandenburger contends that the contrast between σάρξ and πνεῦμα (or νοῦς/ψυχή /σοφία) is of fundamental importance to both writers, that for both the flesh is associated with sinful behaviour (wrong pleasures and passions) and that it appears in both authors as a power (or power-sphere, 'Machtbereich') which opposes and deflects the mind/spirit.[15] Particularly important for Brandenburger's case are Philo's texts *Quod Deus* 140-144 (opposition between flesh and the way of wisdom) and *Gig* 29ff. (the dangers of the flesh and of attraction to its pleasures).

It has to be said, however, that one does not have to read far into Paul and Philo to sense what different thought-worlds they inhabited. Although Paul was undoubtedly influenced to some degree by various forms of popular Hellenistic philosophy, he remained firmly wedded to the notion of the resurrection of the *body* so that all his disparaging references to 'the flesh' and 'our lowly bodies' do not amount to a negative verdict on the material realm; nor does he entertain the hope of the release of the mind/ soul from the body. In fact in most cases 'flesh' and 'body' are terminologically distinct in Paul's letters, with the latter being afforded a particular significance for the present and the future.[16]

---

[13] See, e.g., H. Lietzmann, *Die Briefe des Apostels Paulus*, 36-7; E.R. Goodenough and A.T. Kraabel, 'Paul and the Hellenization of Christianity', in *Religions in Antiquity*, ed. J. Neusner, Leiden 1968, 23-68.

[14] *Fleisch und Geist*, 114-221.

[15] See especially *Fleisch und Geist*, 114-118, 140-154, 177-188.

[16] Only on rare occasions are σάρξ and σῶμα interchangeable (e.g. 2 Cor 4.10-11). Throughout it is clear that the σῶμα is 'for the Lord' and will be raised (1 Cor 6.13-14, 18-20; 15.35ff.; Rom 8.11; 12.1-2), while 'flesh' or 'flesh and blood' will perish (1 Cor 15.50; Rom 8.6-9).

By contrast, Philo, while exegeting Old Testament texts, stands firmly in the Platonic tradition in which the passions and sense-impressions (αἰσθήσεις) of the body ensnare and impede the soul: for him the ideal is when ἄσαρκοι καὶ ἀσώματοι ψυχαί (note that the two adjectives are *synonymous*) roam entirely free (*Gig* 31; cf. *Leg All* 2.54ff.; *Ebr* 71 etc.). Philo's most common anthropological dualism (σῶμα vs. ψυχή/νοῦς) is drawn from Platonic and Stoic philosophy: he uses σάρξ comparatively rarely and in many cases this choice of vocabulary is due to the LXX text he is commenting upon (e.g. Gen 2.24 in *Leg All* 2.49-50; Lev 17.11 in *Det* 84; Gen 6.3 and Lev 18.6 in *Gig* 29ff.; Gen 6.12 in *Quod Deus* 140-144, etc.). In these and other cases σάρξ turns out to be synonymous with σῶμα, and the rare instances of the πνεῦμα-σάρξ contrast (e.g. *Quod Deus* 2; *Quis Heres* 57) do not carry the theological weight which Paul puts on these terms. Nor is it at all clear in what sense σάρξ is viewed by Philo 'als kosmische Macht':[17] in the one text where it takes an active role (*Quod Deus* 140-144) the reference to its attempt to destroy (φθείρειν) arises out of the LXX text (Gen 6.12, κατέφθειρε πᾶσα σάρξ τὴν ὁδὸν αὐτοῦ) and the activity is immediately ascribed to πᾶς ὁ σαρκῶν ἑταῖρος (i.e. human agency).

Thus many of Brandenburger's claimed analogies between Philo and Paul turn out to be unimpressive. He is right, however, to insist that for Philo σάρξ has markedly negative connotations. There are frequent references to the passions/pleasures of the flesh (*Leg All* 3.158; *Gig* 32-40; *Abr* 164; *Quod Deus* 143; *Agric* 97; *Quis Heres* 267-8, etc.) which are invariably evil. This may be explained partly by the equivalence of σάρξ and σῶμα in Philo's thought (and the passions of the body are inimical to the soul, *Quis Heres* 267-8) and partly by the fact that σάρξ was described by Epicurus as the seat of the highest good, ἡδόνη (see Epictetus, *Diss* 1.10.17; Plutarch, *Moralia* 1089d). As E. Schweizer has noted, Epicurus' choice of this vocabulary insured that those writers who took exception to popular Epicurean thought emphasized the dangers of the πάθη or ἡδόναι σαρκός; this can be

[17] *Fleisch und Geist*, 117.

seen not only in Philo's texts listed above, but also in Epictetus (*Diss* 2.23.20-22; 3.7.2-11; 4.1.104), Plutarch (*Moralia* 101b; 107f; 672d-e; and the whole section from 1086c) and others.[18] We shall return to this point below in discussing Paul's usage.

b) *Qumran*. The publication of the Dead Sea Scrolls was soon followed by a number of attempted comparisons with Pauline theology, in which considerable attention was focused on the connection of flesh with sin.[19] The author of the psalm at the end of 1QS acknowledges that he belongs to 'the company of ungodly flesh' (לסוד בשר עול 1QS 11.9) and that he is liable to stumble and to stagger 'because of the sin of flesh' (בעוון בשר 11.12). One of the banners mentioned in the War Rule announces 'the might of War against all sinful flesh' (יד מלחמה בכול בשר עול 1QM 4.3) and exhorts the 'Hero' to 'devour the flesh of the sinner' (תואכל בשר אשמה 1QM 12.12). The Hymns in 1QH are punctuated with confessions of the weakness and sinfulness of man which seem to be intimately associated with his existence as a creature of clay and as *flesh* (see 1QH 4.29; 15.12; 15.21; 18.21). This remarkable Jewish pessimism concerning the sinfulness of flesh prompted comparison with Paul which was further encouraged by two other notable features of the Qumran texts. In the first place, many of the texts portray a dualism which appears to be both cosmic and ethical.[20] This is witnessed most clearly in 1QS 3.13-4.26 where the 'cosmic' battle between the 'Spirit of truth' and the 'Spirit of falsehood' is matched by

---

[18] E. Schweizer, 'Die hellenistische Komponente im neutestamentlichen σάρξ-Begriff', *ZNW* 48 (1957) 237-253; cf. E. de W. Burton, *Spirit, Soul and Flesh*, Chicago 1918, 90, 135-136.

[19] The wealth of literature includes K.G. Kuhn, 'New Light on Temptation, Sin and Flesh in the New Testament', in *The Scrolls and the New Testament*, ed. K. Stendahl, London 1958, 94-113; W.D. Davies, 'Paul and the Dead Sea Scrolls: Flesh and Spirit', in the same volume, 157-182; D. Flusser, 'The Dead Sea Sect and Pre-Pauline Christianity', in *Aspects of the Dead Sea Scrolls*, ed. C. Rabin and Y. Yadin, Jerusalem 1958, 215-266; and J. Pryke, ' "Spirit" and "Flesh" in the Qumran Documents and some New Testament Texts', *RQ* 5 (1964-6), 345-360. Sand, *Fleisch*, 253-273 has a full discussion of all the uses of בשר in the Qumran Scrolls discovered at the time of publication (1967).

[20] For discussion of the content and origins of such dualistic thought see, e.g., P. von der Osten-Sacken, *Gott und Belial: Traditionsgeschichtliche Untersuchungen zum Dualismus in den Texten aus Qumran*, Göttingen 1969.

catalogues of virtues and vices representing their 'ways in the world' (4.2-6, 9-11). A number of features of this passage bear resemblances to Paul's discussion of flesh and Spirit in Gal 5-6 although no suggestion of dependence or direct influence is sufficiently convincing.[21] Secondly, there is a marked emphasis in the Scrolls on the role of the Spirit. Although the ambiguity of the term רוח often leaves it unclear whether the spirit referred to is an aspect of human or divine activity, both 1QS 3-4 and many portions of 1QH show a heightened awareness of the bestowal of the Spirit of God on the community and its leaders in a special eschatological context.[22]

However, such evidence as this must be handled cautiously and with sensitivity to the context of the Qumran theology. In the attempt to draw parallels with Pauline theology a number of misinterpretations have arisen. In particular:

i) Kuhn and others have suggested that the term בשׂר plays a central role in sectarian thought and is used to depict the source or seat of evil.[23] But in fact when the term appears with negative associations it is always in the context of a general indictment of mankind; no single term is particularly prominent and the sinfulness of 'flesh' is merely a function of man's universal rebellion.[24] Meyer has therefore rightly responded to Kuhn by insisting that

---

[21] See the full discussion by Wibbing, *Tugend- und Lasterkataloge*, 86-106.

[22] E.g. 1QS 4.2-6,21; 1QH 7.6-7; 9.32; 12.11-12; 13.18-19; 17.26. For the uses of רוח in the Scrolls see Davies, 'Paul and the Dead Sea Scrolls', 171-182.

[23] Kuhn, 'New Light on Temptation': flesh 'becomes almost synonymous with evil' (101) and is 'the sphere, the realm where ungodliness and sin have effective power' (107). Similar views are expressed by Flusser, 'The Dead Sea Sect', 255 and J. Becker, *Das Heil Gottes. Heils- und Sündenbegriffe in den Qumrantexten und im Neuen Testament*, Göttingen 1964, 111-112.

[24] See the contexts of each of the occurrences of 'sinful flesh' mentioned above; typical is 1QS 11.9 where לסור בשׂר עול is parallel to לאדם רשעה Some scholars have drawn attention to יצר בשׂר in 1QH 10.23, translating it as 'desire of the flesh' (parallel to Paul's ἐπιθυμία σαρκός), Markus, 'Evil Inclination', 9; Jewett, *Paul's Anthropological Terms*, 93. But the context indicates that the phrase is better translated as 'fleshly refuge' (G. Vermes, *The Dead Sea Scrolls in English*, Harmondsworth 1975, 184) or 'creature of flesh' (R.E. Murphy, '"Yeser" in the Qumran Literature', *Biblica* 39 (1958) 334-344, at 341).

'the sinfulness of the flesh is simply the sinfulness of human life'.[25]

ii) Brandenburger, Gundry and others have maintained that the Qumran texts evidence an anthropological dualism between 'spirit' and 'flesh' as distinguishable parts of human nature or an emphatic contrast between human flesh and the Spirit of God; passages such as 1QH 15.21-2 and 4.29-33 are cited in support.[26] But a more careful examination of the texts again renders this analysis questionable; just as the dualism of 1QS 3-4 is between spirit and spirit (not spirit and flesh) so the Hymns use 'the flesh' and 'the perverted spirit' as synonyms.[27] Where the Spirit of God is in antithesis to human weakness and sinfulness there does not appear to be any emphatic or repeated contrast with 'the flesh'.[28]

iii) The same scholars maintain that the Qumran documents envisage salvation in terms of being raised from the 'level' of flesh to that of spirit in a way that might parallel at least some of Paul's statements (Gal 5.24-5; Rom 8.4-11); certainly 1QH 15.16-17 refers to raising the glory of a just man 'from among flesh' (מבשׂר; cf. 1QH 3.19-23).[29] But again the wider context tells against any

---

[25] R. Meyer, art. σάρξ, in *TDNT* VII, 113. A similar verdict is reached by J. Licht, 'The Doctrine of the Thanksgiving Scroll', *IEJ* 6 (1956) 1-13 and F. Nötscher, *Zur theologischen Terminologie der Qumran-Texte*, Bonn 1956, 85-6.

[26] Brandenburger, *Fleisch und Geist*, 86-106; Gundry, *Soma*, 96-107. O. Betz, *Offenbarung und Schriftforschung in der Qumransekte*, Tübingen 1960, 119-126 even uses Pauline terms to describe Qumran anthropology as concerning man κατὰ σάρκα and man κατὰ πνεῦμα.

[27] The 'perverted spirit' is described in 1QH 1.21-3; 3.21; 11.12 etc. רוח is parallel to בשׂר in 1QH 9.16; 15.12-13 and the expression רוח בשׂר is found in 1QH 13.13; 17.25. While Paul can refer to τὸ πνεῦμα τοῦ κόσμου (1 Cor 2.12; cf. Eph 2.2), one can hardly imagine his talking of τὸ πνεῦμα τῆς σαρκός!

[28] There is an effective critique of Brandenburger's argument in H. Hübner, 'Anthropologischer Dualismus in den Hodayoth?', *NTS* 18 (1971-2) 268-284. H. Braun, 'Römer 7, 7-25 und das Selbstverständnis des Qumran-Frommen', *ZTK* 56 (1959) 1-18 rightly insists that 'Fleisch ist in Qumran *eines* der vielen anthropologischen Negativa; bei Paulus ist es *das* Wort' (16).

[29] Brandenburger, *Fleisch und Geist*, 102-105; Gundry, *Soma*, 100-103. Flusser, 'Dead Sea Sect', 256 refers to 'raising from the iniquity of the flesh' as 'the Elect One is purified by the Spirit from his innate carnal pollution'.

decisive release from the sinfulness of the flesh. The confessions of worthlessness and sinfulness which recur throughout 1QS 10-11 and 1QH often reflect the *present* status of the author, even while he acknowledges the grace of God; the righteousness of God has not abolished his existence as a 'creature of clay' and a member of 'ungodly flesh'.[30]

If in all these ways there remain important distinctions to be drawn between the attitude to 'flesh' exhibited at Qumran and in Paul, there are still important similarities which may help us to understand Paul's position better.[31] We have already noted that the unusual emphasis in Qumran on the sinfulness of flesh is a reflection of the remarkable pessimism shown in the texts which emphasize the wickedness and weakness of mankind.[32] Several scholars have pointed out that these repeated 'Niedrigkeits-aussagen' are a reflex of the heightened sense of the election and the grace of God which the sectarians experienced.[33] They could emphasize the universal sinfulness of 'all flesh', including fellow Jews, in order to explain the judgment of God which must come upon all except those he has specially chosen (see esp. 1QM). This emphasis on the mercy of God and the worthlessness of 'all flesh' is expressed *in the context of challenging the general Jewish assumptions of covenant membership*. To be a member of God's elect it was no longer a sufficient condition to be part of the Jewish nation.[34] The

---

[30] 1QH 15.16-17 may refer exclusively to the future. In 1QS 3-4 the two Spirits continue to battle in and over the sectarians. See Sanders, *Paul and Palestinian Judaism*, 272-284.

[31] It is a separate question whether Paul is in any sense dependent on Qumran theology; such dependence is claimed by, e.g., S. Schulz, 'Zur Rechtfertigung aus Gnaden in Qumran und bei Paulus', *ZTK* 56 (1959) 155-185.

[32] To this extent some modification is required for Meyer's statement that 'the anthropological ideas of the Qumran community follow the ancient paths', art. σάρξ, in *TDNT* VII, 114.

[33] Schulz, 'Rechtfertigung', 156-167; Sanders, *Paul and Palestinian Judaism*, 289-298.

[34] One may compare here the pessimistic view of man's sinfulness in the apocalyptic works 4 Ezra and 2 Baruch where the salvation of 'all Israel' is also brought into question. At Qumran Jewish identity was a necessary condition of membership (1QS 6.13 and repeated references to sectarians as 'children of Israel') but not a sufficient condition: God will judge and destroy all wicked Israelites who live outside the sect (CD 1-3; 1QS 1.21-26; 5.10-14 etc.)

sectarian's election was more individual than national, and he could explain his privileged position most clearly against the background of 'sinful flesh'.[35] This judgment on the rest of humanity was also part and parcel of the *apocalyptic* perspective of the Qumran sect. As the community of the elect preparing to fight for God in the final battle it is hardly surprising that they painted 'the lot of Belial' in the blackest colours. What is interesting, however, is the recognition that the community itself had not yet escaped the limitations and rebelliousness of the flesh. The Spirit and righteousness of God had not yet abolished their fleshly weakness, even if they helped to override its effects (1QH 4.29-33; 6.4-6; 7.26-33, etc.). The sectarian still waited for the 'time of visitation' when all spirit of falsehood would be rooted out 'from the bounds of his flesh' (1QS 4.20-21). It will be helpful to compare this form of Jewish apocalyptic, where the battle-lines are sketched out but the decisive event is still awaited, with Paul's apocalyptic perspective, where the cross and resurrection have already inaugurated, although not completed, the apocalyptic event.

Theological Analysis

The comparative studies which we have just been discussing clearly contribute to the theological analysis of Paul's perspective on 'flesh' and 'Spirit'. If we were to decide that Paul's anthropology was wholly dominated by Hellenistic concepts, or that his perspective was no different from, e.g., the Dead Sea Scrolls, this would be an important indication of the theological framework in which to understand his statements. In fact, as we have just indicated, neither of the two main bodies of literature which may appear to be closest to Paul really matches his

---

[35] Sanders, *Paul and Palestinian Judaism*, 270: 'the sectarian conception of the election is that it is an election of individuals rather than of the nation of Israel'; in contrast to other forms of Judaism, 'the covenant is not a birthright, but rather requires a free act of will on the part of an adult'.

thought. And comparison with the use of בשׂר in the Old Testament would also merely point up the distinctive aspects of Paul's terminology.[36] Thus, while benefiting from the comparison and contrast with other writers, we are left with Paul himself and the need to find some explanation for his distinctive uses of these terms. In the last few decades the theological analysis of Paul's anthropology has been dominated by two great scholars – Bultmann and Käsemann – and it will therefore be valuable to lay out their contributions to our subject.

a) *Bultmann*. One of the most influential sections of Bultmann's *Theology of the New Testament* is his discussion of the flesh and sin in Pauline theology (I, 232-246). Bultmann's whole description of Paul's anthropology is characterized by an emphasis on man in relationship to himself (cf. his definition of σῶμα, 197) and man's perverted intent to pursue 'life' without reference to his Creator. Thus the opening statements in the section on 'flesh' already make clear the thrust of Bultmann's position: 'the ultimate sin (eigentliche Sünde) reveals itself to be the false assumption of receiving life not as the gift of the Creator but procuring it by one's own power, of living from one's self rather than from God' (232).

Having established the range of meanings of σάρξ as including 'man's material corporeality' (233) and his 'weakness and transitoriness' (234), Bultmann lays particular stress on flesh as the

---

[36] In common with the OT Paul uses the expression 'all flesh' (Gal 2.16; Rom 3.20; 1 Cor 1.29; cf. Gen 6.12-13; Jer 32.27 etc.), stresses the weakness of flesh in contrast to the power of God (Gal 4.13-14; 1 Cor 15.50; 2 Cor 10.4; Rom 8.3 etc.; cf. Gen 6.3; Ps 56.4; Job 10.4; Is 31.3; 40.6-8 etc.) and warns against trusting in man/flesh (Phil 3.3ff.; cf. Jer 17.5). But (despite Gen 6.12-13) nowhere in the OT does flesh become identified as the seat or sphere of sin, and the occasional contrasts between spirit (of God) and flesh (of man) (Gen 6.2-3; Is 31.3) do not match the weight given to this contrast in Paul. There are only isolated examples of the association between sin and flesh in later Judaism outside of Qumran (Sir 17.31; 23.17; Test Jud 19.4; Test Zeb 9.7; 1 Enoch 1.98; 81.5). Stacey's attempt to describe Paul as a purely 'Hebraic' thinker on this matter founders on the way Paul gives the flesh an active role in sinful hostility to God (esp. Rom 7-8); to dismiss these remarks as Paul 'overreaching himself' in 'desperation' or 'exaggeration' is to evade the real problem (*Pauline View*, 154-180, esp. 163-165).

sphere of the 'outward', the 'visible', 'all that has its nature in external "appearance" ' (234-5, appealing to Rom 2.28-9; 2 Cor 4.18; 5.12). Thus to live ἐν σαρκί is simply to live in the earthly, natural sphere. This reality 'in itself does not involve any ethical or theological judgment' (235-6) although the possibility of another dimension of life 'hovers in the air', while in Rom 7-8 life ἐν σαρκί is 'proleptically denied' and regarded as a 'spurious life' (ein uneigentliches Leben). Bultmann proposes that the reason for this more negative nuance derives from the special meaning of the phrase κατὰ σάρκα (where it modifies verbs):[37] for this phrase 'stamps an existence or an attitude not as natural-human, but as sinful' (237). This is not because σάρξ takes on a new meaning but because κατὰ σάρκα indicates *taking flesh as one's norm*: 'the crucial question is whether "in flesh" only denotes the stage and the possibilities for a man's life or the determinative norm for it – whether a man's life "*in* flesh" is also life "*according* to the flesh" ' (239). And to take flesh as one's norm is precisely what Bultmann has defined as sin, for it means to turn from the Creator to the creation, 'to trust in one's self as being able to procure life by the use of the earthly and through one's own strength and accomplishment' (239).

Having reached this definition of life κατὰ σάρκα, Bultmann goes on to show how this can apply to both (Gentile) lawlessness and (Jewish) religious scrupulosity. The 'passions' and 'desires' of Gal 5 are fleshly in that they reflect 'sensuality and self-seeking' (Selbstsucht) and characterize 'a life of self-reliant pursuit of one's own ends' (239,241). But 'to the category of conduct "according to the flesh" belongs above all zealous fulfilment of the Torah . . . because a man supposes he can thereby achieve righteousness before God by his own strength'(240). Bultmann here appeals to the references to Jewish boasting (Rom 2.23; 3.27), putting confidence in the flesh (Phil 3.3-7) and establishing one's own

---

[37] Where it modifies substantives, κατὰ σάρκα means 'nothing more . . '. than the sphere of the "natural"' (237); but Gal 4.23,29 and, perhaps, 2 Cor 5.16 are recognized as exceptions to this rule.

righteousness through the law (Phil 3.9; Rom 10.3), all symptoms of 'the supposed security which a man achieves out of that which is worldly and apparent, that which he can control and deal with' (243).[38] Thus 'flesh' in Galatians can refer to both observance of the law (3.3) and libertine behaviour (5.19ff.).

As regards Paul's references to the 'desires' and 'works' of the flesh, Bultmann considers that Paul personified 'flesh' and 'sin' 'as if they were demonic rulers – but in such a way that we do not have the right actually to ascribe to him a mythological concept of "flesh" and "sin"' (244). This 'figurative, rhetorical language' is used to show the powerlessness of man, since he has fallen victim to his very attempt to secure life; he has lost to such powers 'the capacity to be the subject of his own actions', (245, sein Subjekt-sein). Hence in describing the *Spirit* (330-340) Bultmann lays considerable stress on the freedom brought by the Spirit – 'release from the compulsion of sin' (332), 'the newly opened possibility of laying hold of "life" ' (336). But he is also at pains to limit the sense in which the Spirit can be thought of as 'power': although Paul shared 'without reflection' popular notions of the Spirit as miraculous power, 'it is clear that to be "led by the Spirit" . . . does not mean to be dragged along willy-nilly (ein entscheidungsloses Hingerissenwerden) . . . but directly presupposes decision in the alternative: "flesh" or "Spirit"' (336). This reflects Bultmann's characteristic emphasis on 'decision' and

---

[38] The same theme is developed in the section on the law, 259-269, as also in Bultmann's other works, particularly his two influential essays, 'Christ the End of the Law', in *Essays Philosophical and Theological*, London 1955, 36-66 and 'Romans 7 and the Anthropology of Paul', in *Existence and Faith. Shorter Writings of R. Bultmann*, ed. S.M. Ogden, London 1961, 147-157. The sin of the Jews is taken to be precisely their zeal to observe the law and to gain credit in the eyes of God; and the law leads to death (Rom 7) not because of transgression but through enticing man to seek life (τὸ ἀγαθόν) from his own resources. Thus, 'it is not evil works or transgressions of the law that first make the Jews objectionable to God; rather the intention to become righteous before him by fulfilling the law is their real sin', ('Romans 7', 149). (The use of the *present* tense in this statement about the Jews, originally published in Germany in 1932, is disturbing).

on faith as obedience (see 314ff.); and it indicates that he sees the Spirit in Paul primarily as the possibility of authentic obedience, a possibility previously unavailable to man trapped in his own self-seeking (the flesh).

As Jewett notes in relation to Bultmann, 'the existential interpretation of the σάρξ-πνεῦμα categories has now become common property for almost all exegetes in contact with present-day discussion of the matter'.[39] The discussions of σάρξ by Robinson, Sand, Schweizer, Kümmel, Thiselton and many others[40] depend heavily on Bultmann's work, particularly his distinction between life ἐν σαρκί and life κατὰ σάρκα, his depiction of the latter as trust in one's own resources and his application of this notion to Jewish boasting in the achievement of law-observance.[41] Since Bultmann's interpretation drew on the Augustinian and Lutheran emphasis on man's sinful self-reliance ('cor incurvatum in se'), it is not surprising that it has won such widespread approval. His depiction of Judaism as merit-earning legalism was also common currency in his day.[42] Jewett himself is firmly in the Bultmannian tradition when he interprets 'boasting in flesh' in Gal 6.12-13 as seeking to justify oneself on the basis of religious zeal, and also when he defines flesh as

[39] Jewett, *Paul's Anthropological Terms*, 67.

[40] J.A.T. Robinson, *The Body*, 25; Sand, *Fleisch*, 135, 190-191; Schweizer, art. σάρξ, in *TDNT* VII, 125ff.; W.G. Kümmel, *Man in the New Testament*, E.T. London 1963, 63; A.T. Thiselton, art. 'Flesh' in *NIDNTT* I, 680-681. Among the commentators on Galatians see esp. Bonnard, *Galates*, 148; Schlier, *Galater*, 243-4; Mussner, *Galaterbrief*, 209.

[41] Deidun, *New Covenant Morality*, 95 defines σάρξ as 'orientation on self' and for Bornkamm ('Freiheit', 134-5) it designates 'die Selbstbehauptung des Menschen, der sich durchsetzt in der Weise der Selbstrechtfertigung aus dem Gesetz oder eigenmächtigen Verachtung des Gesetzes'. Barrett stands in the same tradition when he defines flesh as 'man's innate tendency to egocentricity' and applies this both to the self-concern evident in zeal for the law and the self-centred and loveless behaviour of 'the works of the flesh', *Freedom and Obligation*, 71-77, 84-85; cf. Ebeling, *Truth of the Gospel*, 254-5.

[42] The consensus on Judaism as a religion of works-righteousness, fostered by Weber, Schürer, Billerbeck, Bousset and Bultmann himself is well surveyed by Sanders, *Paul and Palestinian Judaism*, 33-59.

whatever 'lures [man] to substitute his own good for God's'.[43] σάρξ in Galatians can thus be explained as including both legalism (seeking to gain life through obedience to the law) and libertinism ('the desire to gain life through vitality, comfort, security and so forth').[44]

There can be no doubting the clarity and consistency of Bultmann's interpretation of Paul's anthropology. The distinction he draws between life in the natural/human sphere and making that sphere one's 'norm' or 'basis' is an extremely fruitful way of approaching Paul's various statements on σάρξ. But it should be noted that Paul himself does not always observe the distinction between ἐν σαρκί and κατὰ σάρκα (they are synonymous in Rom 7-8). This suggests that there is a danger in attempting to provide too neat a systematization of Paul's 'theology of flesh', and that we must take care to observe the particular contexts in which the term σάρξ appears.[45] This problem is well illustrated by the misleading equivalence Bultmann maintains between 'the flesh' and the 'outward' or 'visible'. The parallel use of these terms in the context of circumcision in Rom 2.28 does *not* entitle us to interpret σάρξ in all other contexts as 'the visible'. In fact many of the works of the flesh are entirely invisible (e.g. envy, jealousy) and much of the Christian's activity (e.g. baptism) is intended to be visible without being 'fleshly'. The legacy of the idealist tradition (flesh as physicality or sensuality) is evident here in Bultmann's theology;[46] and when this provides the means to dismiss Judaism as 'visibly occurring and historically demonstrable' (240) one can also see why Bultmann downplays the church and the sacraments in a quite un-Pauline way.

---

[43] *Paul's Anthropological Terms*, 103.

[44] See the whole section, *Paul's Anthropological Terms*, 95-116, here at 104. His work finds an echo in J. Ziesler, *Pauline Christianity*, Oxford 1983, 74-77.

[45] In this respect Jewett's analysis of Paul's terms letter by letter is an important complement to the schematic presentations of the evidence by Bultmann, Sand and others.

[46] See below for Käsemann's criticism of Bultmann on this point; cf. the comments by Mohrlang, *Matthew and Paul*, 188-189 n.50.

One must also question the generalization that life κατὰ σάρκα designates self-seeking and self-reliance. It is not at all clear that this is what Paul had in mind in designating such varied evils as 'idolatry' and 'hatred' as 'works of the flesh',[47] and very strong objections can be raised to Bultmann's designation of the Jew as the man who seeks to secure his life by his own achievements. Our discussion of the key text in Galatians (2.15ff., see above pp. 76-82) has shown that Paul's attack on works of the law in this letter is not directed against self-righteous merit-earning but against the assumption that Gentile Christians need to become Jewish proselytes.[48] Others have demonstrated the implausibility of Bultmann's interpretation of Romans 7,[49] and have shown that Paul's attack on Jewish 'boasting' does not concern individuals boasting in their own performance of the law but national pride in the special election status of Israel.[50] Bultmann's depiction of Judaism is thus shown to be untrue to Paul's perspective (as well as a caricature of first-century Judaism) and his positing of 'Selbstsucht' as the link between law and flesh must be judged highly questionable.

The decisive factor in Bultmann's whole analysis of Pauline anthropology is his mooring in existentialist philosophy. The most important effect of this is the primary (indeed, almost exclusive) attention given to *the individual*. 'Flesh' and 'Spirit' are defined in terms of the individual's self-understanding, his

---

[47] Jewett's attempt to link all the various 'works of the flesh' as activities which offer man 'the hope of life and power' (*Paul's Anthropological Terms*, 103-104) is painfully forced and artificial.

[48] In the text about 'boasting' (6.12-13), the agitators are not accused of boasting in the flesh in a general sense, but of boasting 'in *your* flesh', that is, in the success of their circumcising mission to the Galatians (not in their own or the Galatians' self-righteous merit before God).

[49] See especially H. Räisänen, 'Zum Gebrauch von ΕΠΙΘΥΜΙΑ und ΕΠΙΘΥΜΕΙΝ bei Paulus', *STh* 33 (1979) 85-99, and Westerholm, 'Letter and Spirit'. Cf. Beker, *Paul the Apostle*, 232-240.

[50] See, e.g., N.T. Wright, 'The Paul of History and the Apostle of Faith', *Tyndale Bulletin* 29 (1978) 61-88; idem, *The Messiah and the People of God*, unpublished Oxford D.Phil. thesis 1980; E.P. Sanders, *Paul, The Law and the Jewish People*; F. Watson, *Paul, Judaism and the Gentiles*.

authentic or perverted relationship to himself and the possibilities
that are (or are not) open to him. Without denying the significance of the individual in Paul's anthropology, we are entitled
to question whether the horizon of Paul's flesh-Spirit
terminology is quite so narrowly circumscribed. Such phrases as
πᾶσα σάρξ (Gal 2.16; Rom 3.20; 1 Cor 1.29) and descriptions of
relationships κατὰ σάρκα (Gal 4.23; Rom 1.3; 4.1; 9.3, 5-9) would
suggest that σάρξ can designate man in relation to the rest of
humanity (not just himself); and, as regards the Spirit, Paul is at
pains to describe its beneficial effect on Christian society, not just
the individual (Gal 5.25ff.). The other result of Bultmann's
existentialism is the tendency to demythologize Paul's remarks
about historical events and their influence on 'the world'. On the
basis that 'every assertion about Christ is also an assertion about
man and vice versa' (191), Bultmann interprets the cross not as an
apocalyptic event which changes the cosmos but as an event of
revelation disclosing the grace of God which 'frees man from
himself'.[51] Similarly the eschatological gift of the Spirit becomes
'the power of futurity' (335), 'the new possibility of genuine,
human life which opens up to him who has surrendered his old
understanding of himself' (336). However much this may be valid
reinterpretation of Paul for today, it remains very doubtful that
the historical and apocalyptic dimensions of Paul's thought can be
eradicated quite so completely in any attempt to represent Paul's
own perspective.[52]

b) *Käsemann.* As a former pupil of Bultmann, much of
Käsemann's work is full of Bultmannian echoes, but there are also
several important points at which he has broken with his

---

[51] 'Christ the End of the Law', 59-60: 'in the cross Paul has become aware that
God's grace frees man from himself in shattering all his self-glory'.

[52] Bultmann's 'Sachkritik' enables him to distinguish what Paul takes over
'without reflection' from what is 'the really characteristic feature of his conception
of the Spirit' (337), but many consider that he thereby emasculates the real Paul.
See C.K. Barrett, *First Adam*, 6,20-21 and N.A. Dahl, 'Rudolf Bultmann's
Theology of the New Testament', in *The Crucified Messiah and Other Essays*,
Minneapolis 1974, 90-128 at 116-120.

teacher.[53] This is particularly evident with regard to Pauline anthropology for Käsemann engages in an extensive critique of Bultmann's views regarding both the role of anthropology in Paul's thought and the interpretation of key anthropological terms.

In his earliest work on this theme, *Leib und Leib Christi*, Käsemann laid particular stress on the cosmic breadth of Paul's thought and on comparison with Gnostic theology: he described 'flesh' in Paul as a cosmic power as well as an anthropological reality, and considered it to be 'etwas wie ein gnostische Aeon' (105).[54] In his later essays the comparison with Gnosticism is dropped in favour of a repeated emphasis on apocalyptic themes as the determining factor in Pauline (and other early Christian) theology.[55] But since apocalyptic theology embraces the whole cosmos and concerns the battle between God and evil powers for sovereignty over the world, this puts Paul's anthropology in a much broader context than Bultmann had allowed. Käsemann repeatedly criticizes Bultmann for making anthropology the 'central point' in Paul and for the exaggerated individualism which results from this.[56] Indeed, in his broad-ranging essay, 'On Paul's Anthropology', he accuses Bultmann of still being victim to the nineteenth-century idealist emphasis on the individual.[57] Käsemann insists that Paul does not see the

[53] On his relationship to Bultmann see 'New Testament Questions of Today', in *New Testament Questions of Today*, E.T. London 1969, 10–11.

[54] *Leib und Leib Christi. Eine Untersuchung zur paulinischen Begrifflichkeit*, Tübingen 1933 (see esp. 100–118).

[55] E.g. in the provocative essays, 'The Beginnings of Christian Theology' and 'On the Subject of Primitive Christian Apocalyptic', in *New Testament Questions*, 82–107 and 108–137.

[56] 'New Testament Questions of Today', 14–15; 'Justification and Salvation History', in *Perspectives on Paul*, 65, 74; '"The Righteousness of God" in Paul', in *New Testament Questions*, 175–177.

[57] 'On Paul's Anthropology', in *Perspectives on Paul*, 1–15. Note especially the following: 'Contemporary theology [in the original – contemporary German theology] is still having to pay for the fact that it is still a victim of the heritage or curse of idealism to a greater degree than it cares to admit. It could have learned as much from Marxism as it did from Kierkegaard and would then have been unable to go on assigning the absolutely decisive role to the individual' (11).

individual as an isolated unit: 'existence is always fundamentally conceived from the angle of the world to which one belongs'.[58] This means that humanity is always caught up in the apocalyptic and cosmological conflict of powers.[59]

One crucial distinction from Bultmann emerges in the interpretation of 'body' (σῶμα). Where Bultmann took this term to designate 'person' in the sense of 'man's relationship to himself', Käsemann insists on the physical/corporeal aspects of the term and so sees it as 'that piece of world which we ourselves are and for which we bear responsibility';[60] it thus takes on crucial significance in Paul's apocalyptic thought since 'our bodily obedience expresses the fact that, in and with us, [God] has recalled to his service the world of which we are a part'.[61]

It is in this framework of thought that Käsemann discusses 'flesh' and 'Spirit'. He insists that these terms 'do not signify . . . the individuation of the individual human being, but primarily that reality which, as the power either of the heavenly or the earthly, determines him from outside, takes possession of him and thereby decides into which of the two dualistically opposed spheres he is to be integrated'.[62] Thus the Spirit, as the earthly presence of the resurrected Lord, is that gift which at the same time claims us (and our bodies) for service to the appointed Lord of the cosmos.[63] Conversely, 'the flesh', which Paul usually carefully distinguishes from 'the body', designates human 'worldliness', that is, being determined by the world. 'Existence is "flesh" in so far as it has given itself over to the world of the flesh, serves that world and allows itself to be determined by it.

---

[58] 'On Paul's Anthropology', 26.

[59] Cf. 'Primitive Christian Apocalyptic', 131-137 and the summary statement, 'Die paulinische Anthropologie ist deshalb die Tiefendimension der paulinischen Kosmologie und Eschatologie', in 'Geist und Geistesgaben im NT', *RGG* II, 1275.

[60] 'Primitive Christian Apocalyptic', 135.

[61] 'Worship and Everyday Life. A note on Romans 12', in *New Testament Questions*, 191.

[62] 'Primitive Christian Apocalyptic', 136.

[63] See the whole article, 'Geist', 1272-1279.

But since confrontation with the creator is characteristic of this world, and since this confrontation has in fact always meant the isolation and rebellion of the creature, "flesh" is also the sphere of the demonic'.[64] From this perspective an explanation can be given for the way Paul uses σάρξ both as an anthropological reality and as a 'power' which has desires and opposes the Spirit. Moreover, since the apocalyptic conflict inaugurated by the resurrection has not yet been resolved, it can be readily understood why the flesh continues to threaten and to tempt the Christian and why the eschatological conflict continues to be worked out in the daily obedience of walking in the Spirit.[65]

Although his views originally aroused great controversy, Käsemann's emphasis on apocalyptic, on the physicality of σῶμα, and on the Spirit and flesh as powers which determine human existence 'from outside' have all won increasing recognition in recent years. Many scholars now concur with his view on the importance of apocalyptic in Paul – not just in isolated motifs but in the whole framework of his theology – and that this cannot be demythologized as 'existential being' without badly distorting his perspective.[66] Although the eschatological significance of the Spirit had long been recognized,[67] it was Käsemann's achievement to put the conflict between flesh and Spirit into this apocalyptic context. Jewett, Martyn and many others have built on this insight in fruitful ways.[68]

Nonetheless some problems and unresolved questions remain. In following Bultmann's basic definition of life κατὰ σάρκα, Käsemann explains Paul's negative uses of σάρξ as 'being determined by the world', or 'the whole person in his fallenness to

---

[64] 'On Paul's Anthropology', 26.

[65] 'On Paul's Anthropology', 26-27; ' "The Righteousness of God" in Paul', 174-182.

[66] See Beker, *Paul the Apostle*, and (on the body) Gundry, *Soma*.

[67] At least since Gunkel (1888) and the religionsgeschichtliche Schule.

[68] Jewett, *Paul's Anthropological Terms*, 93ff.; Martyn, 'Apocalyptic Antinomies', where he describes Spirit and flesh as 'two opposed orbs of power, actively at war with one another since the apocalyptic advent of Christ and of his Spirit', 417.

the world and alienation from God'.[69] But in distancing himself from Bultmann's individualistic interpretation of this situation (man relying on his own resources), Käsemann leaves very ill-defined what it means to be 'determined by the world' or how the 'flesh' operates as a 'cosmic power' to determine and control human beings. Käsemann's concern with apocalyptic rather than individualistic categories is never here spelt out in sufficient detail to explain how Paul envisaged apocalyptic powers like 'flesh' (and 'Spirit') and how their influence is related to such concrete activities as the 'works of the flesh'. At one point he refers to being 'delivered over by the sin of disobedience to the powers of the world' and in another states that the 'will of flesh looks for independence over against the Lord who lays claim totally and unremittingly to our whole self'.[70] But this latter statement about the self and independence reveals that Käsemann is still really working within the Bultmannian-individualistic framework which he so frequently criticizes! He maintains that what is especially characteristic of 'the will of the flesh' is 'the attempt to secure for oneself status before God and a righteousness of one's own in virtue of good works'.[71] Thus in describing the connection between law and flesh, Käsemann falls back on an individualistic interpretation which is not only questionable in itself but also difficult to correlate with the apocalyptic perspective which he elsewhere describes so effectively.

Flesh and Spirit in Galatians

Although comparative studies can shed some light on Paul's use of the terms 'flesh' and 'Spirit', they also serve to underline the peculiarities of his usage. As we have seen, Paul cannot be fitted

---

[69] 'On Paul's Anthropology', 25-26; *Commentary on Romans*, E.T. London 1980, 205.

[70] 'New Testament Questions', 13; ' "The Righteousness of God" in Paul', 179.

[71] ' "The Righteousness of God" in Paul', 179. Cf. *Leib und Leib Christi*, 117-118 and 'Geist', 1275.

neatly into any available 'background', nor does his use of these terms entirely conform to any known pattern. Moreover, even the analysis of his own letters runs into difficulties because of the bewildering variety (and, perhaps, inconsistency) of his own statements on σάρξ and πνεῦμα. Any theological analysis must therefore proceed with caution, giving due but not excessive weight to the 'parallels' in other literature, and carefully investigating the context of each of Paul's statements. Here we will largely confine our attention to Galatians and the particular features of Paul's usage in this letter which were noted at the beginning of this chapter.

1. *The Flesh*

The most important starting-point is the observation that Paul did not invent the term σάρξ but made use of some of the associations it had already gained. As we noted in discussing Philo, one such association was with indulgence, since gratifying the 'desires' or 'passions' of 'the flesh' had become popularly associated with the indulgent life-style which Epicurus was (wrongly) believed to have advocated. We encounter this use of σάρξ and πάθη σαρκός in popular philosophy of the early Christian era (including Hellenistic Judaism)[72] and it appears to lie behind several derogatory references to 'the flesh' in the later documents of the New Testament (1 Pet 2.11; 2 Pet 2.10,18; 1 Jn 2.16; Jude 23). It is very likely that this association was also familiar to Paul (and the Galatians) and accounts for the references to ἐπιθυμίαι and παθήματα in connection with σάρξ (Gal 5.16-17, 24) as well as the occurrences in the list of ἔργα σαρκός of such vices as πορνεία, ἀσέλγεια, μέθαι and κῶμοι.

But to Paul's Jewish mind σάρξ would also have had a number of other, very different, associations. As we noted earlier, one of these was with circumcision, since the description of this act as

---

[72] See above pp. 186-7 and n. 18. Besides Philo see, e.g., 4 Macc 7.18.

'the covenant in your flesh' was well-known in Judaism'.[73] Circumcision is, of course, one of the chief bones of contention in Galatia, and one easy method for Paul to attack this practice would be through its association with 'flesh' (6.12-13). The other Jewish use of the term readily apparent in this letter is in the phrases πᾶσα σάρξ and σὰρξ καὶ αἷμα which denote humanity or mankind: Paul did not consult any 'human being' (σὰρξ καὶ αἷμα) after his conversion (1.16) and insists that 'no one' can be justified (οὐ δικαιωθήσεται πᾶσα σάρξ) by works of the law (2.16; cf. οὐ δικαιοῦται ἄνθρωπος in the same verse).[74]

Thus the simple term σάρξ could be used quite naturally in relation to such diverse entities as 'self-indulgence', 'the tissue cut in circumcision' and 'humanity'! A term with such a wide semantic field is potentially ambiguous. In normal circumstances the context would indicate which sense is implied, but for a skilful writer like Paul such a term also provides opportunities to link disparate entities by word-association and develop his polemic on this basis. Since we have already noted how Paul exploits the ambiguity of a term like πληροῦν, we should be alive to this possibility in the case of σάρξ as well.[75]

Although Paul sometimes employs σάρξ in Galatians without reference to an opposite entity, the uses of the term which are most important for our purposes are those within the πνεῦμα-σάρξ dualism. This dualism is found occasionally in the Old Testament (Gen 6.2-3; Is 31.3), in later Jewish literature (e.g. Sap Sol 7.1-7; 4 Macc 7.13-14; for Philo and Qumran see above) and, perhaps, in pre-Pauline Christianity (Rom 1.3-4; 1 Tim 3.16; cf. Mk 14.38).[76] But the important distinction in Paul's usage in

---

[73] See above n.4.

[74] See above n.36; for 'flesh and blood' as 'humankind' see Sir 14.18; 1 Enoch 15.4 and rabbinic literature *passim*.

[75] A.T. Thiselton detects a deliberate ambiguity in Paul's use of σάρξ in 1 Cor 5.5, 'The Meaning of Σάρξ in I Corinthians 5.5', *SJT* 26 (1973) 204-228.

[76] On the Romans passage see E. Schweizer, 'Röm. 1.3f. und die Gegensatz von Fleisch und Geist vor und bei Paulus', *EvTh* 15 (1955) 563-571.

Galatians is that he employs this dualism within an *apocalyptic* framework. Here Käsemann's insight is of fundamental importance. In this context πνεῦμα is not an anthropological entity nor is it a general term for the spiritual (non-material or divine) realm: it is the eschatological token of the new age, the power that establishes the sovereignty of Christ in the new creation. As its opposite, σάρξ is caught up into the dualism inherent in all apocalyptic thought and is thus associated with 'the world' and 'the present age' which stand in contrast to the new creation. *It is this apocalyptic dualism which gives to σάρξ its negative 'colouring'*: just as the present age is an evil age (1.4), so the flesh is at best inadequate and at worst thoroughly tainted with sin.[77]

Here the comparison with Qumran is instructive. As was noted above, the peculiar pessimism about 'mankind' and 'flesh' in the Dead Sea Scrolls arises from an apocalyptic and sectarian perspective which consigns everyone to doom unless they experience the grace of God within the elect community.[78] For Paul also, 'flesh' is associated with the 'present evil age' since it stands in contrast to the Spirit and the apocalyptic events of the gospel; and his pessimism about the ability of mankind ('all flesh', 2.16) to attain salvation is a reflex of his conviction that the grace of God has been displayed in Christ in a unique and revolutionary way. What distinguishes Paul from Qumran is his more emphatic and self-conscious use of the term 'flesh' and the occasions when he describes the life of the flesh as already *past*. The most striking example of the latter phenomenon is Gal 5.24 where the reference to the *crucifixion* of the flesh also betrays the reason for this unique

---

[77] Even Paul's statements about life ἐν σαρκί are never entirely neutral: it is provisional and unsatisfactory in comparison with 'Christ living in me' (Gal 2.20), being 'in the Lord' (Phlm 16) or being 'with Christ' (Phil 1.21-4). But different contexts give this phrase a variety of connotations; see J.D.G. Dunn, 'Jesus – Flesh and Spirit: An Exposition of Romans 1:3-4' *JTS* n.s. 24 (1973) 40-68.

[78] Apocalyptic pessimism also lies behind the references in 1 Enoch to the censuring of 'all flesh' (1.9) since 'no-one of the flesh can be just before the Lord; for they are merely his own creation' (81.5). The similarity of this phrase to Gal 2.16 (and Rom 3.20) has been noted by Jewett, *Paul's Anthropological Terms*, 97.

view. As we noted at the end of chapter three, the cross is used repeatedly in Galatians as the symbol of the end of the old era (cf. 2.19-20; 5.11; 6.14-15). While the Qumran sectarians still wait for the dawn of God's victory, Paul, in the light of the cross and the eschatological gift of the Spirit, can already announce the death of 'the flesh' or 'the world'.[79] To be sure, σάρξ and κόσμος have not in reality disappeared (see 2.20): the 'eschatological tension' in Paul's thought, which envisages the 'overlap' of the two ages, can accommodate the fact that σάρξ continues as a threatening and tempting reality. But the 'crucifixion' of the flesh indicates that it no longer controls or dominates the Christian's behaviour.

Thus it is only when we see Paul's various statements on 'the flesh' within his own peculiar apocalyptic perspective that we can understand his predominantly negative attitude to 'the flesh' as well as his reference to the crucifixion of the flesh (5.24). The connection with apocalyptic also helps us to see what Paul understood by σάρξ. Having noted the extremely diverse associations this term can have, it may seem foolish to attempt to give any generalizing definition: it may appear that there is no general notion which could link together all its various uses. Nonetheless, the way Paul employs his πνεῦμα-σάρξ dualism in relation to the apocalyptic themes of the letter suggests that he is using σάρξ to designate *what is merely human*, in contrast to the divine activity displayed on the cross and in the gift of the Spirit. The equivalence of ἄνθρωπος and πᾶσα σάρξ in 2.16 already suggests this, as does also a revealing passage in 1 Cor 3.1-4: there Paul describes the Corinthians as σαρκικοί (they are not, as they thought, πνευματικοί) because their behaviour is κατὰ ἄνθρωπον (3.3) – they are 'merely human beings' (οὐκ ἄνθρωποί ἐστε; 3.4). Thus the 'works of the flesh' do not just include sensual vices which

---

[79] See N.A. Dahl, 'The Doctrine of Justification: Its Social Function and Implications', in *Studies in Paul*, 102-104: 'The contrast between "once" and "now" is much more sharply expressed in early Christianity than in the Essene sect . . . For the Qumran sectaries the revelation of God's saving righteousness and his justification of sinners is never linked with any event in history comparable to the death and resurrection of Christ' (103).

were associated with supposed Epicurean indulgence, but also a list of social sins (envy, jealousy, divisiveness, etc.) which Paul lists under this heading as *merely human behaviour*: to display ζῆλος and ἔρις is 'fleshly' because it is just what one expects of human beings who have not been transformed by the Spirit (cf. 1 Cor 3.3). In the same way, Paul can accuse the judaizing Galatians of wanting to 'complete in the flesh' (3.3) not only because of the link between circumcision and flesh but also because (in his view) to commit themselves to Judaism was to enmesh themselves in what had now been shown to be *a merely human religion*.

One might well ask how a Jew like Paul could arrive at such a shockingly negative view of Judaism; but there are a number of clues in this letter which help to explain this phenomenon. In the first place, Paul's description of his former life in Judaism in terms of his zeal for 'the tradition of the fathers' (1.14) is clearly intended to contrast with the direct divine revelation in his call (1.15-16). In the light of such dramatic divine intervention, his former life might well appear to be devotion to *merely human tradition*.[80] Secondly, his depiction of Ishmael's birth κατὰ σάρκα (4.23,29) and his association of Ishmael with unbelieving Jews suggests a criticism of Judaism for being based on human descent: one is born a Jew by mere human parentage, but made a Christian by the creative work of the Spirit of God. Elsewhere Paul often describes Jewish descent with the phrase κατὰ σάρκα (Rom 1.3; 4.1; 9.3,5-9; cf. Rom 11.14 ἡ σάρξ μου and 1 Cor 10.18, ὁ Ἰσραὴλ κατὰ σάρκα) – perhaps alluding to the common Jewish description of kinship in terms of 'flesh of my flesh, bone of my bone'.[81] Jewish identity is thus based on σάρξ, but as the allegory in 4.21-31 makes clear (cf. Rom 9.5-9) this *merely human definition of religious adherence* is far inferior to the divine activity of 'the promise' and

---

[80] Note the emphatic contrast throughout Gal 1 between ἄνθρωπος and θεός (1.1,10-12). Paul's gospel is not κατὰ ἄνθρωπον nor received παρὰ ἀνθρώπου because it came by a revelation of Christ from God: in this context Judaism (1.13-14) appears to be merely κατὰ ἄνθρωπον and thus κατὰ σάρκα.

[81] See, e.g., Gen 2.23; 29.14; 37.27; Judg 9.2; 2 Sam 5.1; 19.12-13; cf. Lev 18.6 and Is 58.7 where בשׂרך means 'kinsman'.

'the Spirit'. Thirdly, one of the major criticisms of Judaism implicit throughout this letter is its exclusion of Gentiles. Having fought so hard against the divisive policies of Peter at Antioch and being committed throughout his ministry to realizing the unity of Jew and Gentile in Christ (3.28), Paul would oppose the Galatians' 'lapse' into Judaism as creating precisely the sort of divisions and exclusions, the διχοστασίαι and αἱρέσεις, which he regarded as symptoms of fleshly behaviour (5.20). The exclusiveness of the agitators, and the enmity and unworthy ζῆλος they created (4.16-18),[82] would merely underline Paul's conviction that Judaism should be placed in the category of 'what is merely human'.[83]

It should be clear that this negative evaluation of 'what is merely human' derives from an apocalyptic perspective (not some perverse misanthropy): in the light of the glory of God's activity in the new age, all human achievements and traditions are put into the shade. Thus Paul's inclusion of Judaism within this category is only made possible by the conviction that the new creation has been inaugurated in (and only in) Christ and his Spirit. The association of Judaism with 'flesh' was certainly aided by the terminological link between σάρξ and circumcision (and physical descent κατὰ σάρκα) but it also reflects Paul's deep-rooted conviction about the human limitations of his former way of life. At this point his difference from Qumran (and indeed all other Jewish literature) is again apparent: to put submission to the law under the negative category 'flesh' signals a break with Jewish covenantal theology even more radical than that evidenced at Qumran. For Paul, Jewish identity was neither *sufficient* nor even *necessary* for membership in God's elect, for Jews and Gentiles alike are part of impotent humanity unless and until they believe in Christ (Gal 2.15-21).

---

[82] With ἐχθρός (4.16) and ζηλοῦν (4.17-18) compare ἔχθραι and ζῆλος in 5.20.

[83] It would be possible, of course, to level the same charge against Paul, since his communities were also exclusive to believers. I suspect he would reply that this is a different matter from the *racial* exclusiveness endemic to the Jewish tradition.

Perhaps the most important feature of this analysis of flesh in Galatians is that it provides a viable alternative to the consensus existentialist interpretation of flesh which chiefly uses individualistic categories (self-centredness, self-dependence, etc.); according to this, flesh is linked with law because doing the works of the law involves supposing one can gain righteousness by one's own strength. We have examined Bultmann's powerful presentation of this case and noted its pervasive influence, even in some crucial aspects of Käsemann's analysis of the matter. But we have also found it unconvincing: neither the vices in the works of the flesh nor the observance of the law can be convincingly subsumed under the category 'egocentricity'. A much more satisfactory solution emerges if we take σάρξ as 'what is merely human' and see its application to the works of the flesh and the law in social rather than purely individualistic terms. The works of the flesh are merely human patterns of behaviour (especially in social relations) while Jewish observance of the law is a merely human way of life, based on human social realities (kinship, traditions of the fathers and racial exclusiveness). Thus while the flesh can be manifested as human weakness (Gal 4.13-14), or self-centred behaviour (5.15), neither of these is itself the heart of Paul's understanding of the term:[84] the looser definition – 'what is merely human' – fits his various uses more comfortably as well as arising quite naturally from his apocalyptic perspective.

2. The Irony of the Spirit-flesh Dualism

Our observations thus far lead us to conclude that Paul uses σάρξ as an 'umbrella-term' under which he can gather such disparate entities as libertine behaviour, circumcision, a range of social vices and life under the law. The apocalyptic framework within which he uses the term does give it some general theological

---

[84] Thus Barrett's definition of 'flesh' as lovelessness, *Freedom and Obligation*, 74-77 covers only one aspect of the term.

content (what is merely human) so that his linkage of these various items is not entirely arbitrary. Nonetheless, there is almost certainly deliberate irony in the way Paul manages to put law–observance in the same category as his list of vices: what might appear on the surface to be entirely distinct forms of activity are here lumped together on the σάρξ side of the πνεῦμα-σάρξ dualism. Paul's argument implies that, far from releasing them from the problems of the flesh, the law only enmeshes them further in that realm![85]

A similar use of irony is evident elsewhere in the letter, especially in Paul's use of the phrase τὰ στοιχεῖα τοῦ κόσμου (4.1-11). Paul maintains that the Galatians' previous worship of idols had enslaved them to such στοιχεῖα, but then goes on to warn them that by becoming proselytes they would again surrender their freedom in turning to ἀσθενῆ καὶ πτωχὰ στοιχεῖα (4.8-9). The meaning of τὰ στοιχεῖα τοῦ κόσμου is at least as much disputed as the meaning of σάρξ, but it is possible that here too Paul is playing on its ambiguity: it can mean both elementary instruction (for 'children' under the ἐπιτρόποι, 4.1ff.) and elemental spirits (the 'gods' of Gentile worship). In any case, the irony in Paul's inclusion of Judaism with paganism under the heading στοιχεῖα is equivalent to, and equally as shocking as, his categorization of both law–observance and libertine behaviour as σάρξ.

We should not ignore the extremes to which Paul's polemic leads him in this letter. By putting Judaism under the category of σάρξ and στοιχεῖα τοῦ κόσμου he appears to be dismissing its value altogether. At one point he almost denies the divine origin of the law (3.19-20) and it is only by the use of studied ambiguity that he is able to claim it for the Christian cause as 'fulfilled' through love. By the time he came to write Romans, Paul's perspective on this point was somewhat clearer and better

---

[85] See the observations of Howard, *Crisis*, 12-14 and Lull, *Spirit in Galatia*, 114-116. But Howard has to read Romans 7 into Galatians to find the thesis that the law leads to 'the works of the flesh' by inciting the desires it forbids.

balanced. As we noted at the beginning of this chapter, Paul carefully distinguishes νόμος from σάρξ in Rom 7-8 (cf. his much more positive comments about Israel in Rom 11), while also insisting that the law is easily misused by sin and the passions of the flesh (Gal 3.19 and 3.22 may refer cryptically to the same phenomenon but are extremely unclear). The whole argument is given much firmer theological underpinning through the Adam–Christ comparison in Rom 5.12-21, for there it is made clear that Israel, for all her many advantages, has not escaped the disastrous effects of Adam's fall.[86] This theme enables Paul to talk of the crucifixion of the παλαιὸς ἄνθρωπος (Rom 6.6; cf. Gal 5.24), which is clearly what he has in mind when he describes Christians as no longer living ἐν σαρκί (Rom 7.5-6; 8.8-9).[87] What we see in Galatians is, therefore, the first and polemically loaded attempt to work out a theological perspective which receives clearer and fuller expression in Romans.

To return to Gal 5-6, our discussion of the flesh has added a further dimension to our understanding of the Spirit-flesh dualism. In chapter four it was suggested that one reason for Paul's choice of the term σάρξ in this passage was that it provided a convenient alternative to ἁμαρτία: the latter term was too closely connected to notions of law-breaking to be helpful in the context of the Galatian dispute. The other term in the dualism, πνεῦμα, was particularly useful since 'the Spirit' marked the dramatic beginning of the Galatians' Christian lives; to present his ethics as 'walking in the Spirit' thus reinforced Paul's basic appeal that they should continue as they had begun. But now we may add a further reason for Paul's choice of the term σάρξ. This term was ambiguous enough to include reference to libertine behav-

---

[86] See Barrett, *First Adam*: 'The legitimate issue of Abraham, through Isaac, became illegitimate, because they were perverted by the fact that, in Adam, they belonged to a perverted universe'.

[87] See Caird, *Language*, 44: 'To be "in the flesh" is the same thing as to be "in Adam", in the old humanity, enslaved to sin and death. Christians are not, in this sense, "in the flesh" (Rom 8:9)'.

211

iour, social disunity and law-observance. Thus when Paul warns
the Galatians about using their freedom as 'an opportunity for the
flesh' (5.13), he does not only have libertine behaviour in mind.
Of more immediate concern to him were the 'fleshly' envy and
rivalry tearing the Galatian churches apart (5.14-15, 19-21, 26) *and*
the risk that they might use their freedom to 'complete in the
flesh' (3.3) through observing the law. Similarly, when he warns
that 'he who sows to his own flesh will reap destruction from the
flesh' (6.8), he is not only thinking of self-indulgence; of more
pressing concern was the Galatians' interest in having their own
flesh circumcised (6.12-13) which he considered to be just as
disastrous as libertine behaviour.[88] Thus Paul's skilful choice of
vocabulary enables him to exploit the semantic ambiguity of
σάρξ within the πνεῦμα-σάρξ dualism, and so continue the
debate about law even within this passage of ethical instruction.[89]

3. *Flesh and Spirit in Indicative and Imperative*

It is clearly impossible to deal with such an enormous topic as the
Pauline combination of indicative and imperative within the
limited space of the remainder of this chapter. Nonetheless, some
observations on the matter can fairly be made on the basis of our
studies in this and the previous chapter.

In relation to the flesh, some explanation is required for the way
Paul envisages σάρξ as a continuing threat to be avoided (5.16-
17) even by Christians who have 'crucified' it with its passions
and desires (5.24). This phenomenon can only be explained when

---

[88] On Gal 6.8 see B. Reicke, 'The Law and This World According to Paul.
Some Thoughts Concerning Gal. 4:1-11', *JBL* 70 (1951) 259-276, at 266.

[89] The point is entirely obscured in most modern translations which translate
σάρξ differently in each context: e.g. NIV on 3.3 'human effort'; 4.23 'in the
ordinary way'; 5.13-6.10 'the sinful nature'; 6.12 'outwardly'. NEB on 3.3 'the
material'; 4.23 'in the course of nature'; 5.13-6.10 'the lower nature'; 6.12 'outward
and bodily'. See the valuable comments by Barrett, *Freedom and Obligation*,
71-2.

it is seen that Paul is not concerned here with a 'fleshly' part of each individual (his physical being or his 'lower nature') but with the influence of an 'era' and its human traditions and assumptions. Flesh can be described as having desires and as being locked in battle with the Spirit, partly because of the popular discussion of the 'desires' and 'passions' of the flesh (see above), and partly because apocalyptic theology lends itself to talk of rival powers in conflict. These descriptions do not, however, amount to the full personification of the flesh.[90] Paul perhaps noted the influence of 'the old aeon' primarily in the real but intangible effects of social pressure and social expectations. His talk of crucifying the flesh suggests a decisive break with such influence on the part of all those who enter the new creation. But since the old aeon continues as the sphere in which the Christian life must be lived, there is always the danger that the Christian will be lured by its false human-centred perspective. It is thus the 'eschatological tension' which necessitates Paul's continuing appeals not to sow to the flesh.[91]

As regards the Spirit, here in Galatians (as elsewhere) a much fuller picture of personified power is evident: the Spirit cries 'Abba' (4.6), leads Christians (5.18) and is displayed in miraculous power in their midst (3.5). The Spirit is no less than the divine power unleashed in the dawning of the new age, the source of new life (εἰ ζῶμεν πνεύματι . . . 5.25). As we noted earlier, such concrete and vigorous language cannot be satisfactorily reduced to 'the new possibility of genuine, human life'. There is surely a fatal weakening of the force of Paul's indicative when Bultmann takes Gal 5.25 to mean that 'the faith bestowed possibility of "living by the Spirit" must be explicitly laid hold of by "walking by the Spirit".'[92] Such (existentialist)

---

[90] Jewett undoubtedly exaggerates the role of σάρξ as a 'cosmic' or 'demonic' power in such passages as Gal 4.21ff., *Paul's Anthropological Terms*, 100-101. The texts in which σάρξ is personified are, in fact, remarkably few in comparison with the range of personal statements made about the Spirit.

[91] See esp. Bornkamm, 'Baptism and New Life in Paul'.

[92] *Theology* I, 333.

emphasis on 'possibility' hardly matches up to the confidence with which Paul describes the transforming work of God.[93]

And yet Bultmann is right to insist that the 'leading' of the Spirit does not represent compulsion or produce automatic obedience. The Spirit given to believers may enlist them in the fight against the flesh (5.16-17) but it does not remove the requirement to work with patience (6.9-10). This understanding of power which involves both gift and obligation has been most effectively described by Käsemann. In his essay on 'the righteousness of God', Käsemann argues that the gift of the Spirit involves the establishment of God's lordship and that this lordship both transforms the human lives it touches and requires from those believers the constant obedience of service: 'The Lord whom we receive in and with our baptism as the Giver of the Spirit, . . . this very Lord urges us on to break through to a service which is perpetually being renewed . . . Only so long as we keep on the pilgrim way and allow ourselves to be recalled daily to the allegiance of Christ, can we abide in the gift which we have received and can it abide, living and powerful, in us'.[94] This brilliantly encapsulates precisely what we have found in Gal 5-6. While Paul can describe his list of virtues as 'the fruit of the Spirit', this does not leave the believer as a purely passive receiver of these gifts:[95] he has to contend against the dangers of conceit (6.3-5) and weariness (6.9) to display this fruit in the Christian

---

[93] T.C. Oden, *Radical Obedience: The Ethics of Rudolf Bultmann*, London 1965, 41ff., expounds the existentialist presuppositions ('Sein ist ein Seinkönnen' – Heidegger) by which 'it is a special feature of the ontology of man that he is always choosing who he is'. The difference between Bultmann and Käsemann on this point is well brought out in their different interpretations of δύναμις in Rom 1.16. For Bultmann this term means 'Kraft', with the accent on possibility; for Käsemann, 'Macht', with the emphasis on prevailing power. See the discussion by Käsemann in ' "The Righteousness of God" in Paul', 173, n.4

[94] ' "The Righteousness of God" in Paul', 175.

[95] This is the impression given by Deidun's definition of the indicative-imperative combination: 'The Christian is under obligation *not to resist* the inward action of God's Spirit which already *impels* him to free obedience', *New Covenant Morality*, 243 (my italics).

community. Neither the indicative (the fruit of the Spirit) nor the imperative (sowing to the Spirit) should be downplayed. Indeed the interplay of human and divine resources is neatly encapsulated in Paul's appeal to 'walk in/by the Spirit' (5.16).

Thus our study of 'flesh' and 'Spirit' takes us to the heart of Paul's ethics in a particularly direct way. It reveals the situation of believers transformed by the power of the new age and enlisted in the service of the Lord and yet required to live out that service in the midst of the lures and temptations of the old age by a constant renewal of their obedience to the truth in faith.

Chapter Seven
Conclusions

Our study of Paul's ethics in Galatians has caused us to range widely over a number of historical and theological questions as well as engaging us in a detailed investigation of the paraenetic section in 5.13-6.10. We are now in a position to provide answers for the questions raised in chapter one and to shed light on some broader issues of Pauline ethics and theology.

The Function of the Paraenetic Material

One aim of this book has been to help to settle the scholarly dispute over the role of Paul's exhortations in 5.13-6.10. It has emphasized the importance of this often neglected section and attempted to define its purpose within the letter and in relation to the historical situation in Galatia. Our conclusions on this matter may best be presented in answer to the four questions listed on p. 26.

i) Is Paul's exhortation related to the argument of the earlier chapters concerning law and faith? Our conclusion is that his exhortation *develops out of and concludes his earlier arguments*; it cannot be understood properly when it is treated as an appendix or an independent paraenetic section. On this point we have established a new angle of approach by highlighting the fact that *a major ingredient in the Galatian dispute is the question of how the members of God's people should live*. When it is seen that the questions of membership and behaviour are bound up together in the Galatian crisis and in Paul's response to it, we may appreciate better that Paul is concerned to conclude his argument with an indication of how to obey the truth. Indeed, we have suggested that his discussion of ethics in terms of faith, love and walking in the Spirit is intended to draw out the implications of justification by faith, and to describe what it means to continue, as they had begun, in the Spirit. Thus it is no surprise to find many points of contact between the exhortation in 5.13-6.10 and the earlier theological arguments: the Spirit-flesh dualism had been anticipated in 3.3 and 4.29; the references to the law complement the argument of the earlier chapters; and several statements in 5.13-24 serve to clarify the moral implications of the 'freedom' heralded throughout the letter. Of course, Paul brings in new themes in 5.13ff. and employs the Spirit-flesh dualism in a new way; but this turn in the argument in fact complements and concludes the earlier chapters. Thus it would be misleading to exaggerate the break in subject-matter at 5.13 and wrong to suggest that this is the first point in the letter where Paul is concerned with ethics. We may also safely conclude that O'Neill's surgery of the text is unnecessary.

ii) Is this section related to a concrete situation in the Galatian churches or should it be considered as an example of general 'paraenesis'? Here we may conclude that this passage is *best understood as having been framed specifically for the current crisis in the Galatian churches*. We have found sufficient evidence to be confident that Paul wrote this passage in this way because its arguments and instructions were relevant to the Galatian crisis and had an important contribution to make towards solving it. This conclusion embraces at least the main themes of 5.13-6.10 and many of its individual details: Paul's terminology (e.g. Spirit, flesh, fulfil) is deliberately and carefully chosen to show the sufficiency of his moral strategy; he uses the catalogue of vices to highlight social and community strife; and many of his maxims are chosen to illustrate the practical value of the fruit of the Spirit. However, upholding the relevance of this whole section need not entail that every detail is a direct reflection of a particular event in the Galatian churches. The traditional character of the catalogues and the 'casual' tone of some of the maxims warn us against concluding that every named vice was currently being displayed in the Galatian churches or that every maxim answers to a recent incident. Thus our conclusions on this matter dispute the inclusion of this passage in a category of general 'paraenesis' (*pace* Dibelius, Vielhauer et al.). But we are not thereby forced to follow Schmithals and others in deducing from the vice-list a congregation captivated by Gnostic morals or 'Hellenistic aspirations' (Jewett); such interpretations, while rightly defending the relevance of 5.13–6.10, err in reading too much into every detail.

iii) Who is Paul addressing in this exhortation and what problems, if any, does he have in view? On this point our whole argument points to the conclusion that *Paul fights on only one front throughout the epistle and that throughout he is concerned with the status and the obedience of Gentile believers.* His exhortation in Gal 5–6 makes best sense when we see that the Galatian crisis required him to draw out the ethical implications of living by faith and walking in the Spirit. The Galatians addressed in these chapters are no different from those who desire to take on 'the yoke of the law', since Paul is attempting to show here how they can 'live to God' without taking on that yoke. In other words, *the problem that lies behind these chapters is not libertinism but moral confusion together with a loss of confidence in Paul's prescription for ethics.* It is precisely because of the Galatians' attraction to the law that Paul has to demonstrate the sufficiency and practical value of his proposal for ethics – 'walking in the Spirit'. This provides an integrated interpretation of the letter which does not suffer the weakness of a 'two-front' hypothesis (Lütgert and Ropes) or posit an unlikely synthesis of 'judaizing' and 'Hellenistic libertinism' (Jewett). It also renders unnecessary any Gnostic hypothesis, which in any case either fails to account for Paul's discussion of the law in Gal 3–4 or concludes that these chapters were irrelevant and incomprehensible to the Galatians (Schmithals and Marxsen). In fact, our conclusion questions whether there is any evidence for antinomian tendencies (Schmithals) or flagrant misconduct (Betz) in Galatia.

iv) What was Paul's purpose in these paragraphs? From the answers we have given to the other three questions we have already reached a number of negative conclusions: Paul did *not* write this exhortation to give a generalized description of Christian ethics, *nor* was he concerned to counter antinomian licence, *nor* was his purpose solely defensive. Any balanced exposition of his purpose should, however, contain the following elements:

a) In the first place, Gal 5.13-6.10 serves as *an appeal to the Galatians to let their lives be directed by the Spirit.* As we have seen, this appeal springs from Paul's concern that, having begun in the Spirit, they should continue to live under the Spirit's control. The urgency of this appeal derives from the danger that the Galatians will look to the law for their moral direction, and from Paul's conviction that in thus becoming like Jews they would jeopardize 'the truth of the gospel' (2.11-21). His appeal is that they should 'obey the truth' under the guidance of the Spirit.

b) 5.13-6.10 also functions as *an assurance that the Spirit can provide adequate moral constraints and directions.* Paul assures the Galatians that the Spirit will not encourage but combat evil in the shape of 'the flesh' and its desires. He insists that the fruit of the Spirit can come under no criticism from the law (of Christ). He also demonstrates how the moral qualities of the Spirit can be applied to a range of possible community problems and thus help to resolve the tensions which currently threaten the Galatian churches. His exhortation is thus designed to demonstrate both the sufficiency and the practical value of the Spirit.

c) In another respect this passage operates as *a warning against moral danger, defined here as 'the flesh'.* The misuse of freedom as an 'opportunity for the flesh' is a real threat and the possibility that the Galatians might end up 'sowing to the flesh' has to be treated as a serious danger. However, while the 'works of the flesh' include licentious behaviour, the passage makes clear that Paul's particular concern is with the 'fleshly' bickering and in-fighting currently prevalent in the Galatian churches. Moreover, on the basis of his previous association of 'law' and 'flesh', Paul is able to include in this warning against 'flesh' a further reprimand of the Galatians' attraction to the law. Thus Paul's warning against 'the flesh' is genuine, but is not to be interpreted in the usual manner as a warning against, or attack upon, libertinism.

This threefold analysis takes good account of the various factors which contributed to Paul's construction of this complex passage. It also combines the strong points of the various theories outlined in chapter one. It acknowledges the defensive tone of some of Paul's statements here, without giving the whole passage a solely apologetic purpose. It gives due weight to the fact that Paul offers serious admonition and instruction in this passage, without requiring us to posit the presence of a libertine party in Galatia. It allows for the traditional character of the vice lists and the general nature of some of the maxims without thereby dismissing the whole passage as unrelated to Galatia. Finally, it includes the maxims of 5.25-6.10 in an integrated explanation of the whole letter which none of the current theories have been able to do in a convincing way.

Observations on Pauline Ethics

It is appropriate now to draw together the threads of our discussion which have a bearing on the character of Paul's ethics. On the basis of the foregoing investigation we may be entitled to draw conclusions only about Galatians, since we cannot assume that this letter is typical of Paul's whole ethical approach. Nonetheless, the insights gained here are worth comparing with the rest of the Pauline correspondence, and so may contribute usefully to some wider debates.

1. *Paraenesis and the use of traditional material*

On the question of the relevance of Paul's material to the Galatian churches, our observations on the catalogue in 5.19-23 and the 'sententiae' in 5.25-6.10 rule out any one-sided solution. We would be wrong to follow Dibelius in taking 5.13-6.10 as 'unconditioned by the particular situation' and as a piece of generalized 'paraenesis' (in Dibelius' technical sense). On the contrary, Paul's instructions have been carefully chosen to reflect not only his theological concerns, but also, to some degree, his awareness of the local situation addressed. But we would also be mistaken to ignore the traditional character of such catalogues and maxims in the attempt to press every detail as a reflection of a Galatian problem. These alternatives are, in fact, the extreme polar positions of a broad spectrum; in between there are a number of possible interpretations which allow for more or less adaptation of paraenetic material to the historical context. As we saw in the conclusion to chapter five, Paul's *mode of expression* cannot, of itself, determine to what extent his ethics are related to a particular situation: a 'general' exhortation can be directed to a particular need, while a 'specific' command can be intended to apply universally.[1] The degree to which Paul's ethics are conditioned by the situation addressed can be determined only by *the context*, not by *the style* of the exhortation; and that means that each passage has to be evaluated on its own merits, taking into account both the literary context of the ethical instruction and the historical context of the letter as a whole. Our conclusions with regard to Gal 5-6 were based on our reconstruction of the Galatian crisis and the theological concerns of the letter. The same method has to be applied to passages like Rom 12-14, Col 3-4, 1 Thess 4-5 (or the letters of James and 1 Peter) before it can be decided how closely they are related to the situations of the churches addressed; and in some cases it may be concluded that parts of the paraenesis are more directly concerned with the historical situation than others (e.g. Rom 13-14 more than Rom 12).[2] Of course such a

---

[1] Schrage, *Einzelgebote*, 37-48 similarly insists that one must not confuse the categories 'aktuell' and 'konkret': 'Wichtiger ist, dass sich bei Paulus sowohl aktuell-situationsbezogene als auch usuelle Mahnungen finden, und vor allem, dass beide eine Konkretheit nicht auschliessen' (45).

[2] It is still a matter of intense dispute how much the material in these chapters is relevant to the Roman church. On Rom 14 see, for instance, R.J. Karris, 'Romans 14.1-15.13 and the Occasion of Romans', *CBQ* 35 (1973) 155-178 and F. Watson, *Paul, Judaism and the Gentiles*, 88ff. Although some even consider Rom 13.1-7 an interpolation it seems to have special relevance to the Roman church in the aftermath of the Claudian expulsion of some Roman Jewish-Christians; see J.I.H. McDonald, 'Romans 13.1-7 and Christian Social Ethics Today', *Modern Churchman* 29 (1987) 19-26.

procedure will sometimes come perilously close to circular reasoning since the reconstruction of the historical context may partly depend on evidence from the paraenetic material; but it need not be invalid if sufficient safeguards, such as the mirror-reading criteria outlined in chapter two, are applied.

We may also draw some tentative conclusions on the related question of Paul's use of ethical traditions (Jewish, Hellenistic and Christian). In many respects Paul's pioneering work in founding and nurturing Hellenistic Christian churches made him an innovator in conceptualizing and presenting a Christian ethic.[3] But such a role inevitably involved the adaptation and application of previous Jewish and Hellenistic moral traditions, for it was unnecessary (and, indeed, wholly impossible) to create an ethical system *de novo*. Paul drew on the Jewish and Christian patterns of thought familiar to him while also being inclined to use terms and forms which could communicate effectively with his Gentile converts. In Galatians 5-6 Paul does not, as far as we know, borrow contemporary Jewish or Hellenistic material *verbatim*. He cites the Old Testament only once (5.14) but uses his citation in a way significantly different from other Jewish traditions (love of neighbour 'fulfils' the whole law). And, as we noted in chapter five, his maxims in this section are not as heavily indebted to Hellenistic moral philosophy as is sometimes claimed. But many of his ideas (e.g. support of teachers), motifs (e.g. sowing and reaping) and forms (e.g. vice and virtue lists) are not original to him. What are unique to Paul are his emphasis within this material and his arrangement of it, both of which are strongly influenced by his understanding of the gospel and the needs of the Galatian situation. Thus we cannot simply assume that traditional material has been uncritically absorbed into Paul's ethics. Once

[3] Houlden comments acutely: 'In so far as Paul was a pioneer in setting things down with pen and ink, he was necessarily striving to capture in words ideas and insights that had not so far had to meet this demanding treatment. It is not surprising . . . that some elements are left over, not integrated with the main structures of his thought. His work is a triumph of creative expression, but its very dynamism left bits of it racing breathlessly behind the main body', *Ethics and the New Testament*, London/Oxford 1973, 25.

again, however, each example in Paul's other letters would have to be examined on its own merits. In some cases one may be led to conclude that Paul has only barely 'Christianized' his material (e.g. Rom 1.18-32; 13.1-7). But it is clear that there is no room for sweeping generalizations on this matter.[4]

2. The theological roots of Paul's ethics

Our investigation (in chapter three) into some of the main theological topics of the letter indicated that there are a number of complementary themes which connect Paul's theology and ethics. In Paul's presentation of justification by faith at the end of Gal 2 it emerges that justification is not a morally barren doctrine (contra Schweitzer et al.). Just as 'the works of the law' concern behaviour in practical matters like meals, so, Paul argues, justification by faith in Christ has important moral implications which Peter was wrong to ignore at Antioch and which the Galatians are in danger of forgetting. Those who are justified by faith are obliged to live by faith, not works of the law: and that means, in particular, not excluding other Christians because of their different social or cultural mores. In this way Paul's theology of justification lies at the root of his subsequent appeals for love, unity and mutual support. But justification by faith is not the only ground of ethics. By appealing to the Galatians' experience of the Spirit, Paul portrays the Christian life under the rubric of 'continuing' or 'walking' in the Spirit, whose chief fruit is love. Moreover, he can arrive at the same result – 'faith', 'love' and 'Spirit' – by arguing through his interpretation of Abrahamic descent: the true sons of Abraham are born of the Spirit and enter a covenant of promise whose fundamental characteristic is 'faith working through love'.

This analysis gives rise to a number of interesting conclusions. It indicates that these various strands in Paul's theology cannot be

---

[4] See Furnish's careful treatment of this matter, *Theology and Ethics in Paul*, 25-92.

fully distinguished or ranked according to their ethical importance: they are interconnected like a web (not, of course, a system) and all drive towards the same definition of ethics. Justification by faith, life in the Spirit, sonship of Abraham are all intertwined in this discussion; even (heavily reworked) covenant motifs appear as well. All these various themes are connected in one way or another to Christ: faith is defined as faith in Christ, the Spirit is 'the Spirit of God's Son' and Christ is Abraham's true 'seed'. Thus in one sense it could be said that all Paul's ethics derive from 'participation in Christ'. But I suspect that this phrase is more an overall description of Paul's theology than a specification of one separable strand within it.

The particular theological themes which Paul uses in Galatians to ground his ethics are brought into prominence by the situation he addressed. The Abrahamic theme was at the heart of his dispute with the opponents, while the justification theme serves to highlight the contrast between a Jewish life-style (works of the law) and faith in Christ. The emphasis on the Spirit arises naturally out of Paul's reference to the Galatians' initial Christian experience and enables him to set up a fundamental Spirit-flesh antithesis which is of great value in his redefinition of ethical categories. When one compares this with other Pauline letters it is noteworthy that these themes recur comparatively little elsewhere (only in a developed form in Rom 3-4, 7-8) while a great range of other motifs can serve to connect theology and ethics. Thus, for example, Paul can appeal to the holiness of the Christian community (1 Thess 4), their involvement in a Christian passover (1 Cor 5), their destiny as judges of the world (1 Cor 6), Christ's ownership of their bodies (1 Cor 6), the humility and obedience of Christ (Phil 2; Rom 5), and baptism as death to sin (Rom 6). The great variety of themes Paul uses as a basis for ethics, and the many different motivations he appeals to, suggest that he could use almost any of the theological themes at his disposal in the service of his ethics.[5] This indicates the flexibility of Paul's mind

---

[5] See the range of theological themes grounding Paul's ethics as listed by Furnish, *Theology and Ethics in Paul*, 112-206 and Schrage, *Ethik*, 161-176. O. Merk gives a full analysis of the various motivations Paul employs, *Handeln aus Glauben. Die Motivierungen der paulinischen Ethik*, Marburg 1968.

but also prompts an important question: to what extent does Paul's theology determine the actual content of his ethics, as opposed to the categories in which it is expressed? Talk of 'obedience', 'death to sin', 'walking in the Spirit', 'holiness' or 'belonging to Christ' can only make a practical impact if one already knows in detail what obedience, holiness, Christ or Spirit actually require.[6] There are, no doubt, some cases where the contents of Paul's ethics are deeply influenced by his theology (e.g. in relation to love and communal fellowship) and others where he is largely rearranging assumed moral values under a Christian rubric.

3. Indicative and Imperative

Furnish once wrote that 'no interpretation of the Pauline ethic can be judged successful which does not grapple with the problem of indicative and imperative in Paul's thought'.[7] Although our study has been restricted to Galatians, it may have shed some worthwhile light on this general issue.

One of the distinctive features of Paul's use of the indicative-imperative combination is his effort to match the content of the two moods: if the indicative is 'you have been freed', the imperative is 'do not become slaves' (5.1), or if the indicative is 'you have life in the Spirit', the imperative is 'walk by the Spirit' (5.25). One explanation of this phenomenon could be given in functional terms. By matching the imperative with the indicative Paul shows the Galatians that there is only one pattern of behaviour which is consistent with their Christian status. As we noted in chapter three, one of the functions of Paul's apocalyptic language is to present the Galatians with the stark either-or choice

---

[6] Cf. Meeks' observation on the common admonition to children, 'Behave yourself'; in itself this contains little moral content, but it is effective within an assumed framework of what is correct behaviour, 'Understanding Early Christian Ethics', *JBL* 105 (1986) 3–11, here at 4.

[7] *Theology and Ethics in Paul*, 279.

between Paul's gospel and any other dissenting opinion. The indicative-imperative combination reinforces this point by suggesting that there is one, and only one, Christian option available to them: they either follow Paul's instructions or jettison their whole Christian faith. If they take on the yoke of slavery (the law) they are denying the Christ who bought their freedom.

The theological analysis of the indicative-imperative pheno-menon focuses on the logic by which these moods can be held together without, apparently, diminishing the force of either. The indicative declares what God has done in Christ (set us free, given us life in the Spirit) or what believers have done in their involvement in this act (crucified the flesh); and this does not appear to be contradicted by, or to render any less necessary, the imperative which appeals for the preservation of freedom or continual resistance to the flesh. As was indicated at the end of the last chapter, we cannot reduce the divine indicative to the mere opening of a new possibility (as is the tendency of Bultmann), nor reduce the Christian's role to purely passive acceptance of a divine act. In that context we noted the fruitfulness of Käsemann's approach where the notion of the Lordship of Christ is shown to include both the empowering of the believer and the necessity of obedience. This is certainly borne out by Paul's discussion of the Spirit in Gal 5-6, where the power and leading of the Spirit and even the gift of the fruit of the Spirit do not diminish but rather enhance the demand to work and to sow to the Spirit. This demand is also clearly related to the continuance of the 'present evil age' and the constant necessity of resisting the desires of 'the flesh'.

One of the most important theological concerns underlying much Pauline scholarship has been the desire to contrast Paul with a 'Pelagian' theology of self-achieved salvation and to distinguish his thought from all forms of 'synergism'. Not only has this contributed to a serious misrepresentation of Judaism, as if it were concerned with man achieving his own salvation; it has also led to many embarrassed attempts to explain the significance Paul att-aches to his moral imperatives, which mostly conclude that Paul saw Christian works as 'evidence' for salvation rather than 'instrumental' in it.[8] In fact, as Moore, Sanders and others have shown, the covenantal structure of most forms of Judaism always ensured a recognition of the priority of God's grace, so that even in Judaism the indicative precedes and grounds the imperative.[9] And our reading of Galatians has confirmed what has already been noted in other contexts,[10] that Paul *does* consider 'eternal life' or 'destruction' as being dependent in some important senses on the 'work' of the believer (5.4, 21; 6.6-10; see further below on judgment by works). Nevertheless, it is important to observe in this context that Paul saw the divine indicative in peculiarly dynamic terms – it was not simply a matter of what God *had* done (in election etc.) but what he *continued to do* in and for the believer. The most effective way of expressing this was by reference to the *Spirit*, since this was a familiar way of denoting God's presence and power. By describing Christian ethics in terms of 'walking in/by the Spirit' Paul could convey this sense of *constant* divine power and direction without, however, diminishing the urgency of his moral imperatives. It is this *constant interplay* between the grace of God and the work of the believer (outside Gal, cf. Phil 2.12-13; 1 Cor 15.9-10 etc.) which makes Paul's ethics of particular interest. It accords with his complex understanding of faith as response, reception, trust, decision *and* obedience (cf. Rom 1.5; 10.16 etc.).

4. *Spirit and flesh in Paul's ethics*

Our investigation has shed some light on Paul's use of the πνεῦμα-σάρξ dualism in this passage of ethical instruction. It has highlighted, for instance, the unique way in which Paul

[8] See, e.g., Gundry, 'Grace', 11: Paul 'makes good works evidential of having received grace through faith, not instrumental in keeping grace through works'.

[9] Moore, *Judaism*; Sanders, *Paul and Palestinian Judaism*.

[10] Donfried, 'Justification and Last Judgment in Paul'; Watson, *Paul, Judaism and the Gentiles*, 64–69, 115-116, 120, etc.

employs this dualism to establish his moral categories. The closest 'parallels', in Philo and the Dead Sea Scrolls, are still some distance away from Paul's usage; and in the rest of Paul's letters only Rom 7-8 approximate to what we find in Galatians, but still with some important differences. There are several factors in the Galatian situation which help to explain Paul's usage:

a) Paul's discussion of the Antioch dispute (2.15-21) reveals his awareness that the traditional language of 'sin' (ἁμαρτία) could be misleading: its association with 'disobedience to the law' could be used against Paul where he took the demands of 'the gospel' to overrule the law's prohibitions ('he makes Christ a servant of sin', 2.17). Rather than attempt to redefine this word, Paul chooses a different term to describe the moral threat – 'the flesh'.

b) Although 'satisfying the desires of the flesh' would be a phrase familiar to the Galatians as denoting self-indulgence, Paul is able to exploit the breadth of this term's semantic field, which could also include such disparate entities as humankind ('all flesh') and the tissue cut in circumcision. He can therefore use σάρξ as an 'umbrella term', and can include in his warnings against 'the flesh' a warning against libertine behaviour, antisocial conduct and law-observance, viewing all as representative of what is 'merely human'.

c) One of the terms not infrequently used in contrast to σάρξ in Jewish and Greek literature (and in the early Christian tradition?) was πνεῦμα. This term was closely associated with the Galatians' understanding of their Christian beginnings (3.2-5) and was thus ideally suited to convey Paul's basic appeal to the Galatians to continue as they had begun. And by using this term (in accordance with Jewish tradition) with reference to God's activity, Paul could assure his converts that what he demanded of them was in accordance with, and made possible by, the divine power at work in and among them.

5. *The nature of Paul's imperatives*

Although it would be unwise to draw generalized conclusions about Paul's ethics from one letter, the way Paul issues specific instructions in Galatians at the same time as he appeals to the leading of the Spirit must certainly be taken into account in any broader discussion of the nature of his imperatives. Clearly, we must avoid the pitfall of attempting to define Paul's ethics within a neat package or as one extreme in a simplistic contrast (e.g. 'libertine' or 'legalistic').[11] We are not entitled to assume that all Paul's ethics fit neatly into any of our categories or that he is always as 'Pauline' as we might like him to be!

One continuing source of confusion in this area is the use of imprecise terminology, and nowhere is this more troublesome than in the debate about whether Paul's ethics are to be characterized as 'legal' (or 'nomistic'), whether his is 'an ethic centred on law'.[12] Often a whole range of different notions are bound up together in such vague terms and, on the basis of our study in Galatians, we may be able to clarify the issues in the following way:

i) Although Paul clearly expects his converts in Galatia to be led by the Spirit, this does not prevent him from spelling out what it means to walk in the Spirit and from issuing direct instructions on the matter. This indicates that there is no fundamental dichotomy in Paul's mind between the 'internal' impulse of the Spirit and 'external' moral instruction. Thus, as Deidun and others point out, when Paul talks of freedom from the slavery of the law, he obviously does not mean freedom from 'external' commands altogether.[13]

ii) Clearly Paul's ethics are not 'legalistic' in the sense that he thought Christians could earn God's grace through obedience;

[11] Drane's title, *Paul: Libertine or Legalist?*, is unfortunate. J. Murphy-O'Connor sets up an equally false antithesis when he asks whether Paul's imperatives are 'comme des préceptes stricts imposant une obligation contraignante' or 'un tracé destiné à aider les efforts trébuchants de ses convertis', *L'Existence chrétienne selon Saint Paul*, Paris 1974, 7.

[12] See, e.g., Mohrlang, *Matthew and Paul*, 35-41; Murphy-O'Connor, *L'Existence chrétienne*, 180 ('L'éthique de Paul n'est donc pas nomistique'); Houlden, *Ethics*, 30 ('the idea of lawfulness'); T.W. Ogletree, *The Use of the Bible in Christian Ethics*, Oxford 1984, 141 ('all sorts of lawlike admonitions').

[13] Deidun, *New Covenant Morality*, 188-217, 251-258, against S. Lyonnet and others; cf. Schrage, *Einzelgebote*, 76-7.

but this was probably not true of any form of contemporary Jewish ethic either, so cannot represent the real contrast with being 'under the law'. It appears, moreover, that Paul does expect judgment to take account of the deeds of the Christian (5.21; 6.3-5, 7-10) and he has no fundamental objection to the idea of a Christian's 'work' (5.6; 6.4). In this respect, as Sanders maintains, Paul's ethics are no less 'legal' than those in most forms of Judaism. [14]

iii) We cannot justly claim that Paul's ethics are always general guidelines rather than specific and authoritative directions. Sometimes his commands are as general as the love-command (5.13-14; 6.2), but sometimes also as specific as the requirement to support Christian teachers (6.6). Love may be the highest, but it is by no means the only imperative. [15] It is true, however, that Paul does not resort to the kind of detail required in 'halakah' to reach precise definitions of right behaviour (1 Cor 7 is the nearest he gets to this). This is particularly striking in the Galatian context where we have suggested that there was some pressure on Paul to provide a detailed description of life in the Spirit. In this respect his ethical approach in this letter is very different from his previous Pharisaic pursuits (1.13-14), although other forms of Judaism showed little interest in Pharisaic-type 'halakah' – e.g., the ethical tracts in the Diaspora. Paul's reluctance to descend to this level may be related to his own flexibility of practice in various cultural contexts (1 Cor 9.19-23) and his corresponding awareness that 'right' and 'wrong' may need to be defined in some circumstances more individually (see 1 Cor 8-10; Rom 14). It may also reflect his confidence in the directive power of the Spirit (elsewhere described in terms of the discernment of a renewed mind, Rom 12.1-2; Phil 1.9-10). Although Paul is prepared to go some way in this letter towards meeting the Galatians' need for a

---

[14] *Paul, The Law, and the Jewish People*, 105-114.

[15] Schrage, *Einzelgebote*, passim. E.J. Schnabel's approach to this problem, *Law and Wisdom from Ben Sira to Paul*, Tübingen 1985, 299-342 is vitiated by his unsupported assumption that law is equivalent to 'binding norms' and wisdom equivalent to 'guiding criteria'.

moral framework, he does not regard it as necessary to give detailed codes of ethics: presumably he was confident that the Spirit would show them how to 'do good to all men' or how to 'bear one another's burdens'. Thus, Paul is not issuing a new 'law of Christ' in any rabbinic sense (*contra* Davies), although he does not eschew every kind of moral rule (*contra* Drane).

iv) Paul's emphasis in this letter on the Spirit may also illustrate a related feature of his ethics. By summing up Christian morality in a list of 'virtues' (the fruit of the Spirit) Paul lays a significant emphasis on the *character* of the moral actor – rather than, for instance, the enumeration of his *duties*. Although he goes on to spell out some implications of these virtues in 5.25-6.10, his concern is with the display of moral character, not simply the observance of a set of duties.[16] In this connection it may be significant that Paul uses the singular 'fruit', and describes the Christian's activity as his 'work' (singular, 6.4). His concern is for the fundamental direction of a person's life, which may be demonstrated in a plethora of activities but cannot be simply equated with them. Using the categories of modern moral philosophy, T.W. Ogletree has highlighted the 'perfectionist' emphasis in Paul's ethics (a concern for the discernment and maturity of the moral actor) which overshadows the 'deontological' elements (enumeration of duties).[17] Of course the rabbis also stressed intentionality and Diaspora Jews seem to have been particularly concerned to interpret the law in terms of Hellenistic virtues (see especially Philo). But Paul's emphasis on the faith, discernment and development of the individual moral actor may well have seemed to him a significant contrast with

---

[16] See Shaw, *The Cost of Authority*, 52 on this passage: 'there is a surprising preference for a model of development rather than an appeal to absolute standards. Here at last is the possibility of replacing the pursuit of conformity by a moral stance that is more exploratory and tolerant; this freedom represents a real alternative to legal observance'.

[17] Ogletree, *Use of the Bible*, 109-116, 135-145. However, his discussion of Paul's ethics in terms of the contrast between 'promise' and 'law' is less helpful and is only tenuously related to the actual text of Paul's letters.

what he, as an ex-Pharisee, considered to be life ὑπὸ νόμον with its primary orientation towards duties.

v) What, then, constituted the Galatians' freedom from 'the yoke of slavery'? Clearly not, in Paul's view, freedom from moral obligation or even from moral instruction. To some extent, the freedom-slavery contrast appears to be an emotive argument designed to alienate the Galatians both from their previous Gentile 'slavery' and from the new 'slavery' advocated by the opponents (4.1-11, 21-31; 5.1). It is rooted in reality, however, because Paul regards those in Christ (Jew and Gentile) as free from some of the Jewish rules on food and calendar observance which restricted Jewish social intercourse with non-Jews. In this way ethics are 'free' from any one cultural definition of morality. But the sense of 'freedom' may also relate to the prevailing tone of Spirit-filled 'enthusiasm' which Paul seems to have created in his Gentile churches. He encouraged them to think that they were no longer immature enough to need a παιδαγωγός (3.23-4.7): such constraints were no longer necessary for those led by the Spirit. And it is here, if anywhere, that Betz may be right to talk of Paul's 'almost naive confidence in the Spirit'. The problem was that such an atmosphere of 'freedom' among Gentiles, who lacked Paul's heritage of assumed moral principles, could easily work against Paul's own wishes: its inherent instability could lead either to the libertinism of the Corinthian church or to the Galatian pursuit of more secure moral directives in the Mosaic law. The later Pauline tradition (Ephesians; Pastorals) clearly found it necessary to modify Paul's 'freedom' in the direction of extensive codes of behaviour and a clearer definition of moral duties.

6. Paul's contrasting statements on the law

Our investigation has shed some light on the intriguing way in which Paul juxtaposes negative statements on the law (freedom from its yoke of slavery) and positive remarks about it (Christian fulfilment of the law). An explanation of this phenomenon could be given on three levels.

In the first place, these anomalies are related to Paul's

argumentative purpose in this letter. Since his main concern is to undermine the Galatians' attraction to the law, most of the letter is taken up with polemical remarks indicating its inferior and merely temporary status. But since the crisis also calls for some defence of Paul's own prescription for ethics, he seizes the opportunity of arguing that the high priority he puts on love is in fact the fulfilment of the whole law. As we noted in chapter four, Paul saves his argument from complete self-contradiction by using the ambiguous terminology of 'fulfilment': in this way he aligns himself with the 'purpose' of the law without implying a commitment to 'observe' all its commands. He also carefully qualifies how Christians fulfil the law – through love alone, and only as the law is redefined as 'the law of Christ'.

Secondly, the tension between Paul's various statements on the law can be explained in relation to the *theological framework* of the letter. In chapter three we outlined the dominant apocalyptic framework and noted its radical contrast between 'the present evil age' and 'the age to come'. But alongside this emphasis on discontinuity run some important strands of salvation-historical continuity, through the figure of Abraham and the presumption of God's constancy of will for Israel. As Sanders rightly points out, 'Paul's attitude towards the law finds its parallel in his attitude towards his own people'.[18] In both cases there is a noticeable ambiguity, since Paul's convictions about the inauguration of a *new age* run alongside his belief that God's ancient purposes find their *fulfilment* in Christ and in the Christian communities.

The third level of explanation concerns Paul's *historical and social context*. What induces Paul to interpret the new age as signalling 'death to the law' is his mission to Gentiles and his refusal to allow his Gentile converts to be forced into becoming proselytes. As a Jew he could scarcely conceive of morality without some reference to the law (or, at least, the will) of God. But in his cross-cultural mission he would not impose on Gentiles some features of the law which were distinctively and uniquely Jewish.

[18] Sanders, 'Jesus, Paul and Judaism', 434.

In discussing the fruit of the Spirit and the concluding phrase in 5.23 we noted some parallels between Paul's approach to this matter and the presentation of ethics in Hellenistic Jewish literature; but Paul is more bold in abandoning some of the distinctive features of Jewish morality which other Diaspora Jews merely downplayed or reinterpreted. Nonetheless, he was neither able nor willing to jettison all the moral values of the law. In establishing Gentile churches in sectarian separation from Judaism, he naturally emphasized *both* the Jewish heritage of his congregations *and* their distinctive Christian practices and beliefs.[19] And this social context inevitably contributed to the ambiguities inherent in his discussion of the law.

Our conclusions on this matter are largely in agreement with the work of Sanders, Dunn and Watson on the social and historical context of Paul's remarks on the law. While accepting much of Räisänen's thesis on the tensions and inconsistencies inherent in Paul's discussion of the law, our analysis of Paul's 'fulfilment' language shows he is not wholly inconsistent;[20] we would also conclude that Räisänen's emphasis on the law as a mainly *personal* problem for Paul is a little exaggerated.[21] Our results imply more serious disagreement with Hübner's proposals: we cannot accept his proposed reinterpretation of Gal 5.14 and his consequent argument that Paul is wholly negative about the law in this letter. Thus, his thesis on development between Galatians and Romans would need to be modified (but not wholly abandoned). Finally we would insist that Galatians provides no support for those who maintain a Pauline 'third use of the law',

---

[19] See Watson, *Paul, Judaism and the Gentiles*, 38–48 on the reinterpretation of religious traditions which is typical of sectarian theology.

[20] Cf. Sanders' response to Räisänen in *Paul, The Law, and the Jewish People*, 147-148. Although Räisänen is often helpful in showing where Paul's arguments are strained or artificial, his rigorous application of logic is occasionally unfair or unsympathetic to Paul's real concerns.

[21] See, e.g., *Paul and the Law*, 12, 83, 133, 137, 139, 201, 221, 224 where Räisänen discusses Paul's 'existential problem' with the law. This needs to be put in the context of Paul's social and historical circumstances, especially his creation and preservation of Gentile congregations.

even in its moral dimensions. Exactly how Jewish or Gentile Christians could 'use' the law Paul leaves tantalizingly vague, but it is clear that their behaviour should primarily be regulated by 'faith' and by their 'obedience to the truth'.

Observations on Pauline Theology

The final question that was broached in chapter one – on the meaning of the antithesis between 'faith' and 'works of the law' – takes us to the heart of the theology of Galatians, and to a central aspect of Pauline theology as a whole. Although such a topic requires a much more extensive treatment than can be offered here, our present study prompts a few pertinent observations.

1. Faith and Law in Galatians

In our analysis of the crisis in Galatia and Paul's response to it we have found no evidence to support the common theological interpretation of this letter, that Paul was fighting to maintain the principle of grace, received as a gift through faith, against the principle of merit, achieved through doing good works. To be sure, Paul does emphasize the grace of God a number of times (1.6,15; 2.21; 5.4), but never in a generalized contrast with works or achievement. 'Faith' is opposed to 'works of the law', not 'works' *simpliciter*, and it is important to realize that Paul's attack on 'works of the law' arises from the debate about Gentiles and whether they need to adopt the Mosaic law. Of course this historical context does not preclude Paul from raising broader theological issues (see below), but it does require us to understand what sort of issues they are and how they relate to his immediate concerns in Galatia.

As we have seen, the historical context of Galatians is the dispute about whether Paul's converts should become proselytes: that is, whether they need to be circumcised in order to enter the Abrahamic family and whether they should observe the Mosaic law as their pattern of life. Paul does not oppose 'the works of the law' because they constitute (or encourage) the legalist's attempt to earn righteousness before God or because they provide quantifiable criteria for evaluating human behaviour. Undoubtedly, if he had been asked if people could earn their salvation by good deeds, Paul, like any good Jew, would have rejected such a crude idea. But in Galatians Paul was not addressing any such abstract theory but the specific attempts of his opponents to make the Galatian Christians 'judaize'. His argument that they are justified by faith and not by works of the law does not constitute a renunciation of 'works' as such, even of 'works' as an important factor in salvation. It was vitally important to Paul that the Galatians' faith should 'work through love' (5.6) and that each man should 'test his own work' (6.4): otherwise they were in danger of 'falling from grace' (5.4) or 'reaping destruction' (6.8). In other words, faith in Galatians is not just 'believing the gospel'; it also includes a commitment to 'obey the truth', and cannot be distinguished from the constant attempt to 'walk in the Spirit'.

This goes a long way to explain the so-called 'antinomy' between 'justification by faith' and 'judgment by works'. If one assumes that Paul sees a fundamental theological antithesis between 'faith' and 'works', this combination of theologoumena looks like an outright contradiction. But Paul does not regard faith in purely passive terms: rather, it has very definite moral aspects which determine how the believer should live 'by faith' or 'by the Spirit'. If Paul calls the Galatians to 'do good to all men' (ἐργαζώμεθα τὸ ἀγαθὸν πρὸς πάντας, 6.10) he is merely calling for the exercise of 'faith which works through love'. Conversely, when he threatens them with exclusion from Christ if they take on the yoke of the law or practise the works of the flesh, he is not introducing a moral standard independent of faith but indicating how they might fail to live by faith or remain true to the Spirit. Thus, just as Peter 'stood condemned' (2.11) because he failed to take seriously what it meant to seek to be justified by faith in Christ (2.15-17), so the deeds for which all Christians are to be judged will be the mark of their success or failure in 'obeying the truth' in faith.

This indicates that, although Sanders rightly interprets 'the works of the law' in Galatians as the demands of the Mosaic law (rather than 'works' in general), he is not right to distinguish so sharply between the requirements for 'getting in' to the people of God and the behaviour required of those who want to 'stay in'. If Paul requires 'faith in Christ', this is not just as an 'entry-requirement', but it is the fundamental determinant of all Christian behaviour. He opposes 'works of the law' not only as entry-requirements but also, and more particularly, as the Torah-centred pattern of life which the Galatians want to adopt. In fact Sanders acknowledges the importance of faith in the *continuing* as well as the *beginning* of the Christian life, but by making such a sharp distinction and by insisting that the debate in Galatians is about 'entry'-conditions, he has misconstrued the letter.[22] Although Paul can still talk of the law in his positive representation of ethics, this is only with careful qualification and using the ambiguous language of 'fulfilling the law'; in actual practice it is very different from the opponents' ideas of 'doing the works of the law'.

Our conclusions are largely, but not entirely, in agreement with Watson's analysis of Galatians. He is correct to emphasize the historical and social realities of the letter and that the debate about the law concerns whether Gentile Christians should live like Jews. He also rightly discerns that the practical issue ultimately at stake in the Galatian crisis was whether Paul's churches should merge with the synagogues and remain as a 'reform-movement' within Judaism or maintain a separate social identity and thus split off as a 'sect' from the parent religion.

One could quibble with some of the finer details of this sociological model: the terms 'reform-movement' and 'sect' are

---

[22] On this point the criticisms of Hübner, *Law in Paul's Thought*, 152 and Gundry, 'Grace', 8-9 are well-aimed. To be sure, Sanders does preface his remark that 'the debate in Galatians is a debate about "entry"' with the proviso that 'I do not mean to imply that the requirement of faith alone for entry . . . is a fleeting one which has no significance for continuing life in the people of God', *Paul, The Law, and the Jewish People*, 20; cf. 114, 159.

not very exact and there are important structural differences between Paul's churches and the Jewish 'sect' at Qumran with which Watson compares them.[23] But there is a much more important problem in the way Watson uses his sociological analysis to minimize the significance of the theological aspects of the letter. His comment on some of the key faith-law antitheses in Galatians is significant: 'the point at issue in all of them is not "theology" as such but the separation of the church from the Jewish community' (67).[24] It is clear that Watson's primary target here is the Lutheran theology which still dominates exegesis of these texts. Elsewhere he insists that his approach 'does not claim to exclude the possibility of *any* theological interpretation of Paul' (20). But his attraction to the sociological notion of 'ideology' – theory used to legitimate established social facts and practices – often leads him to evaluate Paul's various theological statements on the law and Judaism as 'secondary, theological reflection' (31) on primary historical fact. Not surprisingly, his book concludes by asking whether the Paul who struggled to legitimate the existence of his sectarian groups can 'still be seen as the bearer of a message with profound universal significance' (181).

Watson's position is readily understandable as a protest against the individualistic Lutheran theology which has so often been imposed on Paul's texts. He also advances some important historical arguments to support his claim that Paul's theology was subsequent to historical fact: he maintains that Paul began his Christian career as a missionary to Jews and it was only after their rejection of his gospel, and the success he encountered in preaching to Gentiles without requiring law-observance, that he

---

[23] The problems of definition with regard to 'sect' are well-known; see B. Wilson's attempt to classify sect-types, *Sect and Society*, London 1961. One of the major differences between Paul's communities and the Qumran sect is in their attitude to outsiders; see W. Meeks, '"Since then you would need to go out of the world": Group Boundaries in Pauline Christianity', in *Critical History and Biblical Faith: New Testament Perspectives*, ed. T. Ryan, Villanova, Pennsylvania 1979, 4-29.

[24] Cf. *Paul, Judaism and the Gentiles*, 65, 134, 178-9.

constructed a theology to legitimate his activities using an antithesis between faith and works of the law. There are several features of this reconstruction which I would contest – not least on the grounds that Paul's former persecution of Christians out of zeal for the law betrays an awareness that faith in Christ and law-observance were incompatible, an awareness which was merely reinforced when he changed his allegiance on the Damascus road.[25] But even if Watson's historical reconstruction were correct, we would still be entitled to ask whether a document like Galatians (or even more, Romans) does not reflect the continuing *dialectic* between ideas and social conditions which many sociologists regard as a better explanation of such texts than a reductionist notion of ideology.[26] Is it possible that the social context of Paul's Gentile mission both prompted theological conclusions and was itself moulded by theological convictions inherited from Judaism and refashioned 'in Christ'?

The crucial step towards unearthing any such broader theological convictions is the observation that Paul opposes 'the works of the law' in Galatians because they represent imposing a Jewish life-style ('living like a Jew', 2.14ff.) on his Gentile converts. The problem here is not legalism (in the sense of earning merit before God) but cultural imperialism – regarding Jewish identity and Jewish customs as the essential tokens of membership in the

[25] Although we do not really know why Paul's 'zeal for the law' made him persecute Christians (Phil 3.6), his persecuting activity signals his conviction that the Christian movement could not be tolerated within Judaism. Given the traumatic nature of his 'conversion', it is likely that his change of allegiance to the Christian movement contained within it a questioning of his previous wholehearted commitment to the law. Watson's thesis, that Paul first worked as a missionary to Jews without questioning the law, and only subsequently reverted to his pre-Christian opinion that Christian faith and law-observance were in tension, seems unnecessarily complicated. It is also built on rather flimsy evidence (Gal 5.11; 1 Cor 9.20; Rom 11.11ff.) compared to Paul's repeated statements about his call as an apostle to Gentiles (Gal 1.15–16; Rom 1.5; 11.13; 15.16, etc.).

[26] The debate among sociologists about the relationship between social conditions and ideas/ideologies is at least as old as Weber. See the discussion by M. Hill, *A Sociology of Religion*, London 1973 and P. Berger, *The Social Reality of Religion*. Except for those with a rigidly Marxian outlook, most sociologists seem to recognize the importance of the 'dialectic' between events and ideas.

people of God. This indicates that Paul renounces law-observant Judaism not because it is legalistic but because it is nationalistic – bound by its own history and culture to the extent that God's saving activity is envisaged in racial and cultural terms. We have touched on this matter in discussing the flesh-Spirit antithesis. There we noted that one reason for Paul's association of the law with σάρξ was the importance within Jewish religion of kinship-relations (one is born a Jew κατὰ σάρκα) and the racial exclusivism this entails. But we also saw that the flesh-Spirit antithesis expresses a broader theological theme – the contrast between what is 'merely human' and what is consonant with the radical initiative of God in Christ in 'the new age'. It is the combination of Paul's Jewish apocalypticism (the radical contrast between 'the present age' and 'the age to come') and his exclusive Christology (God has inaugurated the new age through the death and resurrection of Christ) which fosters this contrast between 'what is merely human' and what partakes of the new age in the Spirit of Christ. And it is this theological perspective, when combined with his experience of the Gentile mission, which enables Paul to include alongside his man-God or flesh-Spirit antitheses the further antithesis of works of law and faith. The 'works of the law', in that they are culture-bound, are man-centred; they fall into the category of 'what is merely human' in the light of the new values introduced by the new age. Faith, on the other hand, transcends human cultures and unites in Christ Jew and Gentile (as well as slave and free, male and female, 3.28). Faith alone proves to be the means of receiving the Spirit (3.2-5) and it is thus the essential characteristic of those who are open to receive God's revolutionary initiative of grace.

This enables us to understand better Paul's emphasis on grace in Galatians (1.6,15; 2.21; 5.4). To continue under the yoke of the law would be to deny the grace of God (2.21) not because it would involve the legalistic attempt to earn righteousness but because it would entail remaining in a culture-bound tradition which had been rendered obsolete by God's initiative in Christ. Watson himself makes the important observation that 'Paul's view of grace is more "radical" than that of the Judaism he opposes' because Paul's conversionist theology is 'dynamic' in contrast to 'the more static view of grace taken by groups in which membership is determined by birth' (66). This correlates very well with the theological pattern we have been discussing, provided that one remembers that, with his apocalyptic perspective, Paul was apt to dismiss the static view of grace as wholly inadequate when measured against the revolutionary new values of 'the new age' (see below, however, on Rom 9-11). Watson is right to insist that grace is not fundamentally opposed to human activity, although a dynamic view of grace does affect one's perspective on the relationship between divine grace and human activity in important respects (see above pp.226-7). What he fails to explore, however, is the effect of this dynamic view of grace on the believer's attitude to the traditions, cultural norms and social expectations in which he or she has been brought up. In Paul's perspective the grace of God, experienced in Christ, relativizes all such human traditions, including Judaism. In other words, while Paul is not building a general theological contrast between salvation by human achievement and salvation by divine gift, he is propounding a far-reaching contrast between human values and traditions on the one hand and the sovereign initiative of God on the other.

Thus I would join ranks with Sanders, Watson and others in seeking to overthrow the individualistic Lutheran interpretation of Galatians which views Paul as arguing here against the attitude of self-righteousness, that is, dependence on the number or quality of one's works to earn status before God.[27] The argument of Galatians concerns *Jews and Gentiles* and is rooted in the social circumstances of Paul's Gentile congregations. But this does not leave Paul arguing simply that Judaism is wrong because 'it is not Christianity' (Sanders).[28] Even when Sanders fills out this statement with reference to Jewish nationalism, Paul's concern

---

[27] Of course the gospel is aimed to elicit a response from each individual as faith is a personal, not a collective, attribute. Yet it is doubtful whether Paul would have viewed this primarily in terms of a change of *self-understanding*. An exclusive focus on the individual would also obscure the importance for Paul of corporate life and mutual responsibility, which we noted in connection with 5.25-6.10.

[28] *Paul and Palestinian Judaism*, 552.

for Gentiles and his exclusive Christology,[29] he still does not penetrate to the theological depths of Paul's argument. Nor can we explain Paul's attack on Judaism in purely *functional* terms, stating merely that 'it serves to establish and maintain [the] sectarian separation [of Paul's churches]' (Watson).[30] While it does indeed have this social function, it also reflects deep-rooted theological convictions on the sovereign grace of God and the limitations of all human (including Jewish) values and traditions. It would be a mistake to attempt to 'explain' Paul's perspective on Judaism in purely personal terms (as the outcome of his psychological experience) or in purely theological terms (as a theological system worked out in abstract); but it is equally mistaken to attempt a purely sociological 'explanation' (as a mere by-product of, or rationalization for, Paul's social circumstances).[31] Each of these forms of reductionism will give us a distorted image of Paul. It is supremely in Galatians that we find the fascinating interplay between personal experience, social context and theological conviction. The different forms of analysis required to uncover these varied features of the letter should be regarded as mutually illuminating, not mutually exclusive.

2. Galatians and other Pauline letters

Although it is clearly impossible to discuss other texts in proper detail in this conclusion to our investigation, some observations on Paul's treatment of similar themes – law, works, faith, grace –

---

[29] *Paul and Palestinian Judaism*, 541-552; *Paul, The Law, and the Jewish People*. Dunn's criticism of Sanders in 'The New Perspective' in fact adds little to what Sanders himself expounds in the latter book.

[30] *Paul, Judaism and the Gentiles*, 113.

[31] Watson scorns those who take the contrast between a static and dynamic view of the grace of God to be 'a profound insight into the existential plight of humanity, whereas in fact it is merely a by-product of two different patterns of religion, which one might perhaps label "traditional" and "conversionist" respectively', *Paul, Judaism and the Gentiles*, 79. It is hard to see how this statement can avoid the charge of reductionism.

in other letters will prove to be of some value. In some cases it will reveal a similar structure of thought to that we have detected in Galatians, while in others we will find evidence for material difference from Galatians. Since each Pauline letter should be taken on its own terms and not hastily harmonized with the rest of the corpus, this latter category of texts will help to point up the relative uniqueness of the letter we have been studying.

i) *Philippians 3*. Here Paul warns the Philippian church about potential 'judaizing' agents ('the dogs', 3.2) who advocate circumcision ('mutilation'). Whereas in Galatians he responded to this threat with arguments about Abraham, he here presents himself as an exemplar, as one who had every possible Jewish privilege but counted them all as 'loss' for the sake of knowing Christ. The list of privileges includes both tokens of his Jewish status (circumcised on the eighth day, of the people of Israel etc.) and indications of his accomplishment (a zealous persecutor of the church, blameless in his δικαιοσύνη ἐν νόμῳ). What this passage makes clear is that none of these things could be faulted as wrong in themselves (even his zeal) *except* in the light of Christian faith: it is only because of the 'surpassing worth of knowing Christ' that Paul counts these previous tokens of 'gain' as 'loss'. But does this Christian commitment provide a *theological logic* which explains this negative verdict? The majority interpretation has always identified this logic as a renunciation of *self-righteousness*: Paul is accusing his former self (and, by implication, other Jews) of attempting to earn their own righteousness.[32] This is usually supported by reference to 3.9, where Paul contrasts 'my own righteousness, based on law' (ἐμὴν δικαιοσύνην τὴν ἐκ νόμον) with 'the righteousness of God which depends on faith' (τὴν ἐκ θεοῦ δικαιοσύνην ἐπὶ τῇ πίστει). But there are good grounds for questioning whether 'my own righteousness' means 'self-earned righteousness' – not least the fact that most of Paul's Jewish privileges were his by *birth*, not accomplishment, and the fact that he encourages the notion of Christian accom-

---

[32] See, e.g., Bultmann, *Theology* I, 240; Gundry, 'Grace', 14.

plishment elsewhere in this letter (2.12; 3.14–15).[33] It is better to read 'my own righteousness' as an expression of *limitation* rather than an expression of *achievement*: the items in Paul's list are not 'loss' because Paul has achieved them (in self-righteous pride) but because they are *merely his own human characteristics* which do not count as truly significant before *God*. This is why he talks of boasting 'in the flesh' (3.3–4): they are indications of status and achievement *on a merely human level*, rather than what really counts before God. As this passage demonstrates supremely clearly, faith in Christ involves the acknowledgment that the grace of God overturns human expectations and traditions, including Jewish traditions and Jewish cultural norms. The paradoxical gospel of salvation through the crucifixion of a servant (2.6–11) requires that each believer also share in his death (3.10); it overturns his previous value system and exposes it as a 'fleshly' (purely human) phenomenon. Thus while Sanders is right that Paul is not accusing himself of being 'guilty of the attitudinal sin of self-righteousness', he fails to discern that there is a theological principle at stake in this passage deeper than merely putting 'confidence in something other than faith in Christ'.[34] He has made his position vulnerable by failing to provide a good explanation for the phrase 'my own righteousness' (Watson appears to bypass this phrase too). The suggestion offered here is that, as in Galatians, Paul is criticizing his own Judaism because it is too firmly wedded to human cultural and social values. Although he can only make this judgment from the standpoint of Christian faith, it still contains an important theological principle capable of wide application.

ii) *1 Corinthians 1-4*. This passage indeed demonstrates how far-reaching this theological principle can be. Here the topic under debate is not works of the law but wisdom, which Paul

---

[33] Watson, *Paul, Judaism and the Gentiles*, 77–78.

[34] *Paul, The Law, and the Jewish People*, 44; he appears to have left Phil 3.9 out of account when he writes that 'the only thing that is wrong with the old righteousness is that it is not the new one; it has no fault which is described in other terms' (140).

seems to regard as the chief characteristic of Greek culture (1.22-23). These chapters contain a critique of wisdom which is built upon a fundamental contrast between the ways of *God* and the ways of *humankind*. *Human* wisdom and all human-centred boasting are rendered wholly invalid in the light of the gospel (1.19,29; 2.5,13-14; 3.3,18-21).[35] Just as in Galatians the cross constitutes the death of the old world, including the law, so here the antithesis between humankind and God is demonstrated most clearly in the cross: precisely because it represents the foolishness of God it constitutes God's means of salvation, for through it he demolishes the human evaluation of wisdom and power (1.19,25,27-29). Thus the message of the cross, which is a stumbling-block to Jews, is also foolishness to Gentiles (1.23). It overturns the traditions and cultural values of both groups since it represents the radical re-creative initiative of God, who puts human pretensions to shame (including all judgments κατὰ σάρκα, 1.26) and calls into existence even the things that do not exist (1.27-28). God does not work in accordance with human evaluation or human expectation: his working can only be grasped by faith (1.12; 2.5; 3.5).

iii) *Romans*. Recent studies of Rom 1-4 have rightly pointed out the importance of the theme 'Jew and Gentile' in this section of the letter.[36] The gospel is the power of God for salvation for all who believe, 'the Jew first and also the Greek' (1.16); and, though they have the privileges of possessing the law, Jews are not thereby exempt from the judgment of God who judges impartially 'the Jew first and also the Greek' (2.9-11). Paul's critique of Jewish 'boasting in the law' (2.17,23) is not directed against individual Jews seeking credit for good works, but against the national pride that presumes on Israel's election privileges. God's new act of salvation is 'apart from the law' and through faith (3.21ff.)

---

[35] See K. Barth, *The Resurrection of the Dead*, E.T. London 1933, 15-29.

[36] Besides Sanders and Watson, see, e.g., U.Wilckens, *Der Brief an der Römer* I, Zurich/Neukirchen-Vluyn 1978; G. Howard, 'Romans 3.21-31 and the Inclusion of the Gentiles', *HTR* 63 (1970) 223-233.

because faith is not a specifically Jewish characteristic: Jew *and Gentile* are saved through faith (3.30) and thus Abraham's faith renders him the father of both (4.9ff.). God himself is one – not the God of Jews only but also of Gentiles (3.29).

Thus here, as in Galatians, Paul's critique of Judaism focuses on its nationalism, although his argument in Romans leads him into a more extended assault on Israel's national pride – her assumption of a special election status supposedly confirmed by her possession and observance of the law. Yet we also find in Rom 4 a number of remarks which seem to be of a more general nature. In 4.1-6 Paul reflects on 'works' as such (ἔργα, not ἔργα νόμου) and comments that 'for him who works, his reward is not reckoned according to grace, but according to his due' (4.4). Later in the chapter he also makes a generalized comment about faith and grace (διὰ τοῦτο ἐκ πίστεως, ἵνα κατὰ χάριν, 4.16) and describes Abraham's faith as typical of true faith in the God 'who gives life to the dead and calls into existence the things that do not exist' (4.17). These more general comments about 'works' and 'faith' pose something of a problem for commentators. Many read the whole of Rom 1-4 in their light and thus see Paul's real attack on 'works of the law' as directed against the *principle of works*.[37] On the other hand, the recent studies which emphasize the Jew-Gentile context of Paul's attack on works of the law tend to read these statements also as specifically about (Jewish) *works of the law*.[38] A more satisfactory solution would be to admit that the primary thrust of these chapters concerns Jewish law-observance and the faith available to Gentile as well as Jew, but that Paul also makes some subsidiary generalized comments about 'faith as such' and 'works as such'. His point about faith is that it is an attitude of utter dependence on God, which recognizes one's own

---

[37] E.g., Käsemann, *Commentary on Romans*, 105ff.; C.E.B. Cranfield, *A Critical and Exegetical Commentary on the Epistle to the Romans* I, Edinburgh 1975, 224ff. Hübner, *Law in Paul's Thought*, 118ff. argues that Rom 1-3 can only be understood on the basis of Rom 4 (esp. 4.1-8).

[38] Sanders, *Paul, The Law, and the Jewish People*, 32-36; Watson, *Paul, Judaism and the Gentiles*, 135-142.

insufficiency and *therefore* depends on *grace*.[39] His point about works is not that they are wrong in themselves or always express an attitude of self-righteousness, but that the absence or insufficiency of works underlines human inadequacy and thus serves to show up God's grace all the more.[40] Thus in attacking Jewish national pride Paul allows himself some broader reflections on the need for mankind to recognise its insufficiency before God; and in the course of ruling out the adequacy of Jewish works of the law Paul reflects on how God's grace is highlighted and clarified when it is independent of works. In the latter case, Paul is not accusing Jews of seeking to establish credit by amassing good works,[41] but is making an observation on the fact that God's grace is only fully evident where there is no 'work' to be rewarded. He is not analyzing subjective *intentions* but noting an objective *fact*. Nevertheless, those generalizing comments go some way beyond what we have observed in either Galatians or Philippians, where the discussion was always restricted to the law or works of the law.

In recognizing the generalized nature of some of Paul's remarks in Rom 4, we gain a clearer understanding of the relationship between this chapter and the four which follow. If Rom 1-4 is *purely* about Jews and Gentiles, it is difficult to relate these chapters to Rom 5-8.[42] But if Paul's discussion of the Jew-

---

[39] Watson obscures this point by describing Abraham's faith as a 'strenuous human response' (140); Paul's point is that Abraham was strong in faith, knowing that *he could do nothing* about his childlessness.

[40] Nothing in 4.4-5 indicates there is any fault in 'working'. Paul is making a purely factual observation that where works are given their due reward, there is no opportunity for the display of grace. Cf. Mt 20.1-16: those who worked all day in the vineyard were not wrong to work, but the 'grace' of the owner is only seen in his generosity to those who did little work.

[41] Käsemann goes astray when he insists that in 4.5 'ἐργάζεσθαι no longer means "to work" but "to be concerned about works"', *Commentary on Romans*, 110. Hübner's assertion that Paul regards Abraham as a sinner because 'he has sought to be righteous as a result of his works', *Law in Paul's Thought*, 121 is similarly mistaken.

[42] Watson, *Paul, Judaism and the Gentiles*, 142-159 clearly has most difficulty in relating Rom 5-8 to the historical context he proposes as the setting of the whole letter (Jewish and Gentile Christian congregations in Rome).

Gentile problem calls forth some more general observations about humankind, grace and God in Rom 4, we can see better how this leads Paul on to talk about the love of God in Christ crucified (5.6-10), the grace of God in the midst of universal human sinfulness (5.12-21) and baptism, in which the old humanity is crucified (6.6) and new life is given as a gift of grace on the basis of the resurrection of Christ (6.4,8-10,23; cf. 4.17). The generalizing tendency is also evident to some extent in Rom 7, where Paul's comments about the law appear to be applicable to all humanity (not just Israel), as the Adam-echoes in 7.7ff. suggest.

With chapter 9 Paul returns to the more specific issue of Israel, picking up his earlier comments in 3.1ff. on the faithfulness of God.[43] Once again, one of the dominant themes is the relationship between Jews and Gentiles. Paul interprets Scripture as foretelling the 'hardening' of Israel and the influx of Gentiles (9.24ff.) and he re-emphasizes the transcultural nature of faith, in which there is no distinction between Jew and Greek (10.10-13). As Sanders and others have rightly insisted, this context should determine the interpretation of Paul's comment on his fellow Jews seeking to establish 'their own righteousness' (ἰδία δικαιοσύνη 10.3). This phrase does not refer to the problem of *individual self-righteousness*, but to *Jewish national righteousness* which excludes Gentiles (God's righteousness, by contrast, is for *all* who believe).[44] Even more explicitly than in Rom 1-4, Paul is confronting in these chapters the Jewish consciousness of election; only here, as he recalls the divine promises to Israel, he is not able simply to dismiss the problem as nationalistic pride. By

---

[43] Of course there are a number of factors which contributed to the construction of Rom 9-11: some theological (the constancy of God in view of the 'disobedience' of most Jews to the gospel; the witness of Scripture), some personal (Paul's defence of his ministry to Gentiles and assertion of his concern for unbelieving Jews) and some historical (the pride of Gentile believers in Rome; Paul's own impending visit to Jerusalem).

[44] Sanders, *Paul, The Law, and the Jewish People*, 36-43. Cf. N.T. Wright, *The Messiah and the People of God*; G. Howard 'Christ the End of the Law', *JBL* 88 (1969) 331-337.

drawing on Israel's own traditions which talk of 'the remnant' and emphasize God's grace and sovereignty, Paul argues initially that only some within Israel are reckoned as true Israelites (9.6ff.; 11.1ff.); but he eventually reaches the compromise solution that all Israel has fallen into disobedience but will be saved (by faith?) when God has mercy on all (11.25-32).[45] It is precisely this sort of manoeuvre – turning Jewish traditions, especially Scripture, against Judaism itself but then finally asserting the salvation of 'all Israel' – which makes it so difficult to discuss whether or in what sense Paul has 'broken' with Judaism.[46] But it also illustrates Paul's consistent conviction that Jews cannot presume on their election status and that, like the rest of mankind, they must experience God's grace as his mercy on the *disobedient* (11.32; cf. 4.5; 5.12-21). Apart from the final comments on the salvation of 'all Israel', this passage confirms what we have found in Galatians and Philippians, that Paul considers Israel to be on a par with 'what is merely human'; she can claim no ultimate immunity or superiority. This is at the heart of Paul's whole critique of Judaism.[47]

However, as in Rom 4, there are a few statements in these chapters which broach the topic of works in general (rather than works of the law). In 9.32 the context indicates that ἔργα probably stands for ἔργα νόμου (as in the variant reading), but in 9.11-12 and 11.5-6 generalizing remarks are made about 'works' and 'grace'. The former passage concerns Jacob and Esau, whose fate was determined by God's election *in utero* 'before they had done anything, good or bad, in order that God's purpose of election might continue, not because of works but because of his

---

[45] On Paul's various answers to the question of Israel's salvation in Rom 9-11, see, e.g., G. Lüdemann, *Paulus und das Judentum*; H. Hübner, *Gottes Ich und Israel*, Göttingen 1984.

[46] For recent discussion of this issue see, e.g., W.D. Davies, 'Paul and the People of Israel', *NTS* 24 (1977-8) 4-39; H. Räisänen, 'Galatians 2.16 and Paul's Break with Judaism', *NTS* 31 (1985) 543-553.

[47] Thus, against Käsemann's reading of Rom 9-11 as concerning 'the pious man' ('the hidden Jew in all of us'), Wright correctly insists that its real point is 'the hidden Adam in Israel', 'Paul of History', 78 n.34.

call' (9.11). The latter concerns the remnant, 'chosen by grace':
'but if it is by grace it is no longer from works, otherwise grace
would no longer be grace' (11.5-6). This seems to be the same
principle as in 4.4-5: where there are no works, it is apparent that
God is acting purely by grace. Once again, there is no indication
in the context that Paul is accusing Jews of having the perverse
intention of wanting to earn God's favour by good works. He is
merely stating the fact, at a fairly general level of abstraction, that
grace is only shown to be grace where it is not some measured
reward for works.[48]

These observations lead us to conclude that there are some
important differences between Galatians and Romans (although
the basic outlook on Judaism is the same in both letters).[49] The
historical situation in Galatia led Paul to an implicit attack on
law-observant Judaism for its cultural imperialism; he resists the
effort of Jewish Christians to impose the Jewish works of the law
on Gentiles.[50] In Romans, for whatever historical or personal
reasons, Paul addresses himself more directly to Jews and Jewish-
Christians, opposing their national and cultural pride which led
them to presume on God's covenant promises. In both letters
(and in Phil 3) he treats Judaism as a merely human, cultural
phenomenon (Rom 9-11 is a partial exception) and thus sets its
human traditions and achievements in contrast to the grace and
power of God. In Romans Paul's more extended reflections on
these matters led him to make some general observations about
faith and works which are not to be found in the earlier letters.
Though such remarks are subsidiary to the main argument about
Jews and Gentiles, one can understand how they were soon taken

[48] That Paul is not opposed *in principle* to 'works' and 'obedience' is amply
shown by Rom 6 and 12-14.

[49] Thus there is some truth in Hübner's thesis of 'development' between the
two letters. But our analysis differs widely from his interpretation of both
letters!

[50] Mussner's insistence that Paul is not attacking *Jews* but *Jewish-Christians* in
Galatians, *Tractate on the Jews*, E.T. London 1984, 143ff. is of course correct. But
Paul is attacking Jewish-Christians for their Jewish presuppositions, and for
wanting to make Gentile believers live like Jews.

to be the very core of Paul's theology and applied in an individualistic manner. Already in the Pastorals (2 Tim 1.9; Tit 3.4-7) we find the general contrast between 'righteous works' and 'God's grace' represented as the heart of the gospel. And in Eph 2.8-9, where the gospel is summed up as 'by grace through faith', 'not from works lest any man should boast', the focus shifts decisively to the individual and his boasted achievements. This passage is proof that an aversion to individual self-righteous attitudes is not an invention of the Reformation, or even of Augustine!

However, we must still insist that in Galatians *and* in Romans there are no clear indications that Paul is concerned with individual legalistic attitudes. Paul's doctrine of justification by faith has to do with his rejection of Israel's cultural pride, not any presumption that she can amass credit by good works. We may suspect that one reason for the prevalence of the individualistic interpretation of Paul has been its perceived 'relevance' to man's existential situation (it removes the anxiety of the stricken conscience). The irony is that this has led to a distorted reading of Paul's letters and has failed to register the important *social* implications of his real theology.[51] If Jewish Christians went wrong in imposing their Jewish cultural traditions on Gentile believers, Paul's theology could turn out to be a powerful corrective to the cultural (and social) imperialism which has stained, and continues to stain, so much that passes for Christianity. The comprehensive formula in Gal 3.28 (unity of Jew and Gentile, slave and free, male and female) could then be heard to speak to the racial, cultural, social and sexual prejudices which bedevil the church as well as wider society. At the same time Paul's attack on Jewish cultural traditions as 'merely human' could lead the church into a far more critical sifting of her own traditions and a renewed awareness of the danger of complacency for all those who claim to be 'the people of God'.

[51] See Dahl, 'The Doctrine of Justification'; M. Barth, 'Jew and Gentile: The Social Character of Justification in Paul', *JES* 5 (1968) 241-267.

Bibliography

Allison, D.C.,   'The Pauline Epistles and the Synoptic Gospels:
                          the Pattern of the Parallels', *NTS* 28 (1982)
                          1-32.

Althaus, P.,   ' "Dass ihr nicht tut, was ihr wollt". Zur
                          Auslegung von Gal.5, 17', *TLZ* 76 (1951)
                          15-18.

Badenas, R.,   *Christ the End of the Law. Romans 10.4 in Pauline
                          Perspective*, JSNTS 10, Sheffield 1985.

Baeck, L.,   'The Faith of Paul', *JJS* 3 (1952) 93-110.

Bamberger, B.J.   *Proselytism in the Talmudic Period*, New York
                          1968.

Bammel, E.,   'Gottes ΔΙΑΘΗΚΗ (Gal.III.15-17) und das
                          jüdische Rechtsdenken', *NTS* 6 (1959-60)
                          313-319.

                          'νόμος Χριστοῦ', in *Studia Evangelica III*, ed.
                          F.L. Cross, TU 88, Berlin 1964, 120-128.

Bandstra, A.J.,   *The Law and the Elements of the World. An
                          Exegetical Study in Aspects of Paul's Teaching*,
                          Kampen 1964.

Banks, R.,   *Jesus and the Law in the Synoptic Tradition*,
                          SNTSMS 28, Cambridge 1975.

Barclay, J.M.G.,   'Paul and the Law: Observations on Some
                          Recent Debates', *Themelios* 12 (1986) 5-15.

                          'Mirror-Reading a Polemical Letter: Galatians
                          as a Test Case', *JSNT* 31 (1987) 73-93.

Barclay, W.,   *Flesh and Spirit. An Examination of Galatians
                          5.19-23*, London 1962.

Barr, J.,   *The Semantics of Biblical Language*, Oxford
                          1961.

Barrett, C.K.,   'Paul and the "Pillar" Apostles', in *Studia
                          Paulina* (in honorem Johannis de Zwaan),
                          ed. J.N. Sevenster and W.C. van Unnik,
                          Haarlem 1953, 1-19.

From First Adam to Last. A Study in Pauline Theology, London 1962.

The Second Epistle to the Corinthians, Black's New Testament Commentaries, London 1973.

'The Allegory of Abraham, Sarah and Hagar in the Argument of Galatians', in *Rechtfertigung* (Festschrift für E. Käsemann), ed. J. Friedrich et al., Tübingen 1976, 1-16.

Freedom and Obligation. A Study of the Epistle to the Galatians, London 1985.

Barth, K.,   *The Resurrection of the Dead*, E.T. by H.J. Stenning, London 1933.

Barth, M.,   'The Kerygma of Galatians', *Int* 21 (1967) 131-146.

'Jew and Gentile: The Social Character of Justification in Paul', *JES* 5 (1968) 241-267.

Baumgarten, J.,   *Paulus und die Apokalyptik*, WMANT 44, Neukirchen-Vluyn 1975.

Bäumlein, E.,   'Ueber Galat.5, 23', *Theologische Studien und Kritiken*, 1862, 551-553.

Baur, F.C.,   'Die Christuspartei in der korinthischen Gemeinde, der Gegensatz des petrinischen und paulinischen Christenthums in der ältesten Kirche, der Apostel Petrus in Rom', *Tübinger Zeitschrift für Theologie* 4 (1831) 61-206, reprinted in *Ausgewählte Werke in Einzelausgaben* I, Stuttgart 1963.

Paul. The Apostle of Jesus Christ, E.T. by A. Menzies from 2nd German edition, 2 volumes, London/Edinburgh 1876.

Becker, J.,   *Das Heil Gottes. Heils- und Sündenbegriffe in den Qumrantexten und im Neuen Testament*, SUNT 3, Göttingen 1964.

Der Brief an die Galater, Das Neue Testament Deutsch, 8, 15th edition, Göttingen 1981, 1-85.

Beker, J.C.,   *Paul the Apostle. The Triumph of God in Life and Thought*, Philadelphia 1980.

Berger, K.,   'Abraham in den paulinischen Hauptbriefen', *Münchener Theologische Zeitschrift* 17 (1966) 47-89.

Berger, P.L.,   *The Social Reality of Religion*, London 1967.

Berger, P.L., and Luckmann, T., — *The Social Construction of Reality*, London 1967.

Betz, H.D., — 'Spirit, Freedom and Law. Paul's Message to the Galatian Churches', *SEÅ* 39 (1974) 145–160.

'The Literary Composition and Function of Paul's Letter to the Galatians', *NTS* 21 (1974–5) 353–379.

'In Defense of the Spirit: Paul's Letter to the Galatians as a Document of Early Christian Apologetics', in *Aspects of Religious Propaganda in Judaism and Early Christianity*, ed. E. Schüssler-Fiorenza, Notre-Dame, Indiana 1976, 99–114.

Galatians, Hermeneia, Philadelphia 1979.

2 Corinthians 8 and 9, Hermeneia, Philadelphia 1985.

Betz, O., — *Offenbarung und Schriftforschung in der Qumransekte*, WUNT 6, Tübingen 1960.

'Die heilsgeschichtliche Rolle Israels bei Paulus', *Theologische Beiträge* 9 (1978) 1–21.

Bisping, A., — *Erklärung des zweiten Briefes an die Korinther und des Briefes an die Galater*, Münster 1863.

Blank, J., — 'Warum sagt Paulus: "Aus Werken des Gesetzes wird niemand gerecht"?', in *Evangelisch-Katholischer Kommentar zum Neuen Testament, Vorarbeiten Heft 1*, Zürich 1969, 79–95.

Blass, F., and Debrunner, A., — *A Greek Grammar of the New Testament and Other Early Christian Literature*, E.T. and ed. by R.W. Funk from 19th German edition, Chicago 1961.

Bligh, J., — *Galatians in Greek*, Detroit 1966.

Galatians. A Discussion of St. Paul's Epistle, Householder Commentaries, London 1969.

Bonnard, P., — *L'Épître de Saint Paul aux Galates*, Commentaire du Nouveau Testament, 9, 2nd edition, Neuchâtel 1972.

Bonner, S., — *Education in Ancient Rome: From the Elder Cato to the Younger Pliny*, London 1977.

Borgen, P.,   'Observations on the Theme "Paul and Philo".
Paul's Preaching of Circumcision in Galatia
(Gal.5:11)', in *Die paulinische Literatur und
Theologie*, ed. S. Pedersen, Århus 1980, 85-
102.

'Paul Preaches Circumcision and Pleases Men',
in *Paul and Paulinism* (Essays in honour of
C.K. Barrett), ed. M.D. Hooker and S.G.
Wilson, London 1982, 37-46.

'The Early Church and the Hellenistic
Synagogue', *STh* 37 (1983) 55-78.

Bornkamm, G.,   'Die christliche Freiheit (Gal 5)', in *Das Ende des
Gesetzes. Paulusstudien. Gesammelte Aufsätze*
I, 5th edition, München 1966, 133-138.

'Baptism and New Life in Paul (Romans 6)', in
Early Christian Experience, E.T. by P.L.
Hammer, London 1969, 71-86.

Borse, U.,   *Der Standort des Galaterbriefes*, BBB 41, Köln/
Bonn 1972.

Der Brief an die Galater, Regensburger Neues
Testament, Regensburg 1984.

Brandenburger, E.,   *Fleisch und Geist: Paulus und die dualistische
Weisheit*, WMANT 29, Neukirchen-Vluyn
1968.

Braude, W.G.,   *Jewish Proselyting in the First Five Centuries of the
Common Era. The Age of the Tannaim and
Amoraim*, Providence, R.I. 1940.

Braun, H.,   'Römer 7, 7-25 und das Selbstverständnis des
Qumran-Frommen', *ZTK* 56 (1959) 1-18.

Bring, R.,   *Commentary on Galatians*, E.T. by E.
Wahlstrom, Philadelphia 1961.

Brinsmead, B.H.,   *Galatians – Dialogical Response to Opponents*,
SBLDS 65, Chico 1982.

Bruce, F.F.,   *Biblical Exegesis in the Qumran Texts*, London/
Grand Rapids 1959.

'Galatian Problems 1-5', *BJRL* 51 (1969) 292-
309; 52 (1970) 243-266; 53 (1971) 253-271; 54
(1972) 250-267; 55 (1973) 264-284.

*The Epistle of Paul to the Galatians. A
Commentary on the Greek Text*, New
International Greek Testament
Commentary, Exeter 1982.

Büchler, A.,   *Studies in Sin and Atonement in the Rabbinic
Literature of the First Century*, London 1928.

255

Bultmann, R., 'Das Problem der Ethik bei Paulus', *ZNW* 23 (1924) 123-140.

Theology of the New Testament, 2 volumes, E.T. by K. Grobel, London 1952, 1955.

'Christ the End of the Law', in *Essays Philosophical and Theological*, E.T. by J.C.G. Greig, London 1955, 36-66.

'Romans 7 and the Anthropology of Paul', in *Existence and Faith. Shorter Writings of R. Bultmann*, E.T. and ed. by S.M. Ogden, London 1961, 147-157.

'Zur Auslegung von Galater 2, 15-18', in *Exegetica*, ed. E. Dinkler, Tübingen 1967, 394-399.

Burton, E. de W., *Syntax of the Moods and Tenses in New Testament Greek*, 2nd edition, Edinburgh 1894.

Spirit, Soul and Flesh, Chicago 1918.

A Critical and Exegetical Commentary on the Epistle to the Galatians, The International Critical Commentary, Edinburgh 1921.

Byrne, B., *'Sons of God' – 'Seed of Abraham'. A Study of the Idea of the Sonship of God of All Christians in Paul*, AB 83, Rome 1979.

Caird, G.B., *The Language and Imagery of the Bible*, London 1980.

Callaway, J.S., 'Paul's Letter to the Galatians and Plato's *Lysis*', *JBL* 67 (1948) 353- 5.

Cannon, G.E., *The Use of Traditional Materials in Colossians*, Macon, Georgia 1983.

Carr, W., *Angels and Principalities. The Background, Meaning and Development of the Pauline Phrase 'hai archai kai hai exousiai'*, SNTSMS 42, Cambridge 1981.

Carrington, P., *The Primitive Christian Catechism*, Cambridge 1940.

Cole, R.A., *The Epistle of Paul to the Galatians*, Tyndale New Testament Commentaries, London 1965.

Collins, J. (ed.), *Apocalypse: The Morphology of a Genre, Semeia* 14 (1979).

Cranfield, C.E.B.,   'St. Paul and the Law', in *New Testament Issues*, ed. R. Batey, London 1970, 148-172.

A Critical and Exegetical Commentary on the Epistle to the Romans, International Critical Commentary, 2 volumes, Edinburgh 1975, 1979.

Crouch, J.E.,   *The Origin and Intention of the Colossian Haustafel*, FRLANT 109, Göttingen 1972.

Crownfield, F.R.,   'The Singular Problem of the Dual Galatians', *JBL* 64 (1945) 491-500.

Cullmann, O.,   *Salvation in History*, E.T. by S.G. Sowers et al., London 1967.

Dahl, N.A.,   'Der Name Israel: Zur Auslegung von Gal.6, 16', *Judaica* 6 (1950) 161-170.

'Paul's Letter to the Galatians: epistolary genre, content and structure', privately printed at Yale Divinity School 1973.

'Rudolf Bultmann's *Theology of the New Testament*', in *idem, The Crucified Messiah and Other Essays*, Minneapolis 1974, 90-128.

'The Missionary Theology in the Epistle to the Romans', in *idem, Studies in Paul. Theology for the Early Christian Mission*, Minneapolis 1977, 70-94.

'The Doctrine of Justification: Its Social Function and Implications', in *Studies in Paul*, 95-120.

'Contradictions in Scripture', in *Studies in Paul*, 159-177.

Daube, D.,   *The New Testament and Rabbinic Judaism*, London 1956.

Ancient Jewish Law. Three Inaugural Lectures, Leiden 1981.

Davies, W.D.,   *Torah in the Messianic Age and/or the Age to come*, JBLMS 7, Philadelphia 1952.

'Paul and the Dead Sea Scrolls: Flesh and Spirit', in *The Scrolls and the New Testament*, ed. K. Stendahl, London 1958, 157-182.

The Setting of the Sermon on the Mount, Cambridge 1963.

'The Moral Teaching of the Early Church', in *The Use of the Old Testament in the New and Other Essays* (Studies in honour of W.F. Stinespring), ed. J.M. Efird, Durham, N.C. 1972, 310-332.

'Paul and the People of Israel', *NTS* 24 (1977-8) 4-39.

Paul and Rabbinic Judaism. Some Elements in Pauline Theology, 4th edition, Philadelphia 1980.

'Paul and the Law. Reflections on Pitfalls in Interpretation', in *Paul and Paulinism* (Essays in honour of C.K. Barrett), ed. M.D. Hooker and S.G. Wilson, London 1982, 4-16.

Deidun, T.J.,   *New Covenant Morality in Paul*, AB 89, Rome 1981.

Dennison, W.D.,   'Indicative and Imperative: The Basic Structure of Pauline Ethics', *Calvin Theological Journal* 14 (1979) 55-78.

Dibelius, M.,   *From Tradition to Gospel*, E.T. by B.L. Woolf from *Die Formgeschichte des Evangeliums* (Tübingen 1933), London 1934.

A Fresh Approach to the New Testament and Early Christian Literature, E.T., London 1936.

Paul (ed. and completed by W.G. Kümmel), E.T. by F. Clarke, London 1953.

A Commentary on the Epistle of James (revised by H. Greeven), E.T. by M.A. Williams, Hermeneia, Philadelphia 1976.

Dietzfelbinger, C.,   *Paulus und das Alte Testament*, München 1961.

Dodd, C.H.,   *The Bible and the Greeks*, London 1935.

Gospel and Law. The Relation of Faith and Ethics in Early Christianity, Cambridge 1951.

' Ἔννομος Χριστοῦ', in *More New Testament Studies*, Manchester 1968, 134-148.

Donaldson, T.L.,   'Parallels: Use, Misuse and Limitations', *EQ* 55 (1983) 193-210.

Donfried, K.P.,   'Justification and Last Judgment in Paul', *ZNW* 67 (1976) 90-110.

Douglas, M.,   *Purity and Danger*, London 1966.

Drane, J.W.,   'Tradition, Law and Ethics in Pauline Theology', *NT* 16 (1974) 167-178.

Paul: Libertine or Legalist? A Study in the Theology of the Major Pauline Epistles, London 1975.

Dülmen, A. van,   *Die Theologie des Gesetzes bei Paulus*, SBM 5, Stuttgart 1968.

Duncan, G.S.,   *The Epistle of Paul to the Galatians*, Moffatt New Testament Commentary, London 1934.

Dungan, D.L.,   *The Sayings of Jesus in the Churches of Paul*, Oxford 1971.

Dunn, J.D.G.,   'Jesus – Flesh and Spirit: An exposition of Romans 1:3-4', *JTS* n.s. 24 (1973) 40-68.

'Rom.7, 14-25 in the Theology of Paul', *ThZ* 31 (1975) 257-273.

'The Relationship between Paul and Jerusalem according to Galatians 1 and 2', *NTS* 28 (1982) 461-478.

'The New Perspective on Paul', *BJRL* 65 (1983) 95-122.

'The Incident at Antioch (Gal.2:11-18)', *JSNT* 18 (1983) 3-57.

'Works of the Law and the Curse of the Law (Galatians 3.10-14)', *NTS* 31 (1985) 523-542.

Easton, B.S.,   'New Testament Ethical Lists', *JBL* 51 (1932) 1-12.

Ebeling, G.,   *The Truth of the Gospel. An Exposition of Galatians*, E.T. by D. Green, Philadelphia 1985.

Eckert, J.,   *Die urchristliche Verkündigung im Streit zwischen Paulus und seinen Gegnern nach dem Galaterbrief*, BU 6, Regensburg 1971.

Ellicott, C.J.,   *A Critical and Grammatical Commentary on St. Paul's Epistle to the Galatians*, 2nd edition, London 1859.

Elliott, J.H.,   *A Home for the Homeless. A Sociological Exegesis of 1 Peter, Its Situation and Strategy*, London 1982.

Ellis, E.E.,   *Paul's Use of the Old Testament*, Edinburgh 1957.

Enslin, M.S.,   *Christian Beginnings, Part III. The Literature of the Christian Movement*, New York 1956.

Feld, H.,   ' "Christus Diener der Sünde". Zum Ausgang des Streites zwischen Petrus und Paulus', *TQ* 153 (1973) 119-131.

Fenton, J.C.,   'Paul and Mark', in *Studies in the Gospels* (Essays in Memory of R.H. Lightfoot), ed. D.E. Nineham, Oxford 1955, 89-112.

Finn, T.M.,   'The God-fearers Reconsidered', *CBQ* 47 (1985) 75-84.

Fitzmyer, J.A.,   'Paul and the Law', in *To Advance the Gospel.*
                      New Testament Studies, New York 1981,
                      186–201.

Fletcher, D.K.,   *The Singular Argument of Paul's Letter to the*
                      Galatians, Unpublished Ph.D. Dissertation,
                      Princeton 1982.

Flusser, D.,   'The Dead Sea Sect and Pre-Pauline
                      Christianity', in *Aspects of the Dead-Sea*
                      Scrolls, ed. C. Rabin and Y. Yadin,
                      Jerusalem 1958, 215–266.

Foerster, D.,   'Abfassungszeit und Ziel des Galaterbriefes', in
                      Apophoreta (Festschrift für E. Haenchen),
                      ed. W. Eltester and F.H. Kettler, BZNW
                      30, Berlin 1964, 135–141.

Friedrich, G.,   'Das Gesetz des Glaubens Röm 3, 27', *ThZ* 10
                      (1954) 401–417.

Fuller, D.P.,   'Paul and "the Works of the Law"', *Westminster*
                      Theological Journal 38 (1975–6) 28–42.

Furnish, V.P.,   *Theology and Ethics in Paul*, Nashville 1968.
Gaston, L.,   'Israel's Enemies in Pauline Theology', *NTS* 28
                      (1982) 400–423.

Gaventa, B.,   'Galatians 1 and 2: Autobiography as
                      Paradigm', *NT* 28 (1986) 309–326.

Georgi, D.,   *Die Geschichte der Kollekte des Paulus für*
                      Jerusalem, TF 38, Hamburg 1965.

                      The Opponents of Paul in Second Corinthians,
                      E.T., SNTW, Edinburgh 1987.

Goodenough, E.R.,   *Jewish Symbols in the Graeco-Roman Period*, 13
                      volumes, New York 1953–1968.

                      By Light, Light. The Mystic Gospel of Hellenistic
                      Judaism, Amsterdam 1969.

                      An Introduction to Philo Judaeus, 2nd edition,
                      Oxford 1962.

Goodenough, E.R.,   'Paul and the Hellenization of Christianity', in
   and Kraabel,   *Religions in Antiquity* (Essays in Memory of
   A.T.,   E.R. Goodenough), ed. J. Neusner, Leiden
                      1968, 23–68.

Gordon, T.D.,   'The Problem at Galatia', *Int* 41 (1987) 32–43.
Goulder, M.D.,   *Midrash and Lection in Matthew*, London 1974.
Grässer, E.,   *Der Alte Bund im Neuen. Exegetische Studien zur*
                      Israelfrage im Neuen Testament, WUNT 35,
                      Tübingen 1985.

Grayston, K.,   'The Opponents in Philippians 3', *ExT* 97
                      (1985–6) 170–172.

Gundry, R.H.,

'Soma' in Biblical Theology with Emphasis on Pauline Anthropology, SNTSMS 29, Cambridge 1976.

'The Moral Frustration of Paul before his Conversion: Sexual Lust in Romans 7:7-25', in *Pauline Studies* (Essays presented to F.F. Bruce), ed. D.A. Hagner and M.J. Harris, Exeter 1980, 228-245.

'Grace, Works and Staying Saved in Paul', *Biblica* 66 (1985) 1-38.

Gunther, J.J.,

St. Paul's Opponents and their Background, SNT 35, Leiden 1973.

Guthrie, D.,

Galatians, The Century Bible (New Series), London 1969.

Güttgemanns, E.,

Der leidende Apostel und sein Herr. Studien zur paulinischen Christologie, FRLANT 90, Göttingen 1966.

Hahn, F.,

'Das Gesetzesverständnis im Römer- und Galaterbrief', *ZNW* 67 (1976) 29-63.

Hanson, A.T.,

Studies in Paul's Technique and Theology, London 1974.

Harvey, A.E.,

'The Opposition to Paul', in *Studia Evangelica IV*, ed. F.L. Cross, TU 102, Berlin 1968, 319-332.

'Forty Strokes Save One: Social Aspects of Judaizing and Apostasy', in *idem* (ed.), *Alternative Approaches to New Testament Study*, London 1985, 241- 251.

Hatch, E., and Redpath, H.A.,

A Concordance to the Septuagint and the Other Greek Versions of the Old Testament (including the Apocryphal Books), 2 volumes, Oxford 1897.

Haufe, C.,

'Die Stellung des Paulus zum Gesetz', *TLZ* 91 (1966) 171-178.

Hays, R.B.,

The Faith of Jesus Christ. An Investigation of the Narrative Substructure of Galatians 3:1-4:11, SBLDS 56, Chico 1983.

'Christology and Ethics in Galatians: The Law of Christ', *CBQ* (1987) 268- 290.

Hecht, R.D.,

'The Exegetical Contexts of Philo's Interpretation of Circumcision', in *Nourished with Peace* (in memory of S. Sandmel), ed. F.E. Greenspahn et al., Chico 1984, 51-79.

Heiligenthal, R.,   'Soziologische Implikationen der paulinischen Rechtfertigungslehre im Galaterbrief am Beispiel der "Werke des Gesetzes"', *Kairos* 26 (1984) 38- 53.

Hellholm, D. (ed.),   *Apocalypticism in the Mediterranean World and the Near East*, Tübingen 1983.

Hengel, M.,   *Between Jesus and Paul. Studies in the Earliest History of Christianity*, E.T. by J. Bowden, London 1983.

Die Zeloten. Untersuchungen zur jüdischen Freiheitsbewegung in der Zeit von Herodes I bis 70 n.Chr., Leiden 1961.

Judaism and Hellenism. Studies in their Encounter in Palestine during the Early Hellenistic Period, E.T. by J. Bowden, 2 volumes, London 1974.

Hennecke, E. (ed.),   *New Testament Apocrypha*, ed. W. Schneemelcher, E.T. ed. R.McL. Wilson, 2 volumes, London 1963, 1965.

Hill. D.,   *Greek Words and Hebrew Meanings. Studies in the Semantics of Soteriological Terms*, SNTSMS 5, Cambridge 1967.

Hill, M.,   *A Sociology of Religion*, London 1973.

Hirsch, E.,   'Zwei Fragen zu Galater 6', *ZNW* 29 (1930) 192-7.

Hoenig, S.B.,   'Circumcision: The Covenant of Abraham', *JQR* n.s. 53 (1962-3) 322-334.

Hofius, O.,   'Das Gesetz des Mose und das Gesetz Christi', *ZTK* 80 (1983) 262-286.

Holmberg, B.,   *Paul and Power. The Structure of Authority in the Primitive Church as Reflected in the Pauline Epistles*, Philadelphia 1980.

Holtzmann, O.,   'Zu Emanuel Hirsch, Zwei Fragen zu Galater 6', *ZNW* 30 (1931) 76-83.

Hooker, M.D.,   'Interchange in Christ', *JTS* n.s. 22 (1971) 349-361.

'Were there false teachers in Colossae?', in *Christ and Spirit in the New Testament* (In honour of C.F.D. Moule), ed. B. Lindars and S.S. Smalley, Cambridge 1973.

Pauline Pieces, London 1979.

'Paul and "Covenantal Nomism"', in *Paul and Paulinism* (Essays in honour of C.K. Barrett), ed. M.D. Hooker and S.G. Wilson, London 1982, 47-56.

Houlden, J.L., *Ethics and the New Testament*, London 1973.
Howard, G., 'Christ the End of the Law', *JBL* 88 (1969) 331-337.
'Romans 3.21-31 and the Inclusion of the Gentiles', *HTR* 63 (1970) 223-233.
Paul: Crisis in Galatia. A Study in Early Christian Theology, SNTSMS 35, Cambridge 1979.
Hübner, H., 'Anthropologischer Dualismus in den Hodayoth?', *NTS* 18 (1971-2) 268-284.
'Das ganze und das eine Gesetz. Zum Problemkreis Paulus und die Stoa', *KuD* 21 (1975) 239-256.
'Identitätsverlust und paulinische Theologie. Anmerkungen zum Galaterbrief', *KuD* 24 (1978) 181-193.
'Pauli Theologiae Proprium', *NTS* 26 (1979-80) 445-473.
'Der Galaterbrief und das Verhältnis von antiker Rhetorik und Epistolographie', *TLZ* 109 (1984) 241-250.
Law in Paul's Thought, E.T. by J.C.G. Greig, SNTW, Edinburgh 1984.
'Was heisst bei Paulus "Werke des Gesetzes"?', in *Glaube und Eschatologie* (Festschrift für W.G. Kümmel), ed. E. Grässer and O. Merk, Tübingen 1985, 123-133.
Gottes Ich und Israel. Zum Schriftgebrauch des Paulus in Römer 9-11, FRLANT 136, Göttingen 1984.
Hunter, A.M., *Paul and his Predecessors*, revised edition, London 1961.
Hurd, J.C., *The Origin of I Corinthians*, London 1965.
Hurtado, L.W., 'The Jerusalem Collection and the Book of Galatians', *JSNT* 5 (1979) 46-62.
Hyldahl, N., *Die paulinische Chronologie*, ATD 19, Leiden 1986.
Jaubert, A., *La Notion d'Alliance dans le Judaïsme aux Abords de l'Ère Chrétienne*, Paris 1963.
Jeremias, J., 'Chiasmus in den Paulusbriefen', *ZNW* 49 (1958) 145-156.
Jervell, J., 'Die offenbarte und die verborgene Tora. Zur Vorstellung über die neue Tora im Rabbinismus', *STh* 25 (1971) 90-108.

Jewett, R.,

'The Agitators and the Galatian Congregation', *NTS* 17 (1970-71) 198-212.

Paul's Anthropological Terms. A Study of Their Use in Conflict Settings, Leiden 1971.

Dating Paul's Life, London 1979.

Joest, W.,

Gesetz und Freiheit. Das Problem des Tertius Usus Legis bei Luther und die neutestamentliche Paränese, 3rd edition, Göttingen 1961.

Kamlah, E.,

Die Form der katalogischen Paränese im Neuen Testament, WUNT 7, Tübingen 1964.

Karris, R.J.,

'Rom. 14:1-15:13 and the Occasion of Romans', *CBQ* 35 (1973) 155-178.

Käsemann, E.,

Leib und Leib Christi. Eine Untersuchung zur paulinischen Begrifflichkeit, Tübingen 1933.

New Testament Questions of Today, E.T. by W.J. Montague, London 1969: 'New Testament Questions of Today', 1-22; 'The Beginnings of Christian Theology', 82-107; 'On the subject of Primitive Christian Apocalyptic', 108-137; ' "The Righteousness of God" in Paul', 168-182; 'Worship and Everyday Life. A Note on Romans 12', 188-195; 'Principles of the Interpretation of Romans 13', 196-216.

Perspectives on Paul, E.T. by M. Kohl, London 1971: 'On Paul's Anthropology', 1-31; 'Justification and Salvation History in the Epistle to the Romans', 60-78.

'Geist und Geistesgaben im NT', *RGG* II, 1272-1279.

Commentary on Romans, E.T. by G.W. Bromiley, London 1980.

Keck, L.E.,

'Justification of the Ungodly and Ethics', in *Rechtfertigung* (Festschrift für E. Käsemann), ed. J. Friedrich et al., Tübingen 1976, 199-209.

Kennedy, G.,

New Testament Interpretation through Rhetorical Criticism. Chapel Hill 1984.

Kieffer, R.,

Foi et Justification à Antioche. Interpretation d'un Conflit (Ga 2, 14- 21), LD 111, Paris 1982.

Kilpatrick, G.D.,

'Gal 2.14 ὀϱθοποδοῦσιν', in *Neutestamentliche Studien für R. Bultmann*, ed. W. Eltester, 2nd edition, Berlin 1957, 269-274.

Klein, G.,

'Individualgeschichte und Weltgeschichte bei Paulus. Eine Interpretation ihres Verhältnisses im Galaterbrief', *Ev Th* 24 (1964) 126–165.

'Werkruhm und Christusruhm im Galaterbrief und die Frage nach einer Entwicklung des Paulus', in *Studien zum Text und zur Ethik des Neuen Testaments* (Festschrift für H. Greeven), ed. W. Schrage, Berlin 1986, 196–211.

Klijn, A.F.J., and Reinink, G.J.,

Patristic Evidence for Jewish-Christian Sects, SNT 36, Leiden 1973.

Knox, J.,

Chapters in a Life of Paul, London 1954.

Knox, W.L.,

St. Paul and the Church of the Gentiles, Cambridge 1939.

Koester, H.,

'ΓΝΩΜΑΙ ΔΙΑΦΟΡΟΙ. The Origin and Nature of Diversification in the History of Early Christianity', *HTR* 58 (1965) 279–318.

Kraabel, A.T.,

'Paganism and Judaism: The Sardis Evidence', in *Paganisme, Judaisme, Christianisme. Influences et Affrontements dans le Monde Antique*, (Mélanges offerts à M. Simon), Paris 1978, 13–33.

'The Disappearance of the "God-fearers"', *Numen* 28 (1981) 113–126.

Kuhn, K.G.,

'New Light on Temptation, Sin and Flesh in the New Testament', in *The Scrolls and the New Testament*, ed. K. Stendahl, London 1958, 94–113.

Kümmel, W.G.,

Man in the New Testament, E.T. by J.J. Vincent, London 1963.

' "Individualgeschichte" und "Weltgeschichte" in Gal.2:15–21', in *Christ and Spirit in the New Testament* (In honour of C.F.D. Moule), ed. B. Lindars and S.S. Smalley, Cambridge 1973, 157–173.

Introduction to the New Testament, E.T. by H.C. Kee from 17th revised edition, London 1975.

Kuss, O.,

Der Römerbrief, Regensburger Neues Testament, 3 volumes, Regensburg 1963, 1978.

Lagrange, M.-J.,   *Saint Paul, Épître aux Galates*, Études Bibliques, Paris 1950.

Lake, K.,   'Proselytes and God-fearers', in *The Beginnings of Christianity, Part I. The Acts of the Apostles*, volume 5: *Additional Notes*, ed. K. Lake and H.J. Cadbury, London 1933, 74–96.

Lambrecht, J.,   'The Line of Thought in Gal.2.14b–21', *NTS* 24 (1977–8) 484–495.

Laeuchli, S.,   'Monism and Dualism in the Pauline Anthropology', *Biblical Research* 3 (1958) 15–27.

Licht, J.,   'The Doctrine of the Thanksgiving Scroll', *IEJ* 6 (1956) 1–13 and 89–101.

Lietzmann, H.,   *Die Briefe des Apostels Paulus. 1 Die Vier Hauptbriefe*, Handbuch zum Neuen Testament, Band 3.1, Tübingen 1910.

Lightfoot, J.B.,   *Saint Paul's Epistle to the Galatians*, 2nd edition, London 1866.

Ljungman, H.,   *Das Gesetz erfüllen. Matth.5:17ff. und 3:15 untersucht*, Lund 1954.

Lohmeyer, E.,   *Probleme paulinischer Theologie*, Darmstadt 1954.

Lohse, E.,   *Colossians and Philemon*, E.T. by W.R. Poehlmann and R.J. Karris, Hermeneia, Philadelphia 1971.

Longenecker, R.N.,   *Paul: Apostle of Liberty*, New York 1964.

Biblical Exegesis in the Apostolic Period, Grand Rapids 1975.

'The Pedagogical Nature of the Law in Galatians 3:19–4:7', *Journal of the Evangelical Theological Society* 25 (1982) 53–61.

Lüdemann, G.,   *Paul, Apostle to the Gentiles. Studies in Chronology*, E.T. by F.S. Jones, London 1984.

Paulus und das Judentum, München 1983.

Lüdemann, H.,   *Die Anthropologie des Apostels Paulus und ihre Stellung innerhalb seiner Heilslehre*, Kiel 1872.

Lührmann, D.,   *Das Offenbarungsverständnis bei Paulus und in paulinischen Gemeinden*, WMANT 16, Neukirchen-Vluyn 1965.

Der Brief an die Galater, Zürcher Bibelkommentare NT 7, Zürich 1978.

'Tage, Monate, Jahreszeiten, Jahre (Gal 4,10)', in *Werden und Wirken des Alten Testaments* (Festschrift für C. Westermann), ed. R. Albertz et al., Göttingen 1980, 428–445.

Lull, D.J.,   *The Spirit in Galatia. Paul's Interpretation of 'Pneuma' as Divine Power*, SBLDS 49, Chico 1980.

' "The Law was our Pedagogue": A Study in Galatians 3.19-25', *JBL* 105 (1986) 481–498.

Lütgert, W.,   *Gesetz und Geist. Eine Untersuchung zur Vorgeschichte des Galaterbriefes*, Gütersloh 1919.

Luther, M.,   *A Commentary on St. Paul's Epistle to the Galatians*, revised E.T. based on the 'Middleton' edition of 1575, Cambridge 1953.

Luz, U.,   *Das Geschichtsverständnis des Paulus*, BETh 49, München 1968.

'Die Erfüllung des Gesetzes bei Matthäus (Mt 5.17-20)', *ZTK* 75 (1978) 398- 435.

Lyons, G.,   *Pauline Autobiography. Towards a New Understanding*, SBLDS 73, Atlanta 1985.

Maher, M.,   ' "Take my yoke upon you" (Matt XI. 29)', *NTS* 22 (1975-6) 97-103.

Manson, T.W.,   'Jesus, Paul, and the Law', in *Judaism and Christianity III. Law and Religion*, ed. E.I.J. Rosenthal, London 1938, 125-141.

Markus, J.,   'The Evil Inclination in the Letters of Paul', *Irish Biblical Studies* 18 (1986) 8-20.

Martyn, J.L.,   'A Law-Observant Mission to Gentiles: The Background of Galatians', *Michigan Quarterly Review* 22 (1983) 221-236; reprinted in *SJT* 38 (1985) 307-324.

'Apocalyptic Antinomies in Paul's Letter to the Galatians', *NTS* 31 (1985) 410–424.

Marxsen, W.,   *Introduction to the New Testament*, E.T. by G. Buswell from 3rd German edition, Oxford 1968;

Einleitung in das Neue Testament, 4th fully revised edition, Gütersloh 1978.

McDonald, J.I.H.,   'Romans 13.1-7 and Christian Social Ethics Today', *Modern Churchman* 29 (1987) 19-26.

McEleney, N.J.,   'Conversion, Circumcision and the Law', *NTS* 20 (1973-4) 319-341.

Meeks, W.A.,   ' "Since then you would need to go out of the world": Group Boundaries in Pauline Christianity', in *Critical History and Biblical Faith. New Testament Perspectives*, ed. T. Ryan, Villanova, Pennsylvania 1979, 4-29.

'Toward a Social Description of Pauline Christianity', in *Approaches to Ancient Judaism* II, ed. W.S. Green, Missoula 1980, 27-42.

'Social Functions of Apocalyptic Language in Pauline Christianity', in *Apocalypticism in the Mediterranean World and the Near East*, ed. D. Hellholm, Tübingen 1983, 687-705.

The First Urban Christians. The Social World of the Apostle Paul, New Haven/London 1983.

'Understanding Early Christian Ethics', *JBL* 105 (1986) 3-11.

Meier, J.P.,   *Law and History in Matthew's Gospel. A Redactional Study of Mt.5:17-48*, AB 71, Rome 1976.

Merk, O.,   *Handeln aus Glauben. Die Motivierungen der paulinischen Ethik*, Marburg 1968.

'Der Beginn der Paränese im Galaterbrief', *ZNW* 60 (1969) 83-104.

Metzger, B.M.,   *A Textual Commentary on the Greek New Testament*, corrected edition, London 1975.

Meyer, H.A.W.,   *The Epistle to the Galatians*, Critical and Exegetical Commentary on the New Testament, VII, E.T. by G. Venables from 5th German edition, Edinburgh 1884.

Michaelis, W.,   'Judaistische Heidenchristen', *ZNW* 30 (1931) 83-89.

Minear, P.S.,   'The Crucified World: The Enigma of Galatians 6.14', in *Theologia Crucis – Signum Crucis* (Festschrift für E. Dinkler), ed. C. Andresen and G. Klein, Tübingen 1979, 395-407.

Mitchell, S.,   'Population and Land in Roman Galatia', *ANRW* II.7.2, 1053-1081.

Mohrlang, R.,   *Matthew and Paul. A Comparison of Ethical Perspectives*, SNTSMS 48, Cambridge 1984.

Mol, H.,   *Identity and the Sacred*, Oxford 1976.

Montefiore, H.,   'Thou shalt Love thy Neighbour as Thyself', *NT* 5 (1962) 157-170.

Moore, G.F.,   *Judaism in the First Centuries of the Christian Era. The Age of the Tannaim*, 3 volumes, Cambridge, Mass. 1927-1930.

Morgan, W.,   *The Religion and Theology of Paul*, Edinburgh 1917.

Moule, C.F.D.,   ' "Fulness" and "Fill" in the New Testament', *SJT* 4 (1951) 79-86.

An Idiom Book of New Testament Greek, 2nd edition, Cambridge 1959.

'Fulfilment-Words in the New Testament: Use and Abuse', *NTS* 14 (1967-8) 293-320.

'Death "to sin", "to law" and "to the world": A Note on Certain Datives', in *Mélanges Bibliques* (en hommage à B. Rigaux), ed. A. Descamps and A. de Halleux, Gembloux 1970, 367-375.

Munck, J.,   *Paul and the Salvation of Mankind*, E.T. by F. Clarke, London 1959.

Mundle, W.,   'Zur Auslegung von Gal 2, 17-18', *ZNW* 23 (1924) 152-3.

Murphy, R.E.,   ' "Yeser" in the Qumran Literature', *Biblica* 39 (1958) 334-344.

Murphy-O'Connor, J.,   *L'Existence chrétienne selon Saint Paul*, LD 80, Paris 1974.

Mussner, F.,   *Der Galaterbrief*, Herders Theologischer Kommentar zum Neuen Testament, 9, Freiburg 1974.

Theologie der Freiheit nach Paulus, Freiburg 1976.

Tractate on the Jews, E.T. by L. Swidler, London 1984.

Nauck, W.,   'Das οὖν-paräneticum', *ZNW* 49 (1958) 134-5.

Neitzel, H.,   'Zur Interpretation von Galater 2, 11-21' *TQ* 163 (1983) 15-39 and 131-149.

Nock, A.D.,   *Conversion. The Old and New in Religion from Alexander the Great to Augustine of Hippo*, Oxford 1933.

Nolland, J.,   'Uncircumcised Proselytes?' *JSJ* 12 (1981) 173-194.

Nötscher, F.,   *Zur theologischen Terminologie der Qumran-Texte*, BBB 10, Bonn 1956.

O'Donovan,
O.M.T.,
    'The Possibility of a Biblical Ethic', *TSF Bulletin* 67 (1973) 15-23.

Oden, T.C.,
    Radical Obedience. The Ethics of Rudolf Bultmann, London 1965.

Oepke, A.,
    Der Brief des Paulus an die Galater, Theologischer Handkommentar zum Neuen Testament, 9, 5th edition, ed. J. Rohde, Berlin 1984.

Ogletree, T.W.,
    The Use of the Bible in Christian Ethics, Oxford 1984.

O'Neill, J.C.,
    The Recovery of Paul's Letter to the Galatians, London 1972.

Ortkemper, F.-J.,
    Das Kreuz in der Verkündigung des Apostels Paulus, SB 24, 2nd edition, Stuttgart 1968.

    Leben aus dem Glauben. Christliche Grundhaltungen nach Römer 12-13, NA 14, Münster 1980.

Osten-Sacken, P.
von der,
    Gott und Belial. Traditionsgeschichtliche Untersuchungen zum Dualismus in den Texten aus Qumran, SUNT 6, Göttingen 1969.

Perdue, L.G.,
    'Paraenesis and the Epistle of James', *ZNW* 72 (1981) 241-256.

Pfleiderer, O.,
    Paulinism. A Contribution to the History of Primitive Christian Theology, E.T. by E. Peters, 2 volumes, London 1877.

Pryke, J.,
    ' "Spirit" and "Flesh" in the Qumran Documents and Some New Testament Texts', *RQ* 5 (1964-6) 345-360.

Räisänen, H.,
    'Zum Gebrauch von ΕΠΙΘΥΜΙΑ und ΕΠΙΘΥΜΕΙΝ bei Paulus', *STh* 33 (1979) 85-99.

    'Paul's Theological Difficulties with the Law', in *Studia Biblica 1978 III*, ed. E.A. Livingstone, Sheffield 1980, 301-320.

    'Legalism and Salvation by the Law. Paul's Portrayal of the Jewish Religion as a Historical and Theological Problem', in *Die paulinische Literatur und Theologie*, ed. S. Pedersen, Århus 1980, 63-83.

    Paul and the Law, WUNT 29, Tübingen 1983.

    'Galatians 2.16 and Paul's Break with Judaism', *NTS* 31 (1985) 543-553.

Ramsay, W.M.,
    A Historical Commentary on St. Paul's Epistle to the Galatians, 2nd edition, London 1900.

Reicke, B., 'The Law and This World According to Paul.
Some Thoughts Concerning Gal.4:1- 11',
JBL 70 (1951) 259–276.

Resch, A., *Der Paulinismus und die Logia Jesu in ihrem
gegenseitigen Verhältnis untersucht*, Leipzig
1904.

Richardson, P., *Israel in the Apostolic Church*, SNTSMS 10,
Cambridge 1969.
Paul's Ethic of Freedom, Philadelphia 1979.

Riches, J.K., and 'Conceptual Change in the Synoptic
Millar, A., Tradition', in *Alternative Approaches to New
Testament Study*, ed. A.E. Harvey, London
1985, 37–60.

Ridderbos, H.N., *The Epistle to the Galatians*, New International
Commentary on the New Testament, E.T.
by H. Zylstra, Grand Rapids 1956.

Riesenfeld, H., *The Gospel Tradition*, E.T. by E.M. Rowley
and R.A. Kraft, Oxford 1979.

Robb, J.D., 'Galatians V. 23. An Explanation', *ExT* 56
(1944–5) 279–280.

Robertson, A.T., *A Grammar of the Greek New Testament in the
Light of Historical Research*, 3rd edition, New
York 1919.

Robinson, H.W., *The Christian Doctrine of Man*, Edinburgh
1911.

Robinson, J.A.T., *The Body. A Study in Pauline Theology*, SBT 5,
London 1952.

Ropes, J.H., *The Singular Problem of the Epistle to the
Galatians*, HTS 14, Cambridge, Mass.
1929.

Rowland, C., *The Open Heaven. A Study of Apocalyptic in
Judaism and Early Christianity*, London
1982.

Sahlin, H., 'Emendationsvorschläge zum griechischen
Text des Neuen Testaments III', *NT* 25
(1983) 73–88.

Sand, A., *Der Begriff 'Fleisch' in den paulinischen
Hauptbriefen*, BU 6, Regensburg 1967.

Sanders, E.P., *Paul and Palestinian Judaism*, London 1977.
'On the Question of Fulfilling the Law in Paul
and Rabbinic Judaism', in *Donum
Gentilicium* (in honour of D. Daube), ed. E.
Bammel et al., Oxford 1978, 103–126.

'Jesus, Paul and Judaism', in *ANRW* II 25.1, 390–450.

Paul, The Law, and the Jewish People, Philadelphia 1983.

Sandmel, S., 'Parallelomania', *JBL* 81 (1962) 1–13.

Philo's Place in Judaism. A Study of Conceptions of Abraham in Jewish Literature, New York 1971.

Sandt, H.W.M. van de, 'An Explanation of Rom.8,4a', *Bijdragen. Tijdschrift voor Filosofie en Theologie* 37 (1976) 361–378.

Schäfer, P., 'Die Torah der messianischen Zeit', *ZNW* 65 (1974) 27–42.

Schlier, H., *Der Brief an die Galater*, Meyers Kritisch-exegetischer Kommentar über das Neue Testament, 7, 14th edition, Göttingen 1971.

Schmithals, W., 'The Heretics in Galatia', in *Paul and the Gnostics*, E.T. by J.E. Steely, Nashville 1972, 13–64 (revised from 'Die Häretiker in Galatien', *ZNW* 47 (1956) 25–67).

'Judaisten in Galatien?', *ZNW* 74 (1983) 27–58.

Schnabel, E.J., *Law and Wisdom from Ben Sira to Paul*, WUNT 2nd series 16, Tübingen 1985.

Schnackenburg, R., 'Paränese', in *Lexikon für Theologie und Kirche*, VIII, 2nd edition, Freiburg 1963, 80–82.

Schoeps, H.J., *Paul. The Theology of the Apostle in the Light of Jewish Religious History*, E.T. by H. Knight, London 1961.

Jewish Christianity. Factional Disputes in the Early Church, E.T. by D. Hare, Philadelphia 1969.

Schrage, W., *Die konkreten Einzelgebote in der paulinischen Paränese. Ein Beitrag zur neutestamentlichen Ethik*, Gütersloh 1961.

Ethik des Neuen Testaments, GNT 4, Göttingen 1982.

Schrenk, G., 'Was bedeutet "Israel Gottes"?', *Judaica* 5 (1949) 81–94.

'Der Segenswunsch nach der Kampfepistel', *Judaica* 6 (1950) 170–190.

Schulz, A., 'Grundformen urchristlicher Paränese', in *Gestalt und Anspruch des Neuen Testaments*, ed. J. Schreiner and G. Dautzenberg, Würzburg 1969, 249–261.

Schulz, S., 'Zur Rechtfertigung aus Gnaden in Qumran und bei Paulus', *ZNW* 56 (1959) 155-185.

Schuppe, E., παιδαγωγός, *PW* 18, 2375-2385.

Schürer, E., Vermes, G., and Millar, F., *The History of the Jewish People in the Age of Jesus Christ (175 B.C. - A.D. 135)*, E.T. and revision, 3 volumes, Edinburgh 1973, 1979, 1986-7.

Schürmann, H., ' "Das Gesetz des Christus" Gal 6,2. Jesu Verhalten und Wort als letztgültige sittliche Norm nach Paulus', in *Neues Testament und Kirche* (Festschrift für R. Schnackenburg), ed. J. Gnilka, Freiburg 1974, 282-300.

Schweitzer, A., *Paul and His Interpreters*, E.T. by W. Montgomery, London 1912.
The Mysticism of Paul the Apostle, E.T. by W. Montgomery, London 1931.

Schweizer, E., 'Röm. 1.3f. und der Gegensatz von Fleisch und Geist vor und bei Paulus', *EvTh* 15 (1955) 563-571
'Die hellenistische Komponente im neutestamentlichen σάρξ-Begriff', *ZNW* 48 (1957) 237-253.
'Die "Elemente der Welt" Gal 4,3. 9; Kol 2,8. 20', in *Verborum Veritas* (Festschrift für G. Stählin), ed. O. Böcher and K. Haacker, Wuppertal 1970, 245-259.
'Gottesgerechtigkeit und Lasterkataloge bei Paulus (inkl. Kol und Eph)', in *Rechtfertigung* (Festschrift für E. Käsemann), ed. J. Friedrich et al., Tübingen 1976, 461-477.
'Traditional Ethical Patterns in the Pauline and Post-Pauline Letters and their Development', in *Text and Interpretation* (Studies in the New Testament presented to M. Black), ed. E. Best and R. McL. Wilson, Cambridge 1979, 195-209.

Seeberg, A., *Der Katechismus der Urchristenheit*, Leipzig 1903.

Sevenster, J.N., *Paul and Seneca*, SNT 4, Leiden 1961.

Shaw, G., *The Cost of Authority. Manipulation and Freedom in the New Testament*, London 1983.

Sieffert, F., *Der Brief an die Galater*, Meyers Kritisch-exegetischer Kommentar über das Neue Testament, 7, 9th edition, Göttingen 1899.

273

Sjöberg, E., 'Wiedergeburt und Neuschöpfung im palästinischen Judentum', *STh* 4 (1950) 44-85.

Smith, M., 'Goodenough's *Jewish Symbols* in Retrospect', *JBL* 86 (1967) 53-68.

Spicq, C., 'Bénignité, Mansuétude, Douceur, Clémence', *RB* 54 (1947) 321-339.

Stacey, W.D., *The Pauline View of Man in relation to its Judaic and Hellenistic Background*, London 1956.

Stählin, G., 'Galaterbrief', in *RGG* II, 1187-1189.

Stamm, R.T., *The Epistle to the Galatians*, in *The Interpreter's Bible*, volume 10, New York 1953, 429-593.

Stendahl, K., *Paul among Jews and Gentiles*, London 1977.

Stern, M., *Greek and Latin Authors on Jews and Judaism*, 2 volumes, Jerusalem 1974, 1981.

Stoike, D.A., *'The Law of Christ': A Study of Paul's Use of the Expression in Galatians 6:2*, Unpublished Th.D. Dissertation, Claremont 1971.

Strack, H.L., and Billerbeck, P., *Kommentar zum Neuen Testament aus Talmud und Midrasch*, 4 volumes, München 1922-1928.

Strelan, J.G., 'Burden-Bearing and the Law of Christ: A Re-examination of Galatians 6:2', *JBL* 94 (1975) 266-276.

Stuhlmacher, P., *Versöhnung, Gesetz und Gerechtigkeit. Aufsätze zur biblischen Theologie*, Göttingen 1981.

Styler, G.M., 'The Basis of Obligation in Paul's Christology and Ethics', in *Christ and Spirit in the New Testament* (In honour of C.F.D. Moule), ed. B. Lindars and S.S. Smalley, Cambridge 1973. 175-187.

Synofzik, E., *Die Gerichts- und Vergeltungsaussagen bei Paulus. Eine traditionsgeschichtliche Untersuchung*, Göttingen 1977.

Tannehill, R.C., *Dying and Rising with Christ. A Study in Pauline Theology*, BZNW 32, Berlin 1967.

Telford, W.R., *The Barren Temple and the Withered Tree*, JSNTS 1, Sheffield 1980.

Theissen, G., *The Social Setting of Pauline Christianity*, E.T. by J.H. Schütz, SNTW, Edinburgh 1982.

Thiselton, A.C., 'The Meaning of Σάρξ in I Corinthians 5:5', *SJT* 26 (1973) 204-228.

Tyson, J.B., 'Paul's Opponents in Galatia', *NT* 10 (1968) 241-254.

' "Works of Law" in Galatians', *JBL* 92 (1973) 423-431.

Vermes, G.,   *The Dead Sea Scrolls in English*, 2nd edition, Harmondsworth, Middlesex 1975.

Vielhauer, P.,   *Geschichte der urchristlichen Literatur. Einleitung in das Neue Testament, die Apokryphen und die Apostolischen Väter*, Berlin 1975.

'Gesetzesdienst und Stoicheiadienst im Galaterbrief', in *Rechtfertigung* (Festschrift für E. Käsemann), ed. J. Friedrich et al., Tübingen 1976, 543- 555.

Vögtle, A.,   *Die Tugend- und Lasterkataloge im Neuen Testament, exegetisch, religions- und formgeschichtlich untersucht*, NA 16, Münster 1936.

Watson, F.,   *Paul, Judaism and the Gentiles. A Sociological Approach*, SNTSMS 56, Cambridge 1986.

Watson, N.M.,   'Justified by faith; judged by works – an Antinomy?', *NTS* 29 (1983) 209- 221.

Wedderburn, A.J.M.,   'Some Observations on Paul's Use of the Phrases "in Christ" and "with Christ"', *JSNT* 25 (1985) 83-97.

Weder, H.,   *Das Kreuz Jesu bei Paulus*, FRLANT 125, Göttingen 1981.

Wegenast, K.,   *Das Verständnis der Tradition bei Paulus und in den Deuteropaulinen*, WMANT 8, Neukirchen-Vluyn 1962.

Weiss, J.,   *Earliest Christianity. A History of the Period AD 30-150*, E.T. by R.R. Wilson and F.C. Grant, 2 volumes, Gloucester, Mass. 1970.

Wenham, D.,   'The Christian Life: A Life of Tension?', in *Pauline Studies* (Essays presented to F.F. Bruce), ed. D.A. Hagner and M.J. Harris, Exeter 1980, 80-94.

Westerholm, S.,   ' "Letter" and "Spirit": the Foundation of Pauline Ethics', *NTS* 30 (1984) 229-248.

'On Fulfilling the Whole Law (Gal 5.14)', *SEÅ* 51-2 (1986-7) 229-237.

Wette, M.L. de,   *Kurze Erklärung des Briefes an die Galater*, Kurzgefasstes Exegetisches Handbuch zum Neuen Testament, II 3, Leipzig 1841.

White, J.L.,   *The Form and Function of the Body of the Greek Letter*, SBLDS 2, Missoula 1972.

Whiteley, D.E.H., 'Galatians: Then and Now', in *Studia Evangelica VI*, ed. E.A. Livingstone, TU 112, Berlin 1973, 619–627.

Wibbing, S., *Die Tugend- und Lasterkataloge im Neuen Testament und ihre Traditionsgeschichte unter besonderer Berücksichtigung der Qumran-Texte*, BZNW 25, Berlin 1959.

Wilckens, U., 'Was heisst bei Paulus: "Aus Werken des Gesetzes wird kein Mensch gerecht"?', in *Rechtfertigung als Freiheit. Paulusstudien*, Neukirchen-Vluyn 1974, 77–109.

'Zur Entwicklung des paulinischen Gesetzesverständnisses', *NTS* 28 (1982) 154–190.

Der Brief an die Römer, Evangelisch-Katholischer Kommentar zum Neuen Testament, 3 volumes, Zürich/Neukirchen-Vluyn 1978, 1980, 1982.

Wilcox, M., 'The Promise of the "Seed" in the New Testament and the Targumim', *JSNT* 5 (1979) 2–20.

Williams, S.K., 'Justification and the Spirit in Galatians', *JSNT* 29 (1987) 91–100.

Wilson, B., *Sect and Society*, London 1961.

Wilson, R.McL., 'Gnosis, Gnosticism and the New Testament', in *Le Origini dello Gnosticismo*, ed. U. Bianchi, Leiden 1967, 511–527.

'Gnostics – in Galatia?', in *Studia Evangelica IV*, ed. F.L. Cross, TU 102, Berlin 1968, 358–367.

Windisch, H., 'Das Problem des paulinischen Imperativs', *ZNW* 23 (1924) 265–281.

Wright, N.T., 'The Paul of History and the Apostle of Faith', *Tyndale Bulletin* 29 (1978) 61–88.

The Messiah and the People of God, Unpublished D.Phil. Thesis, Oxford 1980.

Colossians and Philemon, Tyndale New Testament Commentaries, Leicester 1986.

Yarbrough, O.L., *Not Like the Gentiles. Marriage Rules in the Letters of Paul*, SBLDS 80, Atlanta 1985.

Young, E.M., ' "Fulfill the Law of Christ". An Examination of Galatians 6:2', *Studia Biblica et Theologica* 7 (1977) 31–42.

Young, N.H.,   *'Paidagogos*: the Social Setting of a Pauline
                    Metaphor', *NT* 29 (1987) 150-176.

Zahn, T.,   *Der Brief des Paulus an die Galater*, Zahns
                    Kommentar zum Neuen Testament, 9,
                    Leipzig 1905.

Ziesler, J.A.,   *The Meaning of Righteousness in Paul. A
                    Linguistic and Theological Enquiry*, SNTSMS
                    20, Cambridge 1972.

                    Pauline Christianity, Oxford 1983.

INDEX OF AUTHORS

INDEX OF REFERENCES

Old Testament